Varronianus

*A Critical and Historical Introduction
to the Philological Study of the Latin Language*

JOHN WILLIAM DONALDSON

CAMBRIDGE
UNIVERSITY PRESS

CAMBRIDGE
UNIVERSITY PRESS

University Printing House, Cambridge, CB2 8BS, United Kingdom

Cambridge University Press is part of the University of Cambridge.
It furthers the University's mission by disseminating knowledge in the pursuit of
education, learning and research at the highest international levels of excellence.

www.cambridge.org
Information on this title: www.cambridge.org/9781108067072

© in this compilation Cambridge University Press 2014

This edition first published 1844
This digitally printed version 2014

ISBN 978-1-108-06707-2 Paperback

This book reproduces the text of the original edition. The content and language reflect
the beliefs, practices and terminology of their time, and have not been updated.

Cambridge University Press wishes to make clear that the book, unless originally published
by Cambridge, is not being republished by, in association or collaboration with,
or with the endorsement or approval of, the original publisher or its successors in title.

CAMBRIDGE LIBRARY COLLECTION
Books of enduring scholarly value

Classics

From the Renaissance to the nineteenth century, Latin and Greek were compulsory subjects in almost all European universities, and most early modern scholars published their research and conducted international correspondence in Latin. Latin had continued in use in Western Europe long after the fall of the Roman empire as the lingua franca of the educated classes and of law, diplomacy, religion and university teaching. The flight of Greek scholars to the West after the fall of Constantinople in 1453 gave impetus to the study of ancient Greek literature and the Greek New Testament. Eventually, just as nineteenth-century reforms of university curricula were beginning to erode this ascendancy, developments in textual criticism and linguistic analysis, and new ways of studying ancient societies, especially archaeology, led to renewed enthusiasm for the Classics. This collection offers works of criticism, interpretation and synthesis by the outstanding scholars of the nineteenth century.

Varronianus

John William Donaldson (1811–61), though somewhat unorthodox in his methods, was an important, if controversial, figure in the development of comparative philology. In this 1844 publication, he attempts to supply young English scholars of Latin with an introductory guide to Latin philology by outlining the origins of the Roman people and, through this, explaining the foundational structures of the Latin language and how they gave rise to Classical Latin. Epigraphic evidence, drawn from the Twelve Tables in particular, is examined as part of the enquiry into Old Latin, and other Italic languages such as Umbrian, Oscan and Etruscan are considered as part of the development of a more standardised Latin language. Although many of the conclusions Donaldson draws are based on limited evidence, the book remains an interesting specimen of early comparative philology. His earlier work on Greek, *The New Cratylus* (1839), is also reissued in this series.

Cambridge University Press has long been a pioneer in the reissuing of out-of-print titles from its own backlist, producing digital reprints of books that are still sought after by scholars and students but could not be reprinted economically using traditional technology. The Cambridge Library Collection extends this activity to a wider range of books which are still of importance to researchers and professionals, either for the source material they contain, or as landmarks in the history of their academic discipline.

Drawing from the world-renowned collections in the Cambridge University Library and other partner libraries, and guided by the advice of experts in each subject area, Cambridge University Press is using state-of-the-art scanning machines in its own Printing House to capture the content of each book selected for inclusion. The files are processed to give a consistently clear, crisp image, and the books finished to the high quality standard for which the Press is recognised around the world. The latest print-on-demand technology ensures that the books will remain available indefinitely, and that orders for single or multiple copies can quickly be supplied.

The Cambridge Library Collection brings back to life books of enduring scholarly value (including out-of-copyright works originally issued by other publishers) across a wide range of disciplines in the humanities and social sciences and in science and technology.

VARRONIANUS.

LONDON:
PRINTED BY ROBSON, LEVEY, AND FRANKLYN,
Great New Street, Fetter Lane.

VARRONIANUS:

A

CRITICAL AND HISTORICAL INTRODUCTION

TO THE

PHILOLOGICAL STUDY

OF

THE LATIN LANGUAGE.

BY THE

REV. JOHN WILLIAM DONALDSON, M.A.

F.R.A.S., F.R.G.S., F.P.S.;
HEAD MASTER OF THE ROYAL SCHOOL, BURY ST. EDMUNDS;
AND LATE
FELLOW, ASSISTANT TUTOR, AND CLASSICAL LECTURER
OF TRINITY COLLEGE, CAMBRIDGE.

Licet omnia Italica pro Romanis habeam. QUINTIL.

CAMBRIDGE:

J. AND J. DEIGHTON;

LONGMAN, BROWN, GREEN, AND LONGMANS, LONDON; J. H. PARKER, OXFORD; AND J. A. G. WEIGEL, LEIPSIG.

MDCCCXLIV.

TO

THE RIGHT REVEREND

CONNOP THIRLWALL, D.D.

LORD BISHOP OF ST. DAVIDS,
PRESIDENT OF THE PHILOLOGICAL SOCIETY,
ETC. ETC.

MY LORD,

IF I had only public reasons for prefixing your Lordship's name to this work, I should not have much difficulty in justifying my dedication. Your position in the first rank of English scholars, your profound and original researches in the highest departments of philology, and, above all, the share which you have had in rendering the great work of Niebuhr accessible to the English student, might well exact such a tribute of respect from any labourer in the same field. But while I express the admiration which I have always felt for your genius and learning, I wish also to take this opportunity of recording some of the most pleasing recollections connected with my residence within the walls of Trinity College, Cambridge. There is no period of that residence to which I do not revert with affection and gratitude, and my warmest acknowledgments are due to many whom I had the happiness to know there. But of all the advantages which I enjoyed at Cambridge, there is no one which I estimate more highly than this — that I was among those who were permitted, some ten or twelve years ago, to attend the crowded lecture-room in which your Lordship first taught the students of the College to understand and appreciate the philosophy of Aristotle. These lectures, combined with the influence which your Lordship possessed among the more intellectual and cultivated members of the College, produced a normal effect of the utmost importance, by which many have benefited. My own share in this benefit I would gladly acknowledge; and I am sure I cannot prize too highly the opportunity by which I was allowed to profit. The philological student travels along a road with many turnings which all end in nothing, or worse; and he has great reason to be thankful, if, at an early part of his career, he meets with a guide who is both willing and able to point out to him the straight and steep and narrow road which leads to the temple of truth. My personal acquaintance with your Lordship has been inconsiderable; but, though I may regret this circumstance on my own account, it will not, I conceive, detract from this testimony to the merits and efficacy of your public teaching.

In this spirit, and writing as a philologer to a philologer, I have presumed to request your acceptance of the present work; and I cannot form a more ambitious hope, than that it may succeed in obtaining your Lordship's approbation.

I have the honour to be,

My Lord,

Your Lordship's faithful servant,

J. W. DONALDSON.

PREFACE.

No person who is conversant with the subject will venture to assert that Latin scholarship is at present flourishing in England. On the contrary, it must be admitted that, while we have lost that practical familiarity with the Latin language which was possessed some forty years ago by every Englishman with any pretensions to scholarship, we have not supplied the deficiency by making ourselves acquainted with the results of modern philology, so far as they have been brought to bear upon the language and literature of ancient Rome. The same impulse which has increased and extended our knowledge of Greek has checked and impoverished our Latinity. The discovery that the Greek is, after all, an easier language than the Latin, and that it may be learned without the aid of its sister idiom, while it has certainly enabled many to penetrate into the arcana of Greek criticism who must otherwise have stopt at the threshold, has at the same time prevented many from facing the difficulties which surround the less attractive literature of Rome, and, by removing one reason for learning Latin, has induced the student to overlook the other and higher considerations which must always confer upon this language its value, its importance, and its dignity.

A return to the Latin scholarship of our ancestors can only be effected by a revival of certain old-fashioned methods and usages, which have been abandoned, perhaps more hastily than wisely, in favour of new habits and new theories. No arguments can make it fashionable for scholars to clothe their thoughts in a classic garb: example will do more than precept; and when some English philologer of sufficient authority shall acquire and exert the faculty of writing Latin with terse and simple elegance, he will not want imitators and followers. With regard, however, to our ignorance of modern Latin philology, it must be owned that our younger students have at least one excuse—namely, that they have no manual of instruction; no means of learning what has been done and is still doing in the higher departments of Italian philology; and if we may judge from the want of information on these subjects which is so frequently conspicuous in the works of our learned authors, our literary travellers, and our classical commentators, this deficiency is deeply rooted, and has been long and sensibly felt. Even those among us who have access to the stores of German literature, would seek in vain for a single book which might serve as the groundwork of their studies in this department. The most comprehensive Roman histories, and the most elaborate Latin grammars, do not satisfy the curiosity of the inquisitive student; and though there is already before the world a great mass of materials, these are scattered through the voluminous works of German and Italian scholars, and are, therefore, of little use to him who is not prepared to select for himself what is really valuable, and to throw aside the crude speculations and vague conjectures by which such researches are too often encumbered and deformed.

These considerations, and the advice of some friends, who have supposed that I might not be unprepared for such an office, have induced me to undertake the work which is now presented to the English student. How far I have accomplished my design must be left to the judgment of others. It has been my wish to produce, within as short a compass as possible, a complete and systematic treatise on the origin of the Romans, and the structure and affinities of their language, — a work which, while it might be practically useful to the intelligent and educated traveller in

Italy, no less than to the reader of Niebuhr and Arnold, might at the same time furnish a few specimens and samples of those deeper researches, the full prosecution of which is reserved for a chosen few.

The most cursory inspection of the table of contents will shew what is the plan of the book, and what information it professes to give. Most earnestly do I hope that it may contribute in some degree to awaken among my countrymen a more thoughtful and manly spirit of Latin philology. In proportion as it effects this object, I shall feel myself excused in having thus ventured to commit to a distant press a work necessarily composed amid the distractions and interruptions of a laborious and engrossing profession.

J. W. D.

THE SCHOOL HALL, BURY ST. EDMUNDS,
25th March, 1844.

CONTENTS.

CHAPTER I.

THE OLD ITALIAN TRIBES CONSIDERED AS RELATED TO EACH OTHER.

SECT.		PAGE
1.	Elements of the population of Rome	1
2.	The LATINS—a composite tribe	2
3.	The Oscans, &c.	3
4.	Alba and Lavinium	4
5.	The SABINES—how related to the Umbrians and Oscans	5
6.	The Umbrians—their ancient greatness	7
7.	Reduced to insignificance by Pelasgian invaders	8
8.	The PELASGIANS—the differences of their position in Italy and Greece respectively	9
9.	They preserve their national integrity in Etruria	10
10.	The ETRUSCANS—the theory of Lepsius, respecting their Pelasgian origin, adopted and confirmed	10
11.	Meaning and ethnical extent of the name "Tyrrhenian"	11
12.	"Rasena" only a corruption of the original form of this name	13
13.	The Etruscan language—a mixture of Pelasgian and Umbrian; the latter prevailing more in the country, the former in the towns	16, 18
14.	The Pelasgian origin of the Etruscans further confirmed by the traditionary history of the Luceres	19
15.	Conclusion	22

CHAPTER II.

THE FOREIGN AFFINITIES OF THE ANCIENT ITALIANS.

1.	Etymology of the word Πελασγός	23
2.	How the Pelasgians came into Europe	25
3.	Thracians, Getæ, and Scythians	27
4.	Scythians and Medes	28

xii   CONTENTS.

SECT.   PAGE
5. Iranian origin of the Sarmatians, Scythians, and Getæ, may be
   shewn (1) generally, and (2) by an examination of the remains
   of the Scythian language 28, 30
6. The Scythians of Herodotus were members of the Sclavonian family . 30
7. Peculiarities of the Scythian language suggested by Aristophanes . 31
8. Names of the Scythian rivers derived and explained . . . 32
9. Names of the Scythian divinities 35
10. Other Scythian words explained 38
11. Successive peopling of Asia and Europe: fate of the Mongolian race . 40
12. The Pelasgians were of Sclavonian origin 41
13. Foreign affinities of the Umbrians, &c. 42
14. Reasons for believing that they were the same race as the Lithu-
    anians 42
15. Further confirmation from etymology 44
16. Celtic tribes intermixed with the Sclavonians and Lithuanians . 45
17. The Sarmatæ probably a branch of the Lithuanian family . . 45

CHAPTER III.

THE UMBRIAN LANGUAGE AS EXHIBITED IN THE EUGUBINE TABLES.

1. The Eugubine Tables 47
2. Peculiarities by which the old Italian alphabets were distinguished . 48
3. The sibilants 49
4. Some remarks on the other letters 52
5. Umbrian grammatical forms 53
6. Selections from the Eugubine Tables, with explanations: Tab I. a, 1 . 56
7. Tab. I. a, 2-6 58
8. Tab. I. b, 13, sqq. 63
9. Extracts from the Litany in Tab. VI. a. 65
10. Umbrian words which approximate to their Latin synonymes . . 67
11. The Todi inscription contains four words of the same class . . 69

CHAPTER IV.

THE SABELLO-OSCAN LANGUAGE.

1. The remains of the Oscan language must be considered as Sabellian
   also 72
2. Alphabetical list of Sabello-Oscan words, with their interpretation . 74
3. The Bantine Table 86
4. Commentary on the Bantine Table 89
5. The "Atellanæ" 97

CONTENTS.   xiii

CHAPTER V.

THE ETRUSCAN LANGUAGE.

SECT.   PAGE
1. Transcriptions of proper names the first clue to an interpretation of the Etruscan language 101
2. Names of Etruscan divinities derived and explained . . . 104
3. Alphabetical list of Etruscan words interpreted 113
4. Etruscan inscriptions—difficulties attending their interpretation . 125
5. Inscriptions in which the Pelasgian element predominates . . 126
6. The great Perugian inscription analysed 130
7. General reflections 135

CHAPTER VI.

THE OLD ROMAN OR LATIN LANGUAGE.

1. Fragments of old Latin not very numerous 137
2. Arvalian Litany 138
3. Chants preserved by Cato 140
4. Fragments of Salian hymns 141
5. Old regal laws 145
6. Remains of the XII. Tables 148
7. Table I. 149
8. Table II. 151
9. Table III. 154
10. Table IV. 155
11. Table V. 156
12. Table VI. 157
13. Table VII. 159
14. Table VIII. 162
15. Table IX. 166
16. Table X. 167
17. Table XI. 169
18. Table XII. 169
19. The Tiburtine inscription 169
20. The epitaphs of the Scipios 171
21. The *Columna Rostrata* 178
22. The Silian and Papirian laws 179
23. The *Senatus-Consultum de Bacchanalibus* 182
24. The old Roman law on the Bantine Table 184

CHAPTER VII.

ANALYSIS OF THE LATIN ALPHABET.

SECT.	PAGE
1. Organic classification of the original Latin alphabet	188
2. The labials	189
3. The gutturals	196
4. The dentals	205
5. The vowels	210
6. The Greek letters used by the Romans	217
7. The numeral signs	223

CHAPTER VIII.

THE LATIN CASE-SYSTEM.

1. Completeness of the Latin case-system	226
2. General scheme of the case-endings	227
3. Latin declensions	227
4. Hypothetical forms of the nominative and accusative plural	229
5. Existing forms—the genitive and dative	231
6. The accusative and ablative	234
7. The vocative and the neuter forms	236
8. Adverbs considered as cases of nouns	238

CHAPTER IX.

THE THEORY OF THE LATIN VERB.

1. The Latin verb generally defective	244
2. The personal inflexions—their consistent anomalies	244
3. Doctrine of the Latin tenses	246
4. The substantive verbs	248
5. Verbs which may be regarded as parathetic compounds	251
6. Tenses of the vowel-verbs which are combinations of the same kind	252
7. Organic derivation of the tenses in the consonant-verb	254
8. Auxiliary tenses of the passive voice	254
9. The modal distinctions—their syntax	255
10. Forms of the infinitive and participle—how connected in derivation and meaning	259
11. The *gerundium* and *gerundivum* shewn to be active and present	260
12. The participle in *-úrus*	264
13. The past tense of the infinitive active	264
14. Differences of conjugation	265

CHAPTER X.

CONSTITUTION AND PATHOLOGY OF THE LATIN LANGUAGE.

SECT.		PAGE
1.	Genius of the Latin language	269
2.	Abbreviations observable in the written forms	270
3.	Ancient testimonies to the difference between the spoken and the written language	273
4.	The poetry of the Augustan age does not represent the genuine Latin pronunciation	275
5.	Which is rather to be derived from an examination of the comic metres	276
6.	The French language is the best modern representative of the spoken Latin	280
7.	The modern Italian not equally so; and why	283
8.	Different dialects of the French language	284
9.	But all these dialects were closely related to the Latin	287
10.	Leading distinctions between the Roman and Romance idioms	289
11.	Importance and value of the Latin language	291

VARRONIANUS.

CHAPTER I.

THE OLD ITALIAN TRIBES CONSIDERED AS RELATED TO EACH OTHER.

§ 1. Elements of the population of Rome. § 2. The LATINS—a composite tribe. § 3. The Oscans, &c. § 4. Alba and Lavinium. § 5. The SABINES—how related to the Umbrians and Oscans. § 6. The Umbrians —their ancient greatness. § 7. Reduced to insignificance by Pelasgian invaders. § 8. The PELASGIANS—the differences of their position in Italy and Greece respectively. § 9. They preserve their national integrity in Etruria. § 10. The ETRUSCANS—the theory of Lepsius, respecting their Pelasgian origin, adopted and confirmed. § 11. Meaning and ethnical extent of the name "Tyrrhenian." § 12. "Rasena" only a corruption of the original form of this name. § 13. The Etruscan language —a mixture of Pelasgian and Umbrian, the latter prevailing more in the country, the former in the towns. § 14. The Pelasgian origin of the Etruscans further confirmed by the traditionary history of the Luceres. § 15. Conclusion.

§ 1. Elements of the population of Rome.

THE sum of all that is known of the earliest history of Rome is comprised in the following enumeration of particulars. A tribe of Latin origin, more or less connected with Alba, settled on the Palatine hill, and in the process of time united itself, by the right of intermarriage and other ties, with a band of Sabine warriors, who had taken up their abode on the Quirinal and Capitoline hills. These two towns admitted into fellowship with themselves a third community, established on the Cælian and Esquiline hills, which seems to have consisted of Pelasgians, either from the Solonian plain, lying between Rome and Lavinium, or from the opposite side of the river near Cære; and the whole body became one city, governed by a king, or *magister populi*, and a senate; the latter being the representatives of the three original elements of the state,—the Latin or Oscan Ramnes, the Sabine Titienses or Quirites, and the Pelasgian Luceres. It appears, moreover, that the Etruscans, on the other side of the Tiber, eventually influenced the destinies of Rome in no slight degree, and the last three kings mentioned in the legendary traditions were of Etruscan origin. In other words, Rome was, during the period referred to by their reigns, subjected to a powerful Etruscan dynasty, from the tyranny of which it had, on two occasions, the good fortune to escape. What Servius planned was for the most part carried into effect by the consular constitution, which followed the expulsion of the last Tarquinius.

As these facts are established by satisfactory evidence, and as we have nothing else on which we can depend with certainty, it follows that in order to investigate the ethnical affinities of the Roman people, and the origin and growth of their language, we must in the first instance inquire who were the Latins, the Sabines, the Pelasgians, and the Etruscans, and what were their relations one with another. After this we shall be able with greater accuracy to examine their respective connexions with the several elements in the original population of Europe.

THE LATINS.

§ 2.
The LATINS—
a composite tribe.

The investigations of Niebuhr and others have made it sufficiently certain that the Pelasgians formed a very important element in the population of ancient Latium. This appears not merely from the primitive traditions, but also, and more strongly, from the mythology, language, and architecture of the country. It has likewise been proved that this Pelasgian population was at an early period partially conquered by a tribe of mountaineers, who are called *Oscans*, and who descended on Latium from the basins of the Nar and the Velinus. The influence of these foreign invaders was most sensibly and durably felt in the language of the country; which in its earliest form presents phenomena not unlike those which have marked the idiom spoken in this country since the Norman conquest. The words relating to husbandry and peaceful life are Pelasgian, and the terms of war and the chase are Oscan.[1]

As it is this foreign element which forms the distinction between the Latins and the Pelasgians, let us in the first place inquire into the origin and affinities of these Oscan conquerors, in order that we may more easily disentangle the complexities of the subject.

§ 3. The Oscans, &c.

The Oscans were known at different times and in different places under the various names of Opicans, Opscans, Ausonians, and Auruncans. The primary denomination was *Op-icus*, derived from *Ops* or *Opis*, the Italian name of the goddess *Earth;* and these people were therefore, in accordance with their name, the *Autochthones*, or aboriginal inhabitants of the district where they are first found. The other denominations are derived from the same word, *Op-s*, by the addition of the endings *-si-cus*, *-sunus*, and

---

[1] Niebuhr, *H. R.* i. p. 82. Müller, *Etrusker*, i. p. 17. This observation must not be pressed too far; for it does not in fact amount to more than *prima facie* evidence. The Opican or Oscan language belongs to the Indo-Germanic family no less than the Pelasgian; the latter, however, was one ingredient in the language of ancient Greece, and it does not appear that any Hellenic tribes were connected with the Oscans; consequently it is fair to say that, as one element in the Latin language resembles the Greek, while the other does not, the Græcising element is Pelasgian.

-sun-icus. The labial is absorbed in *Oscus* and *Αὔσων*, and the *s* has become *r*, according to the regular process, in *Auruncus*.[1]

These aboriginal tribes, having been in the first instance, like the Arcadians in the Peloponnese, driven by their invaders, the Pelasgians, into the mountain fastnesses of the Apennines, at length descended from the interior on both sides, and conquered the people of the plains and the coast. One tribe, the *Ap-uli*, subdued the Daunians and other tribes settled in the south-east, and gave their name to the country; they also extended themselves to the west, and became masters of the country from the bay of Terracina upwards to the Tiber. In this district they bore the well-known names of *Volsci* (=*Apulisici*) and *Æqui* (comp. ἵππος, *equus*, &c.), names still connected with the primary designation of the aborigines.

A more important invasion was that which was occasioned by the pressure of the Sabines on an Oscan people settled in the mountains between Reate and the Fucine lake. These invaders came down the Anio, and conquered the Pelasgians of northern Latium. Their chief seat in the conquered country seems to have been Alba, the *Alp*-ine or mountain city, where they dwelt under the name of *Prisci Latini*, "ancient Latins;" being also called *Casci*, a name which denotes "ancient" or "well-born," and which, like the connected Greek term χαοί, implies that they were a nation of warriors (*N. Crat.* p. 402).

§ 4.
Alba and Lavinium.

The district of Latium, when history first speaks of it, was thus occupied by two races; one a mixed people of Oscan conquerors living in the midst of the Pelasgians whom they had subdued, the other a Pelasgian nation not yet conquered by the invaders. These two nations

[1] See Niebuhr, i. 69, note. Buttmann, *Lexilogus*, i. p. 68, note 1 (p. 154, Fishlake).

formed at first two distinct confederacies: of the former *Alba* was the head, while the place of congress for the latter was *Lavinium*. At the latter place, the *Penates*, or old Pelasgian *Cabeiri*, were worshipped; and even after the Pelasgian league was broken up by the power of Alba, and when Alba became the capital of the united nation of the Latins and sent a colony to Lavinium, the religious sanctity of the place was still maintained, the Penates were still worshipped there, and deputies still met in the temple of Venus. The influence of Alba was, however, so great, that even after its fall, when the Pelasgian Latins partially recovered their independence, there remained a large admixture of foreign elements in the whole population of Latium, and that which was purely Pelasgian in their character and institutions became gradually less and less perceptible, till nothing remained on the south of the Tiber which could claim exemption from the predominating influence of the Oscans.

That the name *Lavinium* is only a dialectical variety of *Latinium* has long been admitted. The original form of the name *Latinus*, which afterwards furnished a denomination for the language of the civilised world, was *Latvinus;* and while the Pelasgian Latins preserved the labial only, the mixed people retained only the dental. The same has been the case in the Pelasgian forms, *liber, libra, bis, ruber*, &c., compared with their Hellenic equivalents, ἐ-λεύθερος, λίτρα, δίς, ἐ-ρυθρός, &c.

THE SABINES.

It has been mentioned that the Sabines dispossessed the Oscans, and compelled them to invade Latium. Our next point is, therefore, to consider the relation in which the Sabines stood to the circumjacent tribes.

§ 5. The SABINES —how related to the Umbrians and Oscans.

The original abode of these Sabines was, according to

Cato,[1] about Amiternum, in the higher Apennines. Issuing from this lofty region, they drove the Umbrians before them on one side and the Oscans on the other, and so took possession of the district which for so many years was known by their name.

It will not be necessary in this place to point out the successive steps by which the Sabine colonies made themselves masters of the whole south and east of Italy, nor to shew how they settled on two of the hills of Rome. It is clear, on every account, that they were not Pelasgians; and our principal object is to inquire how they stood related to the Umbrians and Oscans, on whom they more immediately pressed.

Niebuhr thinks it not improbable that the Sabines and Oscans were only branches of one stock, and mentions many reasons for supposing so.[2] It appears, however, that there are still stronger reasons for concluding that the Sabines were an offshoot of the Umbrian race. This is established not only by the testimony of Zenodotus of Trœzen,[3] who wrote upon the Umbrians, but also by the resemblances of the Sabine and Umbrian languages.[4] It is true that this last remark may be made also with regard to the Sabine and Oscan idioms; for many words which are quoted as Sabine are likewise Oscan.[5] The most plausible theory is, that the Sabines were Umbrians, who were separated from the rest of their nation, and driven into the high Apennines, by the Pelasgians of the north-east; but that, after an interval, they in their turn assumed an offensive position, and descending from their highlands, under the name of *Sabini*, or " worshippers of Sabus the son of Sancus,"[6] attacked their Umbrian brethren on the one

---

[1] Quoted by Dionys. i. 14, p. 40; ii. 49, p. 338. Reiske.
[2] *Hist. Rome*, i. p. 103.　　　[3] Apud Dionys. ii. 49, p. 337.
[4] Servius ad Virg. *Æn.* iii. 235.　　[5] Niebuhr, *ubi supra*.
[6] That this *Sancus* was an Umbrian deity is clear from the Eugubine

side, and the Oscan Latins on the other. At length, however, they sent out so many colonies to the south, among the Oscan nations, that their Umbrian affinities were almost forgotten; and the Sabellian tribes, especially the Samnites, were regarded as members of the Oscan family, from having adopted to a considerable extent the language of the conquered tribes among whom they dwelt.

§ 6. The Umbrians —their ancient greatness.

The Umbrians are always mentioned as one of the most ancient nations of Italy.[1] Though restricted in the historical ages to the left bank of the Tiber, it is clear that in ancient times they occupied the entire northern half of the peninsula, from the Tiber to the Po. Their name, according to the Greek etymology, implied that they had existed before the great rain-floods which had destroyed many an earlier race of men.[2] Cato said that their city Ameria was founded 381 years before Rome.[3] All that we read about them implies that they were a great, a genuine, and an ancient nation.[4] There are distinct traditions to prove that the country, afterwards called Etruria, was originally in the occupation of the Umbrians. The name of the primitive occupants of that country was preserved by the Tuscan river *Umbro*, and the tract of land through which it flowed into the sea was to the last called

Tables. Indeed, both *sabus* and *sancus*, in the old languages of Italy, signified "sacred" or "revered," and were probably epithets regularly applied to the deity. In the Eugubine Tables we have the word *sev-um*, meaning "reverently" (i. a. 5); and *Sansius* is an epithet of the god *Fisus*, or *Fisovius* (vi. b. 3, 5). Comp. the Latin *sev-erus* (σέβ-ω), and *sanctus*. According to this, the name *Sabini* is nearly equivalent to *Sacrani*. The Tables also mention the *picus Martius* of the Sabines, from which the *Piceni* derived their name (*piquier Martier*, v. b. 9, 14); comp. Strabo, v. p. 240.

[1] Niebuhr, i. note 430.
[2] See Plin. *H. N.* iii. 19: "Umbrorum gens antiquissima Italiæ existimatur, ut quos *Ombrios* a Græcis putent dictos, quod inundatione terrarum imbribus superfuissent:" and compare, for the idea, *Psalm* xxix. 10.
[3] Pliny, iii. 14, 19.   [4] Florus, i. 17. Dionys. i. 19.

Umbria.¹ It is expressly stated that Cortona was once Umbrian;² and Camers, the ancient name of Clusium,³ points at once to the Camertes, a great Umbrian tribe.⁴ It is certain also that the Umbrians occupied Picenum, till they were expelled from that region by their brethren the Sabines.⁵

§ 7.
Reduced to insignificance by Pelasgian invaders.

Since history, then, exhibits this once great nation expelled from the best part of its original possessions, driven beyond the Apennines, deprived of all natural barriers to the north, and reduced to insignificance, we are led at once to inquire into the cause of this phenomenon. Livy speaks of the Umbrians as dependent allies of the Tuscans;⁶ and Strabo tells us that the Etruscans and Umbrians maintained a stubborn contest for the possession of the district between the Apennines and the mouth of the Po.⁷ The people which thus ruled and strove with them in the latter period of their history, when they were living within the circumscribed limits of their ultimate possessions, was that which deprived them of a national existence within the fairest portion of their originally wide domains.

There can be no doubt that the Umbrians were invaded and conquered by a stream of Tyrrhenian Pelasgians from the north-east. Before we proceed to shew how these invaders, combined with the conquered Umbrians, made up the great Etrurian nation, it will be convenient to examine generally the course of the Pelasgian invasion of Italy.

¹ Pliny, iii. 5 (8).   ² Dionys. i. 20.
³ Liv. x. 25.   ⁴ Liv. ix. 36.
⁵ Pliny, iii. 13, 14.   ⁶ In books ix. and x.
⁷ P. 216.

THE PELASGIANS.

§ 8. The PELASGIANS—the differences of their position in Italy and Greece respectively.

Without stopping to inquire at present who the Pelasgians were out of Italy, let us take them up where they first make their appearance at the mouth of the Po. We find that they started from this district, and having crossed the Apennines, wrested from the Umbrians the great city Camers, from whence they carried on war all around. Continually pressing towards the south, and, as they advanced, conquering the indigenous tribes, or driving them up into the highlands, they eventually made themselves masters of all the level plains and of the coasts. Though afterwards, as we have seen, invaded in their turn, and in part conquered by the Oscan aborigines, they were for a long time in possession of Latium; and, under the widely diffused name of Œnotrians, they held all the south of Italy, till they were conquered or dispossessed by the spread of the great Sabellian race.

To these Pelasgians were due the most important elements in the ancient civilisation of Italy. It was not their destiny to be exposed throughout their settlements, like their brethren in Greece, to the overruling influence of ruder and more warlike tribes. This was to a certain extent the case in the south; where they were not only overborne by the power of their Sabellian conquerors, but also Hellenised by the Greek colonies which were at an early period established among them. But in Etruria and Latium the Pelasgian nationality was never extinguished: even among the Latins it survived the severest shocks of Oscan invasion. In Etruria it remained to the end the one prevailing characteristic of the people; and Rome herself, though she owed her military greatness to the Sabellian ingredient in her composition, was, to the days of her decline, Pelasgian in all the essentials of her language, her religion, and her law.

§ 9.
Preserve their national integrity in Etruria.

It is easy to see why the Pelasgians retained their national integrity on the north-western coast so much more perfectly than in the south and east. It was because they entered Etruria in a body, and established there the bulk of their nation. All their other settlements were of the nature of colonies; and the density of the population, and its proportion to the number of the conquered mingled with it, varied, of course inversely, with the distance from the main body of the people. In Etruria the Pelasgians were most thickly settled, and next to Etruria in Latium. Consequently, while the Etruscans retained their conquest, and compelled the Sabines, the most vigorous of the dispossessed Umbrians, to direct their energies southwards, and while the Latins were only partially reconquered by the aboriginal tribes, the Pelasgians of the south resigned their national existence, and were merged in the concourse of Sabellian conquerors and Greek colonists.

We have here presumed that the Etruscans were Pelasgians mixed with conquered Umbrians. The next step is to prove this.

THE ETRUSCANS.

§ 10.
The ETRUSCANS—theory of Lepsius, respecting their Pelasgian origin, adopted and confirmed.

To determine the origin of the Etruscans, and the nature of their language, has for many years been considered the most difficult problem in philology. This enigma, however, seems at last to have been solved by Dr. Richard Lepsius,—a worthy pupil of James Grimm and Ottfried Müller,—who has advanced many satisfactory reasons in favour of his hypothesis, that the Etruscans were after all only Tyrrhenians, or Pelasgians, who, invading Italy from the north-east, conquered the Umbrians, and took possession of the western part of the district formerly occupied by that people, but could not protect their own language from the modifying influences of the cognate

Umbrian dialect.[1] In support of this theory, which is in accordance with the opinions elsewhere expressed[2] respecting the early population of Italy, and with the results of the present work, it may be sufficient to adduce the authorities and arguments which follow.

§ 11. Meaning and ethnical extent of the name "Tyrrhenian."

It is clear that the name Τυῤῥηνός or Τυρσηνός, by which the Greeks designated the inhabitants of Etruria, is not directly derived from the name of the Lydian city *Tyrrha*, which occurs only once in ancient tradition.[3] On the contrary, this Greek word, which is identical with the Latin *Tuscus* (for *Tursicus*) and *Etruscus*, and with the Umbrian *Turske*, has been properly explained, even by Dionysius,[4] as referring to the τύρσεις or cyclopean fortifications which every where attest the presence of Pelas-

[1] *Ueber die Tyrrhenischen Pelasger in Etrurien.* Leipsig, 1842. We are indebted to this scholar, who is still, I believe, a young man, for some of the most important contributions which Italian philology has ever received. In his treatise on the Eugubine Tables, which he published in the year 1833, he evinced an extent of knowledge, an accuracy of scholarship, and a maturity of judgment, such as we rarely meet with even among Germans. His collection of Umbrian and Oscan inscriptions (Lipsiæ, 1841) has supplied the greatest want felt by those who are interested in the old languages of Italy; and I expect the most fruitful results from those inquiries into the Egyptian language in which he is now engaged. Unless I am misinformed, Dr. Lepsius has to thank the Chevalier Bunsen for the advantages which he has enjoyed in Italy, in France, and in Egypt. James Grimm, in the second edition of his *Deutsche Mythologie*, which has just reached this country, has confirmed with his great authority the opinions advocated in the text: " Niebuhr (he says, p. 489) hält Tyrrhener und Etrusker von einander, wie ich glaube, mit unrecht."

[2] *N. Crat.* p. 89, sqq.

[3] See Müller, *Etrusk.* i. pp. 71, 72, 80. It is probable that *Tyrrha* and the whole of *Torrhebia* were Pelasgian settlements, of the same kind as the *Larissæ* in Troas and Æolis.

[4] i. 26 : ἀπὸ τῶν ἐρυμάτων, ἃ πρῶτοι τῶν τῇδε οἰκούντων κατεσκευάσαντο. τύρσεις γὰρ καὶ παρὰ Τυῤῥηνοῖς αἱ ἐντείχιοι καὶ στεγαναὶ οἰκήσεις ὀνομάζονται, ὥσπερ παρ' Ἕλλησιν. Tzetzes, *ad Lycophr.* 717 : τύρσις τὸ τεῖχος, ὅτι Τυρσηνοὶ πρῶτον ἔφευρον τὴν τειχοποιΐαν. Comp. *Etym. M.* s. v. τύραννος.

gian *tower-builders*. The word τύρρις or τύρσις, which occurs in Pindar as the name of the great palace of the primeval god Saturn,[1] is identical with the Latin *turris;* and the fact, that the Pelasgians derived their distinguishing epithet from this word, is remarkable, not only as shewing the affinity between the Greek and Latin languages on the one hand, and the Pelasgian in Etruria on the other hand, but also because these colossal structures are always found wherever the Pelasgians make their appearance in Greece. Fortresses in Pelasgian countries received their designation as often from these τύρσεις as from the name *Larissa,* which seems to signify the abode of the *lars* or *prince.* Thus the old Pelasgian Argos had two citadels or ἀκροπόλεις, the one called the *Larissa,* the other τὸ ἄργος, *i.e.* the *arx.*[2] In the neighbourhood, however, was the city *Tiryns,* which is still remarkable for its gigantic cyclopean remains, and in the name of which we may recognise the word τύρρις;[3] and not much further on the other side was *Thyrea,* which Pausanias connects with the fortified city *Thyræon,*[4] in the middle of Pelasgian Arcadia; and further south we have the Messenian *Thuria,* and *Thyrides* at the foot of Tænaron. Then again, in the northern abodes of the Pelasgians, we find *Tyrrheum,* a

[1] *Ol.* ii. 70: ἔτειλαν Διὸς ὁδὸν παρὰ Κρόνου τύρσιν. See also Orph. *Argon.* 151: τύρσιν ἐρυμνῆς Μιλήτοιο. Suidas: τύρσος, τὸ ἐν ὕψει ᾠκοδομημένον. The word τύραννος contains the same root: comp. κοίρανος with κάρα, and the other analogies pointed out in the *New Cratylus,* p. 415, sqq.

[2] Liv. xxxiv. 25: " Utrasque *arces,* nam *duas* habent *Argi.*"

[3] According to Theophrastus (*apud Plin.* vii. 57), the inhabitants of Tiryns were the inventors of the τύρσεις. As early as Homer's time the town was called τειχιόεσσα (*Il.* ii. 559), and its walls are described by Euripides (*Electr.* 1158. *Iph. in Aul.* 152, 1501. *Troad.* 1088) as κυκλώπεια οὐράνια τείχη. The mythological personage *Tiryns* is called " the son of Argos" (Paus. ii. 25), who, according to Steph. Byz., derived his origin from *Pelasgus,* who civilised Arcadia (Pausan. viii. 1), and was the father of Larissa (id. vii. 17), and grandfather of Thessalus (Dionys. i. 17).

[4] It was built by *Thyræus,* the grandson of Pelasgus (Paus. viii. 3).

fortified place not far from the Pelasgian Dodona, and also a *Tirida* in Thrace.[1] At no great distance from the Thessalian *Larissa* and *Argissa* lay the Macedonian *Tyrissa*, a name which reminds us of the Spanish *Turissa in agro Tarraconensi*;[2] and the *Tyrrhenica Tarraco*, with its massive walls,[3] is sufficient to establish the connexion of this latter place with the Tyrrhenians.

One proof of the Italian origin of the name *Tyrrhenian* may be deduced from the existence in Italy of the by-form *Tursici*; and Lepsius agrees with Müller in thinking that the Etruscan capital, Ταρχώνιον, *Tarkynia*, *Tarquinii*, has derived its name from its τύρρεις, or Pelasgian walls.[4] It appears to me that the original form of the word was rather *tarch-* or *trach-* (comp. τραχύς, &c.),[5] and that the guttural was subsequently assibilated and softened into *s*, according to the regular process. The natural transition would be τραχ-, ταρχ-, ταρσ-, ταρρ-. Consequently, the hero *Tarchon* is to be regarded as the real eponymus of the Tyrsenians,—*Tyrrhenus*, *Torrhebus*, *Tiryns*, and *Thyræus*, being only by-forms of the same name.

The most important part, however, of the investigations of Lepsius in this field is his proof of the nonexistence of the *Rasenæ*, whom Niebuhr and Müller agree in considering as the real Etruscans, or the non-Pelasgian conquerors of Etruria. He has shewn the utter inadmissibility of the reading Κρότωνα for Κρηστῶνα, in the celebrated passage of Herodotus,[6] on which Niebuhr and Müller have built

§ 12. "Rasena" only a corruption of the original form of this name.

---

[1] Plin. *H. N.* iv. 18: "Oppidum quondam Diomedis equorum stabulis dirum."

[2] Anton. *Itin.*

[3] Müller, *Etrusker*, i. p. 291. Auson. *Ep.* 24, 88.

[4] Lepsius suggests also, that the *Turres* on the coast near Cære and Alsium may have been a Roman translation of the name Τύρρεις.

[5] Thus Ταρρακίνα was anciently written Τραχίνα (Strabo, v. p. 254).

[6] i. 57. The following is the substance of what Herodotus has told us

so much, and the absolute want of any historical proof that the Pelasgians in Etruria were ever interfered with, until the Gauls invaded the north of Italy. " We hear," he says (p. 22), " of only one Etruscan history. The annals and traditions of the Etruscans go back uninterruptedly to their Pelasgian origin: and can we conceive that their history or tradition should not have preserved some reminiscence of this radical change in the population of the country, if it had really taken place? It is quite unnecessary to prove, that all we hear of the Etruscan organisation, and of the art and science of this people, must refer

respecting the Tyrrhenians and Pelasgians; and his information, though much compressed, is still very valuable. He seems tacitly to draw a distinction between the Pelasgians and the Tyrrhenians. With regard to the former he relates the Lydian story (i. 94: φασὶ δὲ αὐτοὶ Λυδοί), that Atys, son of Manes, king of the Mæonians, had two sons, Lydus and Tyrrhenus. Lydus remained at home, and gave to the Mæonians the name of Lydians; whereas Tyrrhenus sailed to Umbria with a part of the population, and there founded the Tyrrhenian people. In general, Herodotus, when he speaks of the Tyrrhenians, is to be understood as referring to the Etruscans. Of the Pelasgians he says (i. 56, sqq.), that they formed one of the original elements of the population of Greece, the division into Dorians and Ionians corresponding to the opposition of Hellenes to Pelasgians. In the course of his travels he had met with pure Pelasgians in Placie and Scylace on the Hellespont, and also in Creston; and their language differed so far from the Greek that he did not scruple to call it *barbarian* (c. 57). At the same time he seems to have been convinced that the Hellenes owed their greatness to their coalition with these barbarous Pelasgians (c. 58). The text of Herodotus is undoubtedly corrupt in this passage; but the meaning is clear from the context. He says, that " the Hellenes having been separated from the Pelasgians, being weak and starting from small beginnings, have increased in population, principally in consequence of the accession of the Pelasgians and many other barbarous tribes." The reading αὔξηται ἐς πλῆθος τῶν ἐθνέων πολλῶν is manifestly wrong; not only because the position of the article is inadmissible, but also because ἄλλων ἐθνέων βαρβάρων συχνῶν immediately follows. I cannot doubt that we ought to read, αὔξηται ἐς πλῆθος, τῶν Πελασγῶν μάλιστα προσκεχωρηκότων αὐτῷ καὶ ἄλλων ἐθνέων βαρβάρων συχνῶν. The epithet πολλῶν has crept into the text from a marginal explanation of συχνῶν, and τῶν ἐθνέων πολλῶν has consequently taken the place of the abbreviation τῶν ΠΛΓῶν [ΠΛΛῶν] for τῶν Πελασγῶν.

to the Tyrrhenian Pelasgians, and not to the *Rasenæ*, a rude people from the Alps; that the cyclopean architecture, the famous *signa Tuscanica*, the musical skill, the monetary system, and even the writing of the Tuscans, is due to them; that in the Etruscan discipline, in the Etruscan science and literature, in a word, in their history and mythology, we have an inheritance left by Pelasgians, and not by barbarous Rasenæ. If so, how did it happen that, while the uncultivated northern conquerors exchanged their own nationality for these endowments of the subjugated Pelasgians, and even assumed their name—that of the *Tyrrhenians*—they nevertheless did not adopt their language, the original vehicle of all mental cultivation, but translated the thoughts of a foreign tribe into their own barbarous tongue? It seems to me useless to follow any further the consequences to which this hypothesis of a Rasenic conquest of the Pelasgic Tyrrhenians must necessarily lead: thus much will suffice to shew how utterly untenable it is." Lastly, we are indebted to this ingenious author for a confirmation of the happy conjecture by which Lanzi[1] and Cramer[2] had already removed the only difficulty that might seem to leave a doubt upon the subject. After observing that the name Ῥασένα occurs only in a single passage of Dionysius—that it is never mentioned before or after him, either as a name of the people, or as that of an Etruscan hero—and how incredible it is that the Roman writers, who so thoroughly investigated the subject, should have heard nothing of this name, or the tradition on which it rested,—he suggests the probability, that the text of Dionysius,[3] which is often faulty, and

[1] *Saggio*, i. p. 189.

[2] *Ancient Italy*, i. p. 161. It is not a little surprising that this conjecture should have been either unknown to Niebuhr and Müller, or unheeded by them.

[3] The passage runs thus (i. 30): ὠνομάσθαι δ' ὑφ' Ἑλλήνων αὐτὸ τῇ

which in this very passage has Θνοσκόους instead of Θούσκους, presents us with the erroneous reading ‘Ρασένα instead of Ταρασένα or Ταρσένα; so that the difference between the native name of the Tuscans and that by which the Greeks and Romans knew them, consisted only in the substitution of *a* for the Greek *v* and the Roman *u*. As the Greeks called them Τυρσηνοί from the hero Τυρσηνός, they named themselves *Tarsenæ* from the hero *Tarsena*. This change from the *u* to the *a* is seen in the words Ταρχώνιον, *Tarquinii*, and the Spanish *Tarraco;* possibly also *Tarracina*[1] (*Anxur*) in Latium, *Tarrhæ* in Sardinia, and other words, may be considered as containing the same modified root. In this way, the hero Ταρσένα becomes identical with the Τυρσηνός, Τυῤῥηνός, of the Greek legend,[2] and with the *Tarchon* of the Roman story, and is not such a solitary personage as the unknown ‘Ρασένα.[3]

§ 13.
The Etruscan language—a

The difficulty occasioned by the language of the Tuscans is removed by the consideration that it is a mixed

προσηγορίᾳ ταύτῃ οὐδὲν κωλύει, καὶ διὰ τὰς ἐν τύρσεσιν οἰκήσεις καὶ ἀπ' ἀνδρὸς δυνάστου. ‘Ρωμαῖοι μέντοι—'Ετρούσκους καλοῦσι'—πρότερον δ' ἀκριβοῦντες τοὔνομα ὥσπερ ῞Ελληνες Θυοσκόους (l. Θούσκους) ἐκάλουν· αὐτοὶ μέν τοι σφᾶς αὐτοὺς ἀπὸ τῶν ἡγεμόνων τινὸς ‘Ρασένα (l. Ταρσένα) τὸν αὐτὸν ἐκείνῳ τρόπον ὀνομάζουσι.

[1] According to Strabo, v. p. 254, Τραχίνα was the earlier name of Ταῤῥακίνα. *Terracina* is the later pronunciation, resulting perhaps from a wish to Latinise the name. Similarly, *Velaθri* was converted into *Volaterræ*.

[2] The change from Ταρσένα into Τυρσηνός is analogous to the Greek change of *Porsěna* into Πυρσηνός, Πορσήνας, Πορσῖνος (as from πυρσός, πυῤῥός, Πυῤῥός); a change which led Niebuhr into his strange error respecting the quantity of the word (see Macaulay, *Lays of Ancient Rome*, p. 44).

[3] If it be objected, that the word *Raśne* (plur. *Raśneś*) occurs in the great Perugian inscription (below, Chap. V.); in the first place it may be answered, that there is no evidence for identifying this with the ethnic designation of the Tuscans; and if this were necessary, still we might suppose that ‘Ρασένα and *Raśne* were mutilations of Ταρασένα, analogous to the Tuscan *mi* for *esmi*. As far, however, as I can conjecture the meaning of the word *Raśne*, it has nothing whatever to do with this ethnic name.

language—an interpenetration of the Pelasgian and Umbrian idioms. The Pelasgians of the Po invaded and conquered the Umbrians, who remained, however, in their own land in subjection to the Pelasgian aristocracy. Although the Umbrian language, therefore, was in the first instance thrown into the background, it could not be altogether suppressed, but, on the contrary, gradually exerted an influence on the language of the victors, which was the more sensibly felt, because the Pelasgians were separated from their own people, whereas the Umbrians spoke the language of the land and that of the surrounding countries. The Pelasgian invaders stood in the same relation to the Umbrians, as the Normans did to the Saxons after their conquest of England. In both cases a more highly civilised nation settled, as conquerors and with strong national attachments, among a less cultivated race. As the English language was formed by an union of the Norman with the Anglo-Saxon, so the Etruscan arose from the combination of the Pelasgian with the Umbrian. The process of amalgamation in the former case is well known. It did not take place at once. Gradually, however, the language of the conquered people resumed its place even in the cities. The characteristics of this mixed language, as it appeared in the towns, was a preponderating number of Norman words accommodated to the Saxon grammar, as far as it remained. The words were mutilated, lost their terminations, and were pronounced with the accent thrown back, like the Saxon words. The same was the case in Etruria. The Umbrians were perhaps even less cultivated in letters than the Anglo-Saxons, and the oldest written memorials were Pelasgian. But the old language of the country at length began to exert a modifying influence on the idiom of the conquerors. The accent was thrown back, after the Italian custom; the inflexions, no longer understood, were omitted; and a compound language sprung up, which we

mixture of Pelasgian and Umbrian.

must call no longer *Pelasgian*, but *Etruscan*. The Pelasgian element predominated, but was always more and more corrupted by the influence of the Umbrian admixture. The older the fragments of the language, the more Pelasgic are they; the later, the more Etruscan. There were some exceptions,—such, for instance, as Cære, which may have retained the Pelasgian language,—but these were only exceptions to the general rule. Lepsius supposes that the old Pelasgian language gave way to the new compound language at the time when the democratic party in Etruria, supported by the Romans, began to prevail over the Pelasgian aristocracy: this period commences with the fifth century B.C., and includes the downfal of Tarquinii, the Veientine wars, the rise of the Roman colonies (383), the conquest of Perusia (310), and the seditions of Volsinii.

The latter prevailing more in the country, the former in the towns.

As in England the country-people preserved their Saxon longer than the inhabitants of the towns, so it was in Etruria. This appears from the circumstance mentioned by Livy (x. 4) under the year B.C. 301, that some pretended shepherds were detected by a Roman general in Etruria, in consequence of their speaking the town language. The same author mentions (ix. 36), that, in the year B.C. 308, two men brought up at Cære were sent through the Ciminian forest to treat with the Camertians in Umbria. This implies that Umbrian country-people surrounded the Tuscan cities of Cære and Clusium (anciently called *Camars*); and the same fact is implied, with regard to Etruria in general, in the mention of *Penestæ* by Dionysius (ix. 5), and in the *agrestes Etruscorum cohortes* of Livy (ix. 36).

The conclusion arrived at by Lepsius is, therefore, that the Etruscan language is a Pelasgian idiom, gradually destroyed by intermixture with the Umbrian; and he is convinced that this view will be confirmed by every increase of our knowledge with regard to the Etruscan. What we already know of this language proves its connexion with the Græco-Latin dialects on the one hand, and with the Umbrian on the other; and it will be shewn in a subsequent chapter, that some even of those words which appear most barbarous, admit of a very satisfactory explanation from a comparison with corresponding roots in the Indo-Germanic languages.

§ 14. *The Pelasgian origin of the Etruscans further confirmed by the traditionary history of the Luceres.*

In addition, however, to the inferences which Lepsius has drawn from the notices scattered through the pages of ancient writers, and from the Etruscan language as it still appears, we must not overlook the fact that this identification of the Etruscans with the Tyrrhenian Pelasgians most strikingly explains the traditionary history of the *Luceres*. While a great many traditions represent the Luceres, or third Roman tribe, as Pelasgians, just as many more describe the settlers on the Cælian and Esquiline as Etruscans, who fought on the side of Romulus in his war with the Sabines. If, then, it is once ascertained that the Etruscans were Pelasgians, all these diverging traditions flow in the same channel.

It appears that the Oscan or Alban Ramnes on the Palatine[1] had reduced the Pelasgians on the Cælian to a state of dependence or vassalage; what took place in Latium generally was also enacted on the Septimontium. These two communities—one of which we may call Roma, and the other Lucerum—constituted the original city of Rome, which contended on a footing of equality with the Quirites: hence the legend calls *Roma* the daughter of Italus and Leucaria,[2]—of the aboriginal Oscans, and the foreign or Pelasgian Luceres. When Roma admitted

[1] The "Palatini aborigines ex agro Reatino," as Varro calls them (*L. L.* v. § 53).

[2] Plutarch. *Romul.* ii., where we must read Λευκαρίας.

Quirium to the privileges of citizenship, the Quirites naturally took rank above the subject Luceres, and the *celsi Ramnes* still remained at the head of the *populus*. According to one story, they compelled the Luceres to leave their stronghold and descend to the plain.[1] It appears, too, that, together with the Cælian town, the Palatine Romans ruled over the possessions of the Luceres in the Solonian plain, which were called the *Pectuscum Palati*, or "breastwork of the Palatine."[2] Now, it is distinctly said, that the Luceres were first raised to the full privileges of the other burgesses by the first Tarquinius, who both introduced them into the senate, and also gave them representatives among the ministers of religion.[3] And who was this *Lucius Tarquinius* but a *Lucumo* or grandee from the Tuscan city *Tarquinii*, who settled at Rome, and was raised to the throne? Indeed, there seems to be but little reason to doubt that he was the Cæles Vivenna,[4] whose friend and successor Mastarna appears under the name of Servius Tullius.[5] The difference in the policy of the first and second of these Tuscan kings of Rome need not surprise us. Every scattered hint referring to this Tullius, or Mastarna, represents him as connected with that Pelasgian

[1] Varro, *L. L.* v. § 46.
[2] Festus, p. 213, Müller: "Pectuscum Palati dicta est ea regio Urbis, quam Romulus obversam posuit, ea parte in qua plurimum erat agri Romani ad mare versus et qua mollissime adibatur urbs, cum Etruscorum agrum a Romano Tiberis discluderet, ceteræ vicinæ civitates colles aliquos haberent oppositos."
[3] See Niebuhr, i. p. 296; iii. p. 350.
[4] Niebuhr, i. p. 375, note 922; and *Kleine Schriften*, ii. p. 26, sqq.
[5] See the celebrated Lugdunensian Table, Lipsius, *Excurs. ad Tac. Ann.* xi. 24. Müller (*Etrusker*, i. 118-123) ingeniously conjectures that the reigns of the Tarquins mythically represent the predominance of the city Tarquinii, which was for a time interfered with by Mastarna, the representative of the rival city Volsinii. Tarquinii, however, for a while resumed her influence; but at last was obliged to succumb, like the other Tuscan cities, to Clusium.

branch of the Roman population which eventually furnished the greater part of the *plebs*;[1] whereas Vivenna, or Tarquinius, was a patrician or *Lucumo* of the Tuscan city Tarquinii, and his prejudices were of course aristocratic, or rather, as was more fully developed in the case of the second Tarquinius, tyrannical; for only the absolute sovereign of a great nation could have accomplished the wonderful works which were achieved by this Tarquinian Lucumo. There is sufficient reason to believe that Rome stood high as a Tuscan town during the last years of its monarchal history. The Septimontium, if not the capital of southern Etruria,[2] was at least the southern bulwark of the twelve cities, and extended its dominion over a large part of the Sabine territory. The fall of the regal power of Rome has been well ascribed to the downfal of Tarquinii and the rising predominance of Clusium. If Lars Porsena, when he conquered Rome, had really been anxious for the restoration of Superbus, he might easily have replaced him on the throne; but he was so far from doing this, that he did not even grant him an *exsilium* in his own dominions. The vanquished Lucumo of Rome took refuge, not at Clusium, but at Cumæ,[3] with Porsena's great enemy Aristodemus,[4] whom he made his heir, and who subsequently defeated and slew Aruns Porsena, when, with a Clusian army, he made war on Aricia, and endeavoured to found a Tuscan empire in Latium.

[1] See, for instance, Livy, i. 30, where both Tullius and Servilius (Niebuhr, i. note 920) are mentioned as Latin family names.

[2] Niebuhr, i. p. 373.   [3] Cramer's *Italy*, ii. p. 150.

[4] There are many traces of the connexion of the Roman Tuscans with the Greeks. The first Tarquin himself is represented as half a Greek; and Macaulay has pointed out very clearly the Greek features of the second Tarquinian legend (*Lays of Ancient Rome*, p. 80). The equestrian games of the Tarquins, and their reverence for the Delphic oracle, also imply frequent intercourse with Greece, of which we read still more distinctly in the case of Pyrgi, the renowned port of Agylla, or Cære, another Etruscan town, which, like Tarquinii, was intimately connected with Rome.

§ 15.
Conclusion.

This identification of the Etruscans with the Tyrrheno-Pelasgians enables us to come to a fixed conclusion on the subject of the old population of Italy, and the relations of the different tribes to one another. How they stood related to the Transpadane members of the great European family is a subsequent inquiry; but within the limits of Italy proper, we may now say, there were originally two branches of one great family, — the Umbrians, extending from the Po to the Tiber; and the Oscans, occupying the southern half of the peninsula. These nations were invaded by Pelasgians from the north-east. The main body of the invaders settled in Etruria, and established a permanent empire there, which the Umbrians could never throw off. Another great horde of Pelasgians settled in Latium, where they were afterwards partially conquered by the Oscans; and a mixed population of Pelasgians and Oscans extended to the very south of Italy. The Sabines, however, who were members of the great Umbrian family, returned from the hills, to which the Pelasgians had driven them, and pressed upon the other Umbrians, upon the Oscans, and upon those Latins who were a mixture of conquered Pelasgians and Oscan conquerors. The combination of a branch of these Sabines with a branch of the Latins settled on the Tiber constituted the first beginnings of that Roman people which, standing in the midst of all these races, eventually became a point of centralisation for them all.

CHAPTER II.

THE FOREIGN AFFINITIES OF THE ANCIENT ITALIANS.

§ 1. Etymology of the word Πελασγός. § 2. How the Pelasgians came into Europe. § 3. Thracians, Getæ, and Scythians. § 4. Scythians and Medes. § 5. Iranian origin of the Sarmatians, Scythians, and Getæ, may be shewn (1) generally, and (2) by an examination of the remains of the Scythian language. § 6. The Scythians of Herodotus were members of the Sclavonian family. § 7. Peculiarities of the Scythian language suggested by Aristophanes. § 8. Names of the Scythian rivers derived and explained. § 9. Names of the Scythian divinities. § 10. Other Scythian words explained. § 11. Successive peopling of Asia and Europe: fate of the Mongolian race. § 12. The Pelasgians were of Sclavonian origin. § 13. Foreign affinities of the Umbrians, &c. § 14. Reasons for believing that they were the same race as the Lithuanians. § 15. Further confirmation from etymology. § 16. Celtic tribes intermixed with the Sclavonians and Lithuanians. § 17. The Sarmatæ probably a branch of the Lithuanian family.

SINCE the Umbrians, Oscans, &c. must be regarded in the first instance as aboriginal inhabitants, the inquirer, who would pass the limits of Italy and investigate the foreign affinities of the Italians, is first attracted by the Pelasgians. The seats of this race in Greece and elsewhere are well known; but there is no satisfactory record as to the region from which they started on their wide-spread migrations, or the countries which they traversed on their route. According to some they were Cretans, others make them Philistines, others again Egyptians; in fact, there is hardly one ancient nation which has not been noted in its turn as their parent stock. Even their name has received almost every possible etymology. The older scholars derived the

§ 1. Etymology of the word Πελασγός.

name Πελασγός from Peleg;[1] Sturz connects it with πελάζω;[2] Hermann finds the root in πέλαγος, from πελάζω;[3] Wachsmuth[4] and Müller,[5] considering πελαργός to be the original form of the word, give as its etymology πέλω, "to till," and ἄγρος, "the field," looking upon the nation as originally devoted to husbandry. The most common derivation is that which writes Πελαργοί, and interprets it "the storks," either from their wandering habits,[6] their linen dress,[7] or their barbarous speech.[8] Every one of these etymologies admits of an easy confutation. The best answer to them all is to point out a better analysis of the word. Buttmann[9] suggested long ago that the last two syllables were an ethnical designation, connected with the name *Asca-nius*, common in Phrygia, Lydia, and Bithynia, and with the name of *Asia* itself. He also correctly pointed to the relationship between *Ashkenaz*, the son of Gomer, and *Javan*, the biblical progenitor of the Ionians ('ΙάϜονες) (*Gen.* x. 3). Now the first syllable of the word *Pel-asgus* is clearly the same as that of *Pel-ops*. There are two Niobes in Greek mythology, daughters, the one of Phoroneus, the other of Tantalus—the latter is the sister of *Pelops*, the former the mother of *Pelasgus*. The syllable Πελ- stands in the same relation to μελ- that πέδα does to μετά. The original form of the root signifying "blackness"

---

[1] Salmasius *de Hellenistica*, p. 342.

[2] *De Dialect. Macedon.* p. 9.

[3] *Opusc.* ii. p. 174: "πέλαγος enim, a verbo πελάζειν dictum, ut ab Latinis *Venilia*, mare notat; a qua origine etiam πελασγοί, *advenæ*."

[4] *Hellenische Alterthumsk.* i. p. 29, Trans. p. 39. He also, half in jest, refers to πλάζειν, "to lead astray," p. 36.

[5] "Von πέλω (πόλις, πολέω, der Sparte Πέλωρ, und Πελώρια, das Fest der *Bewohnung*) und ἄργος." *Orchom.* p. 125.

[6] Strabo, v. p. 221; viii. p. 397.

[7] Bekker, *Anecd.* p. 229: διὰ τὰς σινδόνας ἃς ἐφόρουν. So also *Etymol. Magn.*

[8] *Philol. Mus.* i. p. 615.   [9] *Lexilogus*, i p. 68, note 1.

was κμελ-;[1] but the labial generally predominated over the guttural element. Of the labial forms, that with the tenuis more usually came to signify " livid" than " black;" as we see in the words πέλιος, πελιδνός, &c. Apollodorus expressly says[2] that Πελιάς was so called because his face was rendered livid (πέλιος) by a kick from a horse; and it is obvious that Πέλ-οψ, which signifies " dark-faced" or " swarthy," is an ethnical designation which differs from the well-known name Αἰθίοψ only in the degree of blackness which is implied. The Αἰθίοπες were the " burntfaced people" (*quos India torret*, as Tibullus says of them, ii. 3, 59), and are described as perfectly black (*Jeremiah* xiii. 23; κυάνεοι, Hes. *Op. et Dies*, 525); whereas the Πέλοπες were only dark in comparison with the Hellenes.[3] On the whole, it can hardly be doubted that the Πελασγοί were, according to the name given them by the old inhabitants of Greece, " the swarthy Asiatics," who were called by the latter part of their name along the coast of Asia Minor. The former part of the name was not necessary there, where all were dark-complexioned.

§ 2. *How the Pelasgians came into Europe.*

Tradition and etymology agree, therefore, in tracing the Pelasgians, so called, to the western and northern coast of Asia Minor. There is, however, little or no reason to doubt that the bulk of the race, to which these " swarthy Asiatics" belonged, entered Europe in the first instance through the wide district of Thrace, which is always mentioned as the most ancient European settlement of this tribe. For although the legends about Pelops and Lydia make it probable that they subsequently crossed over the

---

[1] *New Cratylus*, p. 136. Buttmann's *Lexil.* ii. p. 265.   [2] i. 9, § 8.
[3] Asius makes Pelasgus spring from the *black* earth (ap. Pausan. viii. 1, 4):

ἀντίθεον δὲ Πελασγὸν ἐν ὑψικόμοισιν ὄρεσσι
γαῖα μέλαιν' ἀνέδωκεν, ἵνα θνητῶν γένος εἴη.

But here the adjective is nothing but an *epitheton constans*.

Ægean, making settlements as they sailed along in the islands of the Archipelago, and though the etymology of their name refers to some such migration from the sunny coasts of Asia, it is nearly certain that the main body entered both Greece and Italy from the north-east. The course of their wanderings seems to have been as follows. They passed into this continent from the western side of the Euxine, and spread themselves over Thrace, Macedonia, and Epirus; then, while some of them forced their way into Greece, others, again moving on to the northwest, eventually entered Italy near the mouth of the Po. At some time, however, during the period of their settlement in Thrace, and before they had penetrated to the south of Greece, or had wandered to Italy, they appear to have crossed the Hellespont and peopled the western coast of Asia Minor, where they founded the city of Troy, and established the kingdom of Lydia—names to which the Pelasgians in Italy and Argos looked back with mysterious reverence. There seems to be good reason for believing that the Pelasgians acquired their distinctive character, that of agriculturists and architects, in the fertile plains of Asia Minor, and under that climate which was afterwards so prolific in works of art and genius. Those only of the Pelasgians who claimed a Lydian origin, namely, the Etruscans and Argives, were celebrated as artisans and tower-builders. It might be curious to inquire how the traditionary quarrels between the families of Dardanus and Tantalus contributed to produce the important Lydian migration into Greece; but such an investigation scarcely belongs to our subject.

Beyond these particulars we have no satisfactory data for the migrations of the great Pelasgian people; and if we wish to know their original point of departure in Asia, we must turn to comparative philology and to ethnographical traditions of a different kind.

Our point of departure, in these further researches into the original abode and ethnical affinities of the Pelasgians, is the great country of Thrace, their first European settlement. The Thracians, according to Herodotus, were, next to the Indians, the greatest people in the world;[1] and Scylax tells us that their territory extended from the Strymon to the Ister.[2] Now, among these Thracians we find the two important tribes of Getæ and Mysians, or Mœsians. Of these the geographer Strabo speaks as follows:[3] "The Greeks considered the Getæ to be Thracians. There dwelt, however, on both sides of the Ister as well these Getæ as the Mysi, who are likewise Thracians, and are now called Mœsi, from whom also the Mysi now dwelling among the Lydians, Phrygians, and Trojans, derived their origin." Again, Scylax informs us that the Scythians bordered on the Thracians;[4] and Stephanus of Byzantium says expressly,[5] that the Scythians were of Thracian extraction. The same is implied in what Strabo says on the subject: and it has long been admitted that Σκύθαι and Γέται are the same ethnical name. We thus at once obtain new data, reaching far beyond the limits of Hellenic tradition.

§ 3. Thracians, Getæ, and Scythians.

[1] v. 2.

[2] *Geogr. Vet.,—Script. Min.* i. p. 27. It is singular that the name of the Thracians should seem to bear the same relation to *Tiras*, one of the sons of Japheth, that the ethnical names of the Medes and Ionians do to the names of two of his other sons, *Madai* and *Javan* (*Gen.* x. 2). If it were necessary to seek a connexion between the word Τυρσηνός and the Goth. *Thaúrsós*, Old Norse *Thurs*, O. H. G. *Durs*, according to Grimm's suggestion (*Deutsche Myth.* pp. 23, 489, 2d ed.), we might with still greater safety bring the Thracians and the *Aga-thyrsi* into the same etymology. The Bithynians were Thracians; and there were Medo-Bithynians (Μαιδοὶ ἔθνος Θράκης, Steph. Byz. p. 527) as well as Parthians (οἱ Σκύθαι τοὺς φυγάδας Πάρθους καλοῦσι, Steph. Byz. p. 628) in Thrace.

[3] p. 295. He says also (p. 302), that the Getæ spoke the same language as the Thracians.

[4] *Geogr. Vet.,—S. M.* i. p. 29.

[5] *De Urbibus*, p. 674. Berkel: Σκύθαι ἔθνος Θράκιον.

28   THE FOREIGN AFFINITIES OF   [Ch. II.

For if the Pelasgians can fairly be traced to Thrace as their first traditionary settlement in Europe, and if we can pass from the Thracians to the Getæ, and from the Getæ to the Scythians, we are carried into a new field, in which our speculations immediately receive the support of comparative philology.

§ 4.
Scythians and Medes.

The Scythians of Herodotus are represented as occupying the wide tract of country which lies to the north of the Euxine. Though there are some alleged differences, we can collect that the whole country between Media and the Danube was occupied by a series of cognate tribes. The earliest traditions represent these Scythians as in continual contact and collision with the Medes; and we receive many significant hints that the Scythians and Medes were ultimately connected with one another as kindred races. If we pursue this subject in its details, especially as illustrated by the fragments of the Scythian language which Herodotus and others have preserved, we shall see that the Pelasgians may be traced step by step to a primary settlement in Media or northern Irân.

§ 5.
Iranian origin of the Sarmatians, Scythians, and Getæ, may be shewn generally;

The general proof that Irân, or the country lying between the Caspian, the Euphrates, the Indian Ocean, and the Indus, was the original abode of the Indo-Germanic race, has been given elsewhere.[1] It has also been shewn, that within these limits were spoken two great branches of the one Indo-Germanic language, which stood related to one another in much the same way as the Low and High German; the former being the older, and spoken by the inhabitants of Media, the northern half of this district. To these Medes, or, as they may be called, the *Northern* and *Low Iranians*, we refer, on the one hand, the *Hindus*, who call themselves *Arians* (*áryas*, " well-born"), for this was also

[1] *N. Crat.* p. 80, sqq.

§ 5.] THE ANCIENT ITALIANS. 29

the ancient name of the Medes; and, on the other hand, the following members of the Low-German family:—(*a*) the *Sarmatæ* or *Sauromatæ*, an old Sclavonian tribe, who are expressly called " descendants of the Medes" both by Diodorus[1] and by Pliny,[2] whose name, in the cognate Lithuanian language, signifies " the northern Medes or Matieni,"[3] and who, under the slightly modified name of *Syrmatæ*, dwelt near the Indus;[4] (*b*) the *Sigynnæ*, or Sclavonian Wends, to whom Herodotus ascribes a Median parentage;[5] (*c*) the *Saxons*, *Sacassani*, or *Saca-sunu*, i. e. " sons of the Sacæ," who once occupied Bactriana, as well as the most fertile part of Armenia, and from thence forced their way into Europe;[6] and, above all, (*d*) the *Goths*, who, under the different local names of Γέται, Σ-κύθαι, i. e. *Asa-goths*, Θυσσα-γέται, or Τυρι-γέται, i. e. *Tyras-getæ*, or Goths dwelling by the Dniester, and Μυσοί, Μοισοί, or Μασσα-γέται, i. e. *Mœso-goths*, occupied the whole of the districts which extend from the north-east of Irân to the borders of Thrace.[7]

[1] ii. 43, p. 195. Dind.   [2] *H. N.* vi. 7.
[3] Gatterer ap. Böckh, *C. I.* ii. p. 83.   [4] Plin. *H. N.* vi. 18.
[5] v. 9. Strabo, p. 520.
[6] Plin. *H. N.* vi. 11. Strabo, pp. 73, 507, 509, 511, 513. Among those who fought with *Visvâmitra* are mentioned (*Ramâyana*, i. c. 54, çl. 18), first, the *Pahlavi*, i. e. the Persians, for they were called *Pahlavi* by the Indians; and then a mixed army of *Sacæ* and *Yavani*, who covered the whole earth (*taîr âsit sanvṙtâ bhûmih Çakair-Yavanan-içritaîh*). The Persians called the Scythians in general *Sacæ* (Herod. vii. 64: οἱ γὰρ Πέρσαι πάντας τοὺς Σκύθας καλέουσι Σάκας). A. W. von Schlegel (*ad loc.* Ramây. ii. 2, p. 169) thinks that the name 'ΙάFων, the original form of 'Ιάων, Ἴων, was not brought from Greece, but was learned by the settlers in Asia from the Lydians; and that the *Yavani* here mentioned by the Indian poet were the Greeks in general, who were always so called by the Indians, Persians, and Jews (*Schol. ad Arist. Acharn.* 106: πάντας τοὺς Ἕλληνας Ἰάονας οἱ βάρβαροι ἐκάλουν).

[7] The traditions of the Goths referred not merely to Asia in general, but in particular to their *Midum-heime*, or " Median home," as the point of their departure. (Ritter, *Vorhalle*, p. 473).

<small>and by an examination of the remains of the Scythian language.</small>

Although these general points are already established, the details of the subject have not yet been sufficiently examined, especially as regards the fragments of the language spoken by these northern and western scions of the great Median stock. It is in accordance with the general object of this treatise, that these details should be followed as far as they will lead us; and it is hoped that, by an analysis of all the Scythian words and names which Herodotus and others have preserved, the affinity of the Scythians to the Medes will be confirmed by the most decisive proofs, and that it will appear that the Pelasgians, whom tradition traces to the same regions, were members of the Sclavonian race.

<small>§ 6.
The Scythians of Herodotus were members of the Sclavonian family.</small>

The Scythian words which have been preserved by the ancients are names of rivers, places, and persons; designations of deities; and common terms. Before we consider these separately, it will be as well to inquire if there are not some general principles by which the characteristics of the language may be ascertained.

Niebuhr thinks[1] that the Scythians belonged to the Mongol race; and this is doubtless true of the original Scythians, whom the Medo-Scythians invaded and drove to the north. But these are not the people with whom we are at present concerned, and whose language has been preserved in the fragments which we are about to examine. The Scythians, with whom the Greeks were so well acquainted, were the same in origin with the Getæ and Sauromatæ, who bounded them on either side. That the *Sauro-matæ*, or "northern Medes," were a branch of the Sclavonian family is clear from their connexion with the *Rhoxo-lani;* these are described by Tacitus[2] as a Sarmatian tribe; and the Muscovites are still called *Rosso-lainen,*

---

[1] *Kleine Schriften,* i. p. 361.   [2] *Hist.* i. 79.

or Russian people, by the Finns, who designate themselves as the *Suoma-lainen*.[1] The Sclavonian language may be classed with the oldest branch of the Low-German dialects, which is compared with the Median or Low-Iranian idiom. Consequently, if the Scythians, of whom Herodotus wrote, were of the same race with the Sauromatæ,—and this is implied in his statement that the Sarmatian language was a corruption of the Scythian,[2]—we must conclude that the Scythians were of the same race as the Sclavonians. The first principle, then, which we have to guide us in our examination of the fragments in which the Scythian language is preserved, is this, that the Scythians were members of the widely extended Sclavonian family.[3]

Some other general views are furnished by Aristophanes. It is well known that the police of Athens con-

§ 7.
Peculiarities of the Scythian

[1] Prichard, *Celtic Nations*, p. 16.   [2] iv. 117.
[3] Since writing the above the author has fallen in with an ingenious, but flippant, treatise (*Skythien und die Skythen des Herodot, von Dr. F. L. Lindner*, Stuttgart, 1841), in which the connexion of the Scythians with the Sclavonians is proved on the principle of exhaustion,—the Sclavonians were the only possible descendants of the Scythians, because no other nation could have descended from them. Dr. Lindner does not enter upon the language of the Scythians: he remarks, however, that *Scolotæ* is probably the same word as *Sclavonians;* that *Colatis* is the modern *Galatsch;* and that in the name of the three sons of Targitaos (*Leipoxa-is*, &c.), we have the Sclavonian terminations *-itsch* or *-atsch*. He holds that, according to Herodotus, we have five, and only five, divisions of the Scythian nation,—four in Europe and one in Asia, namely,—

1. The *Scolotæ*, or proper Scythians, between the Danube and the Dnieper.
2. The *Sauromatæ*, between the Dnieper and the Donetz.
3. The *Budini*, in the same district, but to the north of the former.
4. The *Agathyrsi*, in Transylvania.
5. The *Sacæ*, to the east of the Caspian.

There is some good matter in this book of Lindner's; but the self-sufficiency and arrogance of the author would seriously diminish the worth of a much more complete and satisfactory essay on the subject. He has received a severe castigation from Dr. Bobrik, in the *Berlin. Jahrbücher* for August 1842, p. 218, sqq.

32 THE FOREIGN AFFINITIES OF [Ch. II.

language suggested by Aristophanes.

sisted of Scythian bowmen. Accordingly, when the great comedian introduces one of these public servants on the stage, we might expect that, as he imitates the broad dialects of the Bœotians and Megarians, and the pure Doric of the Spartans, he would also give an accurate representation of the broken Greek of these barbarian functionaries.[1] When we mimic the provincialisms of the Highlanders or the Welsh, we are careful to substitute tenues for medials; and in the same way, we may suppose, Aristophanes would represent the leading peculiarities of the Scythian pronunciation of Greek. Now we find that his Scythian bowman in the *Thesmophoriazusæ* consistently omits the final -ς or -ν of Greek words, substitutes the lenis for the aspirate, and once puts ξ for sigma. We should expect, therefore, that the Scythian language would present us with *Visargah* and *Anuswârah*,[2] would repudiate aspirated consonants, and employ ξ instead of the ordinary sibilant. While this is the case with the fragments of the Scythian language which still remain, it is even more remarkable in the old idioms of Italy. In fact, these peculiarities constitute, as we shall see in the sequel, some of the leading features by which the Italian languages are distinguished from the dialects of ancient Greek.

§ 8.
Names of the Scythian rivers derived and explained.

The names of the Scythian rivers, which Herodotus enumerates, will first engage our attention. These names are materially corrupted by the Greek transcription; but with the help of the general principles which have just been stated, we shall be able to analyse them without much difficulty.

Beginning from the European side, the first of these rivers is the *Is-ter*, or, as it is now called, the *Don-au* or

[1] See Niebuhr, *Kleine Schriften*, ii. p. 200 (*über das Ægyptisch-Griechische*).
[2] *N. Crat.* pp. 314, 317.

Dan-ube. If we follow the analogy of our own and other countries, we shall observe that local names very often consist of synonymous elements; from which we may infer that the earlier parts of the word have successively lost their significance. Thus, the words *wick*, *ham*, and *town*, are synonymous, though belonging to different ages of our language; and yet we have compounds such as *Wick-ham* and *Ham[p]-ton-wick*. The words *wan*, *beck*, and *water*, are synonymous; and yet we find a stream in the north of England called *Wans-beck-water*. The words *nagara* and *pura* in Sanscrit both signify " city;" but we find in India a city called *Nag-poor*. In the same way, we believe that both parts of the word *Is-ter* denote " water" or " river." The first part of the word is contained in the name of our own river *Thames*, or *Tam-isis*, the upper part of which is still called the *Is-is*: the second part we shall discuss directly, in speaking of the third Scythian river. The other and more recent name, *Dan-ub-ius*, also contains two elements, each signifying " water" or " river." The latter part is found in the Gaelic *ap*, and in our *Avon*, &c.; the former in most of the Scythian rivers, as will presently appear.

The next river is the *Por-ata* or *Pruth*, which obviously contains the same root as the Greek word πόρος.

The third river is called by Herodotus the Τύρ-ης, and is now known as the *Dnies-ter* or *Danas-ter*. The latter part of this name is the same as the latter part of *Is-ter*. The first part of the compound is the commencement of the other name of the *Is-ter*. In the transcription of Herodotus, either this word is omitted, and the *Danas-ter* is mentioned merely as the *Ter*, or the last syllable of Τύρ-ης represents the first syllable of the *Is-ter*; so that the *Danube* was called the *Is-ter*, and the *Dnies-ter* the *Ter-is*. It is singular that the syllables *Dan-*, *Don-*, or *Dun-*, and *Ter-* or *Tur-*, are used in the Celtic and Pelasgian languages respectively to signify " height," or " hill," or " hill-tower;" and it is to be supposed that this was the origin of their application to the river, which flows rapidly down from its birth-place in the mountains.[1]

The river *Hypan-is* is called, according to the Greek transcription, by a name compounded of the Celtic *Apan* (*Avon*) and the word *is-*, which we have just examined. The first part of the word occurs also in the name of the river *Hypa-caris*, which means the water of *Caris*. The root of the second part of this name appears in the names of the city *Car-cine*, and the river *Ger-rus*, which flowed into the *Car-cinitis sinus* by the same mouth as the *Hypan-is* and *Hypa-caris*. It would also seem that the exceedingly corrupted name *Pan-ticapes* began originally with the same word: the meaning of the last three syllables is absolutely lost, and they will scarcely be sought in the modern name *Ingul-etz*, of which we can only say that the last syllable represents the root *is-;* comp. *Tana-is, Tana-etz*.[2]

The Greeks who dwelt near the mouth of the great river *Borysthenes* naturally pronounced the native name of the river in the manner most convenient to their own articulation; and the name, as it stands, is to all outward appearance a Greek word. This circumstance has deceived the ablest of modern geographers, who derives the first part of the word from Βορῆς or Βορέας. There is little difficulty, however, in shewing that the name is identical with that by which the river is known at the present time, — the *Dnie-per* or *Dana-paris*. It is well known that the northern Greeks were in the habit of substituting the

[1] Coleridge has, with much poetical truth, designated a cataract as " the son of the rock" (*Poems*, vol. ii. p. 131).

[2] The identification of the *Ingul-etz* with the *Pan-ticapes* depends upon the position of the *Hylæa*, or " woodland" district, which must have been on the right bank of the Borysthenes, for the other side of the river is both woodless and waterless (see Lindner, p. 40, sqq.). The name *Ingul* is borne by another river, which may be identified with the *Hypa-caris*.

medial, not only for the tenuis, but even for the aspirate; thus we have βύργος for πύργος, Βερενίκη for Φερενίκη, δανεῖν for θανεῖν, and Βόσ-πορος for Φώσ-φορος. Accordingly, their pronunciation of the word *Dana-paris* (=*Paris-danas*) would be *Dana-baris*, or, by an interchange of the two synonymous elements, *Baris-danas*.[1] But the Greek ear was so familiar to the sequence σθ-, that the *sd-* would inevitably fall into this collocation; and, with a change of vowels, for the same purpose of giving the barbarous name a Greek sound, the compound would become the Hellenic form Βορυσθένης, a word which has hitherto eluded etymological analysis.

The *Tana-is* was the most easterly of Scythian, and indeed of European, rivers. The explanation of the name is implied in what has been already stated. No difficulty can arise from the appearance of a tenuis instead of the medial, which generally appears in the first part of this name; for the Danube, which is most consistently spelt with the medial, is called the *Tun-owe* in the *Niebelungenlied* (v. 6116). The *Tanais* seems to have been the same river which the Cossacks still call the *Donaetz* or *Tanaetz*.

We find the name *Dana-s* in composition not only with the synonymes *Is-*, *Ap-*, *Paris*, and *Ter*, but also with *Rha-*, which occurs in the name of the Asiatic *A-ra-xes*, now the *Rha-*, or *Wolga*. Thus, we have the *E-ri-danus* in Italy, the *Rha-danau* in Prussia, the *Rho-danus* in France, and the name Ῥοῦ-δον, quoted by Ptolemy. In England the name *Dana* occurs by itself as "the *Don*."

§ 9.
Names of the Scythian divinities.

Let us now pass to the names of the Scythian gods, which may be referred without any difficulty to the roots of the Indo-Germanic family of languages. Herodotus informs us (iv. 59), that the names by which the Scythians desig-

---

[1] A similar change has taken place in the name *Berézina*.

nated the Greek divinities, Ἱστίη, Ζεύς, Γῆ, Ἀπόλλων, Οὐρανίη Ἀφροδίτη, and Ποσειδέων, were Ταβιτί, Παπαῖος, Ἀπία, Οἰτόσυρος, Ἀρτίμπασα, and Θαμιμασάδας.

Ἱστίη, or *Vesta*, was the goddess of fire. There can be no doubt why the Medo-Scythians called her *Tabiti*, when we know that in the Zend and Sanscrit languages the root *tab-* or *tap-* signifies " to burn." Compare also the Latin *tab-eo*, the Greek τῖφ-ος, and the German *thau-en*.

Ζεύς, or Ζεὺς πατήρ (*Ju-piter*), was called Παπαῖος, or " the Father," a name by which he was known to the Latins also. The primary labial sounds are appropriated in all languages to express the primary relation of parent and child. The children on whom Psammitichus tried his experiment (Herod. ii. 2) first uttered the articulate sound βε-κός, apparently the first labial followed by the first guttural; and in some articulations, as well as in the order of our alphabet, this is the natural sequence. To this spontaneous utterance of the first labials to designate the parental relation and the primary necessities of infancy, I have referred elsewhere (*N. Crat.* p. 340); and it seems to have struck Delitsch also (*Isagoge*, p. 131), when he speaks of those nouns " quæ aboriginum instar sine verbi semine sponte provenerunt, velut אָב, אֵם, primi labiales balbutientis pueri, Sanscr. *pi-tṛi, ma-tṛi,* &c."

The Scythian name for the goddess of the Earth is Ἀπία. This word actually occurs in Greek, as the name of the country where the Pelasgians ruled: and the root *Ap-* or *Op-* is of frequent occurrence both in Greece and in Italy (Buttmann's *Lexil.* s. v.).

As the Scythian religion appears to have exhibited an elementary character, we should expect that their Apollo would be " the god of the sun." And this seems to be the meaning of his name, as cited by Herodotus. Οἰτό-συρος should signify " the light or life of the sun." The second part of the word at once refers us to the Sanscrit *súrya*, which is also implied in the σύριον ἅρμα of Æschylus (*Pers.* 86. *N. Crat.* p. 576). The first two syllables may be explained as follows. After the loss of the digamma, the sound of *w* at the beginning of a word was often expressed by *o*: thus we have Ὄαξος = Fάξος ; Ὄασις, with its modern equivalent *el Wah;* the Persian interjection ὄα (Æschyl. *Pers.* 116), which is doubtless the Greek representative of the oriental exclamation *wah;* the N. Test. οὐαί = *weh;* and the word οἶστρος, referring to the *whizzing* noise of the gad-fly. Accordingly, Οἰτό-συρος, pronounced *Wito-suros,* signifies the *Uita,* Οἶτος, Αἶσα, or life of the sun: comp. the Russian *Vite*, signifying "a portion;" or if we prefer the cognate idea of light, we may compare the οἰτο- with αἰθή, αἰθός, *uitta, weiss,* "white."

It is by no means clear what were the attributes of the celestial Venus of the Scythians. It seems, however, that the name Ἀρτίμ-πασα must be an approximation to *Ertham-pasa,* "the queen of the earth."

The Scythian name for Neptune may be explained with almost demonstrable certainty. The general observations on the Scythian language have shewn that they preferred the tenuis to the aspirate. The word Θαμιμασάδας must therefore have been pronounced *Tami-masadas.* Now, if we compare this word with the Scythian proper name *Octa-masadas* (Herod. iv. 80), we shall see that *masadas* must be the termination. In the Zend, or old Median language, *Mazdas* (connected with *maz*, "great"), signifies "a god," or "object of worship." So *Or-muzd* is called *Ahura-mazdas,* and a worshipper is termed *Mazda-yasna.* Accordingly, *Tami-masadas* must mean "a god, or object of worship, with regard to *Tami.*" When, therefore, we learn from Pliny, that *Temerinda* is equivalent to *mater maris,* we cannot doubt that *Teme,* or *Tami,* means "the sea," and that *Tami-masadas,* or "Neptune," is, by interpretation, " the god of the sea." It does not appear that the second part of the name *Temerinda* is a distinct word in itself. It seems more probable that it is a feminine termination, analogous to *Larunda*. The word *Tama* probably signifies " broad water;" for the river which is called the *Is-is* while it is narrow, becomes the *Tam-is-is*, or " Thames," when it begins to widen.

That the name of a man, like *Octa-masadas*, should be significant of veneration will not surprise those who recollect the Scythian name *Sparga-pises* (the son of Tomyris, Herod. i. 211), or *Sparga-pithes* (a king of the Agathyrsi, id. iv. 78), which seems to be equivalent to the Sanscrit *Svarga-pati*, " lord of heaven "—*sparga* bearing the same relation to *svarga* that the Persian *açpa* does to the Sanscrit *açva*; and the Zend *çpan*, old Persian *çpaka*, Sclavonian *sabaka*, to the Sanscrit *çva* (*çvan*), Greek κύων.

§ 10.
Other Scythian words explained.

Leaving the names of divinities, we may turn to the scarcely less mythological *Arimaspi*. Herodotus says that they were a one-eyed people (μουνόφθαλμοι), and that their name indicates as much—ἄριμα γὰρ ἓν καλέουσι Σκύθαι, σποῦ δὲ τὸν ὀφθαλμόν. If this be true, we shall have no difficulty in referring the name to the class of languages of which we are speaking; for, with the change of *r* for *d*, so common in Latin (compare *auris, audio; ar-veho*= *ad-veho; arvocito*=*sœpe advoco*, Fest.; *ar-cesso*=*ad-cesso; meridie*=*medi-die*, &c.), *arima* will represent the Sanscrit ordinal *ádima*; and we may compare σποῦ with the root *spic-* or *spec-*, signifying " to spie" or " to see."

Another compound, which may with equal facility be referred to the Indo-Germanic family of languages, is the name by which the Scythians designated the Amazons. Οἰόρπατα, according to Herodotus, is equivalent to ἀνδροκτόνος—ο ἰὸρ γὰρ καλέουσι τὸν ἄνδρα, τὸ δὲ πατά, κτείνειν. Now οἰόρ is clearly the Sanscrit *víra*, the Zend *vairya*, the Latin *vir*, Gothic *vair-s*, Welsh *gwyr*, and the Lithuanian *vyras*. The root *pat* in Sanscrit does not signify primarily " to kill," but " to fall ;" though the causative form *pátyati* constantly means " he kills," *i. e.* " causes to fall." It seems more probable, however, that the Scythian articulation has substituted a tenuis for the *v*-sound, as in the case of *sparga* for *svarga*, mentioned above, and that the verb is to be sought in the common Sanscrit root *vadha*, " to strike," " to kill," " to destroy."

Pliny (*Hist. Nat.* vi. 17) tells us that the Scythian name for Mount Caucasus was *Grou-casus*, i. e. *nive candidus*. The first part of this word is clearly connected with *gelu*, *glacies*, κρύος, κρύ-σταλλος, *kalt*, *cold*, *grau*, and *grey ;* and *casa*, " white," may be compared with *cas-tus*, *casnar* (senex *Oscorum lingua*, Fest.; comp. Varro, *L. L.* vii. § 29), *canus*, &c.

In the tract about rivers, printed among Plutarch's Fragments, we have the following Scythian words, with interpretations annexed. He does not interpret ἀλίνδα, which he describes as a sort of cabbage growing near the Tanais (c. xiv. § 2): we may compare the word with *Temerinda*. He tells us, however, that βριξάβα means κριοῦ μέτωπον (c. xiv. § 4), that φρύξα is equivalent to μισοπόνηρος (c. xiv. § 5), and ἀράξα signifies μισοπάρθενος (c. xxiii. § 2). Of these, βρίξ, " a ram," seems connected with *berbex*, *verbix*, or *vervex*. Ἄβα is probably akin to *caput*, *kapala*, *haupt*, &c.,—the initial guttural having been lost, as in *amo*, Sanscr. *kama-*. We may compare ξά, " to hate," with the German *scheu*. The syllable φρυ (*phru*) probably contains the element of *prav-us* (comp. the German *frevel*); and ἄρα, signifying " a virgin," may perhaps be connected with Ἄρ-τεμις, Etrusc. *Ari-timi-s*.

Herodotus (iv. 52) mentions a fountain the name of which was Σκυθιστὶ μὲν Ἐξαμπαῖος, κατὰ δὲ τὴν Ἑλλήνων γλῶσσαν, Ἱραὶ ὁδοί. Ritter (*Vorhalle*, p. 345) conjectures that the original form of 'Εξαμ-παῖ-ος must have been *Hexen-Pfad*, i. e. *Asen-Pfad*, which he compares with *Siri-pad*, and which denotes, he thinks, the sacred ominous road by which the Cimmerian Buddhists travelled towards the west. Böckh (*Corpus Inscript.* ii. p. 111) supposes the right interpretation to be ἐννέα ὁδοί; so that ἐξάν is "nine." The numeral "nine" is preserved in a very mutilated state in all languages, both Semitic and Indo-Germanic. It may, however, be shewn that it is equivalent in all its expressions to $10-1$; and it would not be difficult to point out the possibility of this in the word ἐξάν, if the reading ἐννέα ὁδοί were really certain.

This examination includes all the Scythian words which have come down to us with an interpretation; and in all of them it has been shewn that they are connected, in the signification assigned to them, with the roots or elements which we find in the Indo-Germanic languages. If we add this result of philology to the traditionary facts which have been recorded of the international relations of the Getæ, Scythæ, Sauromatæ, and Medes, we must conclude that the inhabitants of the northern side of the Euxine, who were known to the Greeks under the general name of Scythians, were members of the Indo-Germanic family, and not Mongolians, as Niebuhr has supposed.

§ 11. Successive peopling of Asia and Europe: fate of the Mongolian race.

The true theory with regard to the successive peopling of Asia and Europe seems to be the following.[1] While the Indo-Germanic or Japhetic race was developing itself within the limits of Irân, and while the Semitic family were spreading from Mesopotamia to Arabia and Egypt, a great population of Tchudes, or Mongolians, had extended

---

[1] See Winning's *Manual*, p. 124, sqq. Rask *über das Alter und die Echtheit der Zend-Sprache*, p. 69, sqq., Hagen's Tr. And, for the affinity of the inhabitants of Northern Asia in particular, see Prichard *on the Ethnography of High Asia* (Journal of R. G. S. x. 2, p. 192, sqq.).

its migrations from the Arctic to the Indian Ocean, and from Greenland over the whole north of America, Asia, and Europe, even as far as Britain, France, and Spain. In proportion, however, as these Tchudes were widely spread, so in proportion were they thinly scattered; their habits were nomadic, and they never formed themselves into large or powerful communities. Consequently, when the Iranians broke forth from their narrow limits, in compacter bodies, and with superior physical and intellectual organisation, they easily mastered or drove before them these rude barbarians of the old world; and in the great breadth of territory which they occupied, the Tchudes have formed only two independent states—the Mantchus in China, and the Turks in Europe. There can be no doubt that they were mixed with the Sarmatians and Getæ, who conquered them on the north of the Euxine; and perhaps the name of *S-colotæ*, or *Asa-Galatæ*, by which the Scythæ called themselves, may point to a Celtic intermixture. But it is obvious, from the arguments which have been adduced, that this Scythian nation, of which Herodotus wrote, did not consist of Tchudes, but of the Indo-Germanic tribes, who conquered them, and who were, as has been shewn, of the same family as the Pelasgians.

It has been proved that the Sarmatians were the parent stock of the Sclavonians; and we find in the Sclavonian dialects ample illustrations of those general principles by which the Scythian languages seem to have been characterised. Making, then, a fresh start from this point, we shall find an amazing number of coincidences between the Sclavonian languages and the Pelasgian element of Greek and Latin: most of these have been pointed out elsewhere; at present it is only necessary to call attention to the fact. So that, whichever way we look at it, we

§ 12.
The Pelasgians were of Sclavonian origin.

shall find new reasons for considering the Pelasgians as a branch of the great Sarmatian or Sclavonian race. The Thracians, Getæ, Scythæ, and Sauromatæ, were so many links in a long chain connecting the Pelasgians with Media; the Sauromatæ were Sclavonians; and the Pelasgian language, as it appears in the oldest forms of Latin, and in certain Greek archaisms, was unquestionably most nearly allied to the Sclavonian: we cannot, therefore, doubt that this was the origin of the Pelasgian people, especially as there is no evidence or argument to the contrary.

§ 13.
Foreign affinities of the Umbrians, &c.

But, to return to Italy, who were the old inhabitants of that peninsula? Whom did the Pelasgians in the first instance conquer or drive to the mountains? What was the origin of that hardy race, which, descending once more to the plain, subjugated Latium, founded Rome, and changed the destiny of the world?

The Umbrians, Oscans, or Sabines—for we must now consider them as only different members of the same family—are never mentioned as foreigners. We know, however, that they must have had their Transpadane affinities as well as their Pelasgian rivals. It is only because they were in Italy before the Pelasgians arrived there, that they are called aborigines. The difference between them and the Pelasgians is in effect this: in examining the ethnical affinities of the latter we have tradition as well as comparative grammar to aid us; whereas the establishment of the Umbrian pedigree depends upon philology alone.

§ 14.
Reasons for believing that they were the same

Among the oldest languages of the Indo-Germanic family not the least remarkable is the Lithuanian, which stands first among the Sclavonian dialects,[1] and bears a

---

[1] See Pott, *Et. Forsch.* i. p. xxxiii.

§ 14.] THE ANCIENT ITALIANS. 43

nearer resemblance to Sanscrit than any European idiom. race as the Lithuanians. It is spoken, in different dialects, by people who live around the south-east corner of the Baltic. One branch of this language is the old Prussian, which used to be indigenous in the *Sam-land* or " Fen-country" between the Memel and the Pregel, along the shore of the *Curische Haf*. Other writers have pointed out the numerous and striking coincidences between the people who spoke this language and the Italian aborigines. Thus the connexion between the Sabine *Cures, Quirinus, Quirites*, &c. and the old Prussian names *Cures, Cour-land, Curische Haf*, &c. has been remarked; it' has been shewn that the wolf (*hirpus*), which was an object of mystic reverence among the Sabines, and was connected with many of their ceremonies and some of their legends, is also regarded as ominous of good luck among the Lettons and Courlanders; the Sabine legend of the rape of the virgins, in the early history of Rome, was invented to explain their marriage ceremonies, which are still preserved among the Courlanders and Lithuanians, where the bride is carried off from her father's house with an appearance of force; even the immortal name of Rome is found in the Prussian *Romowo;* and the connexion of the words *Roma, Romulus, ruma lupæ*, and *ruminalis ficus*, is explained by the Lithuanian *raumu*, gen. *raumens*, signifying " a dug" or " udder."[1] Besides these, a great number of

---

[1] See Festus, p. 266-8, Müller; and Pott, *Etymol. Forsch.* ii. p. 283. According to this etymology, the name *Romanus* ultimately identifies itself with the ethnical denomination *Hirpinus*. The derivation of the word *Roma* is, after all, very uncertain; and there are many who might prefer to connect it with *Groma*, the name given to the *forum*, or point of intersection of the main streets in the original *Roma quadrata*, which was also, by a very significant augury, called *mundus* (see Festus, p. 266; Dionys. i. 88; Bunsen, *Beschreib. d. Stadt Rom*, iii. p. 81; and below, Ch. VII. § 6). The word *groma* or *gruma*, however, is not without its Lithuanian affinities. I cannot agree with Müller (*Etrusk.* ii. p. 152), Pott (*Etym. Forsch.* ii. 101), and

words and forms of words in the Sabine language are explicable most readily from a comparison with the Lithuanian; and the general impression which these arguments leave upon our mind is, that the aborigines of Italy were of the same race as the Lithuanians or old Prussians.

§ 15.
Further confirmation from etymology.

Let us add to this comparison one feature which has not yet been observed. The Lithuanians were not only called by this name, which involves both the aspirated dental *th* and the vocalised labial *u*, but also by the names *Livonian* and *Lettonian*, which omit respectively one or other of these articulations. Now it has been mentioned before, that the name of the Latins exhibits the same phenomenon; for as they were called both *Latins* and *Lavines*, it follows that their original name must have been *Latuinians*, which is only another way of spelling and pronouncing *Lithuanians*. If, therefore, the warrior tribe, which descended upon Latium from Reate and conquered the Pelasgians, gave their name to the country, we see that these aborigines were actually called Lithuanians, and it has been shewn that they and the Sabines were virtually the same stock. Consequently, the old Prussians brought even their name into Italy. And what does this name

Benfey (*Wurzel-Lexikon*, ii. p. 143), who follow the old grammarians and connect this word with the Greek γνῶμα, γνώμη, γνώμων: it is much more reasonable to suppose, with Klenze (*Abhandl*. p. 135, note), that it is a genuine Latin term; and I would suggest that it may be connected with *grumus*, Lithuan. *krúwa*, Lettish *kraut*: comp. κρώμαξ, κλώμαξ, *globus*, *gleba*, &c. The name may have been given to the point of intersection of the main *via* and *limes*, because a heap of stones was there erected as a mark (cf. Charis. i. p. 19). Even in our day it is common to mark the junction of several roads by a cross, an obelisk, or some other erection; to which the *grumus*, or "barrow," was the first rude approximation. If so, it may still be connected with *ruma*; just as μαστός signifies both "a hillock" and "a breast;" and the omission of the initial *g* before a liquid is very common in Latin, comp. *narro* with γνωρίζω, *nosco* with γιγνώσκω, and *norma* with γνώριμος.

§ 17.] THE ANCIENT ITALIANS. 45

signify? Simply, "freemen."[1] For the root signifying "free," in all the European languages consisted of *l-* and a combination of dental and labial, with, of course, a vowel interposed. In most languages the labial is vocalised into *u*, and prefixed to the dental; as in Greek ἐ-λεύθε-ρος, Lithuan. *liaudis*, Germ. *leute*, &c. In the Latin *liber* the labial alone remains.

There are many points of resemblance between these Lithuanians and the Sclavonians on the one hand, and between them and the Celts on the other; and it can scarcely be doubted that in their northern as well as their southern settlements, they were a good deal intermixed with Celtic tribes in the first instance, and subjected to Sclavonian influences afterwards. That this was the case with the Lithuanians, we learn from their authentic and comparatively modern history. It appears, too, that in Italy there was a substratum of Celts before the Lithuanians arrived there; and that the Sclavonian Pelasgians, having subsequently entered the country, absorbed the Lithuanian element into their own language in the northern half of the peninsula, whereas in the south, and especially on the banks of the Tiber, the Lithuanian ingredient predominated, and most materially affected the kindred Pelasgian idiom of ancient Latium.

§ 16. Celtic tribes intermixed with the Sclavonians and Lithuanians.

If it is necessary to go one step further, and identify this Lithuanian race with some one of the tribes which

§ 17. The Sarmatæ probably a

---

[1] By a singular change, the name of the kindred Sclavonians, which in the oldest remains of the language signifies "celebrated," "illustrious" (from *çlava*, "glory," root *çlu*, Sanscr. *çru*, Gr. κλυ-: see 'Safařik and Palacky's *Æltest. Denkm. der Böhm. Spr.* pp. 63, 140), has furnished the modern designation of "a slave," *esclave*, *schiavo*. The Bulgarians, whom Gibbon classes with the Sclavonians (vii. p. 279, ed. Milman), have been still more unfortunate in the secondary application of their name (Gibbon, x. p. 177).

branch of the Lithuanian family. form so many links of the chain between Media and Thrace, it would be only reasonable to select the *Sauromatæ*, whose name receives its interpretation from the Lithuanian language (*Szaure-Mateni*, i. e. " Northern Medes). The Sauromatæ and the Scythæ were undoubtedly kindred tribes;[1] but still there were some marked differences between them, insomuch that Herodotus reckons the Sarmatæ as a separate nation. Between the Pelasgians and the Umbrians, &c. there existed the same affinities, with similar differences; and the ethnographer may acquiesce in the satisfactory assurance that he has Lithuanians by the side of Sclavonians—Sarmatians dwelling in the neighbourhood of Scythians—on the north of the Euxine, on the south coast of the Baltic, and in the richer and more genial peninsula of Italy.

The present inhabitants of Sarmatia are the *Cossacks;* a word which many derive from the ethnic name *Sacæ*. Whatever may be the origin of the term, it is clear that it is no longer a national name; for *Cossacks*, or "freebooting light troops," are found in the Turkish as well as in the Russian armies. The Cossacks who occupy the territory of the ancient Sarmatæ are Sclavonians.

[1] As general designations, the names *Sarmatian* and *Sclavonian* are co-extensive, and include the Scythians as well as the Sauromatæ. In speaking, however, of the Scythians of Herodotus, we are obliged to take the name *Sauromatæ* in a somewhat narrower sense. It is true that some confusion may be created by this change in the application of ethnical names; for we must also limit the name *Sclavonian*, if we wish to oppose it to the term *Lithuanian*. But these difficulties will always beset the terminology of the ethnographer, who has to deal with names as vague and fleeting as the traditions with which they are connected.

CHAPTER III.

THE UMBRIAN LANGUAGE AS EXHIBITED IN THE EUGUBINE TABLES.

§ 1. The Eugubine Tables. § 2. Peculiarities by which the old Italian alphabets were distinguished. § 3. The sibilants. § 4. Some remarks on the other letters. § 5. Umbrian grammatical forms. § 6. Selections from the Eugubine Tables, with explanations: Tab. I. a, 1. § 7. Tab. I. a, 2-6. § 8. Tab. I. b, 13, sqq. § 9. Extracts from the Litany in Tab. VI. a. § 10. Umbrian words which approximate to their Latin synonymes. § 11. The Todi inscription contains four words of the same class.

FROM the preceding investigations it appears that the original inhabitants of ancient Italy may be divided into two great classes, one of which entered the peninsula before the other. It is not necessary to speak here of the Celts, who formed the substratum in all the insular and peninsular districts of Europe; but confining our attention to the more important ingredients of the population, we find only two — the Lithuanians and the Sclavonians. To the former belonged the Umbrians, Oscans, and, the connecting link between them, the Sabines; to the latter the Etruscans, and all the various ramifications of the Pelasgian race.

§ 1. The Eugubine Tables.

The next step will be to examine in detail some of the fragmentary remains of the language spoken by these ancient tribes. The Umbrian claims the precedence, not only on account of the copiousness and importance of the reliques of the language, but also because the Umbrians must be considered as the most important and original of all those ancient Italian tribes with whom the Pelasgians became intermixed either as conquerors or as vassals.

The Eugubine Tables, which contain a living specimen of the Umbrian language, were discovered in the year 1444 in a subterraneous chamber at *La Schieggia*, in the neighbourhood of the ancient city of *Iguvium* (now *Gubbio* or *Ugubio*), which lay at the foot of the Apennines, near the *via Flaminia* (Plin. *H. N.* xxiii. 49). On the mountain, which commanded the city, stood the temple of *Jupiter Apenninus;* and from its connexion with the worship of this deity the city derived its name:— *Iguvium*, Umbr. *Iiovium*, i. e. *Iovium*, Δῖον, Διὸς πόλις. The Tables, which are seven in number, and are in perfect preservation, relate chiefly to matters of religion. From the change of *s* in those of the Tables which are written in the Etruscan or Umbrian character, into *r* in those which are engraved in Roman letters, Lepsius infers (*de Tabb. Eugub.* p. 86, sqq.) that the former were written not later than A.U.C. 400; for it appears that even in proper names the original *s* began to be changed into *r* about A.U.C. 400 (see Cic. *ad Famil.* ix. 21. comp. Liv. iii. cap. 4, 8. Pompon. *in Digg.* i. 2, 2, § 36. Schneider, *Lat. Gr.* i. 1, p. 341, note); and it is reasonable to suppose that the same change took place at a still earlier period in common words. By a similar argument, derived chiefly from the arbitrary insertion of *h* between two vowels in the *Tabulæ Latine scriptæ*, Lepsius infers (p. 93) that these were written about the middle of the sixth century A.U.C., *i. e.* at least two centuries after the *Tabulæ Umbrice scriptæ*.

§ 2.
Peculiarities by which the old Italian alphabets were distinguished.

Before, however, we turn our attention to these Tables, and the forms of words which are found in them, it will be advisable to make a few remarks on the alphabet which was used in ancient Italy.

The general facts with regard to the adaptation of the

Semitic alphabet to express the sounds of the Pelasgian language have been discussed elsewhere.[1] It has there been shewn that the original sixteen characters of the Semitic syllabarium were the following twelve :—

Breathings.	Labials.	Palatals.	Dentals.	
א	ב	ג	ד	Tenues.
ה	ו	ח	ט	Aspirates.
ע	פ	ק	ת	Medials.

with the addition of the three liquids, ל, מ, נ, and the sibilant ס; and it has been proved that these sixteen were the first characters known to the Greeks. They were not, however, sufficient to express the sounds of the old languages of Italy even in the earliest form in which they present themselves to us. The Umbrian alphabet contains twenty letters; the Oscan as many; the Etruscan and the oldest Latin alphabets nineteen. In these Italian alphabets some of the original Semitic letters are omitted, while there is a great increase in the sibilants; for whereas the original sixteen characters furnish only the sibilants s and TH, the old Italian alphabets exhibit not only these, but SH or X, Z, R, and Ṙ. Of these additional sibilants, x is the Hebrew *shin*, z is *zade*, R represents *resh*, and Ṙ is an approximation to the sound of θ.

As these sibilants constitute the distinguishing feature in the old Italian languages, it will be useful to speak more particularly of them, before we turn to the other letters.

§ 3. The sibilants.

(*a*) The primary sibilant s, as used by the Umbrians

---

[1] *N. Crat.* p. 98, sqq.

and Oscans, does not appear to have differed, either in sound or form, from its representative in the Greek alphabet.

(b) The secondary sibilant z, in the Umbrian and Etruscan alphabets, appears to have corresponded to only one of the two values of the Greek ζ. The latter, as we have proved elsewhere, was not only the soft *g* or *j*, or ultimately the sound *sh*, but also equivalent to the combination *sd*, or ultimately, by assimilation, to *ss*. Now the Romans expressed the first sound of the Greek ζ either by *di* or by *j*, and its ultimate articulation (*sh*) by *x*; whereas, on the other hand, they represented ζ = σδ either by a simple *s*, or by its Greek assimilation *ss*. Thus the Etruscan *Kanzna, Venzi, Kazi, Veliza*, are written in Latin *Cæsius, Vensius, Cassius, Vilisa*, and Ζάκυνθος becomes *Saguntus;* while the Greek μάζα, μύζω, ὄβρυζον, πυτίζειν, ἀναγκάζειν, κωμάζειν, may be compared with *massa, musso, obrussa, pytissare, necesse, comissari*. In the Eugubine Tables, words which in the Umbrian characters exhibit a z, give us a corresponding s in those which are written with Latin letters. Thus, for the proper name *Iapuzkum*, as it is written in Umbrian characters, we have in the Latin letters *Iabuske, Iabusker*, &c.

(c) The aspirated Umbrian sibilant ś, for which the Oscans wrote x, expressed the sound *sh* (Germ. *sch*, Fr. *ch*), which was the ultimate articulation of the other sound of the Greek ζ. We may compare it with the Sanscrit श (ç); and, like that Sanscrit sibilant and the Greek ζ, it often appears as a softened guttural. Thus we find *prusesetu* for *prusekatu*, Lat. *pro-secato;* and the termination *-kla, -kle, -klu* (Lat. *-culum*), often appears as *-śla, -śle, -ślu*. As in our own and other languages the gutturals are softened before the vowels *e* and *i*, so in Umbrian the guttural *k* generally becomes ś before the same vowels. The sibilant ś occurs only in contact with vowels, liquids, and *h*; and the prefix *an-*, which drops the *n* before consonants, retains it before vowels and s.

(*d*) The letter R is always to be regarded as a secondary or derived character. In Umbrian it generally represents, at the end of a word, the original sibilant s. When the Eugubine Tables are written in Etruscan characters, we have such forms as, *veres treplanes, tutas Ikuvinas;* but in those which give us Latin letters, we read *verir treplanir, totar Ijovinar*. This change is particularly observable in the inflexions of the Latin passive verb; and the Latin language, in other forms, uses the letter R in the same way as the Umbrian. In fact, the most striking characteristic of the Umbrian language is, its continual employment of the secondary letters R and H, both of which are ultimately derived from sibilants. The former is used in Umbrian, not only in the verb-forms, as in Latin, but also in the declensions, in the Latin forms of which it only occurs in the gen. plural. The letter H is often interposed between vowels both in Umbrian and in Latin. Thus we have in Umbrian the forms *stahito, pihatu,* for *stato, piato,* and *Naharcum* derived from *Nar;* and in Latin, *ahenus, vehemens, cohors, mehe* (Quinctil. i. 5, 2), by the side of *aeneus, vemens* (compare *ve-cors, cle-mens*), *cors, me;* and even *Deheberis* for *Tiberis:* but this, as has been mentioned above, refers to a later epoch both in Umbrian and Latin (see Lepsius, *de Tabb. Eug.* p. 92, and Schneid. *Lat. Gr.* i. 1, p. 118, not. 187).

(*e*) The sibilant Ř is peculiar to the Umbrians. In the Latin transcription it is often represented by the combination *rs*. Sometimes, however, it seems to stand for *si*, as in *festiřa* = *vestisia;* and it also serves as the ultimate assibilation of a guttural, for *teřa* = *dersa* and *tesva* = *dersva* are connected with *dica* and *dextra*. Its real pronunciation was probably similar to that of *θ*, which last occurs only twice in the Eugubine Tables. The frequent substitution of *r* for *d* in Latin indicates a change to that letter through the softened dental *θ*, and we often find ŕ where we should expect a dental, as in *fureńt = furent, kapiŕe = capide, ařveitu = advehito*, &c. Although ŕ is sometimes represented by *rs*, we also occasionally find this letter followed by *s*, as in the words *eturstamu, meŕs*, which in the Latin character are written *eturstahmu, mers*.

§ 4.
Some remarks on the other letters.

Of the other letters it will not be necessary to say much. The most remarkable is the Oscan vowel í, which in the inscriptions appears as a mutilated F; thus, ғ. The same figure was adopted by Claudius to express the middle sound between *i* and *u* with which the Romans pronounced such words as *virtus, vigere*, and *scribere*. In Oscan it appears to have been either a very light *i* (and so distinguished from the vowel ɪ, which generally represents the long *i* of the Romans), or else a very short *u*. In the Oscan inscriptions í is of more frequent occurrence than *i*. Whenever these vowels come together, *i* always precedes. í is almost invariably used to form the diphthongs *úi, aí, eí*, answering to the Greek οι (ῳ), αι (ᾳ), and ει; and *i* very rarely appears before two consonants.

The Oscan letter ᴜ' stands to ᴜ in the same relation as this í to the Oscan ɪ. The former seems to be a sort of very light *o*, which is substituted for it in those inscriptions which are written in the Latin character; whereas the letter *u* seems to represent the long *o* of the Latins, as in *-um* (Gr. -ων) for *orum, likí-tud* for *lice-to, kvaísstur* for *quæstor*, &c.

The Umbrians and Oscans distinguished between ᴜ and ᴠ. The latter was a consonant, and was pronounced like our *w*. It was written as a consonant after ᴋ; but the vowel *u* was preferred, as in Latin, after ǫ.

The letters ʟ and ʙ were of rare occurrence in the

Umbrian language. The former never stands at the beginning of a word, the latter never at the end of one. In the Oscan language we meet with L more frequently.

As the Etruscan alphabet had no medials, those of the Eugubine Tables which are written in Etruscan characters substitute K for G, e. g. *Krapuvi* for *Grabove*. But the Oscan and Umbrian inscriptions when written in Latin characters distinguish between the tenuis and medial gutturals, according to the marks introduced by Sp. Carvilius, viz. C, G.

In the Oscan alphabet D is represented as an inverted R; and the affinity between these letters in the Latin language is well known.

The labial P, which never terminates a word in Latin, stands at the end of many mutilated forms both in Umbrian and Oscan, as in the Umbrian *vitlup* for *vitulibus* (*vitulis*), and the Oscan *nep* for *neque*. In general, it is to be remarked that the letters P, F, R, S, D, and T, all occur as terminations of Umbrian or Oscan words.

§ 5. Umbrian grammatical forms.

The grammatical forms of the Umbrian language are very instructive; and the author of these pages has already made use of them in the solution of the most difficult problem in Latin etymology,— the person-endings of the passive voice (see *New Cratylus*, p. 445). In Umbrian we see the secondary letter *r*, that important element in the formation of Latin words, not only regularly used in the formation of the cases and numbers of nouns which in Latin retain their original *s*, but also appearing in plural verb-forms by the side of the primitive *s*, which is retained in the singular, though the Latin has substituted the *r* in both numbers. The following are the three declensions of Umbrian nouns, according to the scheme given by Müller (*Götting. Gel. Anz.* 1838, p. 58):

I. Decl. *Tota*, a city. II. Decl. *Poplus*, a people.
Nom. *tota*.   *poplus*.
Gen. *tota-r*.   *pople-r*.
Dat. *tote*.   *pople*.
Accus. *totam*.   *poplo-m*.
Abl. *tota*.   *poplu*.

III. Decl. *Ocri-s*, a mountain. *Nome*, a name.
Nom. *ocri(s)*.   *nome*.
Gen. *ocre-r*.   *nomner*.
Dat. *ocre*.   *nomne*.
Accus. *ocrem*.   *nome*.
Abl. *ocri*.   *nome*.

Besides these cases, the Umbrian has a locative, which ends sometimes in *-e*, and sometimes in *-m* or *-me*. Similarly the ancient Latin has two locatives, one in *e = ai* or *ei*, the other in *-im*. It is a question among philologers (below, p. 59), whether the *-f* at the end of plural nouns is a mark of the accusative, or whether it stands as a mutilated element of *-φι, -φιν, -bi, -bus* (see *New Cratylus*, p. 321). The latter is the more reasonable supposition. At all events; this must be the force of *kute-f = caute*, which stands by the side of the locative *sevum*. The genitive plural seems to end in *-rum*, like the Latin (iii. 2).

The verbs generally occur in the imperative mood, as might be expected, since the Tables contain chiefly prayers and injunctions about praying. In these imperatives we mostly recognise a singular in *-tu*, and a plural in *-tutu;* as *fu-tu* (vi. a, 30, &c.), and *fu-tutu* (vi. b, 61), corresponding to *es-to, es-tote*. Verbs of the *-a* conjugation seem occasionally to make their imperative in *-a*, like the Latin. See i. b, 33: *pune purtinsus, karetu; pufe apruf fakurent, puze erus tera; ape erus terust, pustru kupifiatu:* where, though the meaning of particular words may be doubtful, the construction is plain enough: *postquam consecraveris* (?), *cædito* (scil. *popa*); *ubi apris fecerint, ibi preces* (? comp. ἀράς) *dica; quando preces dicaverit, bitumine* (? φωστρῷ) *com-piato*. We often have the perf. subj. both singular and plural, as may be seen in the example just quoted. The pres. subj. too occasionally appears, the person-ending in the singular being generally omitted, as in *arsie* for *ar-sies* = *ad-sies*, and *habia* for *habeas*. The old infinitive, or supine as it is called, is used in Umbrian; and we often find the auxiliary perfect both in the singular and in the plural. See vi. b, 30: *perse touer peskler vasetom est, pesetom est, peretum est, frosetom est, daetom est, touer peskler virseto avirseto vas est:* i. e. *quoniam bonis precibus vacatum est, pacatum est, paratum est, rogatum est, datum est, bonis precibus vertere, avertere fas est*. And we have not only *skrehto est*, but also *skreihtor sent* (vi. a, 15). The active participle seems to end both in *-ens*, like the Latin, and also in *-is*, like that of the Greek verbs in -μι. The following are the forms of *habeo* which are found in the Tables:

Pres. Indic.
3. sing. *habe*[*t*] (i. b, 18; vi. b, 54).

Pres. Subj.
2. sing. *habia*[*s*] (v. a, 17).

Pret. Subj.
2. sing. *habiest* (vi. b, 50); *habus* (*habueris*) (vi. b, 40).
3. plur. *haburent* (vii. a, 52).

Imperat.
2. sing. *habitu* (vi. a, 19); or *habetu* (ii. a, 23).
2. plur. *habituto* (vi. b, 51); or *habetutu* (i. b, 15).

§ 6. Selections from the Eugubine Tables, with explanations.

In interpreting the remains of the Umbrian language, it seems advisable, in the present state of our knowledge, that we should confine our attention to those passages which fall within the reach of a scientific philological examination. Grotefend,[1] indeed, has frankly and boldly presented us with a Latin version of all the Eugubine Tables; but although he has here and there fallen upon some happy conjectures, his performance is for the most part mere guesswork of the vaguest kind, and therefore, for all purposes of scholarship, uninstructive and unsatisfactory. Lassen, by attempting less, has really effected more.[2]

The following extracts are selected from the admirable transcripts of Lepsius, and the arrangement of the Tables is that which he has adopted. The first four Tables, and part of the fifth, are written in the Etruscan or Umbrian character. The others are in Latin letters.

Tab. I. a, 1. Tab. I. a, 1. This Table and its reverse contain the rules for twelve sacrifices to be performed by the *Fratres Atiersii* in honour of the twelve gods. The same rules are given in Tables vi. and vii. and in nearly the same words, the differences being merely dialectical; but the latter Tables add the liturgy to be used on the occasion, and also dwell at greater length on the auguries to be employed, &c. The first Table begins as follows:

Este persklum aves anzeriates enetu, 2. *pernaies pusnaes.*

And in VI. a, 11, we have:

---

[1] *Rudimenta Linguæ Umbricæ*, Particulæ viii. Hannov. 1835-1839.

[2] *Beiträge zur Deutung der Eugubinischen Tafeln*, in the *Rhein. Mus.* for 1833, 4. Of earlier interpretations it is scarcely necessary to speak. It may, however, amuse the reader to know that the recent attempt of a worthy herald, in the sister island, to prove that pure Irish was spoken by the ancient Umbrians and Tuscans, has its parallel in a book published at Ypres in 1614, by Adriaen Schrieck, who finds the ancient language of his own country in the seventh Eugubine Table! (*Van 't Beghin der eerster Volcken van Europen*, t'Ypre, 1614.) The Irish book, however, is the more elaborately ridiculous of the two: indeed, it is the most wonderful discovery of the ὄνου πόκες which is known to the writer of these pages.

Este persklo aveis aseriater enetu.

There can be little doubt as to the meaning of these words. *Este*, which is of constant recurrence in the Tables, is the loc. sing. of the pron. *est*, " that of yours," =*isto*, agreeing with *persklum* or *persklo*, the locative of *persklum* =*preç-culum*, " a prayer." Grotefend derives this noun from *purgo*, and translates it by " *lustrum*." But *pur-go* is a compound of *purus* and *ago* (comp. *castigo*, &c.), whereas the root *pers-*, signifying " pray," is of constant occurrence in Umbrian; and every one, however slightly conversant with etymology, understands the metathesis in a case of this kind. It is the same root as *prec-* in Lat., *prach'-* in Sanscr., *frag-en* in Germ., &c.

The adj. *anzeriates* or *aseriater* seems to be rightly explained by Grotefend. The Salian songs were called *axamenta* or *anxamenta*, from *axo*=*nomino* (Fest. p. 8; see Turneb. *Advers.* xxii. 25), or from *anxare*=*cantare:* and *Jovis Axur* or *Anxur*, the beardless god of Terracina, seems to have been no other than " Jove's augur," *i. e.* Apollo; for Διὸς προφήτης ἐστὶ Λοξίας πατρός (Æschyl. *Eumen.* 19). Consequently *aves anzeriates* are *aves quæ cantant* vel *nominant*, i. e. " augurial birds."

Enetu seems to be the imper. of *ineo*, for *in-ito*, and signifies *indagare* or *inquirere in.*

The adjectives *per-naies*, *pus-naes*, are derived from *per-ne*, *post-ne*, which are locative forms of the prepositions *præ* and *post*, and signify " at the southern and northern side of the temple." The birds are so defined with reference to the practice of the augurs in such cases. See Varro, *L. L.* vii. § 7, p. 119, Müller: " *quocirca* cœlum, qua attuimur, dictum *templum* . . . . Ejus *templi* partes iv. dicuntur, *sinistra* ab oriente, *dextra* ab occasu, *antica* ad meridiem, *postica* ad septentrionem."

The meaning of the whole passage will therefore be:

" At that supplication of yours, inquire of the augurial birds, those in the south, as well as those in the north."

§ 7.
Tab. I. a, 2-6.

Tab. I. a, 2.

Pre-veres treplanes 3. *Iuve Krapuvi tre*[*f*] *buf fetu, arvia ustentu,* 4. *vatuva ferine feitu, heris vinu, heri*[*s*] *puni,* 5. *ukriper Fisiu, tutaper Ikuvina, feitu sevum,* 6. *kutef pesnimu; arepes arves.*—Comp. vi. a, 22. *Pre-vereir treblaneir Iuue Grabovei buf treif fetu.* vi. b, 1. *Arvio fetu, uatuo ferine fetu, poni fetu,* 3. *okriper Fisiu, totaper Iiovina.*

The words *pre-veres* (*vereir*) *treplanes* (*treblaneir*) are easily explained in connexion with (7) *pus-veres treplanes,* (11) *pre-veres tesenakes,* (14) *pus-veres tesenakes,* (20) *pre-veres vehiies,* (24) *pus-veres vehiies.* It is obvious that these passages begin with the prepositions *pre,* " before," and *pus*=*post,* " after," and that they fix the point of time. The prepositions *per,* signifying " for," and *co* or *ku,* signifying " with," are placed after the word which they govern: thus we have *tuta-per Ikuvina*=" pro urbe Iguvina," *vocu-com Ioviu*=" cum foco Jovio." But the prepositions *pre* and *pus* precede, and it seems that they both govern the ablative, contrary to the Latin usage, which places an accus. after *ante* and *post.* The word *veres* (*vereir*) is the abl. plur. of a noun *verus* (cf. i. b, 9), corresponding in root and signification to the Latin *feriæ.* The *v* answers to the *f,* as *vocus, vas,* &c. for *focus, fas,* &c. Lassen (*Rhein. Mus.* 1833, p. 380, sqq.) refers *treplanes, tesenakes, vehiies,* to the numerals *tres, decem,* and *viginti.* Grotefend, more probably, understands the adjectives as describing the carriages used at the particular feasts. Cato (*R. R.* c. 135) mentions the *trebla* as a rustic carriage. *Tensa* is the well-known name of the sumptuous processional chariot in which the images of the gods were carried to the *pulvinar* at the *ludi Circenses* (Festus, p. 364, Müller);[1] and *veia* was the Oscan synonym for *plaustrum* (Festus, p. 368, Müller). It is, therefore, not unreasonable to suppose, that at the *feriæ treblanæ* the expiatory sacrifices were carried for distribution in *treblæ;* at the *feriæ tesenakes* the statues of the gods were conveyed to their *pulvinar* in *tensæ;* and at the *feriæ vehiæ* chariot-races were held, as at the Roman circus. In the Latin Table the adj. derived from *tesna* or *tensa* ends in *-ox -ocis*, like *velox;* in the Umbrian it ends in *-ax -acis*, like *capax.*

The epithet *Krapuvius*, or in the Latin Table *Gra-bovius*, according to Lassen signifies " nourisher or feeder of cattle." The first syllable, he supposes, contains the root *gra-*, implying growth and nourishment, and found in the Sanscr. *grá-ma* (signifying either " a herd of feeding cattle"—*grex*—or *vicus inter pascua*), in the Lat. *grá-men*, in the Goth. *gras*, and in the old Nord. *groa=virescere.* Lassen, too, suggests that *Gradivus* contains the same root. This comparison ought perhaps to have led him to the true explanation of both words. For it is manifest that *Gradivus=gravis* or *grandis Divus;* and it is equally certain that no genuine Latin compound begins with a verbal root. If, therefore, *Gra-bovius* contains the root of *bos, bovis*, the first syllable must be the element of the adjective *gravis* or *grandis;* so that *Grabovius* will be a compound of the same kind as καλλιπάρθενος (see Lobeck, *Paralip.* p. 372). Pott, however, (*Et. Forsch.* ii. p. 201) considers *Grab-ovius* as another form of *Gravi-Jovius.*

Tre or *treif buf* is either *boves tres* or *bobus tribus.* If we have here the accus. plural, we must conclude that this

---

[1] For the metathesis *tesna* or *tesena* for *tensa* we may compare *mesene flusare* in an inscription found near Amiternum (Leps. Tab. xxvii. 46), with *mense flusare* in the Latin inscription quoted by Muratori (p. 587).

case in the Umbrian language ends in *-af, -of, -uf, -ef, -if, -eif*, according to the stem; and the labial termination may be compared with the Sanscrit and Zend change of *s* into *u* at the end of a word (Wilkins, § 51. Bopp, § 76). This is the opinion of Lassen (*Rhein. Mus.* 1833, p. 377). According to Lepsius and Grotefend, on the other hand, all these words are ablatives; and it is obvious that the termination is more easily explained on this hypothesis. There is not much force, however, in the argument that these words must be ablatives because verbs signifying "to sacrifice" are construed with the ablative in good Latin (Virg. *Eclog.* iii. 77. Hor. *Carm.* i. 4, 11). For it is quite clear that *abrons* is an accusative, like the Gothic *vulfans* (see Chap. VIII. § 4), and yet we have both *abrons fakurent* (vii. a, 43) and *abroffetu* (vii. a, 3). See also Pott, *Et. Forsch.* ii. p. 202.

Feitu (*fetu*) is simply *facito*, the guttural being softened down, as in *ditu* for *dicito* (vi. b, 10, &c.).[1]

Arvia seems to be the same as the Latin *arvina*, i. e. "the hard fat which lies between the skin and the flesh" (Servius *ad Virg. Æn.* vii. 627); and *ustentu* is probably *obstineto*, which was the old Latin for *ostendito* (Festus, p. 197, Müll.).

Vatuva ferine feitu must mean "offer up unsalted meal" (*fatuam farinam* or *fatuá fariná*), according to Nonius Marcellus, iv. 291 (quoting Varro, *de Vit. Pop. Rom.* lib. i.): *quod calend. Jun. et publice et privatim fatuam pultem diis mactat*. Grotefend supposes that *ferine* must mean raw flesh, and not *farina*, because "bread" (*puni*) is mentioned in the passage. But in minute directions like these, a difference would be marked between the meal (ἄλευρα) and the bread (ἄρτος); just as the hard fat (*arvina*) is distinguished from the soft fat (*adipes*), if the interpretation suggested below is to be admitted.

Heris vinu, heris puni, "either with bread or wine."

---

[1] According to Pott and Lepsius this imperative stands for *fito=fiat*.

Heris, as a particle of choice, is derived from the Sanscr. root *hri*, " to take ;" Lat. *hir*, " a hand," &c.; and may be compared with *vel*, which is connected with the root of *volo*, as this is with the root of αἱρέω. In fact, *heris* appears to be the participle of the verb, of which the imperative is *heritu* (vi. a, 27, &c.). This verb occurs in the Oscan also (*Tab. Bantin.* 12, &c.).

That *ocriper* (*ucriper*) *Fisiu* means " for the Fisian mount" may be demonstrated from Festus, p. 181, Müller: " Ocrem antiqui, ut Ateius philologus in libro Glossematorum refert, montem confragosum vocabant, ut aput Livium: *Sed qui sunt hi, qui ascendunt altum ocrim? et: celsosque ocris, arvaque putria et mare magnum.* et: *namque Tænari celsos ocris.* et: *haut ut quem Chiro in Pelio docuit ocri.* Unde fortasse etiam ocreæ sint dictæ inæqualiter tuberatæ." From this word are derived the names of some Umbrian towns, e. g. *Ocriculum* and *Interocrea* (cf. *Interamna*). The epithet *Fisius* indicates that the mountain was dedicated to the god *Fisius* or *Fisovius Sansius* (*Fidius Sancus*), a name under which the old Italians worshipped Jupiter in their mountain-temples. Lassen (p. 388) refers to this temple the following lines of Claudian (*de VI. Cons. Honor.* 503, 4):

> Exsuperans delubra Iovis, saxoque minantes
> Apenninigenis cultas pastoribus aras.

He also quotes from the Peutinger inscription: " Iovis Penninus, idem Agubio," where *Iguvium* is obviously referred to. Lepsius thinks that *ocris Fisius* was the citadel of Iguvium.

Tota-per (*tuta-per*) *Ikuvina*, " for the city of Iguvium." It was always understood by previous interpreters that *tuta* or *tota* was nothing more than the fem. of the Lat. *totus*. But Lepsius has clearly proved that it is both an Oscan and an Umbrian substantive, signifying " city," from which the adj. *tuti-cus* is derived, as in the name of the magistrate *meddix tuticus*, i. e. *consul urbanus:* consequently *tuta-per Ikuvina* is simply "*pro urbe Iguvina.*" This substantive, *tota* or *tuta*, is, no doubt, derived from the adject. *totus;* for the idea of a *city* is that of "fulness," "collection," "entirety." Similarly, the Greek πόλις must contain the root πολ- (πολ-ύς) or πλε- (πλέος), signifying the aggregation of the inhabitants in one spot. The derivation of the adjective *tó-tus* is by no means easy; but if we compare it with *in-ví-tus* (from *vel-le*), we may be disposed to connect it with the root of the words *tel-lus, tol-lo, ter-ra, ter-minus* (τέλ-ος, τέρ-μα), &c. *Op-pidum*, another name for "city," is only "a plain" (*ob-ped-um* = ἐπίπεδον); and *oppido*, "entirely" = *in toto*, is synonymous with *plane*. The student will take care not to confuse between this *tó-tus* and the reduplicated form *tŏ-tus* (comp. *to-t-, quŏ-tus*, &c.), which is sufficiently distinguished from it in the line of Lucretius (vi. 652):

Nec *tŏta* pars homo terraï *quŏta tŏtius* unus.

Sevum and *kutef* are two adverbs. The former signifies "with reverence," and contains the root *sev-* (*sev-erus*) or σεβ- (σέβω). The latter is derived from *cav-eo, cautus*, with the affix -*f* = φι, and means "cautiously."

The words *arepes arves* or *ariper arvis*, which conclude almost every prescription in the first Table, are not very easy. That Grotefend's translation *pro ardore* s. *ustione arvigæ* is inadmissible, every sound philologer must at once concede. The following suggests itself as the most probable solution. It appears that the Umbrian participle generally ended in -*es*, -*ez*, or -*eis*, like the old Greek participle of verbs in -μι. Thus we have *tases, tasis*, and *tasez*, for *tacens*. *Vesteis*, too, is obviously a participle (vi. a, 22). As, then, we constantly find the imperative *arveitu* for *advehito*, we may surmise that *arves, arvis*, is the participle for *advehens;* and *arepes, ariper*, on the same principle, will be *adipes;* so that the phrase will signify *adipes advehens* s. *porrigens,* i. e. " offering up the soft fat."

Accordingly, the translation of the whole passage should run thus: " Before the feast, at which the *treblæ* are used, sacrifice three oxen to Jupiter Grabovius, offer up the hard fat, sacrifice with unsalted meal, either with wine or bread, for the Fisian mount, for the city of Iguvium, sacrifice reverently, pray cautiously, holding forth the soft fat of the victims."

§ 8. Tab. I. b, 13, sqq.

The next passage, which deserves notice and admits of a reasonable interpretation, is the following. Many of the intervening sentences, however, are so like that which has just been examined, that they can cause no real difficulty to the student. In i. b, 13, we have

enumek steplatu parfam tesvam.

The first word is a particle of connexion signifying *inde, dein,* " then," " in the next place." It is also written *inumek,* and seems to be compounded of *inum* (the Lat. *enim*) and *ek;* compare the Gothic *inuhthis,* &c.

Steplatu, stiplatu, and *an-stiplatu,* are the imperatives of a verb *stiplo* or *anstiplo,* which seems to be of proper application in matters of augury. In old Latin *stipulus* was synonymous with *stabilis* (Forcell. s. v. *stipulatio*): consequently this verb must signify something like *stabilio* or *firmo,* which last word is used in speaking of omens (Virgil. Georg. iv. 386).

Parfa, which occurs frequently in the Tables, is the augurial *parra,* a kind of owl, which the Italians in general call *civetta,* and the Venetians *parruzza;* and *tesva* means on the right: as will appear from the following considerations. At the beginning of the sixth Table we have, among the auspices, *parfa kurnase dersua, peiqu peica merstu;* which should seem to mean, *parram, cornicem, dextras; picum, picam sinistros.* The Roman augurs used to turn their faces to the south; consequently the east was on their left, and the west on their right. The east was in general the seat of good omens; but in certain cases, and with certain birds, the bad omen of the west, or right hand, might be converted into good. They made a distinction between the birds which gave the omen by their note, and those which gave the omen by their flight; the former were called *oscines*, the latter *alites*. The *parra* and the *picus* were reckoned in both classes, according to Festus (p. 197, Müller). Indeed there must have been some confusion among the augurs themselves, as Cicero seems to admit (*de Divin.* ii. 39): " Haud ignoro, quæ bona sint, sinistra nos dicere, etiamsi dextra sint; sed certe nostri sinistrum nominaverunt, externique dextrum, quia plerumque melius id videbatur." Lutatius says, that the masculine gender indicates the propitious bird, and the feminine the unpropitious; yet the Umbrians seem to have held the *picus* and the *pica* in equal estimation. In constituting a good omen, the Umbrians placed the *picus* on the left, and the *cornix* on the right; while Plautus places them both on the left, but the *parra* on the right, as did the Umbrians (*Asin.* ii. 1, 11):

> Impetritum, inauguratum 'st: quovis admittunt aves,
> Picus, cornix est ab læva; corvus, parra ab dextera.

Prudentius, though not an Umbrian like Plautus, preserves the Umbrian order (*Symmach.* ii. 570):

> Cur Cremeræ in campis, cornice vel oscine parra,
> Nemo deûm monuit perituros Marte sinistra
> Ter centum Fabios, vix stirpe superstite in uno?

Comp. also Horat. iii. *Carm.* xxvii. 1, &c.

Tesva in the Table means " the right," and may be compared with the Gothic *taíhsvó*. In the Latin Table it is written *dersua*, which is nearer to the Lat. *dextra*. The same change is observable in *tera* (i. b, 34) and *dersa* (vii. a, 43), which are equivalent to *dica*, and connected, therefore, with *tesva dersva* (*N. Crat.* p. 374). That *merstus* must mean " propitious" or " salutary," is clear from the passages in which it occurs, as well as from the use of *mers*. A few lines lower we have (i. b, 18): *sve-pis habe purtatutu pue mers est, feitu uru pere mers est.* Comp. vi. b, 54: *so-pir habe esme pople portatu ulo pue mers est, fetu uru pirse mers est.* The meaning seems to be: *si quis habet portatum aliquid ubi salutare est, facito ustionem prout salutare est.* The etymology of *mers* is quite uncertain. Grotefend connects it with *medicus*, Lassen with *merx*.

§ 9. Extracts from the Litany in Tab. VI. a.

A complete examination of the whole of the Eugubine Tables does not fall within the limits of this work, and I will only add a few extracts from the Litany in the sixth Table.

VI. a: 22. *Teio subokau suboko,* 23. *Dei Grabovi, okri-per Fisiu, tota-per Iiovina, erer nomne-per, erar nomne-per; fos sei, paker sei, okre Fisei,* 24. *Tote Iiovine, erer nomne, erar nomne:*

i. e. *te invocavi invoco, Jupiter Grabovi, pro monte Fisio, pro urbe Iguvina, pro illius nomine, pro hujus nomine; bonus sis, propitius sis, monti Fisio, urbi Iguvinæ, illius nomini, hujus nomini.*

VI. a: 24. *Arsie, tio subokau suboko, Dei Grabove:*

i. e. *adsis, te invocavi invoco, J. Gr.*

Arsier, frite tio subokau 25. *suboko D. Gr.*

Here *f-rite* is written for *rite*, just as we have *f-rango* by

F

the side of ῥήγνυμι; f-ragen, f-luo, as well as rogo, luo (λούω); f-ragum, ῥάξ; f-renum, " rein;" f-rigere, rigere; &c.; and in these tables probably f-ri for rus, f-rosetom for rogatum, &c.

VI. a: 26. *D. Gr., orer ose, persei okre Fisie pir orto est, toteme Iovine arsmor dersekor subator sent, pusei nep heritu.*

This passage is somewhat more difficult. It appears to me that the particles *per-sei, pu-sei,* mark the opposition of the *protasis* to the *apodosis,* " as "—" so," *prout—ita.* The chief difficulty here is in the word *arsmo-r,* which, however, occurs very frequently in the Tables. It is clearly the plural of *arsmo.* If we examine one of the numerous passages in which the word is found, we may be inclined to conjecture that it means a man or functionary of some sort. Thus in vi. a, 32, we have: *D. Gr. salvo seritu okrer Fisier, totar Iiovinar nome; nerf, arsmo, veiro, pequo, kastruo, fri, salva seritu;* which must surely mean: *J. Gr. salvum servato nomen ocris Fisii, urbis Iguvinæ, salvas servato vires* (i. e. *nervos*) *arsmorum, virorum, pecuum, castrorum, ruris.* Now Lassen has shewn (*Rhein. Mus.* 1834, p. 151) that *dersecor* must be a derivative from *disseco,* and that, like *mergus, vivus,* from *mergere, vivere,* it must have an active signification. We have the verb *derseco = dis-seco* in the form *dersikust, dersikurent* (*dis-secassit, dis-secaverint*). Consequently, *arsmor dersecor* must mean *arsmi dissecantes,* or *dissicentes* (for *dissico,* 3. conj., see Gronov. *Lect. Plautin.* p. 87). *Subator sent* is either *subacti sunt* or *subjecti sunt.* On the whole, it is most probable that *arsmus* means a priest; but whether the word is derived from *arceo,* because the priest made atonement for the people, or from *arcuma,* because he rode in the little car so called, is quite uncertain. If this supposition be correct, we shall have no great difficulty in translating the passage before us. *Pir* occurs so often in connexion with *vuku=focus*, *asa=ara*, *uretu=urito*, &c. that it must mean "fire." *Orer* is a deponent form of *oro*, after the analogy of *precor*. *Ose* is probably *ore*. *Nep* stands for *nec*, as in Oscan, but does not imply any disjunction: nor did *nec* or *neg* in old Latin; compare *nec-lego*, *nec-quidquam*, &c., and see Festus, p. 162, sub vv. *neclegens* and *nec*. Müller (*Suppl. Annot.* p. 387) supposes that the disjunctive *nec* or *neque*, and the negative *nec* or *neg*, were two distinct particles. To me it appears that *nec* or *neg* is never used for *non* except either as qualifying a single word—*nec-opinans*, *neg-otium*,—in a conditional clause, as in the passages quoted by Festus, and Cato *R. R.* 141,—or in a prohibition as here; in all which cases the Greeks used μή and not οὐ, and the Romans generally *ne* and not *non*. *Nego* is a peculiar case; the Greeks said οὔ φημι οὕτως ἔχειν for φημὶ μὴ οὕτως ἔχειν: and the same principle may be applied to explain οὐχ ἥκιστα, οὐ γὰρ ἄμεινον, &c. In a case like this the Romans seem to have used *nec* as qualifying and converting the whole word, in preference to *non*. Müller supposes that *negritu*, quoted by Festus (p. 165) as signifying *ægritudo* in augurial language, stands for *nec-ritu*. I think it must be a corruption for *ne-gritudo:* see below, Ch. VII. § 5. *Heritu* is the imper. of *hri*, " to take," and here seems to mean " attack" or " afflict." The whole passage then may be rendered: *J. Gr. precor prece, quoniam in ocri Fisio ignis ortus est, in urbe Iguvina sacerdotes dissecantes submissi sunt,—ita ne tu affligas.*

§ 10. Umbrian words which approximate to their Latin synonymes.

This may suffice as far as the direct interpretation of the Tables is concerned. In conclusion, it may be well to give a list of those words in the Umbrian language which approach most closely to their Latin equivalents. And first, with respect to the numerals, which are the least mutable elements in every language. It is clear that *luves* (*duves*), *tuva* (*duva*), and *tris*, *treia*, correspond to *duo* and *tres*, *tria*. Similarly *tupler* (*dupler*) and *tripler* represent *duplus* and *triplus*, and *tuplak* (iii. 14) is *duplice*. It is obvious, too, that *petur* is "four," as in Oscan; see vi. b, 10: *du-pursus, petur-pursus*, i. e. *bifariam, quadrifariam*. As to the ordinals, *prumum* is *primum*, *etre* (*etrama*) is *alter*, and *tertie* (*tertiama*) is *tertius*.

The other words may be given in alphabetical order.

Abrof (*apruf*) (vii. a, 3) = *apros* or *apris; ager* (Tab. xxvii. 21); *alfu* (i. b, 29) = *albus* (ἀλφός); *ander* (*anter*) (vi. b, 47. i. b, 8) = *inter* (sim. in Oscan); *angla* or *ankla* (vi. a, 1) = *aquila* (comp. *anguis* with ἔχις, *unda* with ὕδωρ, &c., see *New Cratylus*, p. 303); *an-tentu* (passim) = *in-tendito; ar-fertur* (vi. a, 3) = *affertur; arputrati* (v. a, 12) = *arbitratu; ar-veitu* (i. b, 6) = *advehito* (cf. *arven* and *arves*); *asa* (vi. a, 9, et passim) = *ara; Asiane* (i. a, 25) = *Asiano; atru* (i. b, 29) = *ater; aveis* (vi. a, 1) = *aves*.

Bue (vi. a, 26, et passim) = *bove*.

Der-sikurent (vi. b, 62) = *dissecaverint; ditu* (vi. b, 10) = *dicito; dupla* (vi. b, 18), so also *numer tupler* (v. a, 19) — comp. *numer prever* (v. a, 18) and *numer tripler* (v. a, 21).

Eru (v. a, 26) = *erit*.

Famerias Pumperias (viii. a, 2) = *familiæ Pompiliæ; feraklu* (Müller, *Etrusk.* i. p. 57, note) = *ferculum; ferehtru* (iii. 16) = *feretrum; ferine* (i. a, 4) = *farina; frater* (v. b, 11).

Homonus (v. b, 10) = *homines*.

Ifont (vi. b, 55) = *ibunt*: the same form occurs in Lucilius Afranius: comp. *erafont* (vi. b, 65), *erahunt* (i. b, 23), *erarunt* (iv. 1); all by-forms of the mutilated future *erunt*.

Kapire (i. a, 29) = *capide*, "with a sacrificial jug;" *kaprum*

(ii. a, 1); *karne* (ii. b, 1); *kastruo* (vi. a, 30, et passim)
= *castrorum*; *kuratu* (v. a, 24) *sve rehte kuratu si*=*si
recte curatum sit*; *kvestur* (v. a, 23)=*quæstor*.

Naratu (ii. a, 8)=*narrato* (Varro wrote *narare*); *nome*
(passim)=*nomen*; *numer* (v. a, 17).

Oui (vi. b, 43), *uve* (ii. 6, 10)=*ovis*.

Pase (vi. a, 30)=*pace*; *pater* (ii. a, 24); *pelsana* (i. a, 26)
= *balsamon*; *pihakler* (v. a, 8)=*piaculum*; *pihatu* (vi.
a, 9)=*piato*; *pir* (i. b, 12)= πῦρ, *fire*; *poplo* (passim)
=*populus*; *porka* (vii. a, 6)=*porca*; *postro* (vi. b, 5)
= φωστρῷ; *prokanurent* (vi. a, 16)=*procinerint*; *pro-
seseto* (vi. a, 56)=*prosecato*; *puemune* (iii. 26)=*pomo-
na*; *puprike* (iii. 27)=*publice*; *pustertiu* (i. b, 40)=
post-tertio.

Rehte (v. a, 24)=*recte*; *ruphra* (i. b, 27)=*rubra*.

Sakra (i. b, 29); *salvo, salva*, &c. (passim); *seritu* (passim),
either *creato* (*New Crat.* p. 444), or *servato* (Müller,
Etrusk. i. p. 55); *sif* (i. a, 7)=*suibus*; *skrehto* (vii. b,
3)=*scriptus*; *sopo* (vi. b, 5)=*sapone*; *stahitu* (vi. b,
56)=*stato*; *strusla* (vi. a, 59)=*stru-cula*, dimin. of
strues; *subator* (vi. a, 27, &c.)=*subacti*; *suboko* (vi. a,
22, &c.)=*sub-voco*; *subra* (v. a, 20)=*supra*; *sve* (v. a,
24)= Osc. *suæ*, Lat. *si*; *seritu* (ii. b, 24), vide *seritu*;
sesna (v. b, 9)=*cesna, cœna*.

Tafle (ii. a, 12)=*tabula*; *tases* (vi. a, 55)=*tacens*; *teku-
ries* (ii. a, 1)=*decuriæ*; *termnu-ko* (vi. b, 53)=*cum
termino*; *tio* (passim)=*te*.

Uretu (iii. 12)=*urito*; *uvikum* (iii. 28)=*cum ove*.

Vas (vi. a, 28)=*fas*; *vatuva* (i. a, 4)=*fatua*; *veiro* (vi. a,
30)=*virorum*; *vinu* (passim)=*vinum*; *vitlu* (ii. a, 21)
=*vitulus*; *voku-kom* (vi. b, 43)=*cum foco*.

In the year 1835 a bronze figure of a man in armour was discovered near *Todi* (*Tuder*), on the borders of Umbria. The inscription, which was detected on the girdle

§ 11.
The Todi inscription contains four words

of the same class.

of the breast-plate, has been interpreted from the Greek, Latin, and Hebrew languages by a number of different scholars. It appears to me to contain four words, which may be added to the above list, as they are all explicable from the roots of the Latin language. The inscription runs thus:

AHALTRVTITISPVNVMPEPE.

The word *titis* occurs in the Eugubine Tables (i. b, 45), and *punum* is obviously the accusative of *punus*, another form of *pune, punes, puni*, which are known to be Umbrian words. It is true that the Latin synonym *panis* and the Eugubine words belong to the *i*-declension; but that is no reason why we should not have a by-form of the *o*-declension, and that this form actually existed in Messapia is well known (Athen. iii. p. 111 c.: πανὸς ἄρτος Μεσσάπιοι). These two words being removed from the middle, the extremities remain, namely, *ahaltru* and *pepe*. With regard to the first it is to be observed that the lengthening of a syllable, by doubling the vowel and inserting the letter *h*, is common in Umbrian (see Leps. *de Tabb. Eugub.* p. 92, sqq.), and the same practice is often remarked in Latin. *Ahaltru*, then, bears the same relation to the Latin *alter* that *ahala* bears to *ala*, *nihil* to *nil*, *vehemens* to *vemens*, &c. It is true that in the Eugubine Tables *etre* seems to represent the meaning, if not the form of *alter;* but this is no reason why there should not be the other equally genuine and ancient form *alter*, or *ahalter*, which is probably the more emphatic word in that language, and corresponds, perhaps, in meaning to the adjective *alienus*. The signification of the word *pepe* suggests itself from the context, and is also supported by analogy. It seems to be a reduplication of the root *pa* (*pá-nis*, *pa-sco*, πα-σάσθαι, πα-τέομαι, &c.), analogous to the reduplication of the root *bi* (or *pi*, πί-νω, &c.) in *bi-bo*. If the Sabines were a warrior tribe of Umbrians, it is reasonable to conclude that their name for " a warrior" would be Umbrian also; now we know that the Sabine name for " a warrior" was *titus* (Fest. p. 366, and below, p. 76), and the warrior tribe at Rome was called the *Titienses* (Liv. i. 13); accordingly, as the Umbrian Propertius calls these the *Tities* (*El.* iv. 1, 31: *Hinc Tities Ramnesque viri Luceresque coloni*),[1] it is not an unfair assumption that *titis*, pl. *tities*, was the Umbrian word for " a warrior." The inscription, then, will run thus: " the warrior eats another's bread;" the position of *ahaltru* being justified by the emphasis which naturally falls upon it. Compare Dante, *Paradiso*, xvii. 58-60:

> Tu proverai sì come sa di sale
> Lo pane *altrui*, et com' è duro calle
> Lo scendere e 'l salir per l' *altrui* scale.

This motto, then, either refers to the practice of serving as mercenaries, so common among the Italians, or expresses the prouder feeling of superiority to the mere agriculturist, which was equally characteristic of the oldest Greek warriors. Compare the scolion of Hybrias the Cretan (*ap.* Athen. xv. 695 F.):

> ἔστι μοι πλοῦτος μέγας δόρυ καὶ ξίφος
> καὶ τὸ καλὸν λαισήϊον πρόβλημα χρωτός·
> τούτῳ μὲν ἀρῶ, τούτῳ θερίζω,
> τούτῳ πατέω τὸν ἀδὺν οἶνον ἀπ' ἀμπέλω,
> τούτῳ δεσπότας μνῴαις κέκλημαι.
> τοὶ δὲ μὴ τολμῶντ' ἔχειν δόρυ καὶ ξίφος, κ.τ.λ.

It is also to be remarked that the *Lucumones*, or "illustrious nobles," among the Tuscans, seem to have distinguished their plebeians as *Aruntes* (ἀροῦντες), i. e. mere ploughmen and agricultural labourers (Klenze, *Phil. Abhandlung.* p. 39, note). In general the prænomen *Aruns* seems to be used in the old mythical history to designate an inferior person (Müller, *Etrusk.* i. p. 405).

---

[1] *Lucmo* in v. 29 is an accurate transcription of the Etruscan *Lauchme*.

CHAPTER IV.

THE SABELLO-OSCAN LANGUAGE.

§ 1. The remains of the Oscan language must be considered as Sabellian also. § 2. Alphabetical list of Sabello-Oscan words, with their interpretation. § 3. The Bantine Table. § 4. Commentary on the Bantine Table. § 5. The "Atellanæ."

§ 1.
The remains of the Oscan language must be considered as Sabellian also.

THE Oscan language is more interesting even than the Umbrian, and the remains which have come down to us are much more easily interpreted than the Eugubine Tables. Indeed, as Niebuhr has remarked (i. *ad not.* 212), " some of the inscriptions may be explained word for word, others in part at least, and that too with perfect certainty, and without any violence." This language had a literature of its own, and survived the Roman conquest of southern Italy. It was spoken in Samnium in the year 459;[1] it was one of the languages of Bruttium in the days of Ennius;[2] the greatest relique of Oscan is the Bantine Table, which was probably engraved about the middle of the seventh century; and the Oscan was the common idiom at Herculaneum and Pompeii, when the volcano at once destroyed and preserved those cities.

Although, as it has been shewn in a previous chapter, the Sabines must be regarded as a branch of the Umbrian stock, who conquered all the Ausonian nations, and though Varro[3] speaks of the Sabine language as different from the

---

[1] Liv. x. 20: " gnaros *linguæ Oscæ* exploratum mittit."

[2] Festus, s. v. *bilingues*, p. 35: " *bilingues Bruttates* Ennius dixit, quod Brutti et Osce et Græce loqui soliti sint."

[3] *L. L.* vii. § 3, p. 130, Müller. Varro was born at Reate (see p. 301 of Müller's edition), and therefore, perhaps, attached peculiar importance to the provincialisms of the *ager Sabinus*.

Oscan, yet, as all the remains of the Sabine and Oscan languages belong to a period when the Sabellian conquerors had mixed themselves up with the conquered Ausonians and had learned their language, it seems reasonable that we should not attempt, at this distance of time, to discriminate between them, but that, recognising generally the original affinity of the Umbrian and Oscan nations, we should consider the Sabine words which have been transmitted to us, as belonging, not so much to the Umbrian idiom, as to the complex Sabello-Oscan language, which prevailed throughout the whole of southern Italy. And this view of the matter is further justified by the fact, that a great many of these words are quoted, not only as Sabine, but also as Oscan. It is true that some particular words are quoted as Sabine, which are not found in Oscan inscriptions, and not known to be Oscan also; but we cannot form any general conclusions from such isolated phenomena, especially as a great many of these words are Latin as well. All that it proves is simply this, that there were provincialisms in the *Sabine territory* properly so called. Still less can we think with Müller (*Etrusk.* i. p. 42), that the Sabine language is the un-Greek element in the Oscan; for many of these words have direct connexions with Greek synonymes, as Müller himself has admitted. There are no Sabine inscriptions as such. The Marsian inscription, quoted by Lanzi, and which Niebuhr thought unintelligible (i. 105, *ad not.* 333), is Oscan, if it ought not rather to be called old Latin.

In the following observations, then, for the materials of which I am largely indebted to Professor Klenze (*Philologische Abhandlungen*, Berlin, 1839), the Sabine and Oscan will be treated in conjunction with one another. Before proceeding to consider the Oscan inscriptions, it may be well to give an alphabetical list of those words which are cited by old writers as Sabine, Oscan, or both.

§ 2.
Alphabetical list of Sabello-Oscan words, with their interpretation.

Alpus, Sab. Fest. p. 4, Müller: "*Album*, quod nos dicimus, a Græco, quod est ἀλφόν, est appellatum. Sabini tamen *alpum* dixerunt."

Aurum, Sab. Fest. p. 9: "*Aurum*—alii a Sabinis translatum putant, quod illi *ausum* dicebant." Vide *Sol*.

Brutus, Osc. "A runaway slave," "a maroon." Strabo, vi. p. 255; Diod. xvi. 15.

Cascus, Casinus, Casnar, Sab. Osc. Varro, *L. L.* vii. § 28: "*Cascum* significat vetus; ejus origo Sabina, quæ usque radices in Oscam linguam egit." § 29: "Item ostendit quod oppidum vocatur *Casinum;* hoc enim ab Sabinis orti Samnites tenuerunt, et nunc nostri etiam nunc *Casinum* forum vetus appellant. Item significant in Atellanis aliquot Pappum senem, quod Osci *Casnar* appellant." These words probably contain the Sanscr. root *cas-*, "white," which also appears in καθαρός, *cas-tus*, &c. *Cānus* is also to be referred to this class (comp. *co-esna, cœna*, &c.), and stands related to *candidus*, as *plēnus* does to *s-plendidus*. According to Pott (*Etym. Forsch.* ii. 109), *cas-nar* is a compound word, containing the roots *cas-*, "old," and *nrĭ*, "man."

Catus, Sab. Varro, *L. L.* vii. § 46: "*Cata* acuta; hoc enim verbo dicunt Sabini."

Crepusculum, Sab. Varro, *L. L.* vi. § 5: "Secundum hoc dicitur *crepusculum* a crepero. Id vocabulum sumpserunt a Sabinis, unde veniunt *Crepusci* nominati Amiterno, qui eo tempore erant nati, ut Lucii prima luce. In Reatino *crepusculum* significat dubium; ab eo res dictæ dubiæ *creperæ*, quod crepusculum dies etiam nunc sit an jam nox, multis dubium." vii. § 77: "*Crepusculum* ab Sabinis, quod id dubium tempus noctis an diei sit." Comp. Festus, s. v. *Decrepitus*, p. 71, Müller. The root of this word seems to be contained in the Sanscr. *kshapas*, Greek κνέφας (see *New Crat.* p. 196).

Cumba, Sab. Festus, p. 64: "*Cumbam* Sabini vocant eam,

quam militares lecticam, unde videtur derivatum esse *cubiculum.*" Comp. Varro, *L. L.* v. § 166, and Gloss. MS. Camberon. (Voss. *Vit. Serm.* p. 419): " *Cumba* dicitur lectica a *cubando.*"

Cupencus, Sab. Serv. *ad Æn.* xii. 538: " Sane sciendum, *cupencum* Sabinorum lingua sacerdotem vocari: sunt autem cupenci Herculis sacerdotes."

Curis, Quiris, Sab. Ovid. *Fast.* ii. 475: " Sive quod hasta *curis* priscis est dicta Sabinis." Varro (*ap. Dion. Hal.* ii. p. 109, Huds.): Κύρεις γὰρ οἱ Σαβῖνοι τὰς αἰχμὰς καλοῦσι· ταῦτα μὲν οὖν Τερέντιος Οὐάρρων γράφει. Macrob. *Sat.* i. 9: " Quirinum quasi bellorum potentem, ab hasta, quam Sabini *curim* vocant." Festus, p. 49: " *Curis* est Sabine hasta. Unde Romulus *Quirinus,* quia eam ferebat, est dictus." Ibid: " *Curitim* Junonem appellabant, quia eandem ferre hastam putabant." p. 63: " Quia matronæ Junonis Curitis in tutela sint, quæ ita appellabatur a ferenda hasta, quæ lingua Sabinorum *Curis* dicebatur." (Comp. Müller, *Etrusk.* ii. p. 45, and Festus, p. 254.) Servius, *Æn.* i. 296: " Romulus autem Quirinus ideo dictus est, vel quod hasta utebatur, quæ Sabinorum lingua *Curis* dicitur: hasta enim, i. e. *curis,* telum longum est, unde et *securis,* quasi *semi-curis.*" Isidor. ix. 2, 84: " Hi et Quirites dicti, quia Quirinus dictus est Romulus; quod semper hasta utebatur, quæ Sabinorum lingua *quiris* dicitur." Cf. Plutarch. *Vit. Romul.* 29. If *curis* meant " a lance," as these authorities indicate, its meaning was derived from the definition of a lance as " a headed or pointed staff." The analogies suggested by Pott (*Et. Forsch.* i. 263, ii. 533) do not lead to any satisfactory result. Some confusion arises in the mind from a comparison of *Quirites,* (*curia*), *curiatii,* " the full citizens or hoplites," with κούρητες, κύριοι, κοίρανοι, κοῦροι, κουρίδιος — words denoting " headship" or " personal rank." Comp. *New Cratylus*, p. 413, sqq.; Welcker, *Theognis*, p. xxxiii.; Lobeck, *Aglaopham.* p. 1144, not. c., and *ad Soph. Aj.* 374, 2d edit. The fight between the *Horatii* and *Curiatii* probably refers to a contest between the *Cūriātii* (κούρητες), " men of the *curia*, and wielders of the spear, or wearers of the helmet," and the *Hŏrātii* (χερνῆτες), " handicraftsmen," *i. e.* the lower order, in which contest, as usual, the latter succeeded in maintaining their just rights. In the old tradition it is uncertain which of the two fought for Alba (Liv. i. 24), *i. e.* whether the Latin or Sabine interest was at that time predominant at Rome. The story about Horatius Cocles admits of a similar interpretation. The Tuscans were repelled at the bridgehead by the three Roman tribes—*Lartius* (*Larth, Lars*, "prince" or "king") representing the head-tribe, *Herminius* the second, and *Horatius* the third. The meaning of the name *Herminius* is far from obvious; it does not sound like a Latin name. Since, however, we know that the later Romans converted Herr-mann into *Arminius* (for the first syllable comp. *herus*, &c., and for the second *ho-min-*, *ne-min-*, &c.), we may well suppose that *Her-minius* represents the same original form, and therefore that, as *Lartius* typifies the nobles, and *Horatius* the common people, so *Herminius* personifies the warriors of Rome. And this explanation of the name is quite in accordance with the meaning of the word *Her-min* in those Low German languages with which the Sabine and other Italian idioms were so intimately connected. Grimm says (*Deutsche Mythol.* p. 328, 2d edit.): " die Sachsen scheinen in *Hirmin* einen *kriegerisch dargestellten Wódan* verehrt zu haben." We find a further confirmation in the fact, that his name was *Titus Herminius;* for not only does *Titus* signify " warrior" (Fest. p. 366, Müller: " *Tituli* milites appellantur quasi *tutuli*, quod patriam tuerentur, unde et *Titi* prænomen ortum est"), but the *Titienses*, or *Tities*, were actually " the Sabine *quirites* (spearmen)," the *second* tribe at Rome. By a similar personification, the senior consul, Valerius, commands *Herminius*, the " warriors," and *Lartius* the " young nobles;" while the other consul, *Lucretius*, represents the *Luceres*, or third class of citizens (Liv. ii. 11). Even Lucretia may be nothing more than a symbol of the third order of the *populus;* so that her ill-treatment by Sextus will be an allegory referring to the oppression of the Luceres, who often approximated to the *plebs*, by the tyrannical Etruscan dynasty. It is also singular that *Lucretius* and *Horatius*, both representatives of the third class, succeed one another in the first consulship. The prænomen of *Spurius Lartius* does not appear to be the Latin *spurius*, " illegitimate," but a Tuscan derivative from *super*, the first vowel being omitted, according to the Tuscan custom, and the second softened into *u*, as in *augur* (also perhaps a Tuscan word) for *aviger*. That *Spurius* was a Tuscan name appears from the derivative *Spurinna*.

Cyprus, Sab. Varro, *L. L.* v. § 159: " Vicus *Cyprius* (Liv. i. 48) a *cypro*, quod ibi Sabini cives additi consederunt, qui a bono omine id appellarunt; nam *cyprum* Sabine *bonum*." The word probably contains the same element as the Persian *khub* (خوب), " good" or " fair."

Dalivus, Osc. Fest. p. 68: "*Dalivum* supinum ait esse Aurelius, Ælius stultum. Oscorum quoque lingua significat insanum. Santra vero dici putat ipsum, quem Græci δείλαιον, *i. e.* propter cujus fatuitatem quis misereri debeat." Comp. Hesych., Δαλίς, μωρός; and see Blomf. *ad Æsch. Eumen.* 318.

Diana, Sab. Vide sub v. *Feronia*.

Dirus, Umbr. et Sab. Serv. *ad Æn.* iii. 235: " Sabini et

Umbri, quæ nos mala *dira* appellant." This word seems to be the same in effect as the Gr. δεινός.

Famel, Osc. Fest. p. 87: "*Famuli* origo ab Oscis dependet, apud quos servus *famel* nominabatur, unde et *familia* vocata." Comp. Müller, *Etrusker*, i. p. 38. Benfey (*Wurzel-Lex.* ii. 20) would connect *fa-mel* for *fag-mel* with the Sanscrit root *bhag'*, " to honour ;" Sclav. *bog*, " god ;" Russ. *bog'-itj*, " to honour."

Fasena, Sab. Varro (*ap. Vet. Orthogr.* p. 2230 P.): " Siquidem, ut testis est Varro, a Sabinis *fasena* dicitur." p. 2238: " Itaque *harenam* justius quis dixerit, quoniam apud antiquos *fasena* erat, et *hordeum*, quia *fordeum*, et, sicut supra diximus, *hircos*, quoniam *firci* erant, et *hædi*, quoniam *fœdi*." The ancients, however, often omitted the aspirate in those words which originally had *f*. Quinctil. *Inst. Orat.* i. 5. § 20: " Parcissime ea (aspiratione) veteres usi sunt etiam in vocalibus, cum *ædos ircosque* dicebant." The *f* is changed into *h* in the proper name *Halesus*—the hero eponymus of the *Falerians*, and founder of *Falisci:* see Turneb. *Adv.* xxi. 3. Below, *Fedus*. For the similar change from *f* to *h* in the Romance languages, see *New Cratylus*, p. 125.

Februum, Sab. Varro, *L. L.* vi. § 13: " *Februum* Sabini purgamentum, et id in sacris nostris verbum." Ovid. *Fast.* ii. 19: " Februa Romani dixere piamina Patres." Fest. p. 85. Also Tuscan; see J. Lyd. *de Mens.* p. 170.

Fedus, Fœdus, Sab. Varro, *L. L.* v. § 97: " *Ircus*, quod Sabini *fircus;* quod illic *fedus*, in Latio rure *edus;* qui in urbe, ut in multis A addito, *aedus.*" Apul. *de Not. Adspir.* p. 94 (Osann.): " M. Terentius scribit *hedum* lingua Sabinorum *fedum* vocatum, Romanosque corrupte *hedus* pro eo quod est *fedus* habuisse, sicut *hircus* pro *fircus*, et *trahere* pro *trafere*." p. 125: " Sabini enim *fircus*, Romani *hircus;* illi *vefere*, Romani *vehere* protulerunt." Fest. p. 84: " *Fœdum* antiqui dicebant pro *hædo, folus* pro *olere, fostem* pro *hoste, fostem* pro *hostia*." Above, *Fasena*.

Feronia, Sab. Varro, *L. L.* v. § 74: " *Feronia, Minerva, Novensides* a Sabinis. Paulo aliter ab eisdem dicimus *Herculem, Vestam, Salutem, Fortunam, Fortem, Fidem*. Et aræ Sabinam linguam olent quæ Tati regis voto sunt Romæ dedicatæ; nam ut Annales dicunt, vovit (1) *Opi*, (2) *Floræ*, (3) *Vediovi Saturno*que, (4) *Soli*, (5) *Lunæ*, (6) *Volcano* et *Summano*, itemque (7) *Larundæ*, (8) *Termino*, (9) *Quirino*, (10) *Vortumno*, (11) *Laribus*, (12) *Dianæ Lucinæ*que. [The figures refer to the xii. altars, according to Müller's view, Festus, p. xliv.: comp. *Etrusk*. ii. p. 64.] E quis nonnulla nomina in utraque lingua habent radices, ut arbores, quæ in confinio natæ in utroque agro serpunt: potest enim Saturnus hic de alia causa esse dictus atque in Sabinis, et sic Diana, et de quibus supra dictum est."

Fides, Sab. Above, s. v. *Feronia*.

Fircus, Sab. Above, *Fedus*.

Flora, Sab. Above, s. v. *Feronia*.

Fors, Fortuna. Ibid.

Gela, Opic. Steph. Byzan. voc. Γέλα: —ὁ δὲ ποταμὸς (Γέλα) ὅτι πολλὴν πάχνην γεννᾷ· ταύτην γὰρ τῇ Ὀπικῶν φωνῇ καὶ Σικέλων γέλαν λέγεσθαι.

Hercules, Sab. Above, s. v. *Feronia*.

Herna, Sab. et Marsic. "A rock." Serv. *ad Virg. Æn*. vii. 684. Compare κραν-αός, κάραν-ον; Gael. *carn;* Irish, *cairneach;* Sclav. *kremeni*.

Idus, Sab. Varro, *L. L.* vi. § 28: " *Idus* ab eo quod Tusci *itus*, vel potius quod Sabini *idus* dicunt."

Irpus, Sab. et Samn. Serv. *ad Æn*. xi. 785: " Nam lupi Sabinorum lingua *hirpi* vocantur." Fest. p. 106: " *Irpini* appellati nomine lupi, quem *irpum* dicunt Samnites; eum enim ducem secuti agros occupavere."

Strabo, v. p. 250 : ἑξῆς δ' εἰσὶν Ἱρπῖνοι, καὐτοὶ Σαυνῖται· τοὔνομα δ' ἔσχον ἀπὸ τοῦ ἡγησαμένου λύκου τῆς ἀποικίας· ἵρπον γὰρ καλοῦσιν οἱ Σαυνῖται τὸν λύκον. Compare the Sanscrit *vrĭkas;* and see *New Cratyl.* p. 349.

Jupiter, Sab. v. *Feronia*.
Lares, Sab. v. *Feronia*.
Larunda, Sab. v. *Feronia*.
Lepestæ, Sab. Varro, *L. L.* v. § 123: " Dictæ *lepestæ*, quæ etiam nunc in diebus sacris Sabinis *vasa vinaria* in mensa deorum sunt posita; apud antiquos scriptores inveni appellari poculi genus λεπαστάν, quare vel inde radices in agrum Sabinum et Romanum sunt profectæ."
Lixula, Sab. Varro, *L. L.* v. § 107 : " Circuli, quod mixta farina et caseo et aqua circuitum æquabiliter fundebant. Hoc quidem qui magis incondite faciebant, vocabant *lixulas* et *semilixulas* vocabulo Sabino, itaque frequentati a Sabinis."
Lucetius, Osc. Serv. *ad Æn.* ix. 570 : " Lingua Osca *Lucetius* est Jupiter dictus, a luce quam præstare dicitur hominibus."
Lucina, Luna. v. *Feronia*.
Mæsius, Osc. Fest. p. 136 : " *Mæsius* lingua Osca mensis *Maius*."
Mamers, Osc. et Sab. Fest. p. 131: " *Mamers, Mamertis* facit, *i. e.* lingua Osca *Mars, Martis*, unde et *Mamertini* in Sicilia dicti, qui Messanæ habitant." id. p. 158 : " Et nomen acceperunt unum, ut dicerentur Mamertini, quod conjectis in sortem duodecim deorum nominibus, *Mamers* forte exierat; qui lingua Oscorum *Mars* significatur." id. p. 131 : " *Mamercus* prænomen Oscum est ab eo, quod hi *Martem Mamertem* appellant." Varro, *L. L.* v. § 73 : " Mars ab eo, quod maribus in bello præest, aut quod ab Sabinis acceptus, ibi (ubi ?) est *Mamers*." The word *má-mers* is easily expli-

cable from the roots of the Latin language as " man-slayer." *Mars* is probably a contraction of *Má-vors*, " man-protector." Compare Δα-Φέρτης; and see *New Crat.* p. 411.

Meddix, Osc. Liv. xxvi. 6: " *Medix* tuticus summus apud Campanos magistratus." Comp. xxiv. 19. (The old reading was *mediastaticus.*) Fest. p. 123 : " *Meddix* apud Oscos nomen magistratus est." Ennius: " Summus ibi capitur *Meddix,* occiditur alter" (*Annal.* viii. 73). In this passage from Ennius, Dacier reads *unus* for *summus.* This appears unnecessary: *Meddix* occurs in the Oscan inscriptions with the epithets *degetasius, fortis,* and *tuticus; summus* may be another epithet of the same kind. The word *Meddix* appears to be connected in origin with the Greek μέδων. The proper name *Mettius* (Fest. p. 158), or *Mettus* (Liv. i. 23), seems to have been this word *Meddix.* At least Livy says that *Mettus* Fuffetius was made *dictator* of Alba; and Festus speaks of Sthennius *Mettius* as *princeps* of the Samnites. So, also, we have ΜΕΔΔΕΙΣ ΟΥΦΕΝΣ (*Meddix Ufens*) in the inscription given by Castelli di Torremuzza, *Sicil. vet. Inscr.* v. 45, p. 55: see Müller, *Etrusk.* ii. p. 69, note. In somewhat later times the Sabello-Oscans called their dictator by the name *embratur,* which is evidently a shortened form of the Latin *im-perator,* or *indu-perator.* Liv. viii. 39 ; ix. 1 ; x. 29. Oros. v. 15: " Postquam sibi Samnites Papium Mutilum *imperatorem* præfecerant." Similarly we have coins with the Oscan inscription, *G. Paapi G. Mutíl Embratur;* which refer to the time of the Social War, when the forces of the confederacy were divided into two armies, each under its own imperator, the Marsi being under the orders of Q. *Popædius Silo,* the Samnites having for their leader this *Gaius Papius Mutilus*, the son of Gaius. Of *tuticus*, see below.

Minerva, Sab. v. *Feronia*.

Multa, Osc. et Sab. Fest. p. 142: " *Multam* Osce dici putant pœnam quidam. M. Varro ait pœnam esse, sed pecuniariam, de qua subtiliter in lib. i. quæstionum epist. i. refert." Cf. p. 144. s. v. *Maximam multam*. Varro, *apud Gell*. xi. 1 : " Vocabulum autem ipsum *multæ* idem M. Varro uno et vicesimo rerum humanarum non Latinum sed Sabinum esse dicit, idque ad suam memoriam mansisse ait in lingua Samnitium, qui sunt a Sabinis orti."

Nar, Sab. Virg. *Æn.* vii. 517 : " Sulfurea *Nar* albus aqua." Ubi Serv. : " Sabini lingua sua *nar* dicunt sulfur."

Ner, nerio, Sab. Suet. *Vit. Tiber*. i. : " Inter cognomina autem et *Neronis* adsumpsit, quo significatur lingua Sabina *fortis* ac *strenuus*." Gell. xiii. 22 : " *Nerio* a veteribus sic declinatur, quasi Anio ; nam proinde ut Anienem, sic Nerienem dixerunt, tertia syllaba producta ; id autem, sive *Nerio* sive *Nerienes* est, Sabinum verbum est, eoque significatur *virtus* et *fortitudo*. Itaque ex Claudiis, quos a Sabinis oriundos accepimus, qui erat egregia atque præstanti fortitudine *Nero* appellatus est. Sed id Sabini accepisse a Græcis videntur, qui vincula et firmamenta membrorum νεῦρα dicunt, unde nos quoque nervos appellamus." Lydus, *de Mens*. iv. 42. Id. *de Magistr*. i. 23. Compare the Sanscr. *nrĭ;* and see above, p. 74, s. v. *Cas-nar*.

Novensides, Ops. Sab. v. *Feronia*.

Panos, Messap. Athen. iii. p. 111 c. : πανὸς ἄρτος Μεσσάπιοι. This is a confirmation of *punus* for *panis* in the Umbrian inscription.

Petora, petorritum, Osc. Fest. p. 206 : " *Petoritum* et Gallicum vehiculum est, et nomen ejus dictum esse existimant a numero IIII. rotarum; alii Osce, quod hi quoque *petora* quattuor vocent; alii Græce, sed αἰολι-κῶς dictum." Comp. Quinctil. *Inst. Orat.* i. 5, § 57. The Æolic Greek wrote πέσσυρες, πέσσαρα, or πίσυρα, or πέτορες, πέτορα. In Gaelic we have *peder.* The Doric Gr. was τέτορες. In general we have τ in Gr. where we have *qv* in Latin, and in these cases we have *p* in Oscan: *e.g.* Osc. *pis,* Lat. *qvis,* Gr. τίς; and the Oscans wrote *Tarpinius, Ampus,* for the Lat. *Tarquinius, Ancus.* But *qv* was so agreeable to the Roman articulation, that we find *qv* in Latin words where we have not τ but π in Greek. Comp. πῇ, πέντε (πέμπε), ἵππος, ἕπομαι, λείπω, λίπα (λιπαρός), ὄπτιλος, ἐνέπει, πατάσσω, πέπτω, ἧπαρ, with *qua, quinque, equus, sequor, linquo, liqueo, oquulus, in-quit* (*quoth* Angl., *quêthan* Anglo-Sax., *gwedyd* Welsh), *quatio, quoquo, jecur.* For *petor-ritum* (*petor,* " four," rad. Sanscrit *ratha,* " a wheel") see Heindorf on Hor. *Sat.* i. 6, 104.

Pipatio, Osc. Fest. p. 212: " *Pipatio* clamor plorantis lingua Oscorum."

Pitpit, Osc. Fest. p. 212: " *Pitpit* Osce quidquid." Above, *Petora.*

Porcus, Sab. Varro, *L. L.* v. § 97: " *Porcus* quod Sabinis dictum *Aprimo Porco-por,* inde porcus; nisi si a Græcis, quod Athenis in libris sacrorum scripta κάπρῳ καὶ πόρκῳ."

Quirinus, Salus, Sab. v. *Feronia.*

Sancus, Sab. Varro, *L. L.* v. § 66: " Ælius Dium Fidium dicebat Diovis filium, ut Græci Διὸς κόρον Castorem, et putabat hunc esse Sancum ab Sabina lingua, et Herculem a Græca."

Saturnus, Sab. v. *Feronia.*

Scensa, Sab. Fest. p. 339: " *Scensas* [Sabini dicebant, quas] nunc cenas, quæ autem nunc prandia, cenas habebant, et pro ceni[s vespernas antiqui]." Comp. Paul. Diac. in p. 338.

Sol, Sab. v. *Feronia;* see also Varro, *L. L.* v. § 68; add Fest. p. 20: " Aureliam familiam, ex Sabinis oriundam, a Sole dictum putant, quod ei publice a populo Romano datus sit locus, in quo sacra faceret Soli, qui ex hoc *Auseli* dicebantur, ut Valesii, Papisii, pro eo quod est Valerii, Papirii." It would seem from this that the Sabine name for the Sun was *Selius,* i. e. ἥλιος, with the usual substitution of the sibilant for the aspirate. The first syllable signifies " to burn," as in Greek. On an Etruscan mirror *Usil* appears as the name of a figure armed with a bow, which probably represents Apollo; and this would seem to confirm Müller's suggestion (see *Berlin. Jahrbücher,* August 1841, p. 222, note) that the whole word *Ausil* was the name of the Sun-god in the Sabine, and perhaps also in the Etruscan language.

Sollo, Osc. Fest. p. 298: "*Sollo* Osce dicitur id quod nos *totum* vocamus. Lucilius: *vasa quoque omnino redimit, non sollo dupundi,* i. e. non tota. Idem Livius. *Sollicuria,* in omni re curiosa. Et *solliferreum* genus teli, totum ferreum. *Sollers* etiam in omni re prudens [comp. Sanscr. *sarvártha*]; et *sollemne,* quod omnibus annis præstari debet."

Strebula, Umbr. Fest. p. 313: "*Strebula* Umbrico nomine Plautus appellat coxendices quas G[ræci μήρια dicunt, quæ] in altaria in[poni solebant, ut Plau]tus ait in Fri[volaria]." Varro, *L. L.* vii. § 67: "*Stribula,* ut Opilius scribit, circum coxendices sunt bovis; id Græcum est ab ejus loci versura." Arnob. *adv. Gent.* vii. 24: " Non enim placet carnem *strebulam* nominari quæ taurorum e coxendicibus demitur."

Strena, Sab. Elpidian., *ap. Lyd. de Mens.* iv. 4: ὁ δὲ Ἐλπιδιανὸς ἐν τῷ περὶ ἑορτῶν στρήναν τὴν ὑγίειαν τῇ Σαβίνων φωνῇ λέγεσθαί φησιν. Comp. Symmach. Ep. x. 35; Festus, p. 313; and the Germ. *strenge*, Engl. *strong*, Lat. *strenuus*, Gr. στρηνής, στρῆνος, &c.

Summanus, Sab. v. *Feronia*.

Supparus, Osc. Varro, *L. L.* v. § 131 : " Indutui alterum quod subtus, a quo subucula; alterum quod supra, a quo *supparus*, nisi id, quod item dicunt Osci."

Tebæ, Sab. Varro, *R. R.* iii. 1, 16: " Nam lingua prisca et in Græcia Æoleis Bœotii sine afflatu vocant collis *tebas;* et in Sabinis, quo e Græcia venerunt Pelasgi, etiamnunc ita dicunt; cujus vestigium in agro Sabino via Salaria non longe a Reate milliarius clivus appellatur *Thebæ*." The word therefore, according to Varro, was Pelasgian as well as Sabine.

Terenum, Sab. Macrob. *Sat.* ii. 14: " A *tereno*, quod est Sabinorum lingua molle, unde *Terentios* quoque dictos putat Varro ad Libonem primo." Comp. the Gr. τέρην.

Terminus, Sab. v. *Feronia*.

Tesqua, Sab. Schol. Hor. *Epist.* i. 14, 19: " Lingua Sabinorum loca difficilia et repleta sentibus sic (*tesqua*) nominantur."

Tuticus, Osc. Liv. xxvi. 6: " Medix *tuticus*." The *Itinerarium Hierosolym.* explains the name of the city *Equus-Tuticus*, which Horace could not fit to his verse (i. *Sat.* 5, 87), by *equus magnus*. Though it is possible, however, that *tuticus* might in a secondary application bear this signification, it is more probable that it is the adj. from *tuta*=*civitas*, and that it means *publicus* or *civicus*.

Trabea, Sab. Lydus *de Mens.* i. 19.

Trafere, Sab. Above, s. v. *Fedus*.

Trimodia, Sab. Schol. Hor. *Serm.* i. 1, 53: " Cumeræ dicuntur vasa minora quæ capiunt quinque sive sex modios, quæ lingua Sabinorum *trimodiæ* dicuntur."

Ungulus, Osc. Fest. p. 375: "Ungulus Oscorum lingua anulus." Comp. Plin. *H. N.* xxxiii. 1.
Vedius, Sab. v. *Feronia.*
Vefere, Sab. v. *Fedus.*
Veia, Osc. Fest. p. 368: "*Veia* apud Oscos dicebatur plaustrum."
Vesperna, Sab. v. *Scensa.*
Vesta, Volcanus, Vertumnus, Sab. v. supra, sub v. *Feronia.*

§ 3.
The Bantine Table.

The most important fragment of the Oscan language is carved on a bronze tablet, which was found in the year 1793 at Oppidum, on the borders of Lucania, and which is called the *Tabula Bantina* on account of the name *Bansæ* occurring in the inscription, which seems to refer to the neighbouring city of Bantia in Apulia. On the other side is a Latin inscription, which will be considered in its proper place.

The Oscan Bantine inscription contains thirty-three lines or fragments of lines. Of these lines four to twenty-six are complete at the beginning; and lines twelve to thirty have preserved the ends entire: consequently there are some twelve or fourteen lines which may be read throughout. Of course, the certainty and facility of the interpretation vary materially with the completeness of the fragment; and while many passages in the intermediate lines may be made out almost word for word, we are left to mere conjecture for the broken words and sentences at the beginning and end. The following is a copy of the Table.

1. . . . . *uo* . . . . . *lici*[*t*]*u*[*d*] . . .
2. . . . . . . *mus . q . moltam . angit . u* . . . .
3. . . . . *deiv . ast . maimas . carneis . senateis . tangi* . . . .

4. *amosi . . cnioc . egmo . com . parascuster .*
    suae . pis . pertemust . p . . . . .
5. *deivatud . sipus . komonei . perum . dolom .*
    mallom . siom . ioc . como . . . . .
6. *cas . amnud . pan . piei . sum . brateis . auti .*
    cadeis . amnud . inim . idic . . . .
7. *tanginud . maimas . carneis . pertumum . piei .*
    ex . comono . pertemem . . . . . .
8. *comono . ni . hipid   pis . pocapi . t . post .*
    post . exac . comono . hafiert . meddis . . .
9. *en . eituas . factud . pous . touto . deivatuns .*
    tanginom . deicans . stom . dat . ei . . .
10. *deicum . pod . valaemom . touticom . tadait .*
    ezum . nep . fepacid . pod . pis . dat . . .
11. *deivaid . docud . malud . suae . pis . contrud .*
    exelc . fefacust . auti . comono . hip . . .
12. *to . estud . n .* ⏀ ⏀ *. in . suae . pis . ionc . fortis .*
    meddis . moltaum . herest . ampert . min
    . . . teis .
13. *eituas . moltas . moltaum . licitud .   suae .*
    pis . pru . meddixud . altrei . castrous . .
    uci . eituas
14. *zicolom . dicust . izic . comonon . hipid . ne .*
    don . op . toutad . petirupert . urust .
    sipus . perum . dolom .
15. *mallom . in . trutum . zico . touto . peremust .*
    petiropert . neip . mais . pomtis .   com .
    preivatud . actud .
16. *pruter . pam . medicat . inom . didist . in . pon .*
    dos . mo . xx . con . preivatud . urust .
    eisucen . ziculud .

17. *zicolom . xxx . nesimum . comonom . ni . hipid . suae . pis . contrud . exeic . fefacust . ionc . suae . pis .*
18. *herest . meddis . moltaum . licitud . ampert . mistreis . aeteis . eituas . licitud.   pon . censtur.*
19. *Bansae . tautam . censazet . pis . ceus . Bantins . fust . censamur . esuf . in . eituam . poizad . ligud .*
20. *aisc . censtur . censaum . anget . uzet . aut . suae . pis . censtomen . nei . cebnust . dolud . mallud .*
21. *in . eizeik . vincter . esuf . comenei . lamatir . prmed . dixud . toutad . praesentid . perum . dolum .*
22. *mallom . in . amiricatud . allo . famelo . in . ei . sivom . paei . eizeis . fust . pa . ean . censto . ust .*
23. *toutico . estud .   pr . suae . praefucus . pod . post . exac . Bansae . fust . suae . pis . op . eizois . com .*
24. *atrud .   .   .   ud . acum . herest . auti . prumedicatud . manimasepum . eizazunc . egmazum .*
25. *pas . ex . aiscen . ligis . scriftas . set . nep . him . pruhipid . mais . zicolois . x . nesimois . suae . pis . contrud .*
26. *exeic . pruhipust . molto . etanto . estud . n . ⊕ . in . suae . pis . ionk . meddis . moltaum . herest . licitud .*
27. *.   .   .   minstreis . aeteis . eituas . moltas . moltaum . licitud   pr . censtur . Bansae*

28. . . . . id . ni . 1 . suae . . . . fust . nep .
censtur . fuid . nei . suae . pr . fust . in .
suae . pis . pr . in . suae .
29. . . . . m . . . iei . q . d . . . im .
nerum . fust . izic . post . eizuc . tr .
ph . ni . fuid . suae . pis .
30. . . . . ist . izik . amprufid . facus .
estud . idic . medicim . eizuk .
31. . . . . um . VI . nesimum .
32. . . . . um . pod .
33. . . . . medicim .

§ 4.
Commentary on the Bantine Table.

In the first line we have only the word liki[t]u[d],[1] i.e. liceto, which occurs in five other passages, and also in the Cippus Abellanus.

In l. 2 we read: Q. moltam angit . u. Q. is the common abbreviation for quæstor, whose business it was to collect such fines: compare *Mus. Ver.* p. 469: QVAISTORES . . . . AIRE . MVLTATICOD . DEDERONT. We have seen above that *multa* s. *molta* is recognised as a Sabello-Oscan word; and it is of course equivalent to the Latin *multa*. As *anter* is the Oscan form of *inter*, we might suppose that *an-git . u* was for *in-igit . o*. But a comparison of the Oscan inscriptions xxiv. 18 (p. 71 Leps.), *meddíss degetasiús araget*, and xxvii. 38 (p. 86 Leps.), *meddís degetasis aragetud multas* (which are obviously, with the common change of *d* to *r*, *meddix degetasius adiget* and *meddix degetasius adigito multas*), would rather shew that *angit . u[d]* is an abbreviation of *adigito*, the dental liquid representing the dental mute.

L. 3: *deivast maimas karneis senateis tangi...* The

---

[1] In the second transcription I have substituted *k* for *c*, for the reasons given by Lepsius (*ad Inscr.* p. 150).

first word is the conjunctive of *divavit*, which occurs in the inscription quoted by Lanzi (*Saggio*, iii. p. 533), and we have the imperative *deivatud* in l. 5, *deivatuns* in l. 9, and *deivaid* in l. 11. *Deivo* must mean " to divide" or " distribute," if we may judge from the context in this passage and in Lanzi's inscription, which runs thus: V. ATII DIVAVIT TUNII IRINII II. T. IRINII PATRII DONO MIIIL I. LIB . . . T. *Maimas karneis* must mean *maximas carnes*, as *mais* in ll. 15, 25, signifies *magis:* comp. the French *mais*. The mutilated *tangi* . . . was probably *tanginud* (l. 7), an ablative case, corresponding to the accus. *tanginom* (l. 9). We have the same phrase, *senateis tanginúd*, in the *Cippus Abellanus*, i. 8; and it is probably equivalent to the *de senatuos sententiad* of the *senatus-consultum de Bacchanalibus*. If so, the root *tag-* (with nasal insertion *ta-n-g-*) occurred in Oscan as well as in Greek.

L. 4: *suæ pis pertemust*. The first two words, *suæ pis*, i. e. *si quis*, are of constant occurrence in this Table. For the form of *suæ*=*si*, see *New Cratylus*, p. 274. So *suad* =*sic* (Müller, *Suppl. Ann. in Fest.* p. 411). *Pertemust* is the perf. subjunctive of a verb *pertimere*, which seems to mean " to portion off" or " divide:" comp. *pertica*, &c. In l. 7 it is used with *maximas karneis;* and it is therefore, perhaps, not unlike *deivo* in meaning.

L. 5: *komonei* seems to be the genitive of a word *com-unus*, synonymous with *com-munis*, and designating the *ager publicus*, i. e. τὸ κοινόν. *Perum dolum mallom siom*=*per dolum malum suum*. The preposition *per-um* seems to be a compound like its synonyme *am-pert* (12, &c.). *Iok komo-*[*no*] is perhaps *hoc com-unum:* *ionc* stands in this inscription for *hunc*.

L. 6: *-kas amnud*. In Lepsius' transcript this is written as one word; but in the original there is a vacant space between the two, and *-kas* is clearly the end of some mutilated word, the beginning of which was broken off from the end of the preceding line. *Amnud* occurs again in this line, and also in the *Cippus Abellanus*, l. 17. It seems to be the abl. of some noun. *Piei*, in this line and the next, must surely be a verb: it is impossible to speak with any degree of confidence about a word which occurs only in this passage; but if the usual change from *qu* to *p* has taken place here, the passage may mean: *quam quiverit, sumat brateis aut kadeis* (perhaps two participles) *ex amne;* and l. 7, [*si senatuis*] *sententiad maximas carnes distribuere quiverit, ex com-uno distribuere* [*liceto*].

L. 8: *ni hipid*, i. e. *ne habeat:* conf. ll. 11, 14, 17; also *pru-hipid* (25) = *præhibeat*, and *pru-hipust* (26) = *præhibuerit*. *Post post* is probably an error of the engraver for *pod post: pod* = *quod* signifies *quando* in l. 23. *Post-esak* = *post-hac: esak* is the accus. neut. pl. of the pronoun *esus*, which we have also in the Eugubine Tables, the *-k*, *-ke*, being subjoined, as in the Latin *hic* = *hi-ce*. This is a most instructive form, as bearing immediately on a difficulty which has long been felt in Latin etymology. The quantity of the last syllables of *anteā, intereā, posteā, postereā*, seems at first sight irreconcilable with the supposition that these words are the prepositions *ante, inter*, &c., followed by the neut. accus. *ea*. And a comparison with *post-hac, adversus hac* (Fest. p. 246, l. 8, &c.), might lead to the supposition that they are ablatives feminine, the regimen of the prepositions being changed, as is certainly the case in Umbrian. This is, at any rate, the opinion of Klenze (*Phil. Abhandl.* p. 45) and Müller (*ad Fest.* p. 247). Another philologer supposes that they may be deduced from the accus. *eam*, on the analogy of *post-quam, ante-quam*, &c. (*Journal of Education*, i. 106). But this opinion has nothing to support it. It is much more reasonable to suppose that the demonstrative pronoun, in Latin as in Oscan, being generally followed by the termination *-ce*, made its neut. pl. in *-a-ce* or *-æc-:* we have an instance of this in the demonstrative *hi-c,* the neut. pl. of which is *hæc,* not *ha-ce* or *ha*. Now as this form has become *ha-c* in *posthac,* and as *qua-ce* has become *quæ,* we may understand that, as *quæ-propter* becomes *quā-propter,* so *ante-ea-ce,* or *ante-eæc,* might become *ant'eā;* and so of the others. At least, there is no other way of explaining the neuter forms *quæ* and *hæc. Post-esa-k* is therefore a synonyme for *post-hæc = post-hac.*

L. 10 : *pod valæmom toutikom tadait ezum nep fepakid pod pis dat,* i. e. [*si quis fecit*] *quod salutem publicam tardet, illud neque fecit, quod quis dat* [*faciendum*]. *Tadait* appears to contain the root of *tædet,* which is connected in sense and etymology with *tardus ;* the *r* is only an assimilation to the *d.* Similarly we have *pigere* interdum pro *tardari,* Festus, p. 213, Müller. *Fepakid* is only an error for *fefakid,* like *docud* for *dolud* in the next line. We see from this and the conjunctive *fefakust,* which follows, that the Oscans formed the preterite of *facio* by reduplication, and not by lengthening the root-syllable (*New Crat.* p. 463).

The passage from l. 11 to the end of the paragraph may be supplied and explained as follows : *suæ pis contrud eseik fefakust, auti komono hip*[*id*], [*molto*] [*etan*]*to estud n.* ⅭⅠↃ ⅭⅠↃ., *in suæ pis ionk fortis meddis moltaum herest ampert mi*[*nstreis ei*]*teis eituas moltas moltaum likitud :* i. e. *si quis adversus hæc fecerit, aut com-unum* (i. e. *agrum publicum*) *habeat* (i. e. *possideat*), *multa tanta esto numi* ⅭⅠↃ.ⅭⅠↃ, *inde si quis hunc validus magistratus multare voluerit per ministros ætuos* (?) *diribitorii* (?) *multas multare liceto.* It is easy to restore *molto etanto* from l. 26 infra. *Multa tanta* refers to what has preceded, like the *siremps lex esto* of the Roman laws. The sum is denoted by the numeral sign, which was subsequently represented by ⅭⅠↃ, just as ɪɪ.s. became ʜ.s. *Fortis meddix = validus magistratus* (see Festus, p. 84, s. v. *forctes*), in other words, " a magistrate of sufficient authority." *Molta-um* is the old infinitive of *multo. Herest* is the second perf. of a verb *hero*, " to choose" or "take" (root *hir*, "a hand," Sanscr. *hrĭ*), which occurs in the Umbrian Tables with a slight variety of meaning. In the Latin Bantine Table (l. 7) we have *quei volet magistratus* in a parallel clause. That *ampert* is a preposition is clear, and it is also obvious that it signifies " by " or " through ;" but that it is to be referred to ἀμφὶ περί, as Grotefend proposes, is not so manifest. I should rather think that *pert* is a termination here, as in *petiropert* (l. 15); and if so, it qualifies the prepos. *am*, corresponding to the German *um*, which is also used with qualifying terminations, whether prepositional or otherwise: compare the Latin *ad-versus*, &c. *Minstreis æteis* is supplied from ll. 18, 27. The word *minis-ter* is the correlative of *magis-ter;* and as *magistri* or *magistratus* were the *higher* public functionaries, so *ministri* were those who did the state service in a *subordinate* capacity — *lictores, viatores*, and such like. The adjective *æteis*, and the word *eituas*, occur again in l. 18 without *moltas;* and it is clear, therefore, that *eituas* is not an adjective agreeing with *moltas*, but rather that it is a gen. depending on *minstreis*. The meaning of these words is altogether uncertain. Klenze takes *eituas* for *istas ;* and Grotefend translates it *ærarii*. It is possible that *æ-teis* may be derived from *æs;* in which case we shall have *æ[s]tuus* by the side of *æs-timus* (preserved in *æs-timo :* see below, Ch. VII. § 5), just as we have both *ædi-tuus* and *ædi-timus* (Festus, p. 13). The word *eitua* may be connected with the root *it-* or *fid*, " to divide" or " distribute." It will be recollected that *idus* was a Sabine, *itus* a Tuscan word: Varro, *L. L.* vi. § 28.

L. 13: *suæ pis pru-meddišud altrei castrous-uci eituas zikolom dicust, izik komonom hipid:* i. e. *si quis præ magistratu alius . . . sicilicum dicaverit, sic comunum habeat.* *Prumeddišud* seems to be much the same as *prumedikatud*, l. 24.

Pru stands for *præ:* so we have *pruter* (l. 16), *pruhipid* (l. 25), for *præter*, *præhibeat*. The *ziculus*, mentioned in this and other passages of the Table, seems to be the *sicilicus* (from *seco*), which was, in land-measuring, $\frac{1}{48}$ of the *juger*, or six hundred square feet (Columella, v. 1, 9): in general it expressed subdivision, and was $\frac{1}{48}$ of the *as*, or ¼ of the *semuncia* in money-reckoning (Fest. p. 366; *Sicilicum dictum quod semunciam secet*, Labb. *Gloss.; Sicilicum*, τέταρτον οὐγκίας, Böckh, *Metrolog. Untersuchung.* p. 160), and also $\frac{1}{48}$ of the *quinaria* (Frontin. *de Aquæd.* c. 28), and of the *hora* (Plin. xviii. 32).

L. 14: *ne donop . toutad . petirupert . urust sipus p. d. m.* The first words here are very obscure. Klenze joins *optoutad*, which he translates *propterea*. *Petirupert* seems to coincide with the Umbrian *petur-pursus* (*Eug. Tab.* vi. b. 11), i. e. *quadri-fariam*. *Urust* is the second perf. of *urvo* s. *urbo* = *aratro definio, circumdo* (Fest. p. 375; Pomponius, *L.* 239, § 6, *de Verb. Signif.*), whence *urbs*, and perhaps *orbis*. *Sipus p. d. m.*, " knowingly and with evil design." *Sipus* = *sibus*, for which see Fest. p. 336.

L. 15: *petiro - pert neip mais pomtis* = *quater neque magis quintis* [*vicibus*]. Ibid.: *kom preivatud aktud* = *cum privato actu*. Fest. p. 17: "*Actus* in geometria minorem partem jugeri, id est centumviginti pedum." Niebuhr, *Hist. of Rom.* ii. *append.* i. *ad not.* 29 : " The *jugerum*, as the very name implies, was a double measure; and the real unit in the Roman land-measure was the *actus*, containing 14,400 square feet, that is, a square of which each side was 120 feet."

L. 16: *pruter pam* = *præter-quam*.

L. 18, sqq.: *pon . kenstur . Bansæ . tautam . kensazet . pis . keus . Bantins . fust . kensamur . esuf . in . eituam . poizad . ligud . aisk . kenstur . kensaum . anget . uzet . aut . suæ . pis . kenstomen . nei . kebnust . dolud . mallud . in . e . izeik . vinkter . esuf . comenei . lamatir . pr . med . dixud .*

toutad . præsentid . perum . dolum . mallum . in . amirika-tud . allo . famelo . in . ei . sivom . paei . eizeis . fust . pa . ean . censto . ust . toutiko . estud. The first words are tolerably clear: *Quum censor* (here *censitor*) *Bantiæ civitatem censassit, quis civis Bantinus fuerit.* The letter *z* represents the combination *ss*, as has been shewn above by a comparison of ὄβρυζα, *obrussa*, &c. The form *keus* for *civis* is etymologically interesting. It proves that *-vis* is the termination of the Latin word: consequently *ke-us, ci-vis*, is composed of the root *ke* (κεῖ-μαι, &c.), and the pronominal affix *-vi-s, -u-s* (see *New Cratylus*, p. 334), and the word means "a squatter," or generally "an inhabitant;" compare θῆτες, *insassen*, &c. (Buttmann, *Lexil.* ii. 111, note). The word *kensamur*, if it is one word, is hardly intelligible. Grotefend understands it as the passive participle *kensamus* for *kensamnus* or *censendus;* but although the participial termination *mn* is often reduced to *n*, I know no instance in which it is represented by *m* only. A comparison of *kensaum . anget . uzet .* in l. 20, and of *kensto . ust .* in l. 22, might rather induce us to suppose that *ur* represents part of this verb *uzet, ust*, and then *kensam* is probably a corruption of *kensaum* the infinitive. It is remarkable that the verb is conjugated in *-ao*, and not like its Latin equivalent in *-eo*. The conjugation seems to be *censo, -as, -ui, -āum, -itus*, like *veto*. What this verb *uzo, uro*, may mean can only be guessed from the context. It seems to be a parallel to *anget;* which, as is shewn above, means *adiget.* It might then be a form of *urgeo*, the guttural being softened, as in the preter *ursi*, and in that case its signification will be "to insist upon," "to exact:" *quum censitor B. civitatem censuerit, censum urgeat, quis civis Bantinus fuerit.* The next words seem to mean, *ibi in diribitorium penset, hac lege*, and here the sentence must end. *Esu-f* seems to correspond exactly to *i-bi*, just as *pu-f* (*Tab. Pomp.* xxiv. 4, 3) answers to *u-bi. Poizad* seems to be *penset*, a form of *pendo*. The analogy is supported by the French *poids* for *pondus*, &c. *Ligud aiske = lege hac*, just as below, 25. *es aisken ligis* must mean *ex hisce legibus*. The next sentence may be rendered: *censitor censitum* (i. e. *ad censendum*) *adiget, urgebit; aut si quis censum illum non compleverit* (?) *dolo malo, inde is statim vincitor*. It is hardly possible to understand *kenstom . en .* except as an abbreviation of the two words *censtom enom*, the latter being the same pronoun which appears in Latin, in the locative case, as the conjunction *enim*, Sanscrit *êna* (*New Crat*. p. 216). Grotefend's supposition that it is a noun in *-men*, like the Umbrian *esunumen*, is inadmissible, because in that case the word must have been *censamen*. The interpretation of *kebnust = kebnuerit* is of course conjectural only; and though there is one etymology by which it might be made to bear the signification which I have given it, yet in a matter of so much uncertainty it is better to leave it as it is. *E . izeic* seems to stand for *Eso izeic*, i. e. *is sic* (*statim, illico*). The Oscans seem to have a verb *vinco*, " to bind," which the Romans imply by their *vinxi*, the form in *-io* having perhaps come into vogue by way of distinction from *vinco*, root *vic*. Of the next words we cannot make much. *Prmed . disud* perhaps stands for *pro meddixud = pro medicatud* (l. 24) *= pro magistratu*. *Toutad præsentid = civitate præsente? In . amirikatud allo . famelo = inde emercato alium famulum?* We know from Festus that *famel* was an Oscan word. *Pa ean kensto ust, toutiko estud = qua eam censitor urget, publicum esto?*

L. 23: *Pr . suæ . præfukus . pod . post . esak . Bansæ . fust :* i. e. *prætor sive præfectus, quando post-hac Bantiæ fuerit. Præfucus* is formed from *præficio*, in the same way as the Umbrian *der-secus* from *dis-seco*. L. 23, sqq. : *suæ pis op-eizois kom atrud . . . ud akum herest, auti prumedikatud manimasepum . . eizazunk eg mazum pas es aisken ligis skriftas set ne . phim pruhipid mais zikolois . x. nesi-*

mois, &c.: i.e. *si quis ob hæc cum atro* .. *o agere voluerit, aut præ magistratu mancipium isthoc elocare* (?), *quas ex hisce legibus scriptas sciet, ne in hoc præhibeat magis sicilicis decem contiguis* (below, Chap. VII. § 6), &c. *Eg-mazun* seems to answer to the Greek ἐκ-μισθοῦν; μισθός, miethe, &c. run through this family of languages. The Table has *ne . phim;* I would rather read *nep him: nep* is used in an absolute prohibition in Umbrian (*Tab. Eug.* vi. a, 27), and *him* appears to be the locative of the pronoun *hi* (see *New Crat.* p. 173). The rest of the paragraph has been explained before.

There is nothing in the last paragraph which seems to require any observation, except that in l. 29 tribunes of the *plebs* seem to be mentioned: *tr. pl. ni fuid = nisi fuit tribunus plebei.*

§ 5. The Atellanæ.

It seems scarcely worth while to enumerate the grammatical forms which may be collected from this inscription, as they are virtually the same with those which occur in the oldest specimens of Latin. It may be desirable, however, before concluding this part of the subject, to make a few remarks on the *Fabulæ Atellanæ*, the only branch of Oscan literature of which we know any thing.

The most important passage respecting the *Fabulæ Atellanæ*,—that in which Livy is speaking (vii. 2) of the introduction of the Tuscan *ludiones* at Rome in the year A. U. C. 390,—has often been misunderstood; and the same has been the fate of a passage in Tacitus (iv. 14), in which the historian mentions the expulsion of the actors from Italy in the year A. U. C. 776. With regard to the latter, Tacitus has caused some confusion by his inaccurate use of the word *histrio;* but Suetonius has the phrase *Atellanarum histrio* (*Nero*, c. 39); and the word had either lost its earlier and more limited signification, or the Atellanæ were then performed by regular *histriones*.

H

Livy says that, among other means of appeasing the anger of the gods in the pestilence of 390 A.U.C., scenic games were for the first time introduced at Rome. Hitherto the Romans had had no public sports except those of the circus—namely, races and wrestling; but now this trivial and foreign amusement was introduced. Etruscan *ludiones* danced gracefully to the sound of the flute without any accompaniment of words, and without any professed mimic action. Afterwards, the Roman youth began to imitate these dances, and accompanied them with unpremeditated jests, after the manner of the Fescennine verses; these effusions gave way to the *satura*, written in verse and set to the flute, which was acted by professed *histriones* with suitable songs and gestures; and then, after a lapse of several years, Livius Andronicus ventured to convert the *satura* into a regular poem, and to make a distinction between the singing (*canticum*) and the dialogue (*diverbia*), the latter alone being reserved to the *histrio*. Upon this, the Roman youth, leaving the regular play to the professed actors, revived the old farces, and acted them as afterpieces (*exodia*) to the regular drama. These farces, he expressly says, were of Oscan origin, and akin to the *Fabulæ Atellanæ;* and they had the peculiar advantage of not affecting the civic rights of the actors.

It is manifest from this passage that the Roman youth were not satisfied with either the Tuscan or the Greek importations, and that it was their wish to revive something not foreign, but national. Of course Livy cannot mean to say that the Oscan farce was not introduced at Rome till after the time of Livius Andronicus Muso, and that it was then imported from *Atella*. For whereas Muso did not represent at Rome till the second Punic war,[1]

---

[1] Porcius Licinius, *apud Aul. Gell.* xvii. 21:

Pœnico bello secundo Muso pinnato gradu
Intulit se bellicosam in Romuli gentem feram.

See also Hor. ii. *Epist.* i. 162.

Atella shared in the fate of Capua ten years before the battle of Zama, and the inhabitants were compelled to migrate to Calatia.[1] Now it appears from the coins of this place that its Oscan name was *Aderla*;[2] and the Romans always pronounced this as Atella, by a change of the medial into a tenuis, as in *Mettus* for *Meddix*, *imperator* for *embratur*, *fuit* for *fuid*, &c. This shews that the name was in early use at Rome; and we may suppose that, as an essential element in the population of Rome was Oscan, the Romans had their Oscan farces from a very early period, and that these farces received a great improvement from the then celebrated city of *Aderla* in Campania. It is also more than probable that these Oscan farces were common in the country life of the old Romans, both before they were introduced into the city,[3] and after the expulsion of the *histriones* by Tiberius.[4] For the mask was the peculiar characteristic of the Atellanæ,[5] and these country farces are always spoken of with especial reference to the masks of the actors.

We may be sure that the Oscan language was not used in these farces when that language ceased to be intelligible to the Romans. The language of the frag-

---

[1] Livy, xxvi. 16, xxii. 61, xxvii. 3.
[2] Lepsius *ad Inscriptiones*, p. 111.
[3] Virgil. *Georg.* ii. 385, sqq.:

> Nec non Ausonii, Troja gens missa, coloni
> Versibus incomptis ludunt risuque soluto,
> Oraque corticibus sumunt horrenda cavatis.

Comp. Horat. ii. *Epist.* i. 139, sqq.

[4] Juvenal, *Sat.* iii. 172, sqq.:

> Ipsa dierum
> Festorum herboso colitur si quando theatro
> Majestas, tandemque redit ad pulpita notum
> Exodium, quum personæ pallentis hiatum
> In gremio matris formidat rusticus infans.

[5] Festus, s. v. *personata fabula*, p. 217: " per Atellanos *qui proprie vocantur personati.*"

ments which have come down to us is pure Latin,[1] and Tacitus describes the Atellana as " Oscum *quondam* ludicrum."[2] Probably, till a comparatively late period, the Atellana abounded in provincial and rustic expressions;[3] but at last it retained no trace of its primitive simplicity, unless we are to seek this in the gross coarseness and obscenity,[4] which seem to have superseded the old-fashioned elegance of the original farce.[5]

[1] See Diomed. iii. pp. 487, 488, Putsch.
[2] *Ann.* iv. 149.   [3] Varro, *L. L.* vii. § 84, p. 152.
[4] Schober, *über die Atellan. Schauspiele*, pp. 281, sqq.
[5] Donat. *de Trag. et Com.* "Atellanæ salibus et jocis compositæ, quæ in se non habent nisi *vetustam elegantiam.*" The *Atellana* as well as the *comœdia* of the Romans derived many of its later features from the Doric farces of the Greeks: see Müller, *Hist. Lit. Gr.* ch. xxix. § 5 (vol. ii. p. 43, note).

CHAPTER V.

THE ETRUSCAN LANGUAGE.

§ 1. Transcriptions of proper names the first clue to an interpretation of the Etruscan language. § 2. Names of Etruscan divinities derived and explained. § 3. Alphabetical list of Etruscan words interpreted. § 4. Etruscan inscriptions — difficulties attending their interpretation. § 5. Inscriptions in which the Pelasgian element predominates. § 6. The great Perugian Inscription analysed. § 7. General reflections.

§ 1. Transcriptions of proper names the first clue to an interpretation of the Etruscan language.

It will not be possible to investigate the remains of the Etruscan language with any reasonable prospect of success, until some scholar shall have furnished us with a body of inscriptions based upon a critical examination of the originals; and even then it is doubtful if we should have a sufficiently copious collection of materials. The theory, however, that the Etruscan language, as we have it, is a Pelasgian idiom corrupted and deformed by contact with the Umbrian, is amply confirmed by an inspection of those remains which admit of approximate interpretation.

The first great clue to the understanding of this mysterious language is furnished by the Etruscan transcriptions of well-known Greek proper names, and by the Etruscan forms of those names which were afterwards adopted by the Romans. This comparison may at least supply some *prima-facie* evidence of the peculiarities of Tuscan articulation, and of the manner in which the language tended to corrupt itself.

It is well known that the Etruscan alphabet possessed no *mediæ*, as they are called. We are not, therefore, surprised to find, that in the transcriptions of Greek proper names the Etruscans have substituted *tenues*. Thus, the Greek names, Ἄδραστος, Τυδεύς, Ὀδυσσεύς, Μελέαγρος, and Πολυδεύκης, are written *Atresthe, Tute, Utuze, Melakre*, and *Pultuke*. But the change in the transcription goes a step further than this; for though they actually possessed the *tenues*, they often convert them into *aspiratæ*. Thus, Ἀγαμέμνων, Ἄδραστος, Θέτις, Περσεύς, Πολυνείκης, Τήλεφος, become *Achmiem, Atresthe, Thethis, Pherse, Phulnike, Thelaphe*. In some cases the Greek *tenues* remain unaltered in the transcription, as in Πηλεύς, *Pele;* Παρθενοπαῖος, *Parthanapæ;* Κάστωρ, *Kastur;* Ἡρακλῆς, *Herkle:* and the Greek *aspiratæ* are also transferred, as in Ἀμφιάραος, *Amphiare*. These transcriptions of Greek names supply us also with a very important fact in regard to the Etruscan syllabarium: namely, that their liquids were really semi-vowels; in other words, that these letters did not require the expression of an articulation-vowel. It has been shewn elsewhere[1] that the semi-vocal nature of the liquid is indicated in most languages by the etymological fact, that it may be articulated by a vowel either preceding or following it. For example: mute + liquid + vowel = mute + vowel + liquid, is an equation which holds good in every etymological problem. Applying this principle to the Etruscan transcriptions, we see that the Etruscan *Ap[u]lu, Ach[i]le, At[a]laent, Erc[u]le, El[e]chs[a]ntre, Men[e]le, M[e]n[e]rva, Phul[u]nices, Ur[e]ste,* &c. are representatives of the Greek Ἀχιλλεύς, Ἀταλάντη, Ἡρακλῆς, Ἀλέξανδρος,

---

[1] *N. Crat.* p. 111. The word *el-em-en-tum*, according to the etymology which has received the sanction of Heindorf (*ad Hor.* i. *Sat.* i. 26), would furnish an additional confirmation of these views. But this etymology cannot be admitted; and the word must be considered as containing the root *ol-* (in *olere, adolescens, indoles, soboles, prôles,* &c.), so that *ele-mentum = ole-mentum*. See Benary in the *Berl. Jahrb.* for August 1841, p. 240.

Μενελέως, Πολυνείκης, Ὀρέστης, and of the Latin *Minerva*, only because the Etruscans did not find it necessary to express in writing the articulation-vowel of the liquids.

If we pass to the consideration of those proper names which are found in the Latin language, we shall observe peculiarities of precisely the same kind. For instance, the medials in *Idus, Tlabonius, Vibius*, &c. are represented in Etruscan by the tenues in *Itus, Tlapuni, Fipi*, &c.; the tenues in *Turius, Velcia*, &c. stand for the aspirates in *Thura, Felche*, &c.; and the articulation-vowels in *Licinius, Tanaquil*, &c. are omitted before or after the liquids in *Lecne, Thanchfil*, &c.

The transcription *Utuze*, for Ὀδυσσεύς, suggests a remark which has been in part anticipated in a former chapter. We see that in this case the Etruscan z corresponds to the Greek -σσ, just as conversely, in the cases there cited, the Greek -ζ is represented by -*ss* in Latin. It was formerly supposed that this Etruscan z was equivalent to x = κs, and this supposition was based on a comparison of *Utuze* with *Ulyxes*. To say nothing, however, of the mistake which was made in assuming that *Utuze* represented *Ulyxes* and not Ὀδυσσεύς, it has been shewn by Lepsius (*Annali dell' Instituto*, viii. p. 168) both that the Etruscans added this z to the guttural κ, as in *šrankzl*, &c. and also, when it was necessary to express the Greek ξ, that they did not use the letter z, but formed a representative for it by a combination of κ or ch with s, as in *Secstinal* = *Sextinia natus*, and *Elchsntre* = Ἀλέξανδρος. Palæographical considerations also indicate that the letter corresponded in form, not to ξ or *x*, but to the Greek *z*. We ought, however, to go a step further than Lepsius has done, and say that the Latin *x* was, after all, in one of its values, a representative of this Etruscan letter. It is true, indeed, that *x* does represent also the combination of a guttural and sibilant; but there are cases, on the other hand, in which *x* is found in Latin words containing roots into which no guttural enters: comp. *rixa* with ἔρις (ἔριδος), ἐρίζω, &c. In these cases it must be supposed to stand as a representative of the Greek ζ in its sound *sh*, and also of the Hebrew *shin*, from which ξῖ has derived its name (see *New Crat.* p. 130). With regard to the name *Ulysses, Ulyxes,* Ὀδυσσεύς, etymology would rather shew that the ultimate form of the *x, ss,* or *z,* was a softened dental. The Tuscan name of this hero was *Nanus,* i. e. "the pygmy" (Müller, *Etrusk.* ii. p. 269); and, according to Eustathius (p. 289, 38), Ὀλυσσεύς or Ὀλισσεύς was the original form of the Greek name. From these data it has been happily conjectured (by Kenrick, *Herod.* p. 281) that the name means ὄ-λιζος, ὄ-λισσος, Æol. for ὀ-λίγος (Eustath. 1160, 16), of which the simplest form is λιτός, *little:* so that Ulysses, in the primitive conception, was a god represented in a diminutive form.

§ 2.
Names of Etruscan divinities derived and explained.

The materials, which are at present available for an approximate philological interpretation of the Tuscan language, may be divided into three classes: (1) the names of deities, &c. whose titles and attributes are familiar to us from the mythology of Greece and Rome; (2) the Tuscan words which have descended to us with an interpretation; and (3) the inscriptions, sepulchral or otherwise, of which we possess accurate transcripts. Let us consider these three in their order.

The Tuscans seem to have worshipped three gods especially as rulers of the sky,—*Janus*, god of the sky in general; *Jupiter*, whom they called *Tina*, god of the day; and *Summanus*, god of the night. Of these, *Janus* and *Tina* are virtually the same designation. The root *dyá* seems to be appropriated in a great many languages to signify "day" or "daylight." See Grimm, *Deut. Mythol.* 2d ed. p. 177. Sometimes it stands absolutely, as in *dies;* sometimes with

§ 2.]   THE ETRUSCAN LANGUAGE.   105

a labial affix, as in the Sanscr. *dyú*, Gr. Ζεύς, Lat. *deus;* sometimes it appears in a secondary form, as in the Hebr. *yóm*, Gr. ἡμέρα; and sometimes it has a dental affix, as in the Gr. Ζήν, Lat. or Tusc. *Janus*. It is sufficiently established that *dj, j, y*, are different forms of the same articulation, which is also expressed by the Greek ζ. The fem. of *Janus* was *Diana: Jupiter* and *Diespiter* were the same word. The Greeks had lost their *j*-sound, except so far as it was implied in ζ; but I have proved elsewhere that the η also contained its ultimate resolution.[1] That *Tina* contains the same root as Ζήν = *Dyan* may be proved by an important Greek analogy. If we compare the Greek interrogative τίς with its Latin equivalent *quis*, admitting, as we must, that they had a common origin, we at once perceive that the Greek form has lost every trace of the labial element of the Latin *qu*, while the guttural is preserved in the softened form τι = *j*. Supposing that *kas* was the proper form of the interrogative after the omission of the labial, then, when *k* was softened into *j* = *di*, as *quare*, &c. became *cur*, &c., in the same way this would become τίς, the tenuis being preferred to the medial.[2] Just so in the

[1] *N. Crat.* pp. 130, 181.
[2] The crude form of τις is τι-ν- (τι-νός, &c.); in other words, it is a compound of two pronominal elements, like εἶς (= ἕν-s), κεῖ-νος, τῆ-νος, ἀ-νά, e-*nim*, é-*na*, &c. Lobeck asserts (*Paralipom.* p. 121, note) that the ν in τι-ν-ός is repugnant to all analogy, the *literæ cliticæ* of the Greeks being dentals only,—as if ν were not a dental! The absurdity of Lobeck's remarks here, and in many other passages of his later writings, will serve to shew how necessary it is that an etymologer should be acquainted with the principles of comparative philology. There are some observations on this subject in the *N. Crat.* p. 38, which more particularly refer to Lobeck (*Aglaopham.* p. 478, note i.), and to a very inferior man, his pupil Ellendt (*Lex. Sophocl.* præfat. p. iii.). From what Lobeck said in his *Paralipomena* (p. 126, note), one felt disposed to hope that his old-fashioned prejudices were beginning to yield to conviction. In his new work, however (*Pathologia*, præf. p. vii. sqq.), he reappears in his original character. The *caution* on which he plumes himself (" ego quoque sæpe vel invitus et ingratis eo adactus sum ut vocabulorum

Etruscan language, which had no medials, $Z\acute{\eta}\nu = dian\text{-}us$ would become *Tina*-[*s*] or *Tinia*-[*s*]. This *Tina* or *Jupiter* of the Tuscans was emphatically the god of light and lightning, and with Juno and Minerva formed a group who were joined together in the special worship of the old Italians. As the Etruscans had no consonant *j*, the name of *Janus* must have been pronounced by them as *Zanus*. This god, whose four-faced statue was brought from Falerii to Rome, indicated the sky, or *templum*, with its four regions. When he appeared as *biceps*, he represented the main regions of the *templum*—the *decumanus* and the *cardo*. And as this augurial reference was intimately connected with the arrangement of the gates in a city or a camp,[1] he became also the god of gates, and his name ultimately signified " a gate" or " archway." *Summanus*, or *Submanus*, was the god of nightly thunders. The usual etymology is *summus manium;* but there is little reason for supposing that it is a common Latin word. As Arnobius considers him identical with Pluto,[2] it seems reasonable to conclude that he was simply the Jupiter Infernus; and as the *Dispater* of the Tuscans was called *Mantus*, and his wife *Mania*, we may conjecture that *Sub-manus* was perhaps in Tuscan *Zuv-manus* or *Jupiter-bonus*, which is the common euphemism in speaking of the infernal deities. The connexion between the nightly thunders, which the

origines abditas conjectura quærerem, *cautior fortasse Cratylis nostris*, quorum curiositati nihil clausum, nihil impervium est,") is only another name for one-sided obstinacy; and whatever value we may set upon Lobeck's actual performances in his own field, we cannot concede to him the right of confining all other scholars to the narrow limits of his Hemsterhusian philology.

[1] See below, Ch. VII. § 6.

[2] The Glossar. Labbæi has *Summanus*, Προμηθεύς; and perhaps Prometheus, as the stealer of fire from heaven, may have been identified with the god of nightly thunders in some forms of mythology. At Colonus, where the infernal deities were especially worshipped, the τιτὰν Προμηθεύς, ὁ πυρφόρος θεός, was reckoned among them (*Œd. Col.* 55).

ancients so greatly feared, and the χθονίαι βρονταί, is obvious. Another gloomy form of the supreme god was *Ve-djus* or *Ve-jovis*, who seems to have represented Apollo in his character of the causer of sudden death. The prefix *Ve-* is a disqualifying negative—the name signifies " the bad Jupiter." He was represented as a young man armed with arrows; his feast was on the nones of March, when an atoning sacrifice was offered up to him; and he was considered, like *Summanus*, as another form of Pluto.

The second of the great Tuscan deities was *Júno* (*Jovino* or *Dyuno*), who was called *Kupra* and *Thalna* in the Etrurian language. Now *Kupra* signifies " good," as has been shewn above; and therefore *Dea kupra* is *Dea bona*, the common euphemism for Proserpine. The name *Thalna* may be analysed with the aid of the principles developed above. The Etruscans had a tendency to employ the aspirates for the tenues, where in other forms, and in Greek especially, the tenues were used. Accordingly, if we articulate between the liquids *ln*, and substitute *t* for *th*, we shall have, as the name of Juno, the goddess of marriage, the form *Tal*[*a*]*na*, which at once suggests the root of *Talassus*, the Roman *Hymen*, the Greek τάλις, Soph. *Antig.* 629. τάλις· ἡ νύμφη, Zonar. p. 1711. τάλις· ἡ μελλόγαμος παρθένος καὶ κατωνομασμένη τινί· οἱ δὲ γυναῖκα γαμετήν· οἱ δὲ νύμφην, Hesych. τήλιδα· οὕτω τὴν συνηρμοσμένην, id. δαλίδας· τὰς μεμνηστευμένας, id. τᾶλιξ· ἔρως, id.: comp. also γάμοιο τέλος, Hom. *Od.* xx. 74, and the epithet Ἥρα τελεία. The Aramæan ταλιθά (תַּלְיְתָא, *Mark* v. 41) is not perhaps to be referred to this class.

The deity *Vulcanus*, who in the Etruscan mythology was one of the chief gods, being one of the nine thundering gods, and who in other mythologies appears in the first rank of divinities, always stands in a near relationship to Juno. In the Greek theogony he appears as her son and defender; he is sometimes the rival, and sometimes the duplicate, of his brother Mars; and it is possible that in the Egyptian calendar he may have been a kind of Jupiter. Here we are only concerned with the form of his Etruscan name, which was *Sethlans*. Applying the same principles as before, we collect that it is only *Se-tal[a]nus*, a masculine form of *Tal[a]na* (=*Juno*) with the prefix *Se-*: comp. the Greek ἥ-λιος, σε-λήνη, with the Latin *Sol*, *Luna*, where the feminine, like *Tal[a]na*, has lost the prefix.

To the two deities *Tina* and *Talna*, whose names, with their adjuncts, I have just examined, the Etruscans added a third, *Minerva*, or, as they called her, *Ménerfa*, *Ménrfa*, who was so closely connected with them in the reverence of this people, that they did not consider a city complete if it had not three gates and three temples dedicated to Jupiter, Juno, and Minerva. She was the goddess of the storms prevalent about the time of the vernal equinox; and her feast, the *quinquatrus*, was held, as that word implied in the Tuscan language, on the fifth day after the ides of March. The name seems to have been synonymous with the Greek μῆτις; the word bears the same relation to *mens* that *luerves* (in the Arval hymn) does to *lues*: this appears from the use of the verb *promenervat* (*pro monet*, Fest. p. 205).

It is easy to explain the names *Sāturnus*, *Vertumnus*, *Mars*, and *Feronia*, from the elements of the Latin language. *Sāturnus*=Κρόνος is connected with *sæ-culum*, as *æ-ternus* with *ævum* (the full form being *ævi-ternus*, Varro, L. L. vi. § 11), *sempi-ternus* with *semper*, and *taci-turnus* with *taceo*. *Vertumnus* is the old participle of *vertor*, " I turn myself." *Márs* is simply " the slayer:" comp. *Má-mers*, " the man-slayer." The attributes of the goddess *Féronia* are by no means accurately known: there seems, however, to be little doubt that she was an elementary goddess, and as such perhaps also a subterraneous deity, so that her name will be connected with *feralis*, φθείρειν, φερσεφόνη, &c.

Λευκοθέα, " the white goddess," had a Tuscan representative in the *Mater matuta*, " mother of the morning," whose attribute is referred to in the Greek name, which designates the pale silvery light of the early dawn. Both goddesses were probably also identical with Εἰλείθυια, *Lucina*, the divinity who brought children from the darkness of the womb into the light of life. *Sothina*, a name which occurs in Etruscan monuments (Lanzi, ii. p. 494), is probably the Etruscan transcription of the Greek Σωωδίνα (" saving from child-bed pains"), which was an epithet of Artemis (see Böckh, *Corp. Inscr.* no. 1595).

Apollo was an adopted Greek name, the Tuscan form being *Apulu*, *Aplu*, *Epul*, or *Epure*. If the " custos Soractis Apollo," to whom the learned Virgil (*Æn.* xi. 786) makes a Tuscan pray, was a native Etruscan god, then his name *Soranus*, and the name of the mountain *Soracte*, must be Tuscan words, and contain the Latin *sol*, with the change from *l* to *r* observable in the form *Epure* for *Epul*: compare also the Sanscr. *Súrya*.

Although *Neptunus* was an important god in the Tuscan pantheon, it is by no means certain that this was the Tuscan form of his name: if it was, then we have another Tuscan word easily explicable from the roots of the Indo-Germanic language; for *Nep-tunus* is clearly connected with νέω, Νηρεύς, νίπτω, &c. The form *Neptumnus* (ap. Grut. p. 460) is simply the participle νιπτόμενος. If the word *Nethuns*, which is found on a Tuscan mirror over a figure manifestly intended for Neptune (*Berlin. Jahrb.* for August 1841, p. 221), is to be considered as the genuine form of the sea-god's name, there will of course be no difficulty in referring it to the same root (see below, § 5, note).

The Tuscan Pluto, as is well known, was called *Man*-

tus, and from him the city *Mantua* derived its name. The etymology of this word is somewhat confused by its contact with the names *manes* and *mania*. That the latter are connected with the old word *manus* = *bonus* can hardly be doubted;[1] and the deprecatory euphemism of such a designation is quite in accordance with the ancient mode of addressing these mysterious functionaries of the lower world. But then it is difficult to explain *Mantus* as a derivative from this *manus*. Now, as he is represented in all the Tuscan monuments as a huge wide-mouthed monster with a *personæ pallentis hiatus*, it seems better to understand his name as signifying "the devourer;" in which sense he may be compared with the yawning and roaring *Charon*.[2] This, at any rate, was the idea conveyed by the *manducus*, another form of *mantus;* for this was an image "*magnis malis ac late dehiscens et ingentem dentibus sonitum faciens*" (Fest. p. 128). The two words may be connected with *ma-n-dere*, μασᾶσθαι, the *n*, which is necessary in *manus, manes*, being here only euphonical: similarly, we have *masucium, edacem a mandendo scilicet* (Fest. p. 139), and *me-n-tum* by the side of ματύαι (= γνάθοι, Hesych.). Compare also *mála, maxilla*, &c. It is not improbable that the Greek, or perhaps Pelasgic, μάν-

---

[1] Varro seems to connect the word *Manius* with *mane*, "morning" (*L. L.* ix. § 60).

[2] See *N. Crat.* p. 364. Another personage of the same kind is Γηρύων, "the caller." As Charon is attended by the three-headed Κέρβερος, so the three-bodied Geryon has a two-headed dog, Ὄρθρος, who is brother to Cerberus (Hesiod. *Theog.* 308, sqq.); that is, "the morning" (ὄρθρος) is brother to "the darkness" (κέρβερος : vide *Schol. Od.* Λ, 14, and Porson *ad l.;* Κέμμερος· ἀχλύς, Hesych.; and Lobeck, *Paralipom.* p. 32). By a similar identity, Geryon lives in the distant west, in Erythia, the land of darkness, just as Charon is placed in Hades; and these two beings, with their respective dogs, both figure in the mythology of Hercules, who appears as the enemy of Pluto, and of his type, Eurystheus. It may be remarked, too, that Pluto is described as an owner of flocks and herds, which is the chief feature in the representations of Geryon.

τις contains this root. The mysterious art of divination was connected, in one at least of its branches, with the rites of the infernal gods. *Teiresias,* the blind prophet, was especially the prophet of the dark regions. Now *Mantua,* according to Virgil, was founded by *Ocnus,* " the bird of omen," who was the son of *Manto,* and through her the grandson of *Teiresias.* This at least is legendary evidence of a connexion between *mantus* and μάντις. The same root is contained in the mythical *mundus* (Müller, *Etrusk.* ii. p. 96).

The name *Ceres* is connected with *creare,* Sanscr. *krĭ.* The Tuscan name *Ancaria* may be explained by a comparison of *ancilla, anclare, oncare,* ἐνεγκεῖν, ἀγκάς, &c.

According to Servius, *Ceres, Pales,* and *Fortuna,* were the three *Penates* of the Etruscans (see Micali, *Storia,* ii. p. 117). The last of these three was one of the most important divinities in Etruria, and especially at Volsinii, where she bore the name *Nortia, Norsia,* or *Nursia,* and was the goddess of the calendar or year (Cincius, *ap. Liv.* vii. 3). The nails, by which the calendar was marked there, pointed to the fixed and unalterable character of the decrees of fate. The *Fortuna* of Antium had the nail as her attribute, and the *clavi trabales* and other implements for fastening marked her partner *Necessitas* (Hor. i. *Carm.* xxxv. 17, sqq.); under the Greek name of Ἄτροπος (*Athrpa*) she is represented on a Tuscan patera as fixing the destiny of Μελέαγρος (*Meliacr*) by driving in a nail; though it is clear from the wings that the name only is Greek, while the figure of the deity is genuine Etruscan (Müller, *Etrusk.* ii. p. 331). From these considerations it seems a safe inference that *Nortia,* or *Nursia,* is simply *ne-vortia, ne-vertia,* the Ἄ-τροπος, or " unturning, unchanging goddess," according to the consistent analogy of *rursus = re-versus, quorsus = quo-versus, introrsus = intra-versus,* &c.: and this supposition receives additional confirmation from the statement mentioned below (§ 3), that *vorsus* was actually a Tuscan word.

The god *Merquurius* appears on the Tuscan monuments as *Turms = Turmus*. This Etruscan name has been well explained by the Jesuit G. P. Secchi (*Annali dell' Instituto*, viii. p. 94, sqq.). It appears that Lycophron, who elsewhere uses genuine Italian names of deities and heroes (as Μάμερτος for Ἄρης, vv. 938, 1410; Νανός for Ὀδυσσεύς, v. 1244), calls the χθόνιος Ἑρμῆς by the name Τερμιεύς (*Alex.* 705, sqq.):

> λίμνην τ᾽ Ἄορνον ἀμφιτορνητὸν βρόχῳ
> καὶ χεῦμα Κωκυτοῖο λαβρωθὲν σκότῳ
> Στυγὸς κελαινῆς νασμόν, ἔνθα Τερμιεὺς
> ὁρκωμότους ἔτευξεν ἀφθίτους ἕδρας
> μέλλων γίγαντας κἀπὶ τιτῆνας περᾶν.

Now *Turmus* certainly does not differ more from this Τερμιεύς than *Euturpe* and *Achle* from their Greek representatives (Bunsen, ibid. p. 175). It might seem, then, that *Turmus* is not the Latin *Terminus*, but rather the Greek Ἑρμῆς; for the Hellenic aspirate being represented in the Pelasgian language, according to rule, by the sibilant, this might pass into τ, as in ἡμέρα, σήμερον, τήμερον; ἕπτα, τέπτα, Hesych.; ἑρμίς, τερμίς, id. &c.

The name *Lar*, *Las*, when it signifies "lord" or "noble," has the addition of a prenominal affix *-t*; when it signifies "god," it is the simple root: the former is *Lars* (*Larth*), gen. *Lartis*; the latter *Lar*, gen. *Laris*. Precisely the same difference is observable in a comparison between Ἄνακες, Ἄνακοι, "the Dios-curi," and ἄνακ-τες, "kings" or "nobles." Some suppose that the English *Lor-d* is connected with the same root; see, however, *New Crat.* p. 418; and as the *Lares* were connected with the Cabiriac and Curetic worship of the more eastern Pelasgians, I would rather seek the etymology in the root λα-, λας-, λαις-, so frequently occurring in the names of places and persons connected with that worship,[1] and expressing the devouring nature of fire. It appears from the word *Lar-va* that the *Lar* was represented as a wide-mouthed figure. There are two feminine forms of the name, *Lar-unda* and *Lar-entia*.

This enumeration of the names of Tuscan divinities shews that, as far as the terms of mythology are concerned (and there are few terms less mutable), the Tuscan language does not absolutely escape from the grasp of etymology. The common words which have been handed down to us present similar traces of affinity to the languages of the Indo-Germanic family. I will examine them in alphabetical order; though, unfortunately, they are not so numerous as to assume the form of a comprehensive vocabulary of the language.

Æsar, " God." Sueton. *Octav.* c. 97 : " Responsum est centum solos dies posthac victurum, quem numerum c littera notaret; futurumque ut inter deos referretur, quod ÆSAR, id est, reliqua pars e Cæsaris nomine, Etrusca lingua *deus* vocaretur." Conf. Dio. Cass. lvi. 29; Hesych. αἰσοί· θεοί, ὑπὸ Τυρρηνῶν. See Ritter, *Vorhalle*, pp. 300, 471, who compares the Cabiric names *Æs-mun*, *Æs-clef*, the proper name *Æsyetes*, *asa* the old form of *ara*, and a great many other words implying " holiness " or " sanctity:" and Grimm, *Deutsche Mythol.* 2d edit. p. 22. Comp. also αἶσα.

Aifil, " age." This word frequently occurs in sepulchral inscriptions with a numeral attached. In one of these we have, *Cf*[*e*]*cfiilf*. *Papa aif* . XXII., with the Latin translation, *Guegilii Papii ætatis* XXII. It is obvious, then, that this word contains the same root as *æv-um*,

§ 3.
Alphabetical list of Etruscan words interpreted.

---

[1] The following are some of the most obvious appearances of this root: Sanscrit, *las*, " to wish;" Latin, *lar-gus;* Greek, λα‑μία, λά‑μος, λάρυγξ, λαῖτμα, &c. Λῆμνος, Λητώ.

æ-tas, αἴϝων, αἰϝεί, &c. The Pelasgo-Tyrrhenian language always inserts the digamma in these cases: compare *Αἴας*, written *Aifas* on the Tuscan monuments.

Arime, "ape." Strabo, xiii. p. 626 D.: καὶ τοὺς πιθήκους φασὶ παρὰ τοῖς Τυῤῥηνοῖς ἀρίμους καλεῖσθαι. Hesych. : ἄριμος· πίθηκος. There is no certainty about this word. The commentators would connect it with the Hebrew חָרֻם (*chárum*), *Levit.* xxi. 18, which signifies " snub-nosed," *simus;* but this is merely fanciful.

Arse-verse. Fest. p. 18: "*Arseverse* averte ignem significat. Tuscorum enim lingua *arse* averte, *verse* ignem constat appellari. Unde Afranius ait: Inscribat aliquis in ostio arseverse." An inscription found at Cortona contains the following words: *Arses vurses Sethlanl tephral ape termnu pisest estu* (Orelli. no. 1384). Müller considers this genuine (*quem quominus genuinum habeamus nihil vetat*); Lepsius will not allow its authenticity, but thinks it is made up of words borrowed from other sources. Be that as it may, the words *arse verse* must be admitted as genuine Etruscan; and they are also cited by Placidus (*Gloss. apud Maium*, p. 434). It seems probable that *arse* is merely the Latin *arce* with the usual softening of the guttural; and *verse* contains the root of πῦρ, *pir, feuer, ber*, &c. Pott (*Et. Forsch.* i. p. 101) seems to prefer taking *verse* as the verb, Lat. *verte*, and *arse* as the noun, comp. *ardere*. If the Cortona inscription is genuine, its meaning must be, "Avert the fire, O consuming Vulcan, from the bounds of this house."

Atrium, "the *cavædium*," or common hall in a Roman house. Varro, *L. L.* v. § 161: "*Cavum ædium* dictum, qui locus tectus intra parietes relinquebatur patulus, qui esset ad communem omnium usum... *Tuscanicum* dictum a Tuscis, posteaquam illorum cavum ædium simulare cœperunt. *Atrium* appellatum ab Atriatibus Tuscis; illinc enim exemplum sumptum." Müller (*Etrusk.* i. p. 256) adopts this etymology (which is also suggested by Festus, p. 13), with the explanation, that the name is not derived from *Atrias* because the people of that place invented it, but from a reference to the geographical position of Atrias, which, standing at the confluence of many rivers, might be supposed to represent the *compluvium* of the atrium. This geographical etymology appears to me very far-fetched and improbable; nor, indeed, do I see the possibility of deriving *atrium* from *atrias;* the converse would be the natural process. There does not appear to be any objection to the etymology suggested by Servius (*ad Æn.* iii. 353), " ab *atro*, propter fumum qui esse solebat in *atriis*:" and we may compare the corresponding Greek term μέλαθρον. If *atrium*, then, was a Tuscan word, the Latin *ater* also was of Pelasgian origin. The connexion of *atrium* with αἴθριον, αἴθουσα, &c., suggested by Scaliger and others, may be adopted, if we derive the word from the Tuscan *atrus*, which signifies " a day."

Balteus, " the military girdle," is stated by Varro (*Antiq. R. Hum.* 18. *ap. Sosip.* i. p. 51) to have been a Tuscan word. It also occurs, with the same meaning, in all the languages of the German family; and we have it still in our word " belt."

Capys, " a falcon." Servius (*ad Æn.* x. 145): " Constat eam (capuam) a Tuscis conditam de viso falconis augurio, qui Tusca lingua *capys* dicitur." Fest. p. 43: " Capuam in Campania quidam a *Capye* appellatam ferunt, quem a pede introrsus curvato nominatum antiqui nostri Falconem vocant." For the meaning of the word *falcones*, see Fest. s. v. p. 88. If *capys* = *falco*, it should seem that *cap-ys* contains the root of *cap-ere;* for this would be the natural derivation of the name.¹

Cassis, " a helmet" (more anciently *cass-ila,* Fest. p. 48). Isidor. *Origg.* xviii. 14: " *Cassidem* autem a Tuscis nominatam dicunt." The proper form was *capsis,* as the same writer tells us; but the assimilation hardly disguises the obvious connexion of the word with *cap-ut, haup-t,* &c. Comp. κοττικαί· αἱ περικεφαλαῖαι, with τῆς κοττίδος· Δωριεῖς δὲ τὴν κεφαλὴν οὕτω καλοῦσιν. J. Pollux, ii. 29.

Falandum, " the sky." Fest. p. 88 : " *Falæ* [φάλαι· ὄρη, σκοπιαί, Hesych.] dictæ ab altitudine, a *falando,* quod apud Etruscos significat cœlum." This is generally connected with φάλανθον, *blond,* &c. Or we might go a step further, and refer it to φάλλω, φαλός, &c., which are obviously derived from φάος : see Lobeck, *Pathol.* p. 87.

Favissa, " an excavation." Fest. p. 88 : " *Favissæ* locum sic appellabant, in quo erat aqua inclusa circa templa. Sunt autem, qui putant, favissas esse in Capitolio cellis cisternisque similes, ubi reponi erant solita ea, quæ in templo vetustate erant facta inutilia." From the analogy of *favissa, mantissa,* and from the circumstance that the Romans seem to have learned to make *favissæ* from the Etruscans, it is inferred that *favissa* was a Tuscan word: see Müller, *ad Festi locum,* and *Etrusk.* ii. p. 239. The word is probably connected with *fovea, bauen,* &c.

---

¹ See *New Cratylus,* p. 550. To the instances there cited the following may be added : (a) כֶּלֶב, " a dog," i. e. " the *yelp*-er." (b) עֹרֵב, " a raven" (*corv-us,* Sanscr. *kârav-*), i. e. " a cawing bird." (c) βοῦς, Sanscr. *gaus,* " the bellowing or lowing animal:" comp. βοάω with γοάω, and the latter with the Hebrew נָגַהּ, *mugire,* " to low like an ox" (1 *Sam.* vi. 12, *Job* vi. 5), and the Latin *ceva,* which, according to Columella (vi. 24), was the name of the cow at Altinum on the Adriatic. (d) χήν, " the goose," i. e. " the gaping bird" (χὴν κεχηνώς, Athen. p. 519 A).

Februum, " a purification." Angrius, *ap. J. Lyd de Mens.* p. 70: " Februum *inferum* esse Thuscorum lingua." Also Sabine: see Varro, *L. L.* vi. § 13. If we compare *febris*, &c., we shall perhaps connect the root with *foveo*=*torreo*, whence *favilla*, &c., and understand the " *torrida* cum mica farra," which, according to Ovid (*Fast.* ii. 24), were called by this name.

Fentha, according to Lactantius (*de Fals. Relig.* i. c. 22, § 9), was the old Italian name of *Fatua*, the feminine form of *Faunus*, " quod mulieribus fata canere consuevisset, ut Faunus viris." The form *Finthia* seems to occur on an old Tuscan monument (*Ann. dell' Instit.* viii. p. 76), and is therefore perhaps a Tuscan word. The analogy of *Fentha* to *Fatua* is the same as that which has been pointed out above in the case of *Mantus*. The *n* is a kind of *anuswárah* very common in Latin: comp. ἔχις, *anguis;* λείπω, *linquo;* λείχω, *lingo;* Sanscr. *tudámi, tundo;* ὕδωρ, *unda;* &c.

Haruspex is generally considered to have been an Etruscan word. Strabo, xvi. p. 762, renders it by ἱεροσκόπος: *asa* or *ara* certainly implied " holiness" in the Tuscan language; and Hesychius has the gloss, ἅρακος· ἱέραξ, Τυρῥηνοί, which shews the same change from ἱερ- to *har*-. If these analogies are not overthrown by the *Inscriptio bilinguis* of Pisaurum (*Fabrett. Inscr.* c. x. n. 171, p. 646; Oliv. *Marm. Pisaur.* n. 27, p. 11; Lanzi, ii. p. 652, n. δ, where [*Caf*]*atius L. f. Ste. haruspex fulguriator* is translated by *Caphates Ls. Ls. Netmfis Trutnft Phruntac*), we may perhaps conclude that *haruspex* was the genuine Pelasgian form, *trutnft* being the Umbro-Tuscan synonyme.

Hister, " an actor." Liv. vii. 2 : " Sine carmine ullo, sine imitandorum carminum actu, ludiones ex Etruria adciti, ad tibicinis modos saltantes, haud indecoros motus more Tusco dabant. Imitari deinde eos juventus, simul inconditis inter se jocularia fundentes versibus cœpere, nec absoni a voce motus erant. Accepta itaque res sæpiusque usurpando excitata. Vernaculis artificibus, quia *hister* Tusco verbo ludio vocabatur, nomen histrionibus inditum: qui non, sicut ante Fescennino versu, similem incompositum temere ac rudem alternis jaciebant; sed inpletas modis saturas, descripto jam ad tibicinem cantu motuque congruenti peragebant." It appears from this, and from all we read of the *hister*, that he was a mimic actor; his dance is compared by Dionysius to the *Sicinnis;* so that the word seems to be synonymous with δεικηλίκτης, and the root is the pronoun *i-* or *hi-* (*N. Crat.* p. 170), which also enters into the cognate words *i-mitor*, ἴ-σος, εἴκ-ων, &c., and appears in the termination of *oleaster*, &c. (Lobeck, *Pathol.* p. 79.)

Itus, " the division of the month." Varro, *L. L.* vi. § 28: " Idus ab eo quod Tusci *itus.*" Cf. Macrob. *Sat.* i. 15. As *itus* was the διχομηνία of the Tuscan lunar month, its connexion with the root *id-* or *fid-* is obvious: comp. *di-vido, vid-uus*, &c. So Horat. iv. *Carm.* xi. 14:

idus tibi sunt agendæ,
Qui dies mensem Veneris marinæ
Findit aprilem.

Læna, " a double cloak." Fest. p. 117 : " Quidam appellatam existimant Tusce, quidam Græce, quam χλανίδα dicunt." If it be a Tuscan word, it is very like the Greek: compare *luridus, lac*, λιαρός, &c., with χλωρός, γά-λα, χ-λιαρός, &c. Varro (*L. L.* v. § 133) derives it from *lana.*

Lanista, " a keeper of gladiators." Isidor. *Origg.* x. p. 247 : " *Lanista* gladiator, *i. e.* carnifex Tusca lingua appellatus." Comp. *lānius*, &c., from the root *lac-.*

Lar, " a lord." Explained above.

Lituus, " an augur's staff, curved at the end;" also " a curved trumpet:" see Cic. *Divin.* ii. 18; Liv. i. 18.

It constantly occurs on Etruscan monuments (see Inghirami, vi. tav. p. 5, 1). Müller justly considers this word an adjective signifying "crooked" (*Etrusk.* ii. p. 212). It contains the root *li-*, found in *li-quis*, *obliquus*, *li-ra*, *li-tus* (πλάγιος), λέχριος, λιάζειν, &c.

Lucumo, whence the Roman prænomen *Lucius* (Valer. Max. *de Nomin.* 18), "a noble." The Tuscan form was *Lauchme*, which the Umbrian Propertius has preserved in his transcription *Lucmo* (*El.* iv. 1, 29): *prima galeritus posuit prætoria Lucmo*. The word contains the root *luc-*, and may therefore be compared with the Greek Γελέοντες, designating, like the Tuscan term, a noble and priestly tribe (*N. Crat.* p. 558). The ἐργάδεις correspond to the *Aruntes*, who are regularly contrasted with the *Lucumones* (above, p. 71).

Ludus. The ancients derived this word from the *Lydian* origin of the Etruscans, from whom the Romans first borrowed their dancers and players. Dionys. *Antiqu.* ii. 71: καλούμενοι πρὸς αὐτῶν ἐπὶ τῆς παιδιᾶς τῆς ὑπὸ Λυδῶν ἐξευρῆσθαι δοκούσης λυδίωνες, εἰκόνες, ὡς ἐμοὶ δοκεῖ, τῶν Σαλίων. Appian, viii. *de Reb. Pun.* c. 66: χορὸς κιθαριστῶν τε καὶ τιτυριστῶν εἰς μιμήματα Τυρρηνικῆς πομπῆς ... Λυδοὺς αὐτοὺς καλοῦσιν, ὅτι (οἶμαι) Τυρρηνοὶ Λυδῶν ἄποικοι. Isidor. p. 1274: "Inde Romani accersitos artifices mutuati sunt, et inde *ludi* a Lydiis vocati sunt." Hesych. ii. p. 506: Λυδοὶ οὗτοι τὰς θέας εὑρεῖν λέγονται, ὅθεν καὶ Ῥωμαῖοι λουδοὺς φασι. Comp. also Valer. Max. ii. 4, 4; Tertull. *de Spect.* v. The derivation from the ethnic name *Lydius* is of course a mere fancy. It does not, however, seem improbable that, as the armed dances as well as the clownish buffooneries of the Romans were derived from Etruria, the name which designated these as jokers and players (*ludiones*) was Etruscan also, like the other name *hister*, which denoted the imitative actor. If so, the word *ludus* was also of Tuscan or Pelasgian origin. Now this word *ludus* is admirably adapted to express all the functions of the Tuscan *ludio*. It is connected with the roots of *lædo* (comp. *cudo, cædo*), λοίδορος, λίζω, λάσθω (=παίζω, Hesych.). Consequently, it expresses on the one hand the amusement afforded by the gesticulations of the ludio (σχηματίζεται ποικίλως εἰς γέλωτα, Appian, u. s.), and on the other hand indicates the innocent brandishing of weapons by the armed *ludio* as compared with the use of arms in actual warfare. This latter sense was preserved by *ludus* to the last, as it signified the school in which the gladiators *played* or fenced with wooden foils (*rudes*) preparatory to the bloody encounters of the *arena*. That the *ludiones* were Tuscans even in the classical age, is clear from Plautus, *Curculio*, i. 2, 60, sqq.: " *péssuli*, heus, péssuli, vós salutó lubens—fíte causá mea *lúdii bárbari; súbsilite*, óbsecro, et míttite istánc foras," punning on the resemblance of *pessuli* to the *præsules* of these Tuscan dancers (see Non. Marc. c. xii. *de Doctorum Indagine*, p. 783, Gottofr.).

Luna, the Tuscan port, probably got its name from the half-moon shape of the harbour. See Pers. vi. 7, 8; Strabo, v. p. 222; Martial, xiii. 30. The Tuscan spelling was perhaps *Losna* (=*Lus-na*), which is found on a patera (see Müller, *Etrusk.* i. p. 294).

Manus or *Manis*, " good." Apparently a Tuscan word: at any rate, the *manes* were Tuscan divinities. Fest. p. 146, s. v. *Manuos;* Serv. *ad Æn.* i. 139, iii. 63. So *cerus manus*, in the Salian song, was *creator bonus*. Fest. p. 122, s. v. *Matrem matutam;* comp. Varro, *L. L.* vii. § 26. We may perhaps recognise the same root in *a-mœnus*, Lithuan. *aimésnis*, Greek ἀ-μείνων= ἀμενίων.

Mantisa, " weighing-meat." Fest. p. 132: " *Mantisa* additamentum dicitur lingua Tusca, quod ponderi adicitur, sed deterius et quod sine ullo usu est. Lucilius: *mantisa obsonia vincit.*" Scaliger and Voss derive it from *manu-tensa*, " eo quod manu porrigitur." It is more probably connected, like *me-n-da*, with the root of μάτην; compare *frustum* with *frustra*.

Nanus, " the pygmy." Lycophr. *Alex.* 1244 : Νάνος πλαναῖσι πάντ' ἐρευνήσας μυχόν. Ubi Tzetzes: ὁ Ὀδυσσεὺς παρὰ τοῖς Τυρσηνοῖς νάνος καλεῖται, δηλοῦντος τοῦ ὀνόματος τὸν πλανήτην. This interpretation seems to be only a guess based on the πλαναῖσι of Lycophron. The considerations mentioned above (§ 1) leave it scarcely doubtful that the Tuscan word, like the Latin *nanus*, refers to the diminutive stature of the hero, which is also implied in his common name *Ulysses*. The Greek words νάνος, νάννος, νάνισκος, ναννάζω, νάνιον, &c. have the same meaning. The word, therefore, being common to the Tuscans, Greeks, and Romans, is indubitably of Pelasgic origin.

Nepos, " a profligate." Fest. p. 165: " *Nepos* luxuriosus a Tuscis dicitur." Probably, as Müller suggests (*Etrusk.* i. p. 277), the word which bears this meaning is not from the same root as the Siculian *nepos*, " a grandson" (Gr. νέπους, ἀ-νέψιος, Germ. *neffe*). Many etymologies have been proposed; but I am not satisfied with any one of them. Might we connect the word with *ne-pŏtis*, Gr. ἀ-κρατής, ἀκόλαστος?

Phruntac=*fulguriator*. See the *Inscriptio bilinguis* quoted above s. v. *Haruspex*. We must consider this Tuscan word as standing either for *Furn-tacius* or for *fulntacius*: in the former case it is connected with the Latin *furnus, fornax*, Greek πῦρ, Germ. *feuer*, &c.; in the latter it may be compared with *ful-geo, ful-men*, φλέγ-ειν, φλό-ξ, &c. It is not impossible that both roots may be ultimately identical: compare *creber, celeber; cresco, glisco;* κραῦροψ, καλαῦροψ; *crus,* σ-κέλος; *culmen, celsus;* κολοφών, κράνιον, κορυφή, &c.

Quinquatrus. Varro, *L. L.* vi. § 14: " *Quinquatrus;* hic dies unus ab nominis errore observatur, proinde ut sint quinque. Dictus, ut ab Tusculanis post diem sextum idus similiter vocatur *Sexatrus,* et post diem septimum *Septimatrus,* sic hic, quod erat post diem quintum idus, *Quinquatrus.*" Festus, p. 254: " *Quinquatrus* appellari quidam putant a numero dierum qui feriis iis celebrantur: qui scilicet errant tam hercule, quam qui triduo Saturnalia et totidem diebus Competalia: nam omnibus his singulis diebus fiunt sacra. Forma autem vocabuli ejus, exemplo multorum populorum Italicorum enuntiata est, quod post diem quintum iduum est is dies festus, ut aput Tusculanos *Triatrus* et *Sexatrus* et *Septimatrus* et Faliscos *Decimatrus.*" See also Gell. *N. A.* ii. 21. From this we infer that in the Tuscan language the numeral *quinque,* or as they probably wrote it *chfinchfe,* signified " five," and *atrus* meant " a day." With this latter word, perhaps connected with αἴθριον, we may compare the Tuscan *atrium,* according to the second of the etymologies proposed above.

Ramnenses, Tities, Luceres. Varro, *L. L.* v. § 55: " Omnia hæc vocabula Tusca, ut Volnius, qui tragœdias Tuscas scripsit, dicebat." See Müller, *Etrusk.* i. p. 380.

Ril, " a year." This word frequently occurs before numerals in sepulchral inscriptions; and, as the word *aifil= ætatis* generally precedes, *ril* is supposed with reason to mean *annum* or *annos.* It is true that this word does not resemble any synonyme in the Indo-Germanic languages; but then, as has been justly observed by Lepsius, there is no connexion between *annus,* ἔτος, and *iár,* and yet the connexion between Greek, Latin, and German is universally admitted.[1] The word *ril* appears to me to contain the root *ra* or *re*, implying "flux" and "motion," which occurs in every language of the family, and which in the Pelasgian dialects sometimes furnished a name for great rivers (above, p. 35). Thus *Tibe-ris*, the Tuscan river, is probably "the mountain-stream;" see below, § 4. The termination *-l* also marks the Tuscan patronymics, and, in the lengthened form *-lius*, serves the same office in Latin (e. g. *Servi-lius* from *Servius*). The Greek patronymic in -δης expresses derivation or extraction, and is akin to the genitive-ending. This termination appears in ῥεῖ-τον, ῥεῖ-θ-ρον, &c., which may therefore be compared with *ri-l*. How well suited this connexion is for the expression of time need not be pointed out to the intelligent reader. The following examples from the Latin language will shew that the etymology is at least not inconsistent with the forms of speech adopted by the ancient Italians. The Latin name for the year—*annus*—of which *annulus* is a diminutive—denotes a circle or cycle—a period—a curve returning to itself. Now as the year was regarded as a number of months, and as the moon-goddess was generally the feminine form of the sun-god, we recognise *Annus* as the god of the sun, and *Anna* as the goddess of the moon; and as she recurred throughout the period of the sun's course, she was further designated by the epithet *perenna*. To this *Anna perenna*, "the ever-circling moon," the ancients dedicated the ides of March, the first full moon of the primitive year, and sacrificed to her, as Macrobius tells us (*Saturn.* i. 12), "ut annare perennareque commode liceat." The idea, therefore, attached to her name was that of a regular flowing, of a constant recurrence. Now this

---

[1] See the other instances of the same kind quoted by Dr. Prichard, *Journal of R. G. S.* ix. 2, p. 209.

is precisely the meaning of the common Latin adjective *perennis;* and *sollennis* (= *quod omnibus annis præstari debet,* Festus, p. 298) has acquired the similar signification of " regular," " customary," and " indispensable." It is, perhaps, worth mentioning that in a Tuscan monument (Micali, *Storia,* pl. 36) Atlas supporting the world is called *A-ril.* If Atlas was the god of the Tuscan year, this may serve to confirm the common interpretation of *ril.*

Stroppus, " a fillet." Fest. p. 313: " *Stroppus* est, ut Ateius philologus existimat, quod Græce στρόφιον vocatur, et quod sacerdotes pro insigni habent in capite. Quidam coronam esse dicunt, aut quod pro corona insigne in caput imponatur, quale sit strophium. Itaque *apud Faliscos* diem festum esse, qui vocetur *struppearia,* quia coronati ambulent. Et *a Tusculanis* [for another instance of the similarity of language between the people of Falerii and Tusculum see under *Quinquatrus*], quod in pulvinari imponatur, Castoris *struppum* vocari." Idem, p. 347: " *Struppi* vocantur in pulvinaribus fasciculi de verbenis facti, qui pro deorum capitibus ponuntur."

Subulo, " a flute-player." Varro, *L. L.* vii. § 35: "*Subulo* dictus quod ita dicunt tibicines Tusci: quocirca radices ejus in Etruria non Latio quærundæ." Fest. p. 309: " *Subulo* Tusce tibicen dicitur; itaque Ennius: *subulo quondam marinas adstabat plagas.*" Compare *sibilo,* σίφων, *si-lenus,* σιφλόω, ἀ-σύφηλος, &c. Fr. *siffler, persifler,* &c.

Toga. If *toga* was the name by which the Tuscans called their outer garment, the verb *tego* must have existed in the Tuscan language; for this is obviously the derivation. That the Tuscans wore *togas,* and that the Romans borrowed this dress from them, is more than probable (Müller, *Etrusker,* i. p. 262). If not, they must, from the expression used by Photius (*Lex.* s. v.), have called it τήβεννα, which was its name in Argos and Arcadia.

Vorsus, " one hundred feet square," is quoted as both Tuscan and Umbrian. *Fragm. de Limit.* ed. Gœs. p. 216: " Primum agri modulum fecerunt quattuor limitibus clausum figuræ, quadratæ similem, plerumque centum pedum in utraque parte, quod Græci πλέθρον appellant, Tusci et Umbri *vorsum.*" For the use of πλέθρον, see Eurip. *Ion.* 1137. The fact that *vorsus* is a Tuscan word confirms the etymologies of *Vertumnus* and *Nortia.*

§ 4. Etruscan inscriptions—difficulties attending their interpretation.

In passing to our third source of information respecting the Tuscan language—the inscriptions which have been preserved—we are at once thrown upon difficulties, which at present, perhaps, are not within the reach of a complete solution. We may, indeed, derive from them some fixed results with regard to the structure of the language, and here and there we may find it possible to offer an explanation of a few words of more frequent occurrence. In general, however, we want a more complete collection of these documents; one, too, in deciphering which the resources of palæography have been carefully and critically applied. When we shall have obtained this, we shall at least know how far we can hope to penetrate into the hitherto unexplored arcana of the mysterious Etruscan language.

Referring to the position, that the Umbrians and Tuscans were so intermixed, that the language of the former had influenced, and indeed corrupted, the language of the latter, it would be well, if possible, to discriminate between those inscriptions which were least subjected to the influences of the Umbrian population, and those which have almost lost their Pelasgic character.

§ 5.
Inscriptions in which the Pelasgian element predominates.

Of all the Etruscan cities the least Umbrian perhaps is *Cære*[1] or *Agylla*, which stands in so many important connexions with Rome. Its foundation by the Pelasgians is attested by a great number of authorities (Serv. *ad Æn.* viii. 478; Strabo, v. p. 220; Dionys. Hal. iii. 58; Plin. *H. N.* iii. 8): its port, Πύργοι, had a purely Pelasgian name, and the Pelasgians had founded there a temple in honour of Εἰλήθυια (Strabo, v. 226; Diod. xv. 14). In the year 534 B.C., the people of Agylla consulted the oracle at Delphi respecting the removal of a curse; and they observed, in the days of Herodotus, the gymnic and equestrian games which the Pythoness prescribed (Herod. i. 167): moreover, they kept up a connexion with Delphi, in the same manner as the cities of Greece, and had a deposit in the bank of the temple (Strabo, v. p. 220).

As the Agyllæans, then, maintained so long a distinct Pelasgian character, we might expect to find some characteristics in the inscriptions of Cære, or Cervetri, by which they might be distinguished from the monuments of northern and eastern Etruria. There is at least one very striking justification of this supposition. On an ancient vase, dug up by General Galassi at Cervetri, the following inscription is traced in very clear and legible characters:

Mi ni keθuma, mi maθu maram liśiai θipurenai;
Eθe erai sie epana, mi neθu nastav heleφu.

It is obvious that there is an heroic rhythm in these lines; the punctuation and division into words are of course conjectural. Not to enter at length into interpretation, which must be mere guess-work,[2] this inscription differs from

---

[1] Lepsius (*die Tyrrh. Pelasger*, p. 28) considers *Cære* an Umbrian and not a Pelasgian word, *-re* being a common ending of the names of Umbrian towns; thus we have *Tute-re* on coins for *Tuder*. The original name was perhaps *Kaiere*, which contains a root expressive of antiquity and nobility.

[2] As no one, however, has attempted to explain this interesting fragment

§ 5.]   THE ETRUSCAN LANGUAGE.   127

those which are found in the Umbro-Etruscan districts, and especially from the Perusian *cippus*, in the much larger proportion of vowels, which are here expressed even before and after liquids, and in the absence of the mutilated terminations in *c, l, r*, which are so common in the other monuments.

There is another inscription, in the museum at Naples, which also begins with *mi ni*, and presents in a shorter

of the old Pelasgian language, I may be allowed to propose the following suggestions, which will serve till some one discovers a more satisfactory clue to the meaning. *Mi* is clearly the mutilated ἐσ-μί. *Ni* is the original negative, which in Latin always appears in a reduplicated or compounded form. *Keθuma* is the primitive form of χθών, χθαμα-λός, χαμαί, *humus*, &c. The difference of quantity in the second *mi* will not prevent us from identifying it with the first, which is lengthened by the ictus. *Maθu* is the Greek μέθυ, Sanscr. *madhu*. *Maram* is the epithet agreeing with *mathu*: it contains the root *mar-*, found in Μάρων (the grandson of Bacchus), and in Ἰσ-μαρος, the site of his vineyards (see *Od*. ix. 196, sqq.), and probably signifying "ruddy" (μαίρω, μαῖρα, &c.). The fact that *Maro* was an agricultural cognomen at Mantua is an argument in favour of the Pelasgian origin of the root. *Lišiai* is the locative of *lišis*, an old word corresponding to *lix*, "ashes mingled with water." Θ*ipurenai* is an adjective in concord with *lišiai*, and probably containing the root of θάπ-τω, τάφ-ρος, &c. *Eθe* is some particle, perhaps the same as *eth* in the Perugian Inscription, l. 3. *Erai* is the locative of *erus*, which constantly occurs in the Eugubine Tables, and also appears in the Perugian Inscription, l. 18. *Sie* (probably pronounced *syé*) is *sies* = *sis* (so *ar-sie* = *ad-sis* in the Eug. Tables); and *epana* may be connected with δάπτω, &c., as *epulæ* is with δαπάνη, *daps*, δεῖπνον, &c., or *ignis* with the root *dah*, "to burn." There can be little doubt that *neθu* means "water" in the Tuscan language. There is an Etruscan mirror in which the figure of Neptune has superscribed the word *Nethuns* = *Nethu-n*[*u*]*s*. The root is *ne-*, and appears under the same development in the next word, *nastav* (comp. ναςμός, ναθμός, O. H. G. *naz*), which is probably a locative in -φι, agreeing with *helefu*, which may be referred to χεῖλος, Æolice χέλλος, Latin *heluo*, &c. Some of these suggestions are more probable than the others; but it would be premature to found any conclusions upon even the most certain of them. Thus much may be inferred, that the inscription confirms what we might have gathered from the shape of the vase,—namely, that it is a sort of funereal lachrymatory, with the same symbolical meaning as that which was found last year at Rougham, near Bury St. Edmunds.

compass the same features with that which has just been quoted. It runs thus:

Mi ni mulvene kevelθu ir pupliana.

Besides these, we have a great number of inscriptions beginning with the syllable *mi*, mostly from *Orvieto* (i. e. *urbs vetus, Volsinii?*); and an inspection of those among them which are most easily interpreted leaves us little reason to doubt that this syllable represents the verb εἰμί, which has suffered decapitation in the same manner as the modern Greek νά for ἵνα. A collection of these inscriptions has been made by Lanzi (*Saggio*, ii. p. 319, *Epitafi scelti fra' piu antichi*, no. 188-200); and Müller thinks (*Etrusk*. i. p. 451) that they are all pure Pelasgian. Some of them, indeed, seem to be almost Greek—at least, they are more nearly akin to Greek than to Latin. Take, for instance, no. 191, which has been adduced both by Müller and by Lepsius, and which runs thus:

Mi kalairu fuius.

Surely this is little else than archaic Greek: εἰμὶ Καλαιροῦ Fυιός. In regard to the last word at any rate, even modern Latin approaches more nearly to the Etruscan type. It is well known that the termination *-al, -ul* in Etruscan indicates a patronymic. Thus a figure of Apollo, found in Picenum, is inscribed, *Jupetrul Epure*, i. e. " Jupiter's son, Apollo." The syllable *-al* corresponds to the Latin form *-alis*, but in its significance as a patronymic it is represented rather by *-i-lius*, as in *Servius, Servilius; Lucius, Lucilius;* &c. According to this analogy, *fi-lius*, from *fio*, is nearer to the Etruscan than φυιός, from the Æolic φυίω (*Et. M.* p. 254, 16).

There is another inscription of this class which deserves particular notice, because, though it is singularly like Greek, it contains a word which is of constant occurrence in the

Umbro-Tuscan monuments. A bronze figure, representing Apollo crowned with laurel, has the following inscription:

Mi phleres Epul . . . phe Aritimi .
Phasti Ruphrua turce clen ceca.

The first sentence must mean: *sum donarium Apollini et Artemidi.* The form *Ari-timi-*, as from *Ar-timi-s,* instead of the Greek Ἄρ-τεμι[δ]ς, is instructive. We might suppose from this that *Ari-timi-s,* the "virgin of the sea" (above, pp. 37, 39), and Ἀρέ-θουσα, "the virgin swiftly flowing," were different types of one and the same goddess. Ἀρτεμής appears to me to be a derivative from Ἄρτεμις. The next words probably contain the name and description of the person who made the offering. The name seems to have been *Fastia Rufrunia.* Lanzi and Müller recognise a verb in *turce,* which is of frequent occurrence on the Etruscan monuments, and translate it by ἐποίει, *dedit,* ἀνέθηκε, or the like. Lanzi goes so far as to suggest the etymology [δε-]δώρηκε. And perhaps we might make a verb of it, were it not for the context. Its position, however, between the proper name and the word *clen,* which in all other inscriptions is immediately appended to the name and description of a person, would induce me to seek the verb in *ceca* (probably a reduplication, like *pepe* on the Todi statue: compare *chu-che* in the Perugian inscription), and to suppose with Niebuhr (i. note 342) that *Turce* is the gentile name *Tusca.* I have cited the inscription principally on account of this word *clen,* which is explained by its contrast to *eter, etera,*—a word clearly expressing the Greek ἕτερος, Latin *alter* (*iterum*), and Umbrian *etre.* Thus we have on the same monument;

La . Fenete   La . Lethial etera
Se . Fenete   La . Lethial clan:

in which, if *etera* means, as is most probable, the *second* in the family, *clan* must mean the *first* or *head* of the family.

K

I would not on this account infer that *clan* was the ordinal corresponding in every case to *primus;* but there will be little difficulty in shewing etymologically its appropriateness as the designation of the *first* of a family. The root, which in the Greek and Latin languages signifies *head, summit, top,* is *cel-, cul-, cli-,* κολ-, κορ-, or κρα-. These are in effect the same root,—compare *glisco, cresco,* &c.; and it is well known, that words denoting height and elevation—or *head-ship,* in fact—are employed to signify *rank.* Now the transition from this to primogeniture—the being first in a family—is easy and natural: compare the " patrio *princeps* donârat nomine regem" of Lucretius (i. 88). Therefore, if *clen* or *clens* (in Latin *clanis* or *clanius*) is connected with the root of *celsus, cul-men, collis, clivus,* κολοφών, κορυφή, κύριος, κοίρανος, κοῦρος, κόρος, κύρβας, κράνιον, &c., it may well be used to signify the first in a family. This etymological analysis will perhaps be complete, if I add that there were two rivers in Italy which bore the name of *Clanis* or *Clanius;* the one running into the Tiber between *Tuder* and *Volsinii,* the other joining the sea near the Tuscan colony of *Vulturnum.* Now the names of rivers in the Pelasgian language seem to have some connexion with roots signifying " height," " hill," or " hill-tower." This has been indicated above in what has been said of the names of the Scythian rivers (Chap. II. § 8). The *Tibe-ris*—the " Tuscan river," as the Latin poets call it—seems to have derived its name from the Pelasgian *Teba,* " a hill," and the root *ri,* " to flow" (see above, Chap. IV. § 2). And the *Clan-is* and *Clan-ius,* which flow down from the Apennines, may well have gained a name of similar import.

§ 6.
The great Perugian Inscription analysed.

The facility with which the philologist dissects the Etruscan words which have been transmitted to us, either with an interpretation, or in such collocation as to render

THE ETRUSCAN LANGUAGE.

their meaning nearly certain, might occasion some surprise to those who are told that there exists a large collection of Etruscan inscriptions which cannot be satisfactorily explained. One cause of the unprofitableness of Tuscan inscriptions is to be attributed to the fact, that these inscriptions, being mostly of a sepulchral or dedicatorial character, are generally made up of proper names and conventional expressions. Consequently they contribute nothing to our knowledge of the Tuscan syntax, and furnish us with very few forms of inflexion. So far as I have heard, we have no historical or legal inscriptions. Those which I have inspected for myself are only monumental epitaphs and the dedications of offerings.

These observations might be justified by an examination of all the inscriptions which have been hitherto published. It will be sufficient, however, in this place to verify them by an analysis of the great inscription which was discovered in the neighbourhood of Perugia in the year 1822. This inscription is engraved on two sides of a block of stone, and consists of forty-five lines in the whole; being by far the most copious of all the extant monuments of the Tuscan language. The writing is singularly legible, and the letters were coloured with red paint.

The following is an accurate transcript of the facsimiles given by Micali (*Tav.* cxx. no. 80) and Vermiglioli (*Antiche Iscrizioni Perugine*, ed. 2, p. 85).

25. *Velthinaś*
26. *Atena zuk-*
27. *i eneski ip-*
28. *a śpelane*
29. *this fulumch-*
30. *va śpel thi-*
31. *rene thi eśt*
32. *ak Velthina*

1. *Eu. lat Tanna La Rezul*
2. *Amev. Achr Lautn Velthinaś E-*
3. *-śt La Afunaś slel eth karu-*
4. *tezan fuśleri tesnś teiś*
5. *Raśneś ipa ama hen naper*
6. XII *Velthina thuraś araś pe-*
7. *raś kemulmleskul zuki en-*
8. *eski eplt ularu*

33. *ak ilune*
34. *turunesk*
35. *unezea zuk-*
36. *i eneski ath-*
37. *umics Afu-*
38. *nas penthn-*
39. *a ama Velth-*
40. *ina Afun*
41. *thuruni ein-*
42. *zeriunak ch-*
43. *a thil Thunch-*
44. *ulthl ich ka*
45. *kechazi chuch-*
46. *e*

9. *Aulesi Velthinas Arznal kl-*
10. *ensi thii thils kuna kenu e-*
11. *plk Felik Larthals Afunes*
12.   *klen Thunchulthe*
13. *falas chiem fusle Velthina*
14. *hintha kape muniklet masu*
15. *naper srankzl thii falsti V-*
16. *elthina hut naper penezs*
17. *masu aknina klel Afuna Vel-*
18. *thinam Lerzinia intemam e-*
19. *r knl Velthina zias Atene*
20. *tesne eka Velthina thuras th-*
21. *aura helu tesne Rasne kei*
22. *tesns teis Rasnes chimth sp-*
23. *el thutas kuna Afunam ena*
24. *hen naper ki knl hareutuse*

Now, if we go through this inscription, and compare the words of which it is composed, we shall find that out of more than a hundred words there are very few which are not obviously proper names, and some of these occur very frequently; so that this monument, comparatively copious as it is, furnishes, after all, only slender materials for a study of the Tuscan language. According to the most probable division of the words, the contents of the inscription may be considered as given in the following vocabulary:

Afun (40); *Afuna* (17); *Afunam* (23); *Afunas* (3, 37); *Afunes* (11); *ak* (32, 33); *Akhr* (2); *aknina* (17); *ama* (5, 39); *Amev* (2); *aras* (6); *Arznal* (9); *Atena* (26); *Atene* (19); *athumics* (36); *Aulesi* (9).

Cha (42); *chiem* (13); *chimth* (22); *chuche* (45).

Einzeriunak (42); *eka* (20); *ena* (23); *eneski* (7, 27); *eplk* (11); *eplt* (8); *er* (18); *est* (2, 31); *eth* (3); *Eu* (1).

§ 6.] THE ETRUSCAN LANGUAGE. 133

Falaś, falśti (13, 15); *Felik* (11); *fulumchva* (29); *fuśle, fuśleri* (13, 4).
Hareutuze (24); *helu* (21); *hen* (5, 24); *hintha* (14); *huṭ* (16).
Ich (44); *ilune* (33); *intemam* (18); *ipa* (5, 27).
Ka (44); *kape* (14); *karutezan* (4); *kechazi* (45); *kei* (21); *kemulmleskul* (7); *kenu* (10); *ki* (24); *klel* (17); *klen, klenśi* (9, 12); *knl* (19, 24); *kuna* (23).
La (1, 3); *Larthalś* (11); *lat* (1); *Lautn* (2); *Lerzinia* (18).
Masu (14, 17); *muniklet* (14).
Naper (5, 15, 16, 24).
Penezś (16); *penthna* (38); *peraś* (6).
Raśne, Raśneś (5, 21, 22); *Rezul* (1).
Slel (3); *śpel, śpelane* (22, 28, 30); *śrankzl* (15).
Tanna (1); *teiś* (4, 22); *tesne, tesnś* (5, 20, 21, 22); *thaura* (20); *thi, this, thii, thil, thilś* (29, 31, 10, 43); *thuraś, thirene, thuruni* (6, 30, 41); *Thunchulthe* (12); *Thunchulthl* (43); *thutaś* (23); *turuneśk* (34).
Velthina, Velthinaś, Velthinam (6, 13, 15, 19, 20, 32, 39, 2, 9, 25, 17).
Ularu (8); *unezea* (35).
Ziaś (19); *zuki* (7, 26, 35).

The first remark to be made respecting this inscription is, that though we have here obviously a different language from that in which the Eugubine Tables are written, still there are many words which in outward form at least resemble the Umbrian phrases. Thus we have *Eu* (v. 1), *velthina* (passim), *est* (2), *karu-* (3), *tesnś* (4), *kape* (14), *muniklet* (14), *turu-* (24), *einzeriu-* (41), &c., which may be compared with *eu, veltu, est, karu, tesenakes, kapi, muneklu, tures, anzeriatu,* &c., in the Eugubine Tables, though it does not at all follow that there is any similarity of meaning in addition to the mere assonance. The word *naper* (5, 15, 16, 24) seems to have the termination *-per*, so common in Umbrian: we may compare it with the Latin *nu-per* (*pro novo*).

With regard to the interpretation of particular words, it seems idle to follow in the steps of the Italian scholars, Vermiglioli, Orioli, and Campanari, the last of whom has given us a Latin translation of the whole inscription. It would, indeed, be easy to found a number of conjectures on the assonances which may be detected in almost every line; but until a complete collection of all the genuine Etruscan inscriptions shall have furnished us with a sufficiently wide field for our researches,—until every extant Tuscan word has been brought within the reach of a philological comparison,—we must be content to say of this great Perugian inscription, that it appears to be a monument in honour of some woman of the family of the *Reza* (*Ræsii*), who were distinguished people in the neighbourhood of Perusia (see Vermiglioli, *Iscriz. Perug.* p. 273). We should probably divide *eu lat.* What the second syllable means can only be guessed: the former may well be the pronoun *eu*, which occurs in the second Eugubine Table (a, 9, b, 2). *Tanna*, or *Thana*, is a common prænomen of women; as such it forms part of the name *Than-chufil* (Lat. *Tanaquil*), the second part of which contains the element of the *Cfilnian* or *Cilnian* name.[1] Perhaps *Thunkulthe* (v. 12), *Thunchulthl* (v. 43), are forms of the same name. *La. Rezul* (for *Larthia Rezul*) is a feminine patronymic—" daughter of the *Lars Ræsius.*" What *amev.* may mean is quite unknown. *Achr.* probably stands for the name *Achrius*, which is found in other Tuscan inscriptions (see Vermiglioli, pp. 175, 220, 233). *Lautn. Vel-*

---

[1] Niebuhr thinks (*Kleine Schriften*, ii. p. 43) that *Tanaquil* is only a diminutive of *Thana*. With this opinion I cannot agree. There is much more truth in the conjecture of Passeri, which he quotes, that *Thana* is a title of honour, nearly equivalent in meaning, though of course not in origin, to the modern Italian *Donna*.

thinas gives another proper name, *Lautnius Velthina*. The latter word occurs no fewer than ten times; and we have, besides the simple *Velthina* (6, &c.), the modifications, *Velthinas* (here and 9) and *Velthinam* (18). We have also *Afunas* (3) and *Afunam* (23). Now as we have here three cases indicating the first declension in Oscan and Latin, it is difficult to conceive how any one should have travelled beyond the limits of the Indo-Germanic family to seek analogies for Etruscan words. The word *Velthina* is either a personal name, like *Cæcina*, &c., or it refers to the old name of Bononia, which was *Felsina* (Plin. iii. 20, xxxiii. 37, xxxvii. 57; Serv. ad *Æn.* x. 198). *La. Afunas* (v. 3) is probably *Larthiæ Aponiæ* (see Vermigl. p. 233). We must compare *slel* (v. 3) with *klel* (in v. 17). *Fusleri* (v. 4) is a form of *fusle* (v. 13). *Tesns teis Rasnes* (vv. 4, 5, and 22) present us with inflexions of *tesne* (v. 20) and *tesne Rasne* (21). *Ipa* may be a preposition (vv. 5, 28); *ama* is probably a noun (vv. 5, 39); the combination *ipa ama* (v. 5) may be compared with *penthna ama* (v. 38). *Zuki eneski* occurs twice (7, 26). For vv. 9, 10, see Müller, *Etrusker*, i. p. 453. *Falaz* (v. 13) may be compared with *falsti* (v. 15). *Eka* often occurs in Tuscan inscriptions (see Müller, *Etrusk.* i. p. 452, note). With *helu* (v. 21) we may compare *helefu* in the Cervetri inscription quoted above, where it is probably in the locative case.

§ 7. General reflections.

This survey of the Etruscan language, brief and imperfect as it necessarily is, may lead us to some general reflections on the subject. When we see so much that is easily explained; when, in fact, there is no great difficulty in dealing with any Etruscan word which has come down to us with an interpretation or clue to its meaning; and when we are puzzled only by inscriptions which are in themselves mere fragments, made up in a great measure of proper names, and mutilated by, we know not how many, conventional abbreviations,— we are entitled to ask, where is the bulk of that language which was spoken by the ancestors of Mæcenas? We talk of dead languages; but this variety of human speech should seem to be not only dead, but buried, and not only buried, but sunk beneath the earth in some necropolis into which no Galassi or Campanari can dig his way. The standard Italian of the present day is the offspring of that Latinity which was spoken by the Etrusco-Romans; but we find no trace of ancient barbarism in any Tuscan writer. Surely it is a fair inference, that the common Etruscan, like the Sabello-Oscan and other dialects, merged in the old Latin, not because the languages were unlike, but because they were sister idioms, and embraced one another as soon as they had discovered their relationship.[1] The only way to escape from the difficulties of this subject is to suppose that the city on the Tiber served as a centre and rallying-point for the languages of Italy as well as for the different tribes who spoke them, and that Rome admitted within her walls, with an inferior franchise, which in time completed itself, both the citizens and the vocabularies of the conquered Italian states.

[1] Among many instances of the possibility at least of such a transition, not the least interesting is the derivation of *Populonia* from *Phupluns*, the Etruscan Bacchus; so that this city, the Etruscan name of which was *Popluna*, is the Dionysopolis of Etruria (see Gerhard in the *Rhein. Mus.* for 1833, p. 135). Now it is clear that as *Nethuns* = *Nethu-nus* is the god of *nethu*, so *Phupluns* = *Poplu-nus* is the god of *poplu*. It seems that the ancients planted the poplar chiefly on account of their vines, and the poplar was sacred to Hercules, who has so many points of contact with Bacchus. Have we not, then, in the word *phupluns* the root of *pŏpulus*, a word quite inexplicable from the Latin language alone? A sort of young, effeminate Hercules, who appears on the coins of Populonia (see Müller, *Etrusk.* i. p. 331), is probably this *Poplunus*. The difference in the quantity of the first syllables of *Pŏpulus* and *Pōpulonia* is not surprising, as the latter is an exotic proper name, and the former a naturalised common term.

CHAPTER VI.

THE OLD ROMAN OR LATIN LANGUAGE.

§ 1. Fragments of old Latin not very numerous. § 2. Arvalian Litany. § 3. Chants preserved by Cato. § 4. Fragments of Salian hymns. § 5. Old regal laws. § 6. Remains of the XII. Tables. § 7. Table I. § 8. Table II. § 9. Table III. § 10. Table IV. § 11. Table V. § 12. Table VI. § 13. Table VII. § 14. Table VIII. § 15. Table IX. § 16. Table X. § 17. Table XI. § 18. Table XII. § 19. The Tiburtine Inscription. § 20. The epitaphs of the Scipios. § 21. The *Columna Rostrata*. § 22. The Silian and Papirian Laws. § 23. The *Senatus-Consultum de Bacchanalibus*. § 24. The old Roman law on the Bantine Table.

§ 1. Fragments of old Latin not very numerous.

HAVING in the preceding chapters given specimens of the languages spoken by those nations which contributed in different proportions to the formation of the Roman people, the next step will be to collect the most interesting remains of the old Roman language,—considered as the offspring of the Umbrian, Oscan, and Tuscan,— such as it was before the predominance of Greek cultivation had begun to work on this rude composite structure. The total loss of the genuine Roman literature[1] will, of course, leave us but a scanty collection of such documents. Indeed, for the earlier centuries we have only a few brief fragments of religious and legal import. As we approach the Punic wars, the inscriptions become more numerous and complete; but then we are drawing near to a period when the Roman language began to lose its leading characteristics under the pressure of foreign influences, and

---

[1] See Macaulay, *Lays of Ancient Rome*, p. 15, sqq.

when it differed little or nothing from that idiom which has become familiar to us from the so-called classical writings of the Augustan age.

Polybius, speaking of the ancient treaty between Rome and Carthage (iii. 22), remarks, that the old Latin language differed so much from that which was spoken in his own time, that the best-informed Romans could not make out some expressions without difficulty, even when they paid the greatest attention: τηλικαύτη γὰρ ἡ διαφορὰ γέγονε τῆς διαλέκτου, καὶ παρὰ ῾Ρωμαίοις, τῆς νῦν πρὸς τὴν ἀρχαίαν, ὥστε τοὺς συνετωτάτους ἔνια μόλις ἐξ ἐπιστάσεως διευκρινεῖν. The great mass of words must, however, have been susceptible of interpretation; for he does not shrink from translating into Greek the substance at least of that very ancient treaty.

Accordingly, we find that the most primitive specimens of Latinity may now-a-days be understood by the scholar, who, after all, possesses greater advantages than Polybius and his contemporary Romans. This will appear if we examine the song of the *Fratres Arvales*, which is one of the most important and ancient specimens of the genuine Roman language. The inscription, in which it is preserved, and which was discovered in the year 1777, is probably not older than A.D. 218; but there is every reason to believe that the *cantilena* itself was the same which was sung in the earliest ages of Rome,—for these litanies very often survive their own significance. The monks read the Latin of their missals without understanding it, and the Parsees of Gujerat cannot interpret their sacred Zend. It appears from the introductory remarks, that this song was confined to the priests, the *Publici* being excluded: " Deinde subselliis marmoreis consederunt; et panes laureatos per Publicos partiti sunt; ibi omnes lumemulia cum rapinis acceperunt, et Deas unguentaverunt, et

Ædes clusa est, omnes foris exierunt: ibi Sacerdotes clusi succincti, libellis acceptis, carmen descindentes tripodaverunt in verba hæc:

1. *Enos Lases juvate* (ter),
2. *Neve luaerve Marmar sins incurrere in pleoris* (ter)
3. *Satur furere* (vel *fufere*) *Mars limen salista berber* (ter)
4. *Semunis alternei* (vel *alternip*) *advocapit conctos* (ter)
5. *Enos Marmor* (vel *Mamor*) *juvato* (ter)
6. *Triumpe, triumpe, triumpe, triumpe, triumpe.*

Post tripodationem, deinde signo dato Publici introierunt, et libellos receperunt." (Orelli, *Inscript. Lat.* i. p. 391, no. 2271.)

There can be little doubt as to the meaning of any single word in this old hymn, which seems to be written in very rude Saturnian verse, the first half of the verse being alone preserved in some cases; as in *Enós Lasés juváte — Enós Mamór juváto.* The last line is a series of trochees *cum anacrusi*, or a still shorter form of the first half of the Saturnian verse.

1. *Enos* is a form of the first person plural, analogous to the German *uns*. *Lases* is the old form of *Lares* (Quinctil. *Institut. Orat.* i. 4. § 13; see Müller *ad Fest.* p. 15).

2. *Luærve* for *luerve-m*, according to a custom of dropping the final M, which lasted till Cato's time (see next §). This form bears the same relation to *luem* that *Minerva* does to *mens*. *Caterva* from *catus* = *acutus* (above, p. 74), and its synonyme *acervus* from *acus*, are derivatives of the same kind. We may also compare *bovem, suem*, &c. with their older forms, *boverem, suerem*, &c. *Marmar, Marmor,*

or *Mamor*, is the Oscan *Mamers*, " man-slayer," i. e. *Mars*. That *Mars*, or *Mars pater*, was addressed as the averter of diseases, bad weather, &c. is clear from Cato, *R. R.* 141. *Sins* is *sinas:* so Tab. Bantin. l. 19: *Bantins* for *Bantinus*, &c. *Ple-ores* is the genuine comparative of *ple-nus*, which bears the same relation to πλεῖος that *unus* does to οἶος. The fullest form would be *ple-iores* = πλείονες : compare βελ-τ-ίων with *mel-ior*, &c.

3. " O Mars, having raged to your satisfaction (comp. Hor. i. *Carm.* ii. 37 : " longo satiate ludo"), put a stop to the scorching heat of the sun." *Limen* for *lumen* may be compared with *plisima* for *plurima* (Fest. p. 205), *scripulum* for *scrupulum*, &c. (see below, Chap. VI. § 5). *Salis* is the original form of *solis:* comp. σέλας, ἥλιος, *Au-selius*, &c. Whether we read *sta* or *ta*, the meaning seems to be " cause to cease," which may be derived from either root. *Berber* is another form of *fervere*.

4. *Semuneis* is *semones*, i. e. *semihemones*. If *alternip* is the right reading, it is an adverb = *alternis*. *Advocapit* is a contraction for *ad vos capite:* the *e* is omitted, as in *duc, fac, fer*, &c. It is not improbable that *ad vo' capite* may be a tmesis for *vos accipite*.

§ 3.
Chants preserved by Cato.

The other extant religious compositions, though few and scanty, contribute to the same conclusion — that the oldest Latin was not so unlike the language with which we are familiar as to defy interpretation. Two reliques of the same kind as the last have been preserved by Cato (*R. R.* 160), who writes thus: " Luxum si quod est, hac cantione sanum fiet. Harundinem prende tibi viridem P. IV. aut V. longam. Mediam diffinde, et duo homines teneant ad coxendices. Incipe cantare in alio: S[anum] F[iet]. In mota et soluta (vulg. *mota væta*) : *daries dardaries astataries*, dic sempiterno (vulg. *dissunapiter* or *dic una pariter*), usquedum coeant . . . . Ad luxum aut ad fracturam alliga, sanum fiet, et tamen quotidie cantato in alio: S. F. vel luxato: vel hoc modo: *havat, havat, havat: ista pista sista: domabo damnaustra et luxato.*" i. e. *haveat, haveat, haveat: istam pestem sistam: domabo damna vestra et luxatum* (see Grotefend, *Rud. L. Umbr.* iv. 13). With regard to the second *excantatio*, which is simple enough, it is only necessary to observe, that the final *m* is omitted both in the accusatives *luxato, pista*, &c. and in the future *sista;* and we are especially told that it was the custom with Cato the Censor to drop the *m* at the termination of the futures of verbs in *-o* and *-io:* thus he wrote *dice, facie*, for *dicam, faciam* (see Quinctil. *Inst. Or.* i. 7, § 23, and cf. ix. 4, § 39; Fest. p. 72. Müll.), *recipie* for *recipiam* (Fest. p. 286), *attinge* for *attingam* (id. p. 26), *ostende* for *ostendam* (id. p. 201), which are all quoted as common examples. He also omitted the *-s* of the nominative, as in *præfamino* for *præfaminus* (used for *præfato:* see *R. R.* 141: "Janum Jovemque vino *præfamino*, sic dicito." cf. 134; and see Fest. p. 87). The words *daries, dar-dar-ies, as-ta-tar-ies*, seem to be a jingling alliteration, the meaning of which must not be pressed too far; Pliny, at least (*H. N.* xvii. 28), does not think them worthy of serious attention; though Grotefend would compare them with *dertier dierir* in the spurious Umbrian inscription (see Leps. p. 52).

§ 4. Fragments of the Salian hymns.

The Salian songs, if any considerable fragments of them had come down to our times, would have furnished us with very interesting specimens of ancient Latinity. Unfortunately they are all lost, with the exception of a few lines and detached words; and with them we have been deprived of the learned commentaries of Ælius Stilo, who was not, however, able to explain them throughout. Varro, vii. § 2: "Ælii, hominis in primo in litteris Latinis exercitati, interpretationem carminum Saliorum videbis et exili littera expeditam et praeterita obscura multa."[1] Of the explanations of Ælius the following have been preserved. Festus, s. v. *Manuos*, p. 146: " *Manuos* in carminibus Saliaribus Ælius Stilo [*et Aurelius*, v. Paul. p. 147] significare ait *bonos:* unde Inferi Di *manes* pro *boni* dicantur a suppliciter eos venerantibus propter metum mortis, ut *immanes* quoque pro valde [non bonis] dicuntur." Id. s. v. *Molucrum*, p. 141: " Molucrum non solum quo molae vertuntur dicitur, id quod Graeci μυληκόρον appellant, sed etiam tumor ventris, qui etiam virginibus incidere solet.... Cloatius etiam [*et Ælius*] in libris sacrorum molucrum esse aiunt lignum quoddam quadratum ubi immolatur. Idem Ælius in explanatione carminum Saliarium eodem nomine appellari ait, quod sub mola supponatur. Aurelius Opilius appellat ubi molatur." Id. s. v. *Pescia*, p. 210: " *Pescia* in Saliari carmine Ælius Stilo dici ait capitia ex pellibus agninis facta, quod Graeci pelle vocent πέσκη [πεσκέων, δερμάτων, Hesych.] neutro genere pluraliter." Id. s. v. *Salias virgines*, p. 329: " Salias virgines Cincius ait esse conducticias, quae ad Salios adhibeantur cum apicibus paludatas, quas Ælius Stilo scripsit sacrificium facere in Regia cum pontifice paludatas cum apicibus in modum Saliorum." There are other references in Festus to the philological interpretations of Ælius; but as the Salian songs are not mentioned in them, we have no right to assume that this particular commentary is quoted: see Festus, s. v. *Manias*, p. 129; s. v. *Monstrum*, p. 138; s. v. *Nebulo*, p. 165; s. v. *Naucum*, p. 166; s. v. *Nusciciosum*, p. 173; s. v. *Novalem agrum*, p. 174; s. v. *Ordinarium hominem*, p. 185; s. v. *Obstitum*, p. 193 (cf. pp. 248, 249); s. v. *Puticulos*, p. 217; s. v. *Portisculus*, p. 234; s. v. *Sonticum*, p. 290; s. v. *Subuculam*, p. 309;

---

[1] Horace, too, alludes to the difficulty of the Salian songs (ii. *Epist.* i. 86): Jam saliare Numae carmen qui laudat, et illud,
Quod *mecum ignorat*, solus vult scire videri, &c.

s. v. *Tongere*, p. 356; s. v. *Tamne* (=*eo usque*), p. 359; s. v. *Victimam*, p. 371.

The following are the remaining fragments of the Salian hymns.

Varro, *L. L.* vii. § 26: " In multis verbis, in quo antiqui dicebant s, postea dictum R; ut in carmine Saliorum sunt hæc:

COZEULODOIZESO [vel *coreulodorieso*]; OMINA [enim] VERO AD PATULA COEMISSE [vel *oremisse*] JAMCUSIANES; DUONUSCERUSES DUNZIANUS VEVET."

This may be written as follows, in the Saturnian metre:

Chŏroí aulódoȓ éso : | ómina énim véro
'Ad pátula' óse' mísse | Jáni cúȓiónes.
Dùónus Cérus ésit, | dúnque Jánus vévet.

i. e. *choroio-aulodos ero; omina enimvero ad patulas aures miserunt Jani curiones. Bonus Cerus* (i. e. *Cerus manus = creator bonus,* Fest. p. 122) *erit donec Janus vivet* (Grotefend, *Rud. L. Umbr.* ii. p. 16).

With regard to the apparently Greek word *choȓoí-aulodos*, it may be sufficient to quote an observation of Varges (*Rhein. Mus.* for 1835, p. 69), who, speaking of his derivation of *ampirvo* (see below) from ἄμπειρα, says: "Vix est quod moneam in Saliari carmine alia quoque vocabula inveniri, quæ originem Græcam manifesto præ se ferant, ut *pescia*, de quo vocabulo vide Fest. et Gutberl. [*de Saliis*], p. 146, et *tripudium*, quod propius esse Græcorum πόδα quam Latinorum *pedem* patet, et recte interpretatur Auson. Popma *de Differ. Verbor.* s. *Saltare.* Item *cosauli* apud Varronem *de L. L.* vii. c. 3. Græcorum χόραυλοι esse videntur, quod verbum Pollux servavit." In this word, as in *cuȓiones,* I have ventured to insert the letter ȓ (above, p. 51).

Varro, *L. L.* vii. § 27: " *Canite,* pro quo in Saliari versu scriptum est *cante,* hoc versu:

DÌVUM ÉMPTA CANTE, DÍVUM | DÉO SÚPPLICÁNTE."

i. e. *Deorum impetu canite, deorum deo supplice canite.* Cf. Macrob. *Sat.* i. 9: " Saliorum carminibus *deorum deus* canitur [*Janus*]."

Festus, s. v. *Mamuri Veturi,* p. 131 : " Probatum opus est maxime Mamuri Veturi, qui præmii loco petiit, ut suum nomen inter carmina Salii canerent."

Id. s. v. *Negumate,* p. 168 : "*Negumate* in carmina Cn. Marci vatis significat *negate,* cum ait : *quàmvís movéntiùm* [*molimentum* Herm. *El. D. M.* p. 614] *du-ónum négumáte.*"

Id. s. v. *Obstinet,* p. 197 : " *Obstinet* dicebant antiqui, quod nunc est ostendit; ut in veteribus carminibus : *sèd jám se cœ́lo cédens* [*Aurora*] *óbstinét suum pátrem.*" Here it will be observed that *se cœlo cedens* = *cœlo secedens,* and that *suum* is a monosyllable (see Fest. p. 301).

Id. s. v. *Præceptat,* p. 205 : " *Præceptat* in Saliari carmine est sæpe præcipit. *Pa* pro patre, et *po* pro potissimum, positum est in Saliari carmine. *Promenervat* item pro monet. *Prædopiont,* præoptant, &c. *Pilumnœ poplœ* in carmine Saliari, Romani, velut pilis assueti : vel quia præcipue pellant hostes."

Id. s. v. *Redantruare,* p. 270 : "*Redantruare* dicitur in Saliorum exsultationibus, quod cum præsul amptruavit, quod est motus edidit, ei referuntur invicem idem motus. Lucilius : *Præsul ut amptruat inde; ita volgu' redamptruat ollim.* Pacuvius :

Promerenda gratia
Simul cum videam Graios nihil mediocriter
Redamptruare, opibusque summis persequi."

According to Varges (*Rhein. Mus.* for 1835, p. 62, sqq.) the fragment of Lucilius ought to be read thus : *Præsul ut ampirvat, sic vulgu' redantruat inde.* He derives *ampirvo* from the Greek ἄμπειρα, which, according to Hesychius (s. v. ἀνάπειρα), was ῥυθμός τις αὐλητικός ; for Dionysius tells us (*Antiq.* ii. 70) that the Salii danced to the flute.

The same name was given to the second part of the Pythian nome (Timosthenes, *ap. Strab.* ix. 3); and Argolus (Græv. *Thesaur.* ix. p. 342) explains the passage in Claudian (vi. *Cons. Hon.* 626-30) by a reference to the Pythian nome. Turnebus (*Advers.* xvii. 8, vol. ii. p. 145) connects *am-pirvo* with the French *pirouetter;* comp. the Oscan *am-pert*= *per;* above, Ch. V. § 4.

Id. p. 290 (*ex Suppl. Ursin.*): "*Sesopia* in augurali et Saliari carmine appellantur, quæ alias esopia pro sedibus dicere habemus nunc adhuc in consuetudine."

Id. s. v. *Sonivio*, ibid.: "*Sonivio* significat in carmine [Saliari et a]ugurali sonanti."

Id. p. 360: "*Tame* in carmine positum est pro *tam*." So also *cume* for *cum*, Terent. Scaur. p. 2661 P., who quotes from the Salian songs.

§ 5. Old regal laws.

The fragments of the oldest Roman laws, though undoubtedly genuine in substance, must be considered as having undergone considerable alteration in the orthography at all events. They are precious memorials of primeval Latinity; but, like the Homeric poems, they not unfrequently exhibit the deformity of an ancient statue, which the false taste of a later age may have daubed over with a coat of coloured plaster.

One of these fragments professes to be as old as the time of Romulus and Tatius. Festus, s. v. *Plorare*, p. 230: "*Plorare, flere* nunc significat, et cum præpositione *implorare*, i. e. *invocare;* sed apud antiquos plane *inclamare*. In regis Romuli et Tatii legibus: *Si nurus ... sacra divis parentum estod.* In Servi Tulli hæc est: *Si parentem puer verberit, ast olle plorasset, puer divis parentum sacer esto;* i. e. *inclamarit, dix[erit diem]*." The restoration of the laws quoted in this passage may be given thus: (1) *Sei nuros [parentem verbussit, ast ole plorasit], sacra diveis parentom estod.* (2) *Sei parentem puer verbesit, ast ole plorasit, puer diveis parentom sacer estod.*

In these fragments two forms deserve to be noticed. If *verberit*, as it is quoted in Festus, were a syncope for *verberarit*, the old form would be *verberasit*. It seems, however, that there was an older form of *verbero*, inflected according to the third conjugation, like *carint* (Plautus, *Mostell.* iv. 1, 1) and *temperint* (*Trucul.* i. 1, 41). The three participles, *verbustus, castus, tempestus* (Fest. p. 362), are further indications of such original forms. Accordingly *verberit* is the modern orthography, not of *verberarit*, but of *verbesit* or *verbussit* (Müller, *Suppl. Annot. in Fest.* p. 393). We should write *ole* = *olle* with one *l*. That this was the primitive orthography is proved, not only by the express testimony of Festus (s. v. *Solitaurilia*, p. 293; id. s. v. *Torum*, p. 355; id. s. v. *ab oloes*, p. 19: " *ab oloes* dicebant pro *ab illis;* antiqui enim litteram non geminabant"), but still more strikingly by the locative *olim*, which retained its orthography long after its derivation had been forgotten.

There are several fragments of the laws of Numa Pompilius. Festus, s. v. *Occisum*, p. 178: " *Occisum* a *necato* distingui quidam, quod alterum a cædendo atque ictu fieri dicunt, alterum sine ictu. Itaque in Numæ Pompili regis legibus scriptum esse: *Si hominem fulmen Jovis occisit, ne supra genua tollitor.* Et alibi: *Homo si fulmine occisus est, ei justa nulla fieri oportet.*" In the old orthography these fragments would run thus: *Sei hemonem fulmin Jobis ocisit, nei supra cenua tolitor. Hemo sei fulmined ocisus escit, eiei jousta nula fieri oportet.* For the form *hemo*, see Müller *ad Fest.* p. 100. *Escit*, an inchoative of *est*, has a future signification: see Müller *ad Fest.* p. 77; and *Suppl. Annot.* p. 386.

Festus (s. v. *Parrici*[*di*] *Quæstores*, p. 221) quotes a short fragment from another law of Numa, which defines the word *parricida:* " *Si qui hominem liberum dolo sciens morti duit, parricidas esto;*" i. e., in the old orthography, *Sei qui hemonem lœbesum* (Fest. p. 121) *dolo sciens mortei duit, pariceidas estod.* The *Parricidi Quæstores* seem to have been the same as the *Perduellionis Duumviri.* The law respecting the punishment of the criminal and his right of appeal, which both Livy and Cicero call a *carmen,* has been thus preserved in Saturnian verse:

> Duúmviri perduélli|ónem júdicánto.
> Si a duúmviris provocásit | provocatióne certáto.
> Si víncent, cáput obnúbito in|félici árbore reste
> Suspéndito, vérberáto | íntra vel éxtra pómœrum.

I have here written *judicanto* for *judicent,* because the final thesis cannot be suppressed (below, § 20). The *v* or *b* is slurred over in *pro'casit, pro'catione,* and *obnu'to,* according to the common Roman pronunciation. Each trochaic tripodia in l. 2 begins with an anacrusis. According to Livy (i. 26), the law belongs to the time of Tullus Hostilius; Cicero, on the other hand (*pro Rabir.* c. 4, § 13), refers it to the legislation of Tarquinius.

Id. s. v. *Pellices,* p. 222: " Cui generi mulierum pœna constituta est a Numa Pompilio hac lege: *Pellex aram Junonis ne tangito; si tanget, Junoni crinibus demissis agnum fœminam cædito.*" i. e. *Pelecs asam Junonis nei tancitud; sei tancet, Junonei crinebos demiseis acnom feminam ceditud.*

Id. s. v. *Opima spolia,* p. 189: " Esse etiam Pompili regis legem opimorum spoliorum talem: *Cujus auspicio classe procincta opima spolia capiuntur, Jovi Feretrio bovem cædito; qui cepit* [ei] *æris* CCC *darier oportet:* [cujus auspicio capiuntur] *secunda spolia, in Martis aram in Campo solitaurilia utra voluerit* (*i. e.* ' vel majora vel lactentia,' SCAL.) *cædito;* [qui cepit, ei æris CC dato]: [cujus auspicio capiuntur] *tertia spolia Janui Quirino agnum marem cædito,* c *qui ceperit ex ære dato: cujus auspicio capta, dis piaculum dato.*" Niebuhr (*H. R.* ii. note 972) explains these gradations of reward by a reference to the scale of pay in the Roman army. The supplements in this passage rest principally on Plutarch, *Vit. Marc.* c. 8 : καὶ λαμβάνειν γέρας, ἀσσάρια τριακόσια τὸν πρῶτον, τὸν δὲ δεύτερον διακόσια, τὸν δὲ τρίτον ἑκατόν.

Plin. *H. N.* xxxii. 2, 10, § 20: " *Pisceis quei squamosei nec sunt, nei polucetod; squamosos omneis præter scarom polucetod.*" Cf. Fest. s. v. *Pollucere,* p. 253 : " *Pollucere merces* [quas cuivis deo liceat], sunt far, polenta, vinum, panis fermentalis, ficus passa, suilla, bubula, agnina, casei, ovilla, alica, sesama, et oleum, pisces quibus est squama, præter scarum : Herculi autem omnia esculenta, poculenta."

Id. s. v. *Termino,* p. 368 : " Denique Numa Pompilius statuit, *Eum qui terminum exarasset et ipsum et boves sacros esse.*" i. e. *Qui terminom ecsaraset, ipsus et boveis sacrei sunto.* (See Dirksen, *Versuche,* p. 334.)

Id. s. v. *Aliuta,* p. 6 : "*Aiuta* antiqui dicebant pro aliter, ... hinc est illud in legibus Numæ Pompili : *Siquisquam aliuta facsit ipsos Jovei sacer estod.*"

§ 6.
Remains of the XII. Tables.

But of all the legal fragments which exhibit the *prisca vetustas verborum* (Cic. *de Oratore,* i. c. 43), the most copious, as well as the most important, are the remains of the Twelve Tables, of which Cicero speaks in such enthusiastic, if not hyperbolical language. These fragments have been more than once collected and explained. In the following extracts I have followed the text of Dirksen (*Uebersicht der bisherigen Versuche zur Kritik und Herstellung des Textes der Zwölf-Tafel-Fragmente*). The object, however, of Dirksen's elaborate work is juristic[1] rather than philological; whereas I have only wished to present these fragments as interesting specimens of old Latinity.

It was probably the intention of the decemvirs to comprise their system in six double Tables; for each successive

---

[1] The student will find a general sketch of the old Roman law in Arnold's *Rome,* i. p. 256, sqq.

pair of Tables seems to refer to matters which are naturally classed together. Thus Tab. i. and ii. relate to the *legis actiones;* Tab. iii. and iv. to the *mancipium, potestas,* and *manus,* or the rights which might be acquired over insolvent debtors, the right of a father over his son, and of a husband over his wife; Tab. v. and vi. to the laws of guardianship, inheritance, and property; Tab. vii. and viii. to *obligationes, delicta,* and *crimina;* Tab. ix. and x. to the *jus publicum* and *jus sacrum;* Tab. xi. and xii. were supplementary to the ten former Tables, both in subject and in date.

Tab. I.

Fr. 1 (i. 1, 2, Gothofredi): SI . IN . JUS . VOCAT . NI . IT . ANTESTATOR . IGITUR . EM . CAPITO . (Porphyrio *ad Hor.* i. *Serm.* 9, 65 : " Adversarius molesti illius Horatium consulit, an permittat se antestari, injecta manu extracturus ad Prætorem, quod vadimonio non paruerit. De hac autem *Lege* XII. *Tabularum* his verbis cautum est: *si vis vocationi testamini, igitur en capito antestari.* Est ergo antestari, scilicet antequam manum injiciat." Cf. Cic. *Legg.* ii. c. 4; Aul. Gell. *N. A.* xx. 1; *Auctor ad Herenn.* ii. c. 13; Non. Marcell. *de Propr. Serm.* c. 1, § 20, s. v. *calvitur.* Lucilius, *Lib.* xvii. : " Si non it, *capito,* inquit, *eum et, si calvitur ergo, Ferto manum*"). It seems probable that the original form of the law was, *si quis in jus vocatus nec it, antestamino, igitur* (i. e. *inde, postea, tum,* Fest. p. 105) *em* (= *eum*) *capito.* Cf. Gronov. *Lect. Plautin.* p. 95.

Fr. 2 (i. 3): SI . CALVITUR . PEDEMVE . STRUIT, . MANUM . ENDO . JACITO . (Festus, p. 313). The word *calvitur* is explained by Gaius, *L.* 233, *pr. D. de Verb. Sign.:* " *Si calvitur* et moretur et frustretur. Inde et *calumniatores* appellati sunt, quia per fraudem et frustrationem alios vexarent litibus." *Pedem struere* is explained by Festus, l. l.: " Alii putant significare *retrorsum ire:* alii, *in aliam partem:* alii *fugere:* alii *gradum augere:* alii *minuere,* cum quis vix pedem pedi præfert, otiose it, remoratur:" and p. 210: "*pedem struit* in XII. significat *fugit,* ut ait Ser. Sulpicius." This fragment seems to have followed close upon the previous one: see the passage of Lucilius, quoted above.

Fr. 3 (i. 4): SI . MORBUS . AEVITASVE . VITIUM . ESCIT, . QUI . IN . JUS . VOCABIT . JUMENTUM . DATO; . SI . NOLET . ARCERAM . NE . STERNITO . (Aul. Gell. *N. A.* xx. 1). *Vitium escit* means *impedimento erit.* *Arcera* is explained by Nonius Marcellus, *de Propr. Serm.* i. § 270: "*Arcera* plaustrum est rusticum, tectum undique quasi *arca.* Hoc vocabulum et apud Varronem et apud M. Tullium invenitur. Hoc autem vehiculi genere *senes et ægroti* vectari solent. Varro γεροντιδιδασκάλῳ: *vehebatur cum uxore vehiculo semel aut bis anno cum arcera: si non vellet non sterneret.*"

Fr. 4 (i. 6): ASSIDUO . VINDEX . ASSIDUUS . ESTO, . PROLETARIO . QUOI . QUIS . VOLET . VINDEX . ESTO . (Aul. Gell. *N. A.* xvi. c. 10; cf. Cicero, *Top.* c. 2, who explains *assiduus* as a synonyme of *locuples,* and derives it, with Ælius, *ab asse dando;* Nonius, *Propr. Serm.* c. 1, § antepen., who explains *proletarius* as equivalent to *plebeius—* "qui tantum *prolem* sufficiat." See Niebuhr, *Hist. Rom.* i. p. 445, note 1041).

Fr. 5 (ix. 2). Festus, p. 348: "*Sanates* dicti sunt, qui supra infraque Romam habitaverunt. Quod nomen his fuit, quia cum defecissent a Romanis, brevi post redierunt in amicitiam, quasi *sanata* mente. Itaque in XII. cautum est, ut ' idem juris esset *Sanatibus* quod *Forctibus,*' id est *bonis* (cf. pp. 84, 102), et qui nunquam defecerant a P. R." Whence we may supply, p. 321: "[Hinc] in XII.: 'NEX[i solutique, ac] FORCTI SANATI[sque idem jus estod'], id est, bonor[um et qui defecerant sociorum]." Where also *sanas* is explained from Cincius, "[quod Priscus] præter opinio-

[nem eos debellavis]set, sanavisse[tque ac cum iis pa]cisci potuisset." Dirksen (p. 164) is wrong in referring these extracts to the epitome of Paulus.

Fr. 6 (i. 17): REM . UBI . PAGUNT, . ORATO . (*Auctor ad Herenn.* ii. c. 13).

Fr. 7 (i. 8): NI . PAGUNT . IN . COMITIO . AUT . IN . FORO . ANTE . MERIDIEM . CAUSAM . CONJICITO, . QUOM . PERORANT . AMBO . PRAESENTES . (id. ibid. and Aul. Gell. xvii. 2). The word *pagunt* is explained by Priscian (x. 5, § 32) as a synonyme of *paciscor;* the common Latin form is *pa-n-go*, but the medial and tenuis of the gutturals were constantly interchanged after the distinction between them was introduced by Sp. Carvilius (Terent. Scaur. p. 2253, Putsch).

Fr. 8 (i. 9): POST . MERIDIEM . PRAESENTI . STLITEM . ADDICITO . (Aul. Gell. xvii. 2).

Fr. 9 (i. 10): SOL . OCCASUS . SUPREMA . TEMPESTAS . ESTO . (id. ibid.). The word *tempestas* is here used for *tempus;* the whole afternoon was called *tempus occiduum*, and the sunset was *suprema tempestas* (Macrob. *Saturn.* i. c. 3). Gellius, to whom we owe these fragments, considers the correct reading to be *sol,* not *solis occasus.* "*Sole occaso,*" he says, "non insuavi *venustate* (vetustate?) est, si quis aurem habeat non sordidam nec proculcatam." But Festus (p. 305), Varro (*L. L.* v. c. 2), and others, consider the phrase to have been *solis occasus.* There is more probability in the reading of Gellius.

Fr. 10 (ii. 1). Aul. Gell. *N. A.* xvi. c. 10: " Sed enim quum *proletarii,* et *assidui,* et *sanates,* et *vades,* et *subvades,* —evanuerint, omnisque illa XII. Tabularum antiquitas— consopita sit," &c.

TAB. II.

Fr. 1. Gaius, *Inst.* iv. § 14: " Pœna autem sacramenti aut quingenaria erat, aut quinquagenaria; nam de rebus mille æris plurisve quingentis assibus, de minoris vero quinquaginta assibus sacramento contendebatur; nam ita lege XII. Tabularum cautum erat. Sed si de libertate hominis controversia erat, etsi pretiosissimus homo esset, tamen ut L. assibus sacramento contenderetur eadem lege cautum est favoris causa ne satisdatione onerarentur adsertores."

Fr. 2 (ii. 2): (*a*) MORBUS . SONTICUS—(*b*) STATUS . DIES . CUM . HOSTE—(*c*) SI . QUID . HORUM . FUAT . UNUM, . JUDICI, . ARBITROVE . REOVE, . DIES . DIFFENSUS . ESTO .
(*a*) Aul. Gell. xx. c. 1 : " Morbum vehementiorem, vim graviter nocendi habentem, Leg. istar. i.e. XII. Tab. scriptores alio in loco non per se *morbum*, sed *morbum sonticum* appellant." Fest. p. 290: "*Sonticum morbum* in XII. significare ait Ælius Stilo certum cum justa causa, quem non nulli putant esse, qui noceat, quod *sontes* significat *nocentes*. Nævius ait: *sonticam esse oportet causam, quam ob rem perdas mulierem*." (*b*) Cic. *de Off.* i. c. 12: "*Hostis* enim majores nostros is dicebatur, quem nunc *peregrinum* dicimus. Indicant XII. Tabulæ ut: *status dies cum hoste;* itemque *adversus hostem æterna auctoritas*." Fest. p. 314: " Status dies [cum hoste] vocatur qui judici causa est constitutus cum peregrino. Ejus enim generis ab antiquis hostes appellabantur, quod erant pari jure cum populo R., atque *hostire* ponebatur pro *æquare*. Plautus in Curculione [i. 1, 5]: *si status condictus cum hoste intercedit dies, tamen est eundum, quo imperant ingratis*." This passage is neglected by Dirksen, but not by Gronovius, *Lectiones Plautinæ*, p. 81. With regard to the original signification of *hostis*, it is very worthy of remark that the Latin *hostis* and the Greek ξένος, starting from opposite points, have interchanged their significations. *Hos-tis* originally signified " a person entertained by another," " one who has food given to him" (comp. *hos-pi*[*t-*]*s*, " the master of the feast," *hostia*, *gasts*, &c. *N. Crat.* p. 579); but at last

it came to mean "a stranger," "a foreigner," and even "an enemy" (see Varro, *L. L.* p. 2, Müller). Whereas ξένος originally denoting "a stranger" (*extraneus*), i. e. "one without" ([ἐ]ξένος), came in the end to signify "an entertainer" and "a friend." I cannot accept Müller's derivation of ξένος (*ad Fest.* p. 102). (*c*) Festus, p. 273: "*Reus* nunc dicitur, qui causam dicit; et item qui quid promisit spoponditve, ac debet. At Gallus Ælius libro ii. *Sign. Verb. qu. ad Jus pertinent*, ait: *Reus est, qui cum altero litem contestatam habet, sive is egit, sive cum eo actum est. Reus stipulando est idem qui stipulator dicitur, quive suo nomine ab altero quid stipulatus est, non is qui alteri adstipulatus est. Reus promittendo est qui suo nomine alteri quid promisit, non qui pro altero quid promisit.* At Capito Ateius in eadem quidem opinione est: sed exemplo adjuvat interpretationem. Nam in secunda Tabula secunda lege in qua scriptum est: *si quid horum fuat unum judici arbitrove reove eo die diffensus esto*, hic uterque, actor reusque, in judicio rei vocantur, itemque accusator de via citur more vetere et consuetudine antiqua." Ulpian. L. lxxiv. *ad Edict.:* " Si quis judicio se sisti promiserit, et valetudine vel tempestate vel vi fluminis prohibitus se sistere non possit, exceptione adjuvatur; nec immerito: cum enim in tali permissione præsentia opus sit, quemadmodum potuit se sistere qui adversa valetudine impeditus est? Et ideo etiam Lex XII. Tab.: *si judex vel alteruter ex litigatoribus morbo sontico impediatur, jubet diem judicii esse diffensum.*" I have restored *diffensus* both in Festus and Ulpian on the authority of Müller, who has shewn (*Suppl. Annot. ad Fest.* p. 401) that *fendo* must have been anciently a synonyme of *ferio* and *trudo*, and consequently that *diffensus esto = differatur.*

Fr. 3 (ii. 3): CUI . TESTIMONIUM . DEFUERIT, . IS . TERTIIS . DIEBUS . OB . PORTUM . OBVAGULATUM . ITO . (Fest. p. 233: "*Portum* in XII. pro *domo* positum omnes fere

consentiunt: si," &c.   Id. p. 375: " *Vagulatio* in lege XII.
[Tab.] significat *quæstionem cum convicio: si*," &c.).

Fr. 4 (ii. 12). " Nam et de furto pacisci lex permittit"
(L. 7. § 14. D. *de Pactis*, Ulp. iv. *ad Edictum*).

TAB. III.

§ 9. Fr. 1 (iii. 4): AERIS . CONFESSI . REBUSQUE . JURE .
Tab. III. JUDICATIS . TRIGINTA . DIES . JUSTI . SUNTO . (Aul. Gell.
xx. c. 1: " Eosque dies Decemviri justos appellaverunt,
velut quoddam justitium, id est juris inter eos quasi interstitionem quandam et cessationem, quibus diebus nihil cum
his agi jure posset." xv. c. 13; cf. Gaius, *Institut.* iii.
§ 78, &c.).

Fr. 2 (iii. 5): POST . DEINDE . MANUS . INJECTIO . ESTO ; .
IN . JUS . DUCITO . (Aul. Gell. xx. c. 1; cf. Gaius, *Inst.* iv.
§ 21).

Fr. 3 (iii. 6): NI . JUDICATUM . FACIT (l. *faxsit*), . AUT .
QUIPS . ENDO . EM . JURE . VINDICIT, . SECUM . DUCITO ; .
VINCITO, . AUT . NERVO . AUT . COMPEDIBUS, . QUINDECIM .
PONDO . NE . MAJORE, . AUT . SI . VOLET . MINORE . VINCITO .
(Aul. Gell. xx. c. 1). We should perhaps read *faxsit* for
facit on account of *vindicit*, for which see Müller, *Suppl.
Ann. ad Fest.* p. 393. For the form *quips* see Gronovius
ad Gell. l.; the proper reading is *ques;* see below, § 23.
For the meaning of *nervus* here comp. Fest. s. v. p. 765.

Fr. 4 (iii. 7): SI . VOLET, . SUO . VIVITO ; . NI . SUO .
VIVIT, . QUI . EM . VINCTUM . HABEBIT, . LIBRAS . FARRIS .
ENDO . DIES . DATO ; . SI . VOLET . PLUS . DATO . (Aul. Gell.
xx. c. 1; and for the meaning of *vivere* compare L. 234,
§ 2. D. *de Verb. Sign.;* Gaius, L. ii. *ad Leg.* XII. *Tab.;*
Donat. *ad Terent. Phorm.* ii. 1, 20). The student will observe that *endo dies* = *indies*.

Fr. 5 (iii. 8). Aul. Gell. *N. A.* xx. 1: " Erat autem jus
interea paciscendi; ac nisi pacti forent, habebantur in vinculis, dies LX.; inter eos dies trinis nundinis continuis ad

Prætorem in comitium producebantur, quantæque pecuniæ judicati essent prædicabatur." From which Ursinus conjectures: *Endoderatim* [rather *interatim*. Festus, p. 111] *pacio estod. Nei cum eo pacit,* XL. *dies vinctom habetod. In ieis diebus tertieis nondineis continueis indu comitium endo joure im procitato, quanteique stlis æstumata siet prædicato.*

Fr. 6 (iii. 9). Aul. Gell. xx. 1: " Tertiis autem nundinis capite pœnas dabant, aut trans Tiberim peregre venum ibant—si plures forent, quibus reus esset judicatus, secare si vellent atque partiri corpus addicti sibi hominis permiserunt—verba ipsa Legis dicam:—TERTIIS, inquit, NUNDINIS PARTIS SECANTO, SI PLUS MINUSVE SECUERUNT, SE FRAUDE ESTO." Cf. Quinctil. *Inst. Or.* iii. c. 6; Tertullian. *Apol.* c. 4. The student will remark that we have here *se* for *sine*, as in the compounds *se-dulo* (= *sine dolo*), *se-paro*, *se-cludo*, &c.

Fr. 7 (iii. 3): ADVERSUS . HOSTEM . AETERNA . AUCTORITAS . (Cic. *de Off.* i. c. 12).

TAB. IV.

Fr. 1 (iv. 1). Cic. *de Legg.* iii. c. 8: " Deinde quum [Trib. pot. ortus] esset cito legatus [*leto datus*, Orelli], tamquam ex XII. Tabulis insignis ad deformitatem puer." From whence we infer that the XII. Tables authorised the exposure of deformed children.

Fr. 2 (iv. 2). From the statement of Dionysius (ii. 26, 27), that the decemvirs in their fourth Table continued the *jus vendendorum liberorum* established in the time of the kings, Ursinus imagines some such passage as this: PATREI . ENDO . FIDIO . VITAE . NECISQUE . POTESTAS . ESTOD, . TERQUE . IN . VENOM . DARIER . JOUS . ESTOD; to which he appends the next fragment.

Fr. 3 (iv. 3): SI . PATER . FILIUM . TER . VENUM . DUIT, . FILIUS . A . PATRE . LIBER . ESTO . (Ulpian, *Fr. Tit.* x. § 1; Gaius, *Inst.* i. § 132; iv. § 79).

Fr. 4 (iv. 4). Aul. Gell. iii. 16: ... " Quoniam Decemviri in decem mensibus gigni hominem, non in undecimo scripsissent;" whence Gothofredus would restore: *si qui ei in* x. *mensibus proximis postumus natus escit, justus esto.*

Tab. V.

§ 11.
Tab. V.

Fr. 1. Gaius, *Inst.* i. § 145: " Loquimur autem exceptis Virginibus Vestalibus, quas etiam veteres in honorem sacerdotii liberas esse voluerunt; itaque etiam lege xii. Tabularum cautum est." Cf. Plutarch, *Vit. Num.* c. 10.

Fr. 2. Id. ii. § 47 : " (Item olim) mulieris quæ in agnatorum tutela erat, res mancipi usucapi non poterant, præterquam si ab ipso tutore (*auctore*) traditæ essent: id ita lege xii. Tabularum cautum erat."

Fr. 3 (v. 1): [PATERFAMILIAS] . UTI . LEGASSIT . SUPER . PECUNIA . TUTELAVE . SUAE . REI, . ITA . JUS . ESTO . (Ulpian, *Fr. Tit.* xi. § 14; Gaius, *Inst.* ii. § 224; Cic. *de Invent. Rhet.* ii. c. 50; Novell. *Justin.* xxii. c. 2, &c.)

Fr. 4 (v. 2): SI . INTESTATO . MORITUR . CUI . SUUS . HERES . NEC . SIT, . ADGNATUS . PROXIMUS . FAMILIAM . HABETO. (Ulpian, *Fr. Tit.* xxvi. § 1; cf. Gaius, *Inst.* iii. § 9, &c.)

Fr. 5 (v. 3): SI . ADGNATUS . NEC . ESCIT, . GENTILIS . FAMILIAM . NANXITOR. (*Collatio Legg. Mosaic. et Rom. Tit.* xvi. § 4; cf. Gaius, *Inst.* iii. § 17.) I have written *nanxitor* for *nancitor* on the authority of Müller, *ad Fest.* p. 166, " *nanxitor* in xii., nactus erit, præhenderit;" where he remarks, " *nancitor* quomodo futurum exactum esse possit, non intelligo, nisi correcta una littera. Ab antiquo verbo *nancio* fut. ex. fit *nanxo*, sicut a capio capso; idque translatum in pass. form. efficit *nanxitur* vel *nanxitor*, ut a turbasso fit turbassitur."

Fr. 6 (v. 7). Gaius, *Inst.* i. § 155: " Quibus testamento quidem tutor datus non sit, iis ex lege xii. agnati sunt tutores; qui vocantur legitimi." Cf. § 157, where he says that this applied to women also.

Fr. 7 (v. 8): SI . FURIOSUS . AUT . PRODIGUS . ESCIT, . AST . EI . CUSTOS . NEC . ESCIT, . ADGNATORUM . GENTILIUMQUE . IN . EO . PEQVUNIAQUE . EJUS . POTESTAS . ESTO. (Cicer. *de Invent. Rhet.* ii. c. 50, gives the bulk of this passage; *aut prodigus* is inserted on the authority of Ulpian, § 3, i. *de Curationibus;* and *ast ei custos nec escit* is derived from Festus, p. 162 : "*Nec* conjunctionem grammatici fere dicunt esse disjunctivam, ut *nec legit nec scribit,* cum si diligentius inspiciatur, ut fecit Sinnius Capito, intelligi possit eam positam esse ab antiquis pro *non,* ut et in XII. est: *ast ei custos nec escit.*") For *nec* see above, Ch. III. § 9, and below, Ch. VII. § 5.

Fr. 8 (v. 4). Ulpian, *Frag. Tit.* xxix. § 1 ; *L.* 195, § 1. D. *de Verb. Sign.:* " Civis Romani liberti hereditatem lex XII. Tab. patrono defert, si intestato sine suo herede libertus decesserit—Lex: EX EA FAMILIA, inquit, IN EAM FAMILIAM." Gothofredus proposes the following restoration of the law: *si libertus intestato moritur cui suus heres nec escit, ast patronus patronive liberi escint, ex ea familia in eam familiam proximo pecunia adduitor.*

Fr. 9 (v. 5) and 10 (v. 6). From the numerous passages which refer the law *de ercti-ciscunda* (as the word must have been originally written) *familia* to the XII. Tables (see Hugo, *Gesch. d. Röm. R.* i. p. 229), we may perhaps suppose the law to have been: *si heredes partem quisque suam habere malint, familiæ ercti-ciscundæ tris arbitros sumunto.*

TAB. VI.

Fr. 1 (vi. 1): CUM . NEXUM . FACIET . MANCIPIUMQUE, . UTI . LINGUA . NUNCUPASSIT, . ITA . JUS . ESTO. (Festus, p. 173; Cic. *de Off.* iii. 16, *de Orator.* i. 57.) *Nuncupare* =*nominare:* Festus, l. l.; Varro, *L. L.* vi. § 60, p. 95, Müller.

Fr. 2 (vi. 2). Cic. *de Offic.* iii. 16 : " Nam cum ex XII. Tabulis satis esset *ea præstari quæ essent lingua nuncupata, quæ qui infitiatus esset dupli pœnam subiret;* a jureconsultis etiam reticentiæ pœna est constituta."

Fr. 3 (vi. 5). Cic. *Topic.* c. 4 : " Quod in re pari valet, valeat in hac, quæ par est; ut: *Quoniam usus auctoritas fundi biennium est, sit etiam ædium:* at in lege ædes non appellantur, et sunt *ceterarum rerum omnium, quarum annuus est usus.*" Cf. Cic. *pro Cæcina,* c. 19 ; Gaius, *Instit.* ii. § 42 ; and Boethius *ad Top.* l. c. p. 509, Orelli.

Fr. 4 (vi. 6). Gaius, *Inst.* i. § 111 : "Usu in manum conveniebat, quæ anno continuo nupta perseverabat :—itaque lege XII. Tab. cautum [erat], *si qua nollet eo modo in manum mariti conve*[nire, ut quotan]*nis trinoctio abesset, atque* [ita usum] *cujusque anni interrumperet.*" Cf. Aul. Gell. iii. 2 ; Macrob. *Saturn.* i. 3.

Fr. 5 (vi. 7) : SI . QUI . IN . JURE . MANUM . CONSERUNT. (Aul. Gell. xx. c. 10).

Fr. 6 (vi. 8). From Liv. iii. 44, Dionys. Hal. xi. c. 30, &c., we may infer a law : *prætor secundum libertatem vindicias dato.*

Fr. 7 (vi. 9) : TIGNUM . JUNCTUM . AEDIBUS . VINEAEVE, . E . CONCAPITE . NE . SOLVITO . (Fest. p. 364). A great number of emendations of this passage have been proposed. The reading which I have adopted is the same as Müller's, except that I prefer *concapite* to his *concape :* compare *procapis=progenies,* " quæ ab uno capite procedit" (Fest. p. 225). In the same way as we have *capes, capitis* m.= *miles; caput, capitis* n.=*vertex;* so we have *concapis, concapitis* f.=*continua capitum junctura.* (Comp. Madvig, *Beilage zu seiner Latein. Sprachl.* p. 33.)

Fr. 8 (vi. 10). L. 1. *pr. D. de tigno juncto,* Ulpian, L. xxxvii. *ad Edictum :* " Quod providenter lex [XII. Tab.] effecit, ne vel ædificia sub hoc prætextu diruantur, vel vinearum cultura turbetur ; sed in eum qui convictus est junxisse, in duplum dat actionem." Where *tignum* is defined as signifying in the xii. Tables: *omnis materia ex qua ædificium constet, vineæque necessaria.*

Fr. 9 (vi. 11): QUANDOQUE . SARPTA, . DONEC . DEMPTA . ERUNT . (Fest. p. 384). The word *sarpta* (which Müller understands of the *ipsa sarpta*, i. e. *sarmenta putata*) is explained by Festus, l. l. : " *sarpiuntur* vineæ, i. e. putantur," &c. p. *322* : " [sarpta vinea putata, i.] e. pura [facta —] inde etiam [sarmenta script]ores dici pu[tant; sarpere enim a]ntiqui pro pur[gare dicebant]." The sentence in the fragment probably ended with *vindicare jus esto.*

Tab. VII.

Fr. 1 (viii. 1). Varro, *L. L.* v. § 22, p. 9: " *Ambitus* est quod circumeundo teritur, nam *ambitus* circumitus, ab eoque xii. Tabularum interpretes *ambitum* parietis circumitum esse describunt." Volusius Mæcianus, apud Gronov. *de Sestertio*, p. 398: " *Sestertius* duos asses et semissem. Lex etiam xii. Tabularum argumento est, in qua duo pedes et semis *sestertius pes* vocatur." Festus, p. 16 (cf. p. 5) : " *Ambitus* proprie dicitur inter vicinorum ædificia locus duorum pedum et semipedis ad circumeundi facultatem relictus." The law itself, therefore, probably ran thus: *inter vicinorum ædificia ambitus parietum sestertius pes esto.*

Fr. *2* (viii. 3). Gaius (lib. iv. *ad Leg.* xii. *Tab. L. fin. D. finium regundorum*) refers to a law of Solon, which he quotes in Greek, and describes as in some measure the type of the corresponding law of the xii. Tables, which regulates digging, fencing, and building near the borders of a piece of ground.

Fr. 3 (viii. 6): HORTUS — HEREDIUM — TUGURIUM (Plin. *H. N.* xix. 4, § 1: " In xii. Tab. leg. nostrar. nusquam nominatur *villa;* semper in significatione ea *hortus,* in *horti* vero *heredium.*" Festus, p. 355: " [*Tugu-*]*ria* a tecto appellantur [domicilia rusticorum] sordida—quo nomine [Messalla in explana]tione xii. ait etiam .... significari.") Properly speaking, the *vicus* (signifying " several houses joined together") included the *villa* (= *vicula*, Döderl. *Syn. u. Et.* iii. 5), which was the residence of the proprietor, and the adjoining *tuguria*, in which the *coloni partiarii* lived. All persons living in the same *vicus* were called *vicini*; and the first fragment in this table refers to the *ambitus* between the houses of those who lived on the same estate. The pasture-land left common to the *vicini* was called *compascuus ager* (Festus, p. 40). It is not improbable that the words *compescere* and *impescere* occurred in the xii. Tables. See, however, Dirksen, p. 534. *Ager* is defined as "locus qui sine villa est" (Ulpian, L. 27. *Pr. D. de V. S.*). But in a remarkable passage in Festus (p. 371), the *vicus* is similarly described in its opposition to the *villa* or *prædium*. The passage is as follows (see Müller, *Suppl. Ann.* p. 413): " Vici appellari incipiunt ab agris, [et sunt eorum hominum,] qui ibi villas non habent, ut Marsi aut Peligni, sed ex vicis partim habent rempublicam, [ubi] et jus dicitur, partim nihil eorum, et tamen ibi nundinæ aguntur negotii gerendi causa, et magistri vici, item magistri pagi, [in iis] quotannis fiunt. Altero, cum id genus officiorum [significatur], quæ continentia sunt in oppidis, quæve itineribus regionibusve distributa inter se distant, nominibusque dissimilibus discriminis causa sunt dispartita. Tertio, cum id genus ædificiorum definitur, quæ in oppido prive, id est in suo quisque loco proprio, ita ædificat, ut in eo ædificio pervium sit, quo itinere habitatores ad suam quisque habitationem habeat accessum: qui non dicuntur vicani, sicut ii, qui aut in oppidi vicis, aut ii, qui in agris sunt, vicani appellantur." Festus here describes (1) the *vicus rusticus*, (2) a street in a town, as the *vicus Cyprius*, and (3) a particular kind of insulated house (*insula*) in the city.

Fr. 4 and 5 (viii. 4, 5). Cicero *de Legg.* i. c. 21:

" Usucapionem XII. Tabulæ intra quinque pedes esse noluerunt." Non. Marcell. *de Propr. Serm.* c. 5, § 34, quotes, as the words of the law: SI JURGANT. " *Si jurgant*, inquit. Benevolorum concertatio non *lis*, ut inimicorum, sed *jurgium* dicitur." Ursinus supposes the law to have been: *si vicini inter se jurgassint, intra* V. *pedes usucapio ne esto.*

Fr. 6 (viii. 10). L. 8. D. *de Servit. Præd. Rustic.:* " Viæ latitudo ex lege XII. Tab. in porrectum octo pedes habet; in anfractum, id est, ubi flexum est, sedecim." Varro, *L. L.* vii. § 15, p. 124: "*Anfractum* est flexum, ab origine duplici dictum, ab ambitu et frangendo; ab eo leges jubent, in directo pedum VIII. esse, in anfracto XVI., id est in flexu."

Fr. 7 (viii. 11). Cicero *pro Cæcina*, c. 19: " Si via sit immunita, jubet (lex), qua velit agere jumentum." Cf. Festus, p. 21, s. v. *Amsegetes*. Müller and Huschke express their surprise that Dirksen and other learned jurists should have overlooked the passage in Festus, which contains the best materials for the restoration of this law. Festus (s. v. *Viæ*, p. 371) says: " Viæ sunt et publicæ, per [quas ire, agere veher]e omnibus licet: privatæ quibus [vehiculum immittere non licet] præter, eorum quorum sunt privatæ. [In XII. est: AMSEGETES] VIAS MUNIUNTO, DONICUM LAPIDES ESCUNT: [NI MUNIERINT,] QUA VOLET JUMENTA AGITO." See Müller, *Suppl. Annot.* p. 414.

Fr. 8 (viii. 9). L. 5. D. *ne quid in l. publ.* Paulus, Lib. xvi. *ad Sabinum:* " Si per publicum locum rivus aquæductus privato nocebit, erit actio privato ex lege XII. Tab. ut noxæ domino caveatur." L. 21. D. *de Statuliber.* Pompon. L. vii. *ex Plautio:* SI . AQUA . PLUVIA . NOCET.

Fr. 9 (viii. 7). L. 1, § 8. D. *de Arboribus cædend.* Ulp. L. lxxi. *ad Edict.:* " Lex XII. Tab. efficere voluit, ut xv. pedes altius rami arboris circumcidantur." From which, and Festus, p. 348, it is proposed to restore the law: *si*

M

arbor in vicini agrum impendet, altius a terra pedes xv. *sublucator.*

Fr. 10 (viii. 8). Plin. *H. N.* xvi. c. 5: " Cautum est præterea lege xii. Tab., ut glandem in alienum fundum procidentem liceret colligere." The English law makes a similar provision respecting rabbit-burrows.

Fr. 11 (vi. 4). § 1, 41, i. *de Rer. Divis.:* " Venditæ vero res et traditæ non aliter emptori adquiruntur, quam si is venditori pretium solverit, vel alio modo satisfecerit, veluti expromissore, aut pignore dato. Quod cavetur quidem et lege xii. Tab., tamen recte dicitur et jure gentium, i. e. jure naturali, effici."

Fr. 12 (vi. 3). Ulpian, *Fr.* tit. 2, § 4 : " Sub hac conditione liber esse jussus, si decem millia heredi dederit, etsi ab herede abalienatus sit, emptori dando pecuniam, ad libertatem perveniet: idque lex xii. Tab. jubet." Cf. Fest. s. v. *Statuliber.* p. 314.

Tab. VIII.

§ 14.
Tab. VIII.

Fr. 1 (viii. 8). Cic. *de Republ.* iv. 10: " Nostræ xii. Tabulæ, quum perpaucas res capite sanxissent, in his hanc quoque sanciendam putaverunt: *si quis occentavisset, sive carmen condidisset, quod infamiam faceret flagitiumve alteri.*" Festus, p. 181: " *Occentassint* antiqui dicebant quod nunc *convitium fecerint* dicimus, quod id clare, et cum quodam canore fit, ut procul exaudiri possit. Quod turpe habetur, quia non sine causa fieri putatur. Inde cantilenam dici querellam, non cantus jucunditatem puto." Plautus, *Curcul.* i. 2, 57; Horat. ii. *Serm.* 1, 80; ii. *Epist.* 1, 152. Gothofredus would restore the law thus: *si quis pipulo* (= *ploratu,* Fest. p. 253; cf. p. 212, s. v. *pipatio*) *occentassit, carmenve condidisset,* &c. *fuste ferito.*

Fr. 2 (vii. 9): si . membrum . rupit . ni . cum . eo . pacit, . talio . esto. (Fest. p. 363: " Permittit lex parem vindictam." Aul. Gell. xx. 1; Gaius, *Inst.* iii. § 223).

Fr. 3 (vii. 10). Gaius, *Inst.* iii. § 223 : " Propter os vero fractum aut conlisum ccc. assium pœna erat (ex lege XII. Tab.), velut si libero os fractum erat; at si servo, CL." Cf. Aul. Gell. xx. 1.

Fr. 4 (vii. 7): SI . INJURIAM . FAXIT . ALTERI, . VIGINTI . QUINQUE . AERIS . POENAE . SUNTO . (Aul. Gell. xx. 1; cf. Gaius, *Inst.* iii. § 223). Fest. p. 371: "*Viginti quinque pœnas* in XII. significat viginti quinque asses." Here *pœnas=poinas* is the old form of the genitive singular and nominative plural.

Fr. 5 (vii. 2): RUPITIAS . [QUI . FAXIT] . SARCITO . (Fest. s. vv. pp. 265, 322) i. e. *qui damnum dederit præstato.*

Fr. 6 (vii. 5). L. 1, pr. D. *si Quadrup. Paup. fec. dic.* Ulp. xviii. *ad Edict.:* " Si quadrupes pauperiem fecisse dicetur, actio ex lege XII. Tab. descendit; quæ lex voluit aut dari id quod nocuit, id est, id animal, quod noxiam commisit, aut æstimationem noxiæ offerre."

Fr. 7 (vii. 5). L. 14, § 3. D. *de Præscr. Verb.:* " Si glans ex arbore tua in meum fundum cadat, eamque ego immisso pecore depascam, Aristo scribit non sibi occurrere legitimam actionem, qua experiri possim, nam neque ex lege XII. Tab. de pastu pecoris, quia non in tuo pascitur, neque de pauperie neque de damni injuriæ agi posse."

Fr. 8 (vii. 3): QUI . FRUGES . EXCANTASSIT . (Plin. *H. N.* xxviii. c. 2). NEVE . ALIENAM . SEGETEM . PELLEXERIS . (Serv. *ad Virg. Ecl.* viii. 99). Cf. Seneca, *Nat. Quæst.* iv. 7, &c.

Fr. 9 (vii. 4). Plin. *H. N.* xviii. c. 3: " Frugem quidem aratro quæsitam furtim noctu pavisse ac secuisse, puberi XII. Tabulis capitale erat, suspensumque Cereri necari jubebant; gravius quam in homicidio convictum: impubem prætoris arbitratu verberari, noxiamque duplione decerni."

Fr. 10 (vii. 6). L. 9. D. *de Incend. Ruina Naufr.* Gaius, iv. *ad* XII. *Tab.:* " Qui *ædes acervumve frumenti* juxta domum positum *combusserit, vinctus verberatus igni necari* jubetur, si modo sciens prudensque id commiserit: si vero *casu,* id est, negligentia, aut *noxiam sarcire* jubetur, aut si minus *idoneus* sit, levius castigatur: appellatione autem *ædium* omnes species ædificii continentur."

Fr. 11 (ii. 11). Plin. *H. N.* xvii. 1: " Fuit et arborum cura legibus priscis; cautumque est xii. Tabulis, ut qui injuria cecidisset alienas, lueret in singulas æris xxv."

Fr. 12 (ii. 4): si . nox . furtum . factum . sit, . si . im . occisit, . jure . caesus . esto . (Macrob. *Saturn.* i. c. 4). Here *nox=noctu;* Aul. Gell. viii. c. 1.

Fr. 13 (ii. 8). L. 54, § 2. d. *de furt.* Gaius, Lib. xiii. *ad Edict. Provinc.:* " Furem interdiu deprehensum non aliter occidere lex xii. Tab. permisit, quam si telo se defendat."

Fr. 14 (ii. 5-7). Aul. Gell. xi. c. 18: " Ex ceteris autem manifestis furibus liberos verberari addicique jusserunt (decemviri) ei, cui factum furtum esset, si modo id luci fecissent, neque se telo defendissent: servos item furti manifesti prensos verberibus affici et e saxo præcipitari; sed pueros impuberes prætoris arbitratu verberari voluerunt, noxamque ab his factam sarciri." Cf. Gaius, iii. § 189. For the last part, cf. Fr. 9.

Fr. 15 (ii. 9). Gaius, *Inst.* iii. § 191, 192: " Concepti et oblati (furti) poena ex lege xii. Tab. tripli est,—præcipit (lex) ut qui quærere velit, nudus quærat linteo cinctus, lancem habens; qui si quid invenerit, jubet id lex furtum manifestum esse." Cf. Aul. Gell. xi. 18, xvi. 10.

Fr. 16 (ii. 10): si . adorat . furto . quod . nec . manifestum . escit . (Fest. p. 162. Gaius, *Inst.* iii. § 190: " Nec manifesti furti per leg. xii. Tab. dupli irrogatur"). For the use of *adoro,* see Fest. p. 19: " *Adorare* apud antiquos significabat *agere,* unde et legati *oratores* dicuntur, quia mandata populi *agunt :*" add, Fest. s. v. *oratores,* p. 182; Varro, *L. L.* vi. § 76, vii. § 41, &c.

Fr. 17 (ii. 13). Gaius, *Inst.* ii. § 45: " Furtivam (rem) lex xii. Tab. usucapi prohibet."

Fr. 18 (iii. 2). Cato, *R. R. prooem.*: " Majores nostri sic habuerunt, itaque in legibus posuerunt, furem dupli damnari, foeneratorem quadrupli." Tacit. *Annal.* vi. 16: " Nam primo xii. Tabulis sanctum, ne quis unciario foenere amplius exerceret." See Niebuhr, *H. R.* iii. 50, sqq., who has proved that the *foenus unciarium* was $\frac{1}{12}$ of the principal, *i. e.* $8\frac{1}{3}$ per cent for the old year of ten months, and therefore 10 per cent for the civil year.

Fr. 19 (iii. 1). Paulus, *Rec. Sent.* ii. tit. 12, § 11: " Ex causa depositi lege xii. Tab. in duplum actio datur."

Fr. 20 (vii. 16). L. i. § 2. D. *de suspect. Tutoribus:* " Sciendum est suspecti crimen e lege xii. Tab. descendere." L. 55, § 1. D. *de Admin. et Peric. Tutor.:* " Sed si ipsi tutores rem pupilli furati sunt, videamus, an ea actione, quæ proponitur ex lege xii. Tab. adversus tutorem in duplum, singuli in solidum teneantur."

Fr. 21 (vii. 17): PATRONUS . SI . CLIENTI . FRAUDEM . FECERIT . SACER . ESTO . (Servius, on Virgil's words, *Æneid.* vi. 609: " pulsatusve parens, et fraus innexa clienti"). I can suppose that the original had *fraudem frausus siet:* see Festus, p. 91, and Gronov. *Lect. Plaut.* p. 33, *ad Asin.* ii. 2, 20.

Fr. 22 (vii. 11): QUI . SE . SIERIT . TESTARIER, . LIBRIPENSVE . FUERIT, . NI . TESTIMONIUM . FARIATUR(?), . IMPROBUS . INTESTABILISQUE . ESTO . (Aul. Gell. xv. 13).

Fr. 23 (vii. 12). Aul. Gell. xx. 1: " An putas, si non illa ex xii. Tab. de testimoniis falsis poena abolevisset, et si nunc quoque, ut antea, qui falsum testimonium dixisse convictus esset, e saxo Tarpeio dejiceretur, mentituros fuisse pro testimonio tam multos quam videmus ?"

Fr. 24 (vii. 13). Pliny, in the passage quoted in Fr. 9, implies that involuntary homicide was but slightly punished. The fine in such a case seems to have been a ram

(Serv. *ad Virg. Ecl.* iv. 43); and the law has been restored thus (with the help of Cic. *de Orat.* iii. 39, *Top.* 17): *si quis hominem liberum dolo sciens morti dedit, parricida esto: at si telum manu fugit pro capite occisi et natis ejus arietem subjicito.*

Fr. 25 (vii. 14). From Plin. *H. N.* xxviii. 2, and L. 236, pr. D. *de Verb. Sign.*, the following law has been restored: QUI . MALUM . CARMEN . INCANTASSIT . [CERERI . SACER . ESTO]. [QUI] . MALUM . VENENUM . [FAXIT . DUITVE . PARRICIDA . ESTO].

Fr. 26 (ix. 6). Porcius Latro, *Declam. in Catilin.* c. 19: " Primum XII. Tabulis cautum esse cognoscimus, *ne quis in urbe cœtus nocturnos agitaret.*" Which Ursinus restores thus: *qui calim endo urbe nox coit, coiverit, capital estod.*

Fr. 27 (viii. 2). L. 4. D. *de Colleg. et Corporibus:* " Sodales sunt, qui ejusdem collegii sunt; quam Græci ἑταιρίαν vocant. His autem potestatem facit lex, pactionem quam velint sibi ferre, dum ne quid ex publica lege corrumpant."

Tab. IX.

§ 15.
Tab. IX.

Fr. 1 (ix. 1). Cicero *pro Domo*, c. 17: " Vetant XII. Tabulæ leges privis hominibus irrogari."

Fr. 2 (ix. 4). Cicero *de Legibus*, iii. 19: " Tum leges præclarissimæ de XII. Tabulis translatæ duæ: quarum . . . altera de capite civis rogari, nisi maximo comitatu, vetat." Cf. Cicero *pro Sextio*, c. 30.

Fr. 3 (ix. 3). Aul. Gell, xx. 1: " Dure autem scriptum esse in istis legibus (sc. XII. Tab.) quid existimari potest? nisi duram esse legem putas, quæ judicem arbitrumve jure datum, qui ob rem dicendam pecuniam accepisse convictus est, capite pœnitur." Cf. Cicero, *Verr. Act.* ii. lib. ii. c. 32.

Fr. 4 (ix. 5). L. 2, § 23. D. *de Orig. Jur.:* " Quæstores constituebantur a populo, qui capitalibus rebus præessent: hi appellabantur *Quæstores parricidii;* quorum etiam meminit lex XII. Tabularum." Cicero *de Republ.* ii. 31: " Provocationem autem etiam a regibus fuisse declarant pontificii libri, significant nostri etiam augurales; itemque ab omni judicio pœnaque provocari licere, indicant XII. Tabulæ compluribus legibus." See above, p. 147.

Fr. 5 (ix. 7). L. 3, pr. D. *ad Leg. Jul. Majestat.:* " Lex XII. Tab. jubet eum qui hostem concitaverit, quive hosti civem tradiderit, capite puniri."

Tab. X.

Fr. 1 (x. 2): HOMINEM . MORTUUM . IN . URBE . NE . SEPELITO . NEVE . URITO . (Cicero *de Legibus,* ii. 23).

Fr. 2 (x. 4, 5): HOC . PLUS . NE . FACITO . — ROGUM . ASCIA . NE . POLITO . (id. ibid).

Fr. 3 and 4 (x. 6, 7): " Extenuato igitur sumtu, tribus riciniis, et vinclis purpuræ, et decem tibicinibus tollit (lex XII. Tab.) etiam lamentationem: MULIERES . GENAS . NE . RADUNTO; . NEVE . LESSUM . FUNERIS . ERGO . HABENTO ." (id. ibid). For *ricinium* (=*vestimentum quadratum*) see Fest. s. v. p. 274, and for *radere genas* (=*unguibus lacerare malas*), id. p. 273. From Servius *ad Æn.* xii. 606, it would appear that the full fragment would be, *mulieres genas ne radunto, faciem ne carpunto,* &c.

Fr. 5 (x. 8): " Cetera item funebria, quibus luctus augetur, XII. sustulerunt: HOMINI, . inquit, MORTUO . NE . OSSA . LEGITO, . QUO . POST . FUNUS . FACIAT . Excipit bellicam peregrinamque mortem" (Cic. *de Leg.* ii. 24).

Fr. 6 (x. 9, 10): " Hæc præterea sunt in legibus de unctura, quibus SERVILIS . UNCTURA . tollitur, omnisque CIRCUMPOTATIO: quæ et recte tolluntur, neque tollerentur nisi fuissent. NE . SUMTUOSA . RESPERSIO; . NE . LONGAE . CORONAE, . NEC . ACERRAE . prætereantur" (Cic. *de Legibus,* ii. 24). For *acerra* see Fest. p. 18: " *Acerra* ara quæ ante mortuum poni solebat, in qua odores incendebant. Alii dicunt arculam esse thurariam, scilicet ubi thus reponebant." Festus, s. v. *Murrata potione* (p. 158), seems also to refer to this law, which, according to Gothofredus, ran thus: *Servilis unctura omnisque circumpotatio auferitor. Murrata potio mortuo ne inditor. Ne longæ coronæ, neve acerræ præferuntor.*

Fr. 7 (x. 11): QUI . CORONAM . PARIT . IPSE, . PECUNIAVE . EJUS, . VIRTUTIS . ERGO . DUITOR . EI . (Plin. *H. N.* xxi. 3; cf. Cic. *de Leg.* ii. 24).

Fr. 8 (x. 12). Cic. *de Leg.* ii. 24: " Ut uni plura (funera) fierent, lectique plures sternerentur, id quoque ne fieret *lege* sancitum est."

Fr. 9 (x. 13): NEVE . AURUM . ADDITO . QUOI . AURO . DENTES . VINCTI . ESCUNT, . AST . IM . CUM . ILLO . SEPELIRE . UREREVE . SE . FRAUDE . ESTO . (Cic. *de Leg.* ii. 24). *Se,* it need hardly be observed, is an old particle equivalent in meaning to *sine.* They both spring from the same pronominal root, and are distinguished only by case-endings, which are often convergent in signification. *Se* = *sed* is an ablative form, which in later Latin appears only in composition (*se-motus, se-gregatus, se-dulus,* &c. *Sine* accords in form with the Sanscrit instrumental, and was used as a separate preposition to the latest period of the language. The same is the case with the Greek κά and κατά; the former being used only in composition in later Greek (as κάπετον, Pind. *O.* viii. 38), while the latter retains to the end its regular prepositional functions.

Fr. 10 (x. 14). Id. ibid.: " Rogum bustumve novum vetat (lex XII. Tab.) propius LX. pedes adici ædeis alienas, invito domino."

Fr. 11 (x. 15). Id. ibid.: " Quod autem FORUM, id est vestibulum sepulchri, BUSTUMVE . USUCAPI . vetat (lex XII. Tab.) tuetur jus sepulchrorum." Comp. Festus, s. v. *Forum,* p. 84.

Tab. XI.

Fr. 1 (xi. 2). Liv. iv. c. 4: "Hoc ipsum, *ne connubium patribus cum plebe esset*, non Decemviri tulerunt?" Cf. Dion. Hal. x. c. 60, xi. c. 28.

§ 17. Tab. XI.

Tab. XII.

Fr. 1 (xii. 1). Gaius, *Inst.* iv. § 28: "Lege autem introducta est pignoris capio, velut lege XII. Tab. adversus eum, qui hostiam emisset, nec pretium redderet; item adversus eum, qui mercedem non redderet pro eo jumento, quod quis ideo locasset, ut inde pecuniam acceptam in dapem, id est in sacrificium, inpenderet."

§ 18. Tab. XII.

Fr. 2 (xii. 4): "In lege antiqua, si servus sciente domino furtum fecit, vel aliam noxiam commisit, servi nomine actio est noxalis, nec dominus suo nomine tenetur. SI . SERVUS . FURTUM . FAXIT, . NOXIAMVE . NOCUIT." (L. ii. § 1. D. *de Noxal. Actionibus*).

Fr. 3 (xii. 3): SI . VINDICIAM . FALSAM . TULIT, . STLITIS . [ET . VINDICIARUM . PRAE]TOR . ARBITROS . TRES . DATO, . EORUM . ARBITRIO . [POSSESSOR sive REUS] . FRUCTUS . DUPLIONE . DAMNUM . DECIDITO . (Festus, s. v. *Vindiciæ*, p. 376. I have introduced the corrections and additions of Müller). Cf. Theodos. *Cod.* iv. 18, 1.

Fr. 4 (xii. 2). L. 3. D. *de Litigios.*: "Rem, de qua controversia est, prohibemur in sacrum dedicare; alioquin dupli pœnam patimur."

Fr. 5 (xi. 1). Liv. vii. 17: "In XII. Tabulis legem esse, ut, quodcunque postremum populus jussisset, id jus ratumque esset."

These remains of the XII. Tables, though referring to an early period of Roman history, are merely quotations, and as such less satisfactory to the philological antiquary than monumental relics even of a later date. The oldest,

§ 19. The Tiburtine Inscription.

however, of these authentic documents is not earlier than the second Samnite war. It is a *senatus-consultum*, " which gives to the Tiburtines the assurance that the senate would receive as true and valid their justification in reply to the charges against their fidelity, and that it had given no credit, even before, to these charges" (Niebuhr, *H. R.* iii. p. 264, tr.).[1] The inscription was engraved on a bronze table, which was found at Tivoli in the sixteenth century, near the site of the Temple of Hercules. About a hundred years ago it was in the possession of the Barberini family, but is now lost; at least, Niebuhr was unable to discover it, though he sought for it in all the Italian collections, into which the lost treasures of the house of Barberini were likely to have found their way. Niebuhr's transcript (from Gruter, p. 499), compared with Haubold's (*Monumenta Legalia*, p. 81), is as follows.

1. *L. Cornelius Cn. F. Praetor Senatum consuluit a. d.* III. *Nonas Maias sub aede Kastorus:*
2. *scribendo adfuerunt A. Manlius A. F. Sex. Julius, Lucius Postumius S.[2] F.*
3. *Quod Teiburtes verba fecerunt,—quibusque de rebus vos purgavistis, ea Senatus*
4. *animum advortit, ita utei aequom fuit: nosque ea ita audiveramus*
5. *ut vos deixsistis vobeis nontiata esse: ea nos animum nostrum*
6. *non indoucebamus ita facta esse propter ea quod scibamus*

---

[1] Visconti supposed that this inscription was not older than the Marsian war; but there can be little doubt that Niebuhr's view is correct: see *Beschreibung der Stadt Rom*, iii. pp. 125, 659.

[2] Niebuhr prefers *L.*

7. *ea vos merito nostro facere non potuisse: neque vos dignos esse,*
8. *quei ea faceretis, neque id vobeis neque rei poplicae vostrae*
9. *oitile esse facere: et postquam vostra verba Senatus audivit,*
10. *tanto magis animum nostrum indoucimus, ita utei ante*
11. *arbitrabamur de eieis rebus af vobeis peccatum non esse.*
12. *Quonque de eieis rebus Senatuei purgatei estis, credimus vosque*
13. *animum vostrum indoucere oportet, item vos populo*
14. *Romano purgatos fore.*

With the exception of a few peculiarities of spelling, as *af* for *ab*, *quonque* for *cumque* (comp. *-cunque*), *deixsistis* for *dixistis*, &c. there is nothing in the phraseology of this inscription which is unclassical or obscure. The expressions *animum advertere*, "to observe," *animum inducere*, "to think," seem to belong to the conventional terminology of those days. After *fecerunt* in l. 3 we ought perhaps to add D. E. R. I. C. *i.e.* "de ea re (*patres*) ita censuerunt" (cf. Cic. *ad Fam.* viii. 8).

§ 20. The epitaphs of the Scipios.

The L. Cornelius, the son of Cnæus, who is mentioned as prætor in this inscription, is the same L. Cornelius Scipio Barbatus, whose sarcophagus is one of the most interesting monuments at Rome. The inscription upon that monument expressly states that he had been prætor. All the extant epitaphs of the Scipios have been given by Bunsen (*Beschreibung der Stadt Rom*, iii. p. 616, sqq.), who does not, however, enter upon any criticism of the text. It will be as well to cite here the three oldest of them, which are composed in the Saturnian metre.

(*a*) Epitaph on L. Cornelius Scipio, who was consul in A.U.C. 456.

Cornelio' Cn. F. Scipio
Cornélius Lúcius | Scípió Barbátus
Gnaívod pátre prognátus | fórtis vír sapiénsque,
Quoíus fórma vírtu|teí paríssuma fúit.
Cònsúl censór Aidílis | quí fúit apúd vos,
Taùrásiá' Cisaúna' | Sámnió' cépit,
Sùbígit ómne Loúcana' | ópsidésque abdoúcit.[1]

(*b*) Epitaph on the son of the above, who was ædile in A.U.C. 466; consul, 494.

L. Cornelio' L. F. Scipio
Aidiles . Cosol . Cesor .
Hònc oíno' ploírumé co|séntiúnt R[ománi]
Duònóro' óptumó' | fúise víro'
Lúciom Scípiónem. | Filiós Barbáti
Cònsól, Censór, Aidíles | híc fuét [apúd vos].
Hèc cépit Córsicá | 'Alería'que úrbe',
Dèdét tempéstatébus | aidé' meréto.[2]

(*c*) Epitaph on the Flamen Dialis P. Scipio, son of the elder Africanus, and adoptive father of the younger.

Queì ápice', insígne diális | fláminís gesístei,
Mòrs pérfecít tua ut éssent | ómniá brévia,
Honos fáma vírtúsque | glória átque ingénium.

---

[1] See Arnold, *History of Rome*, ii. p. 326.

[2] Bunsen, l. l.: "In return for the delivery of his fleet in a storm off Corsica he built the temple of which Ovid speaks (*Fast.* iv. 193):

Te quoque, Tempestas, *meritam* delubra fatemur,
   Quum pene est Corsis diruta classis aquis."

The same passage is quoted by Funccius, *de Origine et Pueritia L. L.* p. 326.

Quíbus sei ín longá licuíset | tíbe útier víta,
Facíle fácteis súperáses | glóriám majórum.
Quà ré lubéns te in grémiu', | Scípio, récipit térra,
Públi, prógnátum | Públió, Cornéli.[1]

It will be observed, that in these interesting monuments we have both that *anusvárah*, or dropping of the final *m*, which led to ecthlipsis (e.g. *duonoro'* for *bonorum*), and also the *visarga*, or evanescence of the nominative *s* (as in *Cornelio* for *Cornelius*). We may remark, too, that *n* seems not to have been pronounced before *s:* thus we have *cosol*, *cesor*, for *consul, censor*, according to the practice of writing *cos.* for *consul* (Diomed. p. 428, Putsch). The phraseology, however, does not differ in any important particulars from the Latin language with which we are familiar.

The metre in which these inscriptions are composed is deserving of notice. That they are written in Saturnian verse has long been perceived; Niebuhr, indeed, thinks that they " are nothing else than either complete nenias, or the beginnings of them" (*H. R.* i. p. 253). It is not, however, so generally agreed how we ought to read and divide the verses. For instance, Niebuhr maintains that *patre*, in *a*, 2, is " beyond doubt an interpolation;" to me it appears necessary to the verse. He thinks that there is no ecthlipsis in *apice'*, *c*, 1; I cannot scan the line without it. These are only samples of the many differences of opinion which might arise upon these short inscriptions: it will therefore, perhaps, be desirable that a few general remarks should be made on the Saturnian metre itself, and that these remarks should be applied to the epitaphs before

---

[1] Bunsen, l.l.: "Cicero bears testimony to the truth of these noble words in his *Cato Maj.* § 11: Quam fuit imbecillus Africani filius, is qui te adoptavit? Quam tenui aut nulla potius valetudine? Quod ni ita fuisset, altera ille exstitisset lumen civitatis; ad paternam enim magnitudinem animi doctrina uberior accesserat."

us, which are the oldest Latin specimens of the Saturnian lay.[1]

That the Saturnian metre was either a native of Italy, or naturalised there at a very early period, has been sufficiently shewn by Mr. Macaulay (*Lays of Ancient Rome*, p. 23). It is, perhaps, not too much to say, that this metre,—which may be defined in its pure form as a brace of trochaic tripodiæ, preceded by an anacrusis,—is the most natural and obvious of all rhythmical intonations. There is no language which is altogether without it; though, of course, it varies in elegance and harmony with the particular languages in which it is found, and with the degree of literary advancement possessed by the poets who have written in it. The Umbrians had this verse as well as the Latins; at least there can be no doubt that the beginning of the vi. Eugubine Table is pervaded by a Saturnian rhythm, though the laws of quantity which the Latins borrowed from the Greeks are altogether neglected in it. The following may serve as a sample:

'Esté perskló aveís a|sériáter enétu.
Pàrfá kurnáse dérsva | peíqu peíca mérstu,
Poei ángla áseriáto est | éso trémnu sérse.

These verses are, in fact, more regular than many of the Latin specimens. The only rule which can be laid down for the genuine Latin Saturnian is, that the *ictus* must occur three times in each member of the verse,[2] and that any *thesis*, except the last, may be omitted (see Müller, *Suppl. Annot. ad Fest.* p. 396). The *anacrusis*, at the beginning of the line, is often necessary in languages which,

---

[1] Livy's transcript of the inscription of T. Quinctius is confessedly imperfect; the historian says: " his *ferme* incisa litteris fuit" (vi. 29).

[2] To this necessity for a triple recurrence of the *ictus* in the genuine Italian metre I would refer the word *tripudium* = *triplex pulsatio*. *Pudio* meant " to strike with the foot," " to spurn" (comp. *re-pudio*).

like the Latin and our own, have but a few words which begin with an ictus. When the Greek metres became established among the Romans, it would seem that the conventional pronunciation of many words was changed to suit the exigencies of the new versification, and no line began with an anacrusis unless it had that commencement in the Greek model: but this seems not to have been the case in the genuine Roman verses, which begin with an unemphatic thesis whenever the convenience of the writer demands such a prefix. We have seen above (§ 2), that the first trochaic tripodia of the Saturnius *cum anacrusi*, and even an amphibrachys (= *trochæus cum anacrusi*[1]),

---

[1] In the common books on metres this would be called a single foot, i. e. an *amphibrachys*. It appears to me that many of the difficulties, which the student has felt in his first attempts to understand the rules of metre, have been occasioned by the practice of inventing names for the residuary forms of common rhythms. Thus, the last state of the logaœdic verse is called a *choriambus*; and the student falls into inextricable confusion when he endeavours to explain to himself the concurrence of choriambi and dactyls in the commonest measures of Horace's odes. Some commentators would persuade us that we are to scan thus: *Mæce|nas atavis | edite reg|ibus;* and *Sic te | diva potens | Cypri*. But how can we connect the rhythm of the choriambus with such a termination? If we examine any of the Glyconics of Sophocles, who was considered a master in this species of verse, we shall observe that his choriambi appear in contact with dactyls and trochees, and not with iambi. Take, for instance, *Œd. Col.* 510, sqq.:

δεινὸν | μὲν τὸ πά|λαι || κείμενον | ἤ||δη κακὸν | ὦ || ξεῖν' ἐπε|γείρειν ||
ὅ|μως δ' ἔρα|μαι πυ|θέσθαι ||
τί | τοῦτο | τᾶς δειλ|αί||ας ἀπό|ρου φα|νείσας ||
ἀλ|γηδόνος | ᾇ ξυν|έστας ||
μὴ | πρὸς ξενί|ας ἀν|οίξῃς ||
τᾶς | σᾶς, πέπον, | ἔργ' ἀν|αιδῆ ||
τό | τοι πολὺ | καὶ || μηδαμὰ | λῆγον ||
χρή|ζω, ξέν', | ὀρθὸν ἄκ|ουσμ' ἀκ|οῦσαι. ||

Here we see that the rhythm is dactylic or trochaic—these two being considered identical in some metrical systems—and that the long syllable after the dactyl is occasionally equivalent to the ictus of the trochee. We may apply the same principle to the choriambic metres in Horace, which differ only in could form a verse. And conversely, if the anacrusis was wanting, the Saturnius could extend itself to a triplet of the number of imperfect trochees which follow the dactyls in this logaœdic rhythm. Thus we have nothing but dactyls in

Sic te | díva po|téns Cypri : ||

we have one imperfect trochee or dactyl in

Sic fra|trés Hele|naé || lúcida | sídera ; ||

and two imperfect feet of the same kind in

Tu ne | quaésie|rís || scíre ne|fás || quém mihi | quém tibi. ||

The cretic bears the same relation to the trochaic dipodia that the choriambus does to the dactylic dipodia, or logaœdic verse; and it was in consequence of this reduction of the trochaic dipodia to the cretic that the ancient writers on music were enabled to find a rhythmical identity between the dactyl and the trochaic dipodia (see Müller, *Liter. of Greece*, i. p. 228). It appears to me that this view of the question is calculated to settle the dispute between those who reject and those who maintain the termination of a line in the middle of a word. If every compound foot is a sort of conclusion to the rhythm, many rhythms must end in the middle of a word; and therefore such a cæsura cannot be in itself objectionable. We can hardly take any strophe in Pindar without finding some illustration of this. As a specimen, I will subjoin the first strophe of the ix. Olympian ode, with its divisions according to the rhythm :

τὸ μὲν | 'Αρχιλό|χου μέ|λος ||
φω|νᾶεν Ὀ|λυμπί|ου || καλλί|νικος ὁ | τριπλό|ος κε|χλαδώς ||
ἄρκε|σε κρόνι|ον παρ' || ὄχθον | ἁγεμο|νεῦσαι ||
κωμά|ζοντι φί|λοις Ἐ||φαρμόσ|τῳ σὺν ἑ|ταίροις ||
ἀλλὰ | νῦν ἑκα|ταβό||λων Μοι|σᾶν ἀπὸ | τόξων ||
Διά τε | φοινι|κοστερό|παν σεμ|νόν τ' ἐπί|νειμαι ||
ἀκρω|τήριον | Ἄλιδος ||
τοι|οῖσδε βέ|λεσσιν ||
τὸ | δή ποτε | Λυδὸς | ἥ||ρως Πέ|λοψ ||
ἐ|ξάρατο | κάλ||λιστον | ἕδνον | Ἱπποδα|μείας. ||

In general, it seems unreasonable to call a number of syllables in which the ictus occurs more than once by the name of "foot" (*pes*); for the foot, so called, is defined by the stamp of the foot which marks the ictus, and therefore, as above suggested, the half-Saturnius would be called *tri-pudium*, because it consisted of three feet. For instance, if 'Αρχιλόχου μέλος had no ictus except on the first and fourth syllables of 'Αρχιλόχου. we might scan it as two dactyls; but if, as the analogy of -νᾶεν Ὀλυμπίου would seem to indicate, it had an ictus on the last syllable of μέλος, we must scan the words as a dactyl + trochee + ictus.

tripodiæ. We have instances of both practices in the old Latin translation of an epigram, which was written, probably by Leonidas of Tarentum, at the dedication of the spoils taken in the battles of Heraclea and Asculum (B.C. 280, 279), and which should be scanned as follows:

*Quì ántedhác invícti | fúvére víri | páter óptime Olýmpi ||
Hòs égo in púgna víci ||
Victúsque súm ab ísdem ||*

Niebuhr suggests (iii. note 841) that the first line is an attempt at an hexameter, and the last two an imitation of the shorter verse; and this remark shews the discernment which is always so remarkable in this great scholar. The author of this translation, which was probably made soon after the original, could not write in hexameter verse, but he represented the hexameter of the original by a lengthened form of the Saturnius, and indicated the two penthemimers of the pentameter by writing their meaning in two truncated Saturnians, taking care to indicate by the *anacrusis* that there was really a break in the rhythm of the original pentameter, although it might be called a single line according to the Greek system of metres.

To return, however, to the epitaphs of the Scipios. The scansion of the lines which I have adopted is sufficiently indicated by the metrical marks placed over the words. It is only necessary to add a few explanatory observations. With the exception of a. 3, b. 3, and c. 7, every line begins with an anacrusis, or unaccentuated thesis; and it seems to be a matter of indifference whether this is one long or two short syllables. The vowel *i* is often pronounced like *y* before a vowel, as in *Lúcyus* (a. 1), *Lúcyom* (b. 3), *dyális* (c. 1), *brévya* (c. 2), *ingényum* (c. 3), *útyer* (c. 4), *grémyu* (c. 6), *Scípyo* (ibid.). And *u* is pronounced like *w* in c. 2. The rules of synalœpha and ecthlipsis are sometimes attended to (as in a. 6), and sometimes neglected

N

(as in b. 5, c. 4). The quantity of *fúisse* and *víro'* in b. 2, may be justified on general principles; for *fuisse* is properly *fuvisse*, and *viro* is written *veiro* in Umbrian. But there is no consistency in the syllabic measurement of the words; for we have *fŭet* in b. 4. *Facile*, in c. 5, makes a thesis in consequence of that short pronunciation which is indicated by the old form *facul* (Fest. p. 87, Müller). As all the other verbs in epitaph *a* are in the perfect tense, it seems that *subigit* and *abdoucit*, in the last line, must be perfect also. *Indoucimus* is perhaps a perfect in the Tiburtine inscription (l. 10): " postquam senatus audivit, tanto magis—*indoucimus;*" and *subigit* was probably pronounced *sŭbĭgĭt*. The beginning of b. seems to have been the conventional phraseology in these monumental nenias. The sepulchre of A. Attilius Calatinus, which stood near those of the Scipios at the *Porta Capena* (Cic. *Tusc. Disp.* i. 7, § 13), bore an inscription beginning in much the same way:

Hŏnc oíno ploírumé co|séntiónt géntes.
Pŏpŭli primárium | fúisse vírum.

(Comp. Cic. *de Finibus*, ii. 35, § 116; *Cato M.* 17, 61).

§ 21.
The *Columna Rostrata*.

The *Columna Rostrata*, as it is called, was found at the foot of the Capitol in the year 1565. Its partial destruction by lightning is mentioned by Livy (xlii. 20); and it was still standing, probably in the existing copy, when Servius wrote (*ad Virgil. Georg.* iii. 29). It refers to the well-known exploits of C. Duilius, who was consul B.C. 260, A.U.C. 494. This inscription, with the supplements of Ciacconi, and a commentary, was published by Funck, in his treatise *de Orig. et Puer. L. L.* p. 302, sqq. It is here given with the restorations of Grotefend (Orelli, no. 549).

[*C. Duilios, M. F. M. N. Consol advorsum Poenos en Siceliad Sicest*]*ano*[*s socios*

Rom. obsidioned crave]*d exemet leciones r*[*e-
fecet dumque Poenei m*]*aximosque macistratos
l*[*ecionumque duceis ex n*]*ovem castreis exfo-
ciunt Macel*[*am opidom opp*]*ucnandod cesset
enque eodem mac*[*istratod bene r*]*em navebos
marid consol primos c*[*eset socios*] *clasesque na-
vales primos ornavet pa*[*ravetque*] *cumque eis
navebos claseis Poenicas om*[*neis et max*]*su-
mas copias Cartaciniensis praesente*[*d sumod*]
Dictatored ol[*or*]*om in altod marid pucn*[*ad
vicet*] xxx*que navi*[*s cepe*]*t cum socieis septem*[*milibos quinresm*]*osque triresmosque na-
veis* [XIV. *merset. tonc aur*]*om captom numei*
ⅭⅭⅭ *D C* . . . [*pondod arcen*]*tom captom
praeda numei* cccIↄↄↄ [*pondod crave*] *captom
aes* cccIↄↄↄ cccIↄↄↄ cccIↄↄↄ cccIↄↄↄ cccIↄↄↄ
cccIↄↄↄ cccIↄↄↄ cccIↄↄↄ cccIↄↄↄ cccIↄↄↄ
cccIↄↄↄ cccIↄↄↄ cccIↄↄↄ cccIↄↄↄ cccIↄↄↄ
cccIↄↄↄ cccIↄↄↄ cccIↄↄↄ cccIↄↄↄ . . . . .
[*is qu*]*oque navaled praedad poplom* [*Rom.
deitavet atque*] *Cartacini*[*ens*]*is* [*ince*]*nuos
d*[*uxet triumpod cum* xxx *rostr*]*eis* [*clasis*]
Carta[*ciniensis captai quorum erco* S. P. Q. R.
hanc colomnam eei P.].

§ 22. The Silian and Papirian Laws.

Festus has preserved two interesting fragments of laws which are nearly contemporary with the *Columna Rostrata*. The first of these is the *Lex Silia de publicis ponderibus*, which was passed in the year B.C. 244, A.U.C. 510. Festus s. v. *Publica pondera*, p. 246: " Publica pondera [ad legitimam normam exacta fuisse] ex ea causa Junius . . . . .

[collegi]t quod duo Silii P. et M. Trib. pleb. rogarint his verbis:

> *Ex ponderibus publicis, quibus hac tempestate populus oetier solet, uti coaequetur*[1] *sedulum,*[2] *uti quadrantal vini octoginta pondo siet; congius vini decem p. siet; sex sextari congius siet vini; duo de quinquaginta sextari quadrantal siet vini; sextarius aequus aequo cum librario siet;*[3] *sex dequimque*[4] *librari in modio sient.*
>
> *Si quis magistratus adversus hac d. m. pondera modiosque vasaque publica modica, majora, minorave faxit, jusseritve*[5] *fieri, dolumve adduit quo ea fiant, eum quis volet magistratus*[6] *multare, dum minore parti familias taxat,*[7] *liceto; sive quis im*[8] *sacrum judicare voluerit, liceto.*"

The Latinity of this fragment requires a few remarks. (1) *coæquetur*. In the Pompeian Inscription (Orelli, no. 4348) we have: *mensuras exæquandas*. (2) *Sedulum*. Scaliger suggests *se dolo m*. i. e. *sine dolo malo*. But *sedulo* or *sedulum* itself signifies " sine fraude indiligentiæve culpa" (Müller *ad l.*), and the law refers to the care and honesty of those who were to test the weights and measures. For *sedulus*, see Döderl. *Syn. u. Et.* i. p. 118. (3) " Nihil intelligo nisi *librarius* qui hic significatur *sextarius frumenti* erat." Müller. (4) *Sex dequimque* = *sex decimque*, the *qu* being written instead of *c*. (5) The editions have *jussit ve re*, for which Müller writes *jussitve;* Haubold (*Monumenta Legalia*) proposes *jusseritve*, " propter sequens *re;*" and I have adopted this reading on account of the word *faxit*, which precedes. (6) *Quis volet magistratus.* Cf. *Tab. Bantin. Osc.* 12. *Lat.* 7. (7) *Dum minore parti familias taxat.* Compare the Latin Bantine Inscription, l. 10: [dum minoris] *partus familias taxsat.* Cato, *apud Aul. Gell.* vii. 3: " Quæ lex est tam acerba quæ dicat, si quis illud facere voluerit, mille nummi *dimidium familiæ* multa esto?" The abl. *parti* (which occurs in Lucretius) and the genitive *partus* (comp. *Castorus* in the Bantine Inscription, *ejus, cujus*, &c.) depend on *multare* and *multam*, which are implied in the sentence. For *taxat*, see Fest. p. 356. These passages shew the origin of the particle *dumtaxat*, which is used by the classical writers to signify " provided one estimates it," " estimating it accurately," " only," " at least," " so far as that goes," &c.[1] (8) *Im=eum.* Fest. p. 103.

The *Lex Papiria de Sacramento*, which is to be referred to the year B.C. 243, A.U.C. 511, is thus cited by Festus s. v. *Sacramentum*, p. 344: " Sacramentum æs significat, quod pœnæ nomine penditur, sive eo quis interrogatur, sive contenditur. Id in aliis rebus quinquaginta assium est, in aliis rebus quingentorum inter eos, qui judicio inter se contenderent. Qua de re lege L. Papiri Tr. pl. sanctum est his verbis:

> *Quicunque Praetor post hac factus erit qui inter cives jus dicet, tres viros Capitales populum rogato, hique tres viri [capitales], quicunque [posthac fa]cti erunt, sacramenta ex[igunto], judicantoque, eodemque jure sunto, uti ex legibus plebeique scitis exigere, judicareque, esseque oportet.*"

---

[1] It is scarcely necessary to point out the absurdity of the derivation proposed by A. Grotefend (*Ausf. Gramm. d. Lat. Spr.* § 124): " *duntaxat* aus *dum taceo* (cetera) *sat* (est hoc)!"

§ 23.
The Senatus Consultum de Bacchanalibus.

The *Senatus Consultum de Bacchanalibus*, which is referred to by Livy (xxxix. 14), and which belongs to the year B.C. 186, A.U.C. 568, was found at *Terra de Teriolo* in Calabria, in 1640, and is now at Vienna, where I have carefully examined it. A facsimile of the inscription, with the commentary of Matthæus Ægyptius, will be found in Drakenborch's *Livy*, vol. vii. p. 197, sqq.

1. [Q.] *Marcius L. F. S. Postumius L. F. Cos. Senatum consoluerunt N.*[1] *Octob. apud aedem*
2. *Duelonai sc.*[2] *arf.*[3] *M. Claudi M. F. L. Valeri P. F. Q. Minuci C. F. de Bacanalibus quei foideratei*
3. *Esent ita exdeicendum censuere neiquis eorum Sacanal*[4] *habuise velet sei ques*[5]
4. *esent quei sibei deicerent necesus*[6] *ese Bacanal habere eeis utei ad pr. urbanum*
5. *Romam venirent deque eeis rebus ubei eorum v tr a*[7] *audita esent utei senatus*
6. *noster decerneret dum ne minus senatoribus c. adesent [quom e]a res cosoleretur*
7. *Bacas*[8] *vir ne quis adiese*[9] *velet ceivis Romanus neve nominus Latin[i] neve socium*
8. *quisquam nisei pr. urbanum adiesent isque de senatuos sententiad dum ne*
9. *minus senatoribus c. adesent quom ea res cosoleretur iousisent censuere*
10. *sacerdos ne quis vir eset magister neque vir neque mulier quisquam eset*

---

[1] *Nonis.* [2] *scribendo.* [3] *adfuerunt.* [4] *Bacchanal.*
[5] *ques = quei.* See Klenze, *Legis Serviliæ Fr.* p. 12, not. 2; Fest p. 261.
[6] *necessum.* [7] l. *verba.* [8] i.e. *Bacchas.* [9] *adiisse.*

11. *neve pecuniam quisquam eorum comoinem habuise velet neve magistratum*
12. *neve pro magistratuo neque virum neque mulierem quiquam*[1] *fecise velet*
13. *neve post hac inter sed*[2] *conjourase neve comvovise neve conspondise*
14. *neve conpromesise velet neve quisquam fidem inter sed dedise velet*
15. *sacra in oquoltod*[3] *ne quisquam fecise velet neve in poplicod neve in*
16. *preivatod neve exstrad urbem sacra quisquam fecise velet nisei*
17. *pr. urbanum adieset isque de senatuos sententiad dum ne minus*
18. *senatoribus c. adesent quom ea res cosoleretur iousisent censuere*
19. *homines plous v. oinversei*[4] *virei atque mulieres sacra ne quisquam*
20. *fecise velet neve interibei*[5] *virei plous duobus mulieribus plous tribus*
21. *arfuise velent nisei de pr. urbani senatuosque sententiad utei suprad*
22. *scriptum est haice utei in coventionid*[6] *exdeicatis ne minus trinum*
23. *noundinum senatuosque sententiam utei scientes esetis eorum*
24. *sententia ita fuit sei ques*[7] *esent quei arvorsum ead fuisent quam suprad*

---

[1] *quisquam.* [2] i.e. *se*, as in l. 14. [3] *occulto.* [4] *universi.*
[5] = *interea.* [6] *contione.* [7] *ques* = *quei.*

25. *scriptum est eeis rem caputalem faciendam censuere atque utei*
26. *hoce in tabolam ahenam inceideretis ita senatus aiquom censuit*
27. *uteique eam figier joubeatis ubei facilumed*[1] *gnoscier potisit*[2] *atque*
28. *utei ea Bacanalia sei qua sunt exstrad quam sei quid ibei sacri est*
29. *ita utei suprad scriptum est in diebus* x *quibus vobeis tabelai*[3] *datai*
30. *erunt faciatis utei dismota sient in agro Teurano.*[4]

§ 24.
The old Roman law on the Bantine Table.

The Roman law on the Bantine Table is probably not older than the middle of the seventh century. The chief reason for introducing it here, is its connexion in locality, if not in import, with the most important fragment of the Oscan language (above, p. 86). Klenze divides it into four sections. His transcription and supplements are as follows (*Rhein. Mus.* for 1828, p. 28, sqq.; *Phil. Abhandl.* p. 7, sqq.).

CAP. 1. On the degradation of offenders.

1. . . . . . . *e . in poplico joudicio nesep*
2. . . . . . *o . neive quis mag. testumonium poplice eid[em sinito den]ontiari*
3. . . . . . *dato neive is in poplico luuci praetextam neive soleas habeto neive quis*

---

[1] *facillime.*   [2] = *potis-sit* = *possit.*   [3] = *tabellæ.*
[4] *in agro Teurano.* Strabo, p. 254 c : ὑπὲρ δὲ τῶν Θουρίων καὶ ἡ Ταυριάνη χώρα λεγομένη ἵδρυται.

4. [*mag. prove. mag. prove quo imperio potestateve erit qu*]*eiquomque comitia conciliumve habebit eum sufragium ferre nei sinito.*

L. 2. See Quinctil. v. 7, § 9: " Duo sunt genera testium, aut *voluntariorum* aut quibus in judiciis publicis *lege denuntiatur.*"

L. 3. *luuci,* " by day." Plaut. *Cas.* iv. 2, 7: " Tandem ut veniamus *luci.*" Cic. *Phil.* xii. 10, § 25: " Quis audeat *luci*—illustrem aggredi ?"

CAP. 2. On the punishment of judges and senators who violate the law.

5. [*seiquis joudex queiquomque ex hace lege*] *plebeive scito factus erit senatorve fecerit gesseritve quo ex hace lege*
6. [*minus fiant quae fieri oportet quaeve fieri oportu*]*erit oportebitve non fecerit sciens d. m., seive advorsus hance legem fecerit.*
7. [*gesseritve sciens d. m. ei multa esto* . . . *eamque pequniam*] *quei volet magistratus exsigito sei postulabit quei petet pr. recuperatores*
8. [*dato* . . . . *facit*]*oque eum sei ita pareat condumnari popul. facitoque joudicetur sei condemnatus*
9. [*fuerit ut pequnia redigatur*] *ad Q. urb*[*an.*] *aut bona ejus poplice possideantur facito . seiquis mag. multam inrogare volet*
10. [*apud populum dum minoris*] *partus familias taxsat liceto eiq. omnium rerum siremps lexs esto quasei sei is haace lege*

11. [*condemnatus fuerit*]

L. 10. *dum minoris partus familias taxsat.* See above, § 22, on the Lex Silia. *Partus* is the genitive case, like *Castorus,* cap. 3, l. 15. *Siremps* is explained by Festus, p. 344: "*Siremps* ponitur pro eadem, vel, proinde ac ea, quasi *similis res ipsa.* Cato in dissuadendo legem . . . . relicta est: Et præterea rogas, quemquam adversus ea si populus condempnaverit, uti siremps lex siet, quasi adversus leges fecisset."

CAP. 3. On binding the judges and magistrates by an oath to observe the law.

12. [*Cos. Pr. . . . qu*]*ei nunc est is in diebus* v *proxsumeis quibus queique eorum sciet h. l. popolum plebemve*

13. [*joussisse jouranto — —*] *Dic. cos. pr. mag. eq. cens. aid. tr. pl. q.* IIIvir *cap.* IIIIvir *a. d. a. joudex ex h. l. plebive scito*

14. [*factus queiquomque eorum p*]*osthac factus erit eis in diebus* v *proxsumeis quibus quisque eorum mag. inperiumve inierit, jouranto*

15. [*— — in ae*]*de Castorus palam luci in forum vorsus et eidem in diebus* v *apud Q. jouranto per Jovem deosque*

16. [*penateis sese quae ex h. l. oport*]*ebit facturum neque sese advorsum h. l. facturum scientem d. m. neque seese facturum neque intercesurum*

17. [*ne ex h. l. fiant quae oportet. Qu*]*ei ex h. l. non jouraverit is magistratum inperiumve nei petito neive gerito neive habeto neive in senatu*

18. [*si adfuerit sententiam dicere e*]*um quis sinito*

neive eum censor in senatum legito. Quei ex
h. l. joudicaverit is facito apud Q. urb.
19. [nomen ejus quei jouraverit sc]riptum siet.
Quaestorque ea nomina accipito et eos quei
ex h. l. apud sed jourarint facito in taboleis
20. [popliceis scriptos habeat].

L. 13. i. e. *Dictator, consul, praetor, magister equitum, censor, aedilis, tribunus plebei, quaestor, triumvir capitalis, triumvir agris dandis adsignandis.*

L. 15. *palam luci in forum versus.* See Cic. *de Offic.* iii. 24.

CAP. 4. On the oath of the senators.

21. [*Senatores quei sententi*]*am deixer*[*in*]*t post hance legem rogatam eis in diebus* x *proxsumeis quibus quisque* [*eorum sciet h. l.*]
22. [*populum plebemve joussisse j*]*ouranto apud quaestorem ad aerarium palam luci per Jovem de*[*osqu*]*e penate*[*is sese quae oportebit*]
23. [*facturum — — neque se*]*se advorsum hance legem facturum esse neque seese* [*facturum*]
24. — — *se hoice leegei fi* — —

L. 21. *eis = ii.* See above, p. 182.

L. 22. *ad aerarium.* See Liv. xxix. 37. *Per Jovem deosque penateis.* Comp. Cic. *Acad.* iv. 20.

CHAPTER VII.

ANALYSIS OF THE LATIN ALPHABET.

§ 1. Organic classification of the original Latin alphabet. § 2. The labials. § 3. The gutturals. § 4. The dentals. § 5. The vowels. § 6. The Greek letters used by the Romans. § 7. The numeral signs.

§ 1.
Organic classification of the original Latin alphabet.

THE genuine Latin alphabet,—or that set of characters which expressed in writing the sounds of the Roman language before it had borrowed from the Greek a number of words, and the means of exhibiting them to the eye,—may be considered as consisting of nineteen letters; that is, of the representatives of the original Cadmean syllabarium (which consisted of sixteen letters);—the secondary vowels, or vocalised consonants, I and U, and the secondary sibilant $x = sh$, being added as a necessary appendix.

If we distribute these nineteen letters according to their natural or organic classification, we shall have the following arrangement:—

CONSONANTS.

	Labials.	Gutturals.	Dentals.
Medials . . .	B	G	D
Aspirates . .	F	H	R
Tenues . . .	P	Qv	T
Liquids . . .	M		L, N
Sibilants . . .		X, S	

ANALYSIS OF THE LATIN ALPHABET.

VOWELS.

Vowels of Articulations.	Heaviest. A	Lightest. E	Medium. O
Vocalised Consonants	Vocalised Labial. U	Vocalised Guttural, or Dental. I	

It will be most convenient, as well as most methodical, to consider these letters according to this classification, which will be justified by the investigation itself.

LABIALS.

The labials consist of three mutes and the liquid M. The regular changes of the labial mutes, in the principal languages of the Indo-Germanic family, have been thus indicated by James Grimm, to whom we owe the discovery of a most important law (*Deutsche Gramm.* i. p. 584), which may be stated thus in its application to all three orders of mutes:

§ 2. The labials.

In Greek, Latin, Sanscrit.		In Gothic.		In Old High German.
Medial	corresponds to	*Tenuis*	and to	*Aspirate.*
Aspirate	,,	,,	*Medial*	,,	*Tenuis.*
Tenuis	,,	,,	*Aspirate*	,,	*Medial.*

This law, applied to the labials only, may be expressed in the following table:

Latin, (Greek, Sanscrit) .	B	F	P
Gothic	P	B	F
Old High German . . .	F	P	B (V)

To take the instances given by Grimm himself,—the first column is confirmed, as far as the Latin language is concerned, by the following examples: *cannabis* (κάνναβις), Old Norse *hanpr*, Old High German *hanaf; turba* (θορύβη), Goth. *thaúrp*, O. H. G. *dorof; stabulum*, O. N. *stöpull*, O. H. G. *staphol*. To which may be added, *labi*, Anglo-Saxon *slipan*, O. H. G. *sliuffan*. These instances are confined to the occurrence of the labials in the middle of words; for there are no German words beginning with P, and no H. G. words beginning with F.

The second column is supported as follows: Initials— *fagus* (φηγός), O. N. *beyki*, O. H. D. *puocha; fero* (φέρω), Goth. *baíra*, O. H. G. *piru; fui* (φύω), Ang.-Sax. *bëon*, O. H. G. *pim; flare*, Goth. *blasan*, O. H. G. *plasan; fra-ngere* (ῥήγνυμι), Goth. *brikan*, O. H. G. *prëchan; folium* (φύλλον), O. N. *blad*, O. H. G. *plat; frater* (φρητήρ), Goth. *brothar*, O. H. G. *pruoder*. The Latin language furnishes no instances of this rule in its application to the middle sounds. In νεφέλη, κεφαλή, γράφειν, and such like, the Latin equivalents present *b* or *p;* compare *nebula, caput, s-cribere*. The reason for this is to be sought in the aversion of the Roman ear from F as a middle sound.

The third column rests on the following induction: Initials—*pes (pedis)*, Goth. *fótus*, O. H. G. *vuoz; piscis*, Goth. *fisks*, O. H. G. *visc; pater*, Goth. *fadrs*, O. H. G. *vatar; plenus*, Goth. *fulls*, O. H. G. *vol; pecus*, Goth. *faíhu*, O. H. G. *vihu; palma*, Angl.-Sax. *folma*, O. H. G. *volma; pellis*, Goth. *fill*, O. H. G. *vël; pullus*, Goth. *fula*, O. H. G. *volo; primus*, Goth. *frumists*, O. H. G. *vromist*. Middle sounds—*sopor*, O. N. *svefn*, O. Sax. *suëlhan; septem*, Angl.-Sax. *sëfon*, Goth. *sibun; afer*, Angl.-Sax. *ëofor*, O. H. G. *ëbar; super*, Goth. *ufar*, O. N. *yfir*, O. H. G. *ubar; rapina*, Angl.-Sax. *reáf*, O. H. G. *roub*.

These may be taken as proofs of the general application of Grimm's rule to the Latin labials. If, however, we examine the use of the separate letters more minutely, we shall find great vacillation even within the limits of the Latin language itself.

The medial B seems to have approximated in many cases to the sound of v; at other times it came more nearly to P. We find in old Latin the forms *Duillius, duonus, duellum*, &c. by the side of *Billius, bonus, bellum*, &c. Now, there is no doubt that the proper abbreviation of these forms would be e. g. *donus* or *vonus*, and so on. The labial representative *bonus*, therefore, shews a sort of indifference between the occasional pronunciation of B and V. This view is confirmed by a comparison of *duis*, which must have been the original form, with δίς on the one hand, and *bis, bes, vi-ginti* on the other. This appears particularly in the change from Latin to Italian, as in *habere = avere, habebam = aveva*, &c. The commutation of *b* and *v* in the Spanish language gave occasion to Scaliger's epigram:

<blockquote>
*Haud temere antiquas mutat Vasconia voces
Cui nihil est aliud vivere quam bibere.*
</blockquote>

The interchange of B and P may be remarked in *burrus*, πυρρός; *Balantium, Palatium; bitumen, pitumen* (comp. *pituita*); &c. In many Latin words the B stands for a φ (=P'H) in the Greek synonyme: compare *balæna, albus, ambo, nebula, tenebræ, umbilicus*, &c., with φάλαινα, ἀλφός, ἄμφω, νεφέλη, δνοφεραί, ὀμφαλός, &c.

The ancient Romans did not use B, as the Greeks did, to form a fulcrum between two liquids (comp. μεσημερία, μεσημβρία; μέλι, [μ]βλίττω; ἔ-μολον, μέμβλωκα; μόρος, ἄμβροτος; &c.): but in the derivative idioms there are many instances of this insertion; compare *numerus, nombre; camera, chambre*, &c.; and even when *r* is substituted for some other liquid, as in *hominem*, Sp. *hombre*; or when a third liquid is retained, as in *cumulare*, Fr. *combler*.

It is hardly necessary to remark, that the genuine Etruscan element in the Latin language must have been altogether without the medial B.

When B or V is followed by the vocalised guttural J, we

sometimes remark that, in the derived languages, this guttural supersedes the labial, and is pronounced alone: so we have *cavea* (= *cavja*), *cage; cambiare, changer; Dibio, Dijon; rabies, rage; rubere* (=*rubjere*), *rougir;* &c.

The labial F and the guttural Q$_v$ are the most characteristic letters in the Latin alphabet. Of the latter I will speak in its place, merely remarking here that its resemblance to F consists in the fact that they are both compound letters, although used from the earliest period as exponents of simple sounds.

In considering the Latin F, we must be careful not to confuse it with the Greek φ on the one hand, or with the modern v on the other. It is true that F corresponds to φ in a number of words, such as *fagus, fama, fero, fallo, fari, fascis, frater, frigus, fucus, fugio, fui, fulgeo, fur* (Müller, *Etrusk.* i. p. 20); but we must consider these words as an approach to a foreign articulation; for in a great number of words, in which the F has subsequently been commuted for H, we can find no trace of connexion with the Greek φ: such are *fariolus, fasena, fedus, fircus, folus, fordeum, fostis, fostia, forctis, vefo, trafo* (Müller, *Etrusk.* i. p. 44).

It is generally laid down that F and V are both labiodental aspirates, and that they differ only as the tenuis differs from the medial; and one philologer has distinctly asserted their identity, meaning perhaps that in Latin F = the English v, and U = the English w. If, however, we analyse some of the phenomena of comparative philology in which the Latin F appears, and then refer to Quinctilian's description of the sound of this letter, we may be disposed to believe that in many cases the English v formed only a part of the sound. Quinctilian says (xii. 10, § 27, 29) that the Roman language suffered in comparison with the Greek from having only v and F, instead of the Greek *v* and φ, "*quibus nullæ apud eos* (*Græcos*) *dulcius spirant. Nam et illa, quæ est sexta nostrarum, pæne non humana voce, vel omnino non voce potius inter discrimina dentium efflanda est: quæ etiam, cum vocalem proxima accipit, quassa quodammodo: utique, quoties aliquam consonantem frangit, ut in hoc ipso* FRANGIT, *multo fit horridior.*" Not to repeat here what has been stated at length elsewhere (*N. Crat.* p. 124), it will be sufficient to make the following observations: (*a*) the Latin F, though not = v, contained that letter, and was a cognate sound with it:[1] this is proved by a comparison of *con-ferre, con-viva*, &c. with *com-bibere, im-primis*, &c. (*b*) It appears from Quinctilian that in his time the Latin F contained, in addition to the labial v, some dental sibilant; and the sibilant is known to have been the condition in which the guttural passed into the mere aspirate. (*c*) A comparison of the Greek θήρ with its Latin synonyme *fera* would produce great difficulty, if we could not suppose a coexistence of the sibilant with the labial in the latter; such a concurrence we have in the Russian synonyme *svera*, Lettish *svehrs*, Old Prussian *svirs*. (*d*) The Sabine words mentioned above (such as *fircus*), the more modern representatives of which substitute an aspirate for the F, prove that the F must have contained a guttural aspirate; for no labial can pass into a guttural, though a compound of labial and guttural may be represented by the guttural only. (*e*) Those words in the Romance languages which present an aspirate for the F which their Latin synonymes retained to the last,—such as *falco*, " hawk;" *foris*, Fr. " hors;" *facere, formosus, fumus*, &c., Sp. " hacer," " hermoso," " humo," &c.,— prove that, to the last, the Latin F contained some guttural element, in addition to the labial of which it was in part composed. It seems to me that F must have been sv, or, ultimately,

[1] In the same way as F seems to represent φ in the instances cited above, v also appears as a substitute both for φ and π. Compare *valgus, vallus, veru, virgo*, and *vitricus*, with φολκός, *palus*, πείρω, παρθένος, and *pater* (Buttmann, *Lexil*. s. v. φολκός).

hv, and that v must have corresponded to our English w. With regard to the Greek φ, there can be no doubt that it was a distinct *p'h*, like the middle sound in *hap-hazard, shep-herd;* reduplications like πέφυκα (*pe-p'huka*), and contacts like Σαπφώ (*Sapp'ho*), sufficiently prove this. The forms of Latin words which seem to substitute f for this φ must be referred to the Pelasgian element in the Latin language: the Tuscans, as we have seen, were by no means averse from this sound; and the Romans were obliged to express it by the written representative of a very different articulation.

Of the tenuis p it is not necessary to say much. If we compare the Latin forms with their Greek equivalents, we observe that p, or pp, is used as a substitute for the φ (p'h) of which I have just spoken. Thus *puniceus, caput, napura, prosper,* &c., correspond to φοινίκεος, κεφάλη, ναφρόν, πρόσφορος, &c., and *cruppellarii, cippus, -lappa, stroppus, supparum, s-cloppus, topper,* &c., answer to κρύφαλον, κέφαλον, ἀκαλήφη, στρόφιον, ὑφασία, κόλαφος, σ-τυφρός, σ-τυφελός (*tapfer*), &c. For the inferences deducible from this commutation, see *N. Crat.* p. 135.

In the languages derived from the Latin, p very often passes into v. This is most regular in the French: comp. *aperire, aprilis, capillus, episcopus, habere, lepus, opera, pauper, recipere,* &c., with *ouvrir, avril, cheveu, évêque, avoir, lièvre, œuvre, pauvre, recevoir,* &c.

P is often inserted as a fulcrum to the labial m when a liquid follows: thus we have *sumo, sum-p-si, sumptus; promo, prom-p-si, promptus.*

Contact with the guttural j will convert p into ch = j. Compare *rupes, roche; sapiam, sache;* &c. Conversely, but by a similar process, the termination *-quam* has become *-piam.*

The labial liquid m occasionally takes the place of one or other of the labial mutes, even within the limits of the

§ 2.]   ANALYSIS OF THE LATIN ALPHABET.   195

Latin language itself. It stands by the side of B in *fama*, *glomus*, *hiems*, *melior*, *tumeo*, &c., compared with *fabula*, *globus*, *hibernus*, *bonus* (*benus*, *bene*, *bellus*, &c., βελτίων, βέντιστος, &c.), *tuber*, &c. I am not aware that we have any example of the commutation of M with the labio-dental F. With V it is not uncommon: comp. *Mulciber*, *Vulcanus*; *pro-mulgare*, *pro-vulgare* (compare *di-vulgare*); &c. This is still more remarkable if we extend the comparison to cognate languages: thus *Mars*, *mas* (*maris*), may be compared with Φάρης, Φάρρην, *vir*, *virtus*, " war," *wehren*, " warrior," Ὀαρίων, and *Minne* " Minion," &c., with *Venus*, *Winnesjäfte*, &c. (*Abhandl. Berl. Ak.* 1826, p. 58). So also μά-ντις may be compared with *vatis*; at least, Plautus writes *mantiscinari* for *vaticinari*. The changes of P into M are generally observable in assimilations such as *summus* for *supimus*, *supremus*: in Greek, and in the passage between Greek and Latin, this change is common enough; thus we have μετά by the side of πέδα, and μόλυβδος by the side of *plumbum*. In fact, M and N are more nearly akin to the medials B and D than to the tenues, and a thick articulation will always give the medials for the liquids.

At the end of Latin words M is very often omitted in writing, and seems to have been still more frequently neglected in pronunciation. With regard to the written omissions, it was the rule to omit in the present tense of active verbs the important M which characterises the first person in many of the other tenses. In fact, the only verbs which retain it in the present tense are *su-m* and *inqua-m*: and it is mentioned as a custom of Cato the Censor, that he used also to elide the M at the termination of the futures of verbs in *-o* and *-io* (see Ch. VI. § 3). The metrical ecthlipsis, which disregards the final *-m* when a vowel follows, may be explained by supposing a sort of *anusvârah* in the Latin language.

GUTTURALS.

§ 3. The gutturals.

The Roman gutturals are three,—the medial G, the aspirate H, and the labio-guttural tenuis Qv. The regular changes of this order of mutes, as far as the Latin language is concerned, are proved by the following examples; the law itself, as applied to the gutturals, being expressed thus:

Latin, (Greek, Sanscrit)	G	H	C
Gothic	K	G	H, G.
Old High German	CH	K	H, G.

1st column. Initials: *granum*, O. N. *korn*, O. H. G. *chorn; genus, kuni, chunni; gena*, O. N. *kinn*, O. H. G. *chinni; genu, knê, chnio; gelu, gelidus*, Gothic *kalds*, O. H. G. *chalt; gustare, kiusan, chiosan*. Middle sounds: *ego, ik, ih (ich); ager, akrs, achar; magnus, mikils, michil; jugum, juk, joch; mulgere*, O. N. *miólka*, O. H. G. *mëlchan*.

2d column. Initials: *hanser, gans, kans; heri, hesternus, gistra, këstar; hortus, gards, karto; hostis, gasts, kast; homo, guma, komo*. H is of rare occurrence as a middle sound in Latin; we may, however, compare *via, veha*, with *weg; veho* with Goth. *aigan; traho* with Anglo-Sax. *dragan*, &c.

3d column (in which I have substituted C for Qv, because the latter belongs to a different class of comparisons). Initials: *claudus, halt, halz; caput, haubith, houbit; cor, haírto, hërza; canis, hunths, hund*. Middle sounds: *lux, liuhad, licht; tacere, thahan, dagen; decem*, Goth. *taíhun*, Lith. *deszimts*.

Originally the Romans made no distinction between the gutturals C and G; the former was the only sign used; and although Ausonius says (*Idyll.* xii. *de litteris*, v. 21): *gammæ vice functa prius* C (see also Festus, s. vv. *prodigia, orcum*) thereby implying that C expressed both the medial G and the tenuis K, there is reason to believe that in the older times the Romans pronounced C as a medial, and used Q as

§ 3.]   ANALYSIS OF THE LATIN ALPHABET.   197

their only tenuis guttural. This appears from the forms *macestratus, leciones*, &c., on the Duillian monument, and still more strikingly from the fact that the prænomens *Gaïus, Gnæus* (Γάϊος, Γενναῖος), were to the last indicated by the initials *C.* and *Cn.;* for in the case of a proper name the old character would survive the change of application. When, however, the Romans began to distinguish between the pure tenuis κ and the labial tenuis ǫ, they introduced a distinction between c and g, which was marked by the addition of a tail to the old character c, the letter thus modified being used to represent the medial, and the old form being transferred from the medials to the tenues. The author of this change was Sp. Carvilius, a freedman and namesake of the celebrated Sp. Carvilius Ruga, who, in A.U.C. 523, B.C. 231, furnished the first example of a divorce. See Plutarch, *Quæst. Rom.* p. 277 D.: τὸ Κ πρὸς τὸ Γ συγγένειαν ἔχει παρ' αὐτοῖς [the Romans], ὀψὲ γὰρ ἐχρήσαντο τῷ γάμμα Καρβιλίου Σπορίου προσεξευρόντος. Id. p. 278 E.: ὀψὲ ἤρξαντο μισθοῦ διδάσκειν, καὶ πρῶτος ἀνέῳξε γραμματοδιδασκαλεῖον Σπόριος Καρβίλιος ἀπελεύθερος Καρβιλίου τοῦ πρώτου γαμετὴν ἐκβαλόντος. From the position in the alphabet assigned to this new character,—namely, the seventh place, corresponding to that of the Greek z,—there is reason to believe that the Roman c still retained the hard *g*-sound, while the new character represented the soft sibilant pronunciation of the English J and the Greek z, which is also expressed by the modern Italian *gi*.

The Latin H was a strong guttural aspirate, corresponding in position and in power to the Greek χ. It is true that this character sometimes indicates a mere *spiritus asper;* and in this use it is either dropt or prefixed, according to the articulation. In general, however, it was the strongest and purest of the Roman aspirated gutturals. Graff has remarked (*Abhandl. Berl. Ak.* 1839, p. 12) that there are three classes of aspirates—the guttural (H), *i. e.* the *spiritus;* the labial (w), *i. e.* the *flatus;* and the dental (s), *i. e.* the *sibilatus:* and he says that the Latin language entirely wants the first, whereas it possesses the labial aspirate in its Q, and the dental perhaps in its x. This appears to me to be neither a clear nor a correct statement. With regard to H in particular, there can be no doubt that it is a strong guttural, quite as much so as the Greek χ. This is established by the following comparison. The Latin H answers to χ in the words *hiems* ($\chi\epsilon\iota\mu\omega\nu$), *hibernus* ($\chi\epsilon\iota\mu\epsilon\rho\iota\nu o\varsigma$), *hio* ($\chi a\iota\nu\omega$), *humi* ($\chi\acute{a}\mu a\iota$), *hortus* ($\chi\acute{o}\rho\tau o\varsigma$), &c. It represents the guttural c in *trah-o, trac-si, veh-o, vec-si,* &c. In a word, it corresponds to the hard Sanscrit *h,* for which, in the cognate Gothic and Greek words, either *g, k,* or γ, κ, χ, are substituted (comp. *N. Crat.* p. 128).

With regard to Q or Qv, a character almost peculiar to the Latin alphabet, a longer investigation will be necessary. It has been a common opinion with philologers that there were different classes of the tenuis guttural, varying with the vowel which articulated them; thus, $\kappa\acute{a}\pi\pi a,$ *kaph,* was followed only by *a;* H (*heth*) only by *e;* $\chi\hat{\iota}$ only by *i;* $\kappa\acute{o}\pi\pi a,$ *koph,* only by *o;* and Q only by *u.* Lepsius (*Zwei Abhandl.* p. 18-31) has given a more rational and systematic form to this opinion, by supposing that there were three fundamental vowels, *a, i, u;* that *i* was subsequently split up into *i, e,* and *u* into *o, u;* that one of the three fundamental vowels was prefixed to each row of mutes in the old organic syllabarium, so that all the medials were articulated with *a,* all the aspirates with *i,* and all the tenues with *u.* This form of the opinion, however, is by no means sufficient to explain the peculiarities of the Roman Qv; and if it were, still it could not be adopted, as it runs counter to the results of a more scientific investigation into the origin of *i* and *u.*

The difficulty which has been felt in dealing with the Latin Q has proceeded chiefly from the supposition that

§ 3.] ANALYSIS OF THE LATIN ALPHABET. 199

the accompanying *u* or *v* must be either a distinct vowel or a distinct consonant; for if it is a vowel, then either it ought to form a diphthong with the accompanying vowel, or a distinct syllable with the Q; and neither of these cases ever happens: if, on the other hand, it is a consonant, the vowel preceding the Q ought to be long by position; and this is never the case even in the most ancient writers (see Graff, *Abh. Berl. Ak.* 1839 : " über den Buchstaben Q (Qv)")

It appears to me unnecessary to assume that the accompanying U is either a distinct vowel or a distinct consonant. And herein consists the peculiarity of the Roman Q : it cannot be articulated without the *u*, and yet the *u* has no distinct existence. The true explanation, I conceive, is the following. No attentive student of the Latin authors can have failed to observe how great a tendency there is in this language to introduce sounds consisting of an union of the guttural and labial. Such a sound is the digamma, which may be considered to have been the leading characteristic of the Pelasgian language both in Italy and in Greece. Now there are four states of this sound, besides its original condition, in which both guttural and labial have their full power: the first is when the labial predominates, and this is expressed by the letter F $= sv \; (hv)$; the second is when the guttural predominates, and this is expressed by Qv; the third is when the guttural alone is sounded, and in this state it becomes the strong guttural H or K; the fourth is when the labial alone is articulated, and from this we have the letter v.

The great difference between F and Qv consists in this, that in the latter it is necessary to express both the ingredients of the double sound, whereas they are both represented by one character in the former. Hence it has happened, that, while the guttural element of F has been overlooked by many philologers, they have over-estimated the independent value of the labial which accompanies Q.

A sound bearing the same relation to the medials that Qv does to the tenues is occasionally formed by the addition of *v* to G. This occurs only after *n* and *r:* thus we find *tinguo, unguo, urgueo*, by the side of *tingo, ungo, urgeo*. The former were probably the original words, the latter being subsequent modifications: compare *guerra*, " war," *guardire*, " ward," &c. with the French pronunciation of *guerre, guardir*, &c. (*N. Crat.* p. 120.)

When the labial ingredient of Qv is actually vocalised into *u*, the Q is expressed in classical Latin by the new tenuis C = κ; thus *quojus, quoi*, the original gen. and dat. of *qui*, become *cujus, cui; quare* becomes *cur; quom* is turned into *cum; sequundus, oquulus, torquular* (comp. *torqueo*), *quiris* (cf. *Quirinus*), &c., are converted into *secundus, oculus, torcular, curis*, &c. This is also the case when *u* is represented by the similar Roman sound of the *o*. Thus *colo* must have been originally *quolo;* for Q is the initial of *quolonia* on coins, and *in-quilinus* is obviously derived from *in-colo*. It is known, too, that *coquus* must have been pronounced *quoquus* even in Cicero's time; for he made no difference in pronunciation between the particle *quoque* and the vocative of *coquus:* see Quinctil. vi. 3, § 47: " Quæ Ciceroni aliquando .... exciderunt, ut dixit, quum is candidatus, qui coqui filius habebatur, coram eo suffragium ab alio peteret: ego *quoque* tibi favebo." The change of *qva* into *cu* is particularly remarkable when a syllable is shortened, on account of the heavier form in which it occurs; as when *quatio* in composition becomes *con-cutio, per-cutio*, &c.

The two constituent parts of Qv often exist separately in different forms of the same root: thus we have *conniveo, connixi; fio* (φύω), *facio, factus; fluo, fluxi; foveo, focus;*

juvo, jucundus; lavo, lacus; struo, struxi; vivo, vixi. The last is a double instance; for there can be no doubt of the connexion between "quick" and *vivus* (for *qviqvus*). Compare *eleven, twelve,* with *undecim, duodecim.* Bopp's opinion, therefore (*Vergleich. Gramm.* pp. 18, 98), that there is some natural connexion between *v* and *k* in themselves, is altogether unfounded.

In the comparison between Latin and Sanscrit we seldom find that Qv is represented by a Sanscrit κ, but that it usually stands in cognate words where the Sanscrit has a *palatal* guttural or sibilant (*N. Crat.* p. 108): compare *quatuor,* Sanscr. *chatur; s-quama,* Sanscr. *chad,* " tegere ;" *quumulus,* Sanscr. *chi,* " accumulare ;" *oc-cultus (ob-quultus),* Sanscr. *jal,* " tegere ;" *sequor,* Sanscr. *sajj; pequus,* Sanscr. *paçu; equus,* Sanscr. *açva;* &c. When Qv stands by the side of a Sanscrit *k*, it is either when that letter is followed by *e* or *i*,— in which case the guttural approximates to the palatal,— or when the *k* stands before *u* or *v*. There are some instances in which the Qv is represented by the labial P in Greek and Sanscrit; and this is particularly remarkable in cases where the Qv occurs twice in the Latin word: compare the Latin *quinque, quoquo (coquo), aqua, loquor,* &c., with the Sanscrit and Greek *panchan,* πέμπε, *pach,* πέπω, *áp, lap,* &c.; also *equus, oquulus, sequor, linquo,* &c., with ἵππος, ὄμμα, ἕπομαι, λείπω, &c.

Quinctilian says that the Latin Q is derived from the Greek κόππα (i. 4, § 9); and there can be no doubt that they have a common origin. Now this Greek κόππα, which is of rare occurrence, is found, where it occurs in Greek inscriptions, only before *o*. Thus we have ϙοριν- θοθεν (Böckh, *C. I.* no. 29), ὄρϙον (n. 37), λυϙοδορκας (n. 166); and on coins we have ϙορινθος, Συραϙοσιων, &c. The explanation of this is simple: the letter *o* before a vowel expressed the sound of *w*, so far as the mouth of a Greek could convey this sound: compare οἶστρος, ῥοῖβδος, which imitate the *whizzing* noises of the wings of the gad-fly and the bird; ὄα which represents the Persian lamentation *wa!* &c. Consequently, the syllable ϙο must be regarded as the residuum of a syllable pronounced *kwa*, which was probably the pronunciation of the Latin Qv. At any rate, it is sufficiently evident from the single word λυϙοδορκας that ϙ and κ could not have been identical at the time when the inscription was carved; otherwise we should have had either λυκοδορκας or λυϙοδορϙας. In fact, the word λυκος must have been originally λυϙοος (*luqvus*), otherwise the labial in the Latin *lupus* would be inexplicable. Perhaps, too, as Graff suggests (u. s. p. 10, note 7), there are other Greek words containing the syllable κο or κυ, which must have been written with ϙ in the older state of the language. He selects the following, of which the Sanscrit equivalents have the palatals ç, *ch*: κόσμος, κόγχος, κόρση, κῶνος, κυανός, Sanscrit *çudh*, " purificari;" *çankha,* " concha;" *çirsha,* " caput;" *çó,* " acuere," Lat. *qvurvus; chyáma,* " violaceus." The passage from Qv into ϙο, κυ, &c. may be illustrated also by the converse change from κυ to *qu* in " liquorice," from γλυκυῤῥίζα, &c., while the English articulation of " can" has entirely obliterated all traces of the Q in the Latin *queo,* originally *queno* (cf. *ne-quinont* for *ne-queunt*), though the Greek κοννῶ (Æsch. *Suppl.* 75) and the German *können* still preserve this sound by implication.

If we examine the changes which have taken place in the gutturals in their passage from the Roman to the Romance languages, we are first struck by the general tendency to soften down or assibilate the tenuis c. The former process is effected by a change of c into CH: compare the Latin *caballus, cadere, camera, canis, casa, castus,* &c. with the French *cheval, cheoir, chambre, chien, chez,*

§ 3.] ANALYSIS OF THE LATIN ALPHABET. 203

chaste, &c. Of the assibilation of c we have many instances: such are, *facimus*, Fr. *faisons; licere, loisir; placere, plaisir*, &c.

Another change in the Romance languages is the omission of c when it is followed by a T: comp. *dictus*, It. *ditto*, Fr. *dit; pectus*, It. *petto*, Fr. *poitrine*, &c. c also disappears in French when in the Latin form it was followed by R. Compare *lacrima, sacramentum*, &c. with *larme, serment*, &c. It is neglected in the same language when it stands between two vowels, especially when one or both are *u* (*o*) or *i:* compare *apicula, corbicula, focus, jocus, locus, nocere, paucus, vices*, &c. with *abeille, corbeille, feu, jeu, lieu, nuire, peu, fois*, &c.

In some cases the French converts the tenuis c into the medial G. Compare *aigre, aveugle, maigre*, &c. with *acer, aboculus, macer*, &c.

G is often omitted in the middle of French words: compare *legere, Ligeris, mais, maistre*, &c., with *lire, Loire, magis, magister*, &c.

The French and Italians generally neglect the guttural H. The old hard sound of this aspirate is quite unknown to them.

Although the sibilant is in some cases akin to the dental class, the Latin sibilants x and s must be considered as belonging altogether to the gutturals. The Romans had a dental sibilant in their R, of which I shall speak directly; but these two seem to have in themselves no connexion with the dentals, beyond the circumstance that R is frequently derived from s by the substitution of a dental articulation, in the same way as θ stands for σ in θάλασσα for σάλασσα, &c., and as the lisping Englishman says *yeth* for *yes*.

If we consider x in its common acceptation, it is a direct combination of the guttural c or G with the sibilant s. This must, of course, be its power in *rexi, flexi*, &c.

But it was not always equivalent to this combination either in sound or in origin. Sometimes it stands for the dental ζ=*dj*, as in *rixa* compared with ἔριδ-ς, ἐρίζω, &c. And even when it was derived immediately from a guttural and s, the sibilant seems to have overpowered the guttural, which was either lost altogether or pronounced only as an aspiration. We have traces of this in the modern Italian pronunciation of *Alessandro, vissi*, &c. The Greek ξῖ derived its name from the Hebrew *shin*, and perhaps occasionally represented it in sound. A sibilant or aspirate often changes its place: thus the Gothic *hv* is in English *wh*, the Greek *hr* is the Latin *rh*, and the Greek ξ=κσ- might occasionally be σκ-: compare the transposition in the oriental words *Iscander, Scanderoon, Candahar*, all derived from the Greek Ἀλέ-ξανδρος. The last of these words is a mutilation which reminds us of the modern Scotch division of the name *Alexander* into the two abbreviations *Alick* and *Saunders* or *Sandy*. When the transposition was once effected, the softening of the guttural was obvious and easy: compare σχέτλιος, " scathe," *schade;* χάρμη, " s-kirmish," *schirm*, &c.

The Latin s is principally remarkable as standing at the beginning of words, the Greek equivalents of which have only an aspirate: compare *sal, sex, septem, sol, sylva, simul, sedere, sequi, somnus*, &c., with ἅλς, ἕξ, ἕπτα, ἥλιος, ὑλϜη, ἅμα, ἕζεσθαι, ἕπομαι, ὕπνος, &c. Though in some cases even this aspirate has vanished: as in ἄναξ, εἰ, ἐλλός, &c., compared with *senex, si, sileo*, &c. It frequently happens that in the more modern forms of the Roman language an original s has been superseded by the dental sibilant R. Thus Quinctilian tells us (i. 4, § 13) that *Valesius, Fusius, arbos, labos, vapos, clamos*, and *lases* (cf. Fest. s. v.), were the original forms of *Valerius, Furius, arbor, labor, vapor, clamor*, and *lares;* and it is clear that *honor, honestus*, are only different forms of *onus, onustus*. It is rather surprising that the Jurist Pomponius (*Digg.* i. 2, 2, § 36) should have attributed to Appius Claudius Cæcus (consul I. A.U.C. 447, B.C. 307; consul II. A.U.C. 458, B.C. 296) the invention of a letter which is the initial of the names *Roma* and *Romulus*. He can only mean that Appius was the first to introduce the practice of substituting R for S in proper names, a change which he might have made in his censorship. It appears, from what Cicero says, that L. Papirius Crassus, who was consul in A.U.C. 418, B.C. 336, was the first of his name who did not call himself *Papisius* (*ad Famil.* ix. 21): "How came you to suppose," says Cicero, writing to L. Papirius Pætus, "that there never was a Papirius of patrician rank, when it is certain that they were *patricii minorum gentium?* To begin with the first of these, I will instance L. Papirius Mugillanus, who, in the year of the city 312, was censor with L. Sempronius Atratinus, who had previously (A.U.C. 310) been his colleague in the consulship. But your family-name at that time was *Papisius*. After him there were thirteen of your ancestors who were curule magistrates before L. Papirius Crassus, the first of your family that disused the name *Papisius*. This Papirius in the year was chosen *dictator* in A.U.C. 415, with L. Papirius Cursor for his *magister equitum*, and four years afterwards he was elected consul with K. Duilius." We must conclude, therefore, that Appius Claudius used his censorial authority to sanction a practice, which had already come into vogue, and which was intimately connected with the peculiarities of the Roman articulation. In fact, the Romans were to the last remarkable for the same tendency to rhotacism, which is characteristic of the Umbrian, Dorian, and Old Norse dialects.

DENTALS.

The Romans had five dentals or linguals: the mutes D and T, the liquids L and N, and the secondary letter R,

§ 4. The dentals.

which in most alphabets is considered a liquid, but in the Latin stands for an aspiration or assibilation of the medial D. Grimm's law, as applied to the dentals, stands thus:

Latin, (Greek, Sanscrit) .	D		T
Gothic	T	D	Z, TH
Old High German . . .	Z	T	D

The following examples will serve to establish the rule.

1st column. Initials: *dingua, lingua, tuggo, zunga; deus,* O. N. *týr,* O. H. G. *ziu; dens, dentis,* Goth. *tunthus,* O. H. G. *zand; domare, tamjan, zemen; dolus,* O. N. *tál, zála; ducere,* Goth. *tiuhan,* O. H. G. *ziohan; duo, tva, zuei; dextra, taíhsvó, zësawa.* Middle sounds: *sedes, sedere, sitan, sizan; e-dere, itan, ëzan; videre, vitan, wizan; odium, hatis, haz; u-n-da, vató, wazar; sudor, sveiti, sweiz; pedes, fótjus, vuozi.*

2d column. The Latin has no θ; and when the R stands for the D, there are generally other coexistent forms in which the medial is found. For the purpose of comparison Grimm has selected some Latin words in which a Latin F stands by the side of the Greek θ. Initials: *fores* (θύρα), *daúr, tor; fera* (θήρ), O. N. *dýr,* O. H. G. *tior.* Middle sounds: *audere, ausus* (θαῤῥεῖν), *gadaúran, turran; mathu,* Tusc. (Gr. μέθυ), Anglo-Sax. *mëdo,* O. H. G. *mëtu.*

3d column. Initials: *tu,* Gothic *thu;* O. H. G. *dú; tener,* O. N. *thunnr,* O. H. G. *dunni; tendere,* Goth. *thanjan,* O. H. G. *denen; tacere, thahan, dagen; tolerare, thulan, dolen; tectum, thak, dach.* Middle sounds: *frater, bróthar, pruoder; rota,* O. N. *hradhr* ("celer"), O. H. G. *hrad* ("rota"); *a-l-ter* (Umbr. Tusc. *etre*), *anthar, andar; iterum, vithra, widar.*

Of the commutations of the dentals with one another in the Latin language alone, the most constant is the interchange of D with L or R. D becomes L in *delicare* (Fest. pp. 70, 73), *impelimenta, levir, Melica* (Fest. p. 124), *ol-*

facit, for *dedicare*, *impedimenta*, δαήρ, *Medica*, *odefacit*; and is assimilated to L in such words as *mala*, *ralla*, *scala*, *sella*, from *ma-n-do*, *rado*, *sca-n-do*, *sedeo* : the converse change is observable in Ὀδυσσεύς, Πολυδεύκης, δάκρυον (*dacrima*, Fest. p. 68), δαψιλής, *dingua* (O. H. G. *zunga*), *Capitodium*, *meditari*, *kadamitas*, *adauda*, &c., the more genuine forms of which are preserved in the *Ulysses* (ὀλίγος), *Pol-lux* (comp. δευκές, Hesych. with *lux*), *lacryma* (*liqueo*), *lapsilis* (λάπτω), *lingua* (λείχειν), *Capitolium*, μελετᾶν, *calamitas*, *alauda*, &c. : δέω, on the contrary, is a more ancient form than *ligare* (see *N. Crat.* p. 189). This change takes place within the limits of the Greek language also: comp. δείδω with δειλός, δᾷς (δᾷδος) with δαλός, &c., though in many of these cases there is the residue of an original assimilation, as in κάλός, root καδ-, cf. κάζω, &c. The change is also observable in the passage from Latin to the Romance languages : thus *Digentia* has become *Licenza*, and the people of *Madrid* call themselves *Madrilenos*. The other dentals, T and N, are also sometimes converted into L : as in *Thetis*, *Thelis* ; *Nympha*, *Lympha*, &c. (see Varro, *L. L.* vii. § 87). In some cases there is a passage from δ to λ in Greek, as in ἄδην, ἄλις (compare *satis*); and the Greek θ in θώρηξ is represented by an *l* in *lorica*. There is an interchange of N and R in *æreus*, *æneus*; in *murus*, *munio*; in δῶρον, *donum*; πλήρης (Etr. *phleres*), *plenus*, &c. The ablative or adverbial D has become N in *longuinquus*, *propinquus*, from *longe[d]*, *prope[d]* ; compare *antiquus*, *posticus*, from *antea*, *postea*, *amicus* from *amo* (*amao*), &c.

The change from D to R has been often pointed out, in such common instances as *aur-is* compared with *aud-io*, *apor* for *apud*, *meridie* for *media die*, *ar-vocat* for *ad-vocat*, &c. The verb *arcesso*, which is also written *accerso*, furnishes a double example of the change : the original form was *ad-ced-so* = *accedere sino*; in *arcesso* the first *d* is changed into *r*, and the second assimilated to *s:* in *accerso* the first *d* is assimilated to *c*, and the second changed to *r*.

N is principally remarkable in Latin from its use as a sort of *anusvárah* (see *N. Crat.* p. 303). In this use it is inserted, generally before the second consonant of the root, as in *tu-n-do*, root *tud-; fi-n-do*, root *fid-*, &c.; but sometimes after it, as in *ster-n-o*, root *ster-*, *stra-; sper-n-o*, root *sper-*, *spre-; pó-n-o*, root *pos-*, &c.

Conversely, N becomes evanescent in certain cases, particularly before s and v. Thus *consul* is written *cosol* (abbreviated into *cos*); and we find *cesor, infas, vicies, vicesimus*, for *censor, infans, viciens, vicensumus*. This omission of N is regular in the Greek participles in -εις, and in other words, *e.g.* ὀδούς; it seems also to have been the rule in Umbrian. The most important instance of the omission of N before V is furnished by the common word *contio*, derived from *conventio* through the form *coventio*,[1] which is found in old inscriptions. Similarly, *convent* becomes *covent* ("*Covent*-garden," &c.), *Confluentes* is turned into *Coblenz*, and *fünf* into "five." In English the prefix *con* is shortened into *co-* before all consonants, in spite of the remonstrances of Bentley.

With regard to the changes experienced by the dentals in the passage from Latin to the Romance dialects, the following instances may suffice. D and T when preceded and followed by vowels are frequently dropt in the French forms of Latin words: (a) D: *cauda* (It. *coda*, Sp. *cola*), Fr. *queue; fides*, Fr. *foi; media-nocte*, Fr. *mi-nuit; nudus*, Fr. *nu; vadum*, Fr. *gué; videre*, Fr. *voir*.[2] (b) T: *ad-satis*, Fr. *as-sez* (originally *assetz*); *amatus*, Fr. *aimé; Catalauni*, Fr. *Châlons; pater*, Fr. *père; vita*, Fr. *vie*. On the con-

---

[1] *Contio* stands related to *coventio* as *nuntius* to *novi-ven-tius;* comp. *nov-i-tius*.

[2] The French sometimes drop the D before a guttural in words of German extraction, as in *Huguenot* for *Eidgenossen*.

trary, D is sometimes inserted as a fulcrum between the liquids *n* and *r*, as in *cendre, gendre, tendre*, from *ciner-is, gener, tener; viendr-ai, tiendr-ai*, for *venir-ai (venire habeo), tener-ai (tenere habeo)*, &c.; *vendredi* for *Veneris die*, &c. This will remind the classical student of the similar insertion in the Greek ἀν-δ-ρός, &c.; and both the Greeks and the Romans apply the same principle to the labials also.

The indistinctness with which the French pronounce N at the end of a word has given rise to some etymological, or rather orthographical, inconsistencies in that language. Not the least remarkable of these is the appearance of S instead of M or N in the first person of many verb-forms. If we compare *suis* with the Italian *sono* on the one hand, and the Spanish *soy* on the other, we may doubt whether the s in this and other French forms is the ultimate resolution of the nasal N, or an arbitrary orthographic appendage. The whole question is one which demands a formal examination.

L, N, R, are frequently interchanged as the Latin passes into the Romance idiom. L passes into R[1] in *apótre, epítre, titre*, &c., from *apostolus, epistola, titulus*, &c.;—N into L in *alma, Barcelona, Bologna, Lebrixa*, from *anima, Barcino, Bononia, Nebrissa;*—N into R in *diacre* from *diaconus*.

L is a representation of D in *Giles* from *Ægidius*, in *ellera* for *edera*, and in *Versiglia* for *Vesidia*.

The Italians vocalise L into I when it follows certain consonants: compare *clamare, clarus, clavis, flos, Florentia, fluctus, flumen, obliquus, Placentia, planus, plenus*, &c., with *chiamare, chiaro, chiave, fiore, Fiorenze, Firenze, fiotto, fiume, bieco* (Fr. *biais*, Engl. "bias"), *Piacenza, piano, pieno*, &c.

---

[1] *Ad-ûlare* seems to be an instance of the converse change from R to L: for this compound is from *ad* and *ula* = οὐρά, and refers, like the Greek σαίνειν (= σείειν, " to shake or wag "), to the dog blandishing, fawning, and wagging his tail. The older etymologers connect it with *ad-oro;* but this is another word similarly formed from *ad* and *os*, and corresponding literally to the Greek προς-κυνέω.

The French vocalise the Latin L into U, which seems to have been in the first instance only an affection of the previous vowel, into which the L was subsequently absorbed. Thus *alter* was first written *aultre*, and then *autre*. This affection of a preceding vowel by the liquid which follows is not uncommon in other languages. The Greeks in some of their dialects pronounced the vowel broad before or after ρ: comp. φρασί with φρεσί, &c.: and the common people in Dorsetshire pronounce *o* like *a* when it is followed by *r* and another consonant; thus *George* is pronounced *Gearge*, *storm*, *starm*, &c. The French absorption of the L is almost universal: it is regular in the dative of the article *au*=à *le*, *aux*=à *les*; in the plurals of nouns in *l*, as *animales*, *animaux*; *canales*, *canaux*, &c. But it is also found in a number of other words, in which the vowel preceding *l* is not *a*; even when it is *u*: compare *aliquis unus*, *altare*, ἐλεημοσύνη, *Bulgare*, *felix* (like ὁ μακαρίτης, used in speaking of the dead), *ulna*, &c., with the French *aucun*, *autel*, *aumóne*, *bougre*, *feu* (anciently written *feux* and *feulx*), *aune*, &c.

VOWELS.

§ 5.
The vowels.

The philological student must always bear in mind that there are two distinct classes of vowels; the one containing the vowels of articulation, A, E, O; the other comprising the vocalised consonants I and U. In other words, there are only three distinct vowels, A, I, U; for E and O differ from A in weight only.

The original alphabet is a syllabarium consisting of breathings and consonants, which are articulated by the sound A. Now the character A in its original application denotes the lightest of the breathings, the character E the heaviest of them, and the character O a breathing which is intermediate in weight. Consequently, on the principle that the lightest vowel always co-exists with the heaviest form (see *N. Crat.* pp. 104, 300, 451), when these breathings were no longer indicated by distinct characters, A would represent the heaviest articulation-vowel, E the lightest, and O that which stands between them in point of weight. That this is actually the order of the articulation-vowels, considered in respect to the weight of the combinations in which they are found, is clearly established by an examination of the existing forms in the most perfect of the Indo-Germanic languages.

The vowels I and U result from the vocalisation, not of breathings,—as is the case with A, E, O,—but of mutes. The former is the ultimate state of the softened or assibilated gutturals and dentals, the latter is the residuum of the labials (*N. Crat.* p. 115, sqq.). But, though they are of different origin from A and its subordinates, they must be considered, especially in the Latin language, as occasionally approximating in sound to the vowels derived from breathings, and as representing them in certain cases, where forms of an intermediate weight require an intermediate weight of vowels. This will be best shewn by examples, from which it will appear that the vowels I and U have shades of value, or rather that they admit of subdivision into other vowels, differing from them in weight, as E and O differ from A, but not expressed in different characters, at least in the existing written remains of the Latin language.

It has been remarked that the *a* of the root-syllable is changed into *i* or *e* in secondary formations according to a fixed rule: namely, the *a* becomes *i* when the root-syllable in the longer form remains otherwise unchanged; but the *a* is turned into *e* when the root-syllable is followed immediately by an adscititious consonant, or when the consonant following the root-vowel is thrown back upon the vowel by some consonantal vowel like *i*, or $e = y$ (see Bopp, *Vergleich. Gramm.* p. 5; Rosen, *Journal of Education*, viii. p. 344; *N. Crat.* p. 300). The following examples may suffice to establish this:

A	I	E
amicus	in-imicus	"enmity."
arma		in-ermis.
ars		in-ers.
barba		im-berbis.
caput	oc-ciput	bi-ceps.
	prin-cipium	præ-ceps.
	sin-ciput	prin-ceps.
cado	ce-cidi.	
	stilli-cidium.	
cano	ce-cini	con-centus.
	tubi-cinis	tubi-cen.
facio	con-ficio	con-fectus.
	pro-ficiscor	pro-fectus.
factum		pro-fecto.
fallo		fe-felli.
fastus		pro-festus.
gradior		re-gredior.
jacio	ab-jicio	ab-jectus.
taceo	con-ticesco.	
tango	con-tingo.	

The cause of the change from I to E is further shewn by the change back again from E to I when the root is not followed by two consonants: thus, *bi-ceps*, &c., become *bi-cipitis*, &c. in the genitive; and similarly *tubi-cen*[s] makes *tubi-cinis*. Another change from I to E is to be remarked in the transformation of the diphthongs AI, OI into AE and OE.

The next comparison, in point of weight, which suggests itself is that between the secondary vowels I and U; and in order to make this comparison satisfactorily, it will be well to consider first their subdivisions. It appears, then, that there are three distinct uses of each of these vowels: I is (1) a very long vowel, the representative of

§ 5.]   ANALYSIS OF THE LATIN ALPHABET.   213

the diphthong AI = AE; (2) a vowel of medium length, frequently, as we have seen above, the representative of *a*, the first part of that diphthong; (3) a very short vowel, approximating to the sound of the shortest U, and used chiefly before R. Similarly, U is (1) a very long vowel, the representative of the diphthong OI = OE; (2) a vowel of medium length, generally answering to O, the first part of that diphthong; (3) a very short vowel, approximating to the sound of the shortest I, and used chiefly before L. The old Italians had separate characters for I_3 and U_3, which differed from the other characters by the addition of certain marks: I_3 was written ⌐, like a mutilated F, and U_3 was written V. It is remarkable that the emperor Claudius, when he introduced his new letters into the Roman alphabet to express the consonant v, the Greek ψ, and the modification I_3, while he inverted the digamma (thus ⅎ) to express the first, and joined two sigmas (thus)c) to express the second, which was consequently called *antisigma* (Priscian, p. 545; Putsch, i. p. 40, Krehl), was contented to borrow the third from the old alphabet of the Oscans.

The following examples will justify the subdivision which I have made of the vowels I and U.

I_1.—In composition we find this long vowel in the root-syllable of words which contain the diphthong *ai = ae*. Thus, from *æs-timo* we have *ex-istimo*; from *æquus* we have *in-iquus*; *cædo, con-cido, oc-cido*; *quæro, in-quiro*; &c.

I_2.—This is the commonest power of the Roman I. It is, however, a representative of A in other cases besides those given above: thus, *inter* stands for the old *antar*, *ille* represents the Sanscrit *anya*, old Latin *ollus*, &c.

I_3.—The sound of this letter is indicated by a passage in Velius Longus (p. 2235, Putsch): " Unde fit, ut sæpe aliud scribamus, aliud enuntiemus, sicut supra (p. 2219) locutus sum de *viro* et *virtute*, ubi I scribitur et pæne V enuntiatur; unde Ti. Claudius novam quandam litteram excogitavit, similem ei notæ, quam pro aspiratione Græci ponunt, per quam scriberentur eæ voces, quæ neque secundum exilitatem litteræ I, neque secundum pinguitudinem litteræ v sonant, ut in *viro* et *virtute*, neque rursus secundum latum litteræ sonum enuntiarentur, ut in eo quod est *legere, scribere.*" From this passage we learn that I before R was pronounced somewhat like U, as is the case with us; and we also draw the important inference that *legere* and *scribere* must have been pronounced *lire* and *scrire*. In *augur* and the proper name *Spurius* this pronunciation seems to be expressed by the vowel U. The latter is a derivative from *super*, and is equivalent in meaning to *Superbus* (above, Chap. IV. § 2); the former is a derivative from *avi-gero*, as may be proved by a curious analogy between the derivatives of *avis*, " a bird," and *æ-s*, " a weight or burden." For as *ædi-ti-mus* means a person who is conversant with a temple (Fest. p. 13 = *ædis intimus*), so *avi-timus* would mean " conversant with birds," *æs-timus*, " conversant with weights;" hence, as augury and weighing were the two most usual means of forming a judgment, both *au-tumo* and *æs-tumo* signified " to judge." Comp. the use of *con-templor, con-sidero*. Again, as *æ-ger* signifies " bearing a burden," or " burdened," and *ne-ger*, " not able to bear," or " weak" (Fest. p. 165, s. v. *ne-gritu*[*do*]), so *augur* would mean " bearing a bird," or " dealing with birds" (*belli-ger*, &c.) : comp. *au-spex*, &c.

The existence of such a short vowel as I_3 is necessary for the explanation of those forms in which I appears to be lighter than E. Thus, from *lego, rego, teneo*, we have *col-ligo, di-rigo, re-tineo;* and the I thus introduced is so short, that it is omitted altogether in some compounds of *rego*, as *per*[*r*]-*go, sur*[*r*]-*go*. In the rustic pronunciation of the Italians I was frequently dropped (as in *ame*, from *animus*), and the E, on the other hand, was lengthened improperly; see Cic. *de Orat.* iii. 12, § 46: " Quare Cotta

§ 5.]   ANALYSIS OF THE LATIN ALPHABET.   215

noster, cujus tu illa lata, Sulpici, nonnumquam imitaris, ut *iota* litteram tollas, et E plenissimum dicas, non mihi oratores antiquos, sed messores videtur imitari."

U_1.—The interchange of the diphthong *oi* = *oe* with this value of U is of constant occurrence. Thus we have *oinos, unus; moenus, munus;* &c.; and in Bœotian Greek ἔμυ for ἐμοί (Apollon. *de Pronom.* p. 364). The observation of some of these changes leads to interesting etymologies; as, for instance, in the case of the word *prœlium,* formerly written *proilium* (see Muretus, *Var. Lect.* vi. 4). The Greeks, like the Highlanders of Scotland, placed their best-armed soldiers in the first line, and by these the battle was begun and generally decided. Hence these ἥρωες or ὁπλῖται were called πρυλέες,—which is interpreted πρόμαχοι (see Hermann, *Opusc.* iv. p. 289; Müller, *Dor.* iii. 12, § 10), and is undoubtedly another form of προ-ιλέες; and hence the skirmish or battle between the van of the two armies was termed προ-ίλιον or *prœlium*. This etymology is confirmed by the obvious derivation of *milites*. The Greek language expressed large numbers in terms derived from common objects: thus, χίλιοι, "a thousand," is connected with χιλός, "a heap of fodder;" and μύριοι, "ten thousand," with μύρω, "to pour forth water." Similarly, the Latin *m-ile*, "a thousand," means only "a large number," "a crowd" (ὁμ-ιλία); and *m-il-ites* are "those who march in a large body" (compare *pari-etes*, "those which go round," scil. the house), i. e. "the common soldiers." So that we have three classes of warriors: (1) the πρυλέες, i. e. προ-ιλέες or ἥρωες, "the choice troops who fought in the van;" (2) the [*ha*]*m-ilites,* or "common soldiers, who marched in a body;" (3) the *equ-ites,* or "cavalry, who went on horseback."

In the same way as the diphthong AI becomes I_1, the diphthong AU becomes U_1: comp. *causa, ac-cuso; claudo, in-cludo;* &c. The same is the case with the Greek diphthong ου, Θουκυδίδης, *Thucydides*, &c.; and even with its Latin equivalent *ou*,—thus we have *indouco* for *indūco* on the bronze table of Tivoli (above, Chap. VI. § 19). The diphthong AU is sometimes represented by *ó = au*, as in Sanscrit: comp. *plaudo, ex-plodo; Claudius, Clodius;* &c. In *ob-oedio*, from *audio*, AU is represented by the lighter diphthong OI; and it is a further proof of the tendency to interchange between u_1 and i_1, that the diphthong OI = OE, which is so often represented by u_1, also appears as i_1: thus, *oiconomus* is written *iconomus*, ὁδοιδόκος appears as *hodidocus*, Οἰνόμαος as *Inomaus*, κοιμητήριον as *cimeterium*, &c. Sometimes, on the contrary, OE is represented by the first vowel only, as in *diocesis, poema*, &c., from διοίκησις, ποίημα, &c. (see Gifanius, in *Mureti Opp.* i. p. 550, Ruhnken.) With regard to ποιέω, the omission of the ι was common enough in Greek (see Porson, *Tracts*, p. 63; Dindorf, *ad Arist. Nub.* 1448, *Acharn.* 410).

U_2.—This is the common short U of the Romans. It corresponds generally to the short O of the Greeks; and nouns of the o-declension always exhibit this U in Latin: comp. λύκος, *lupus;* ἵππος, *equus;* &c. It is probably a remnant of the Etruscan U.

U_3.—This letter, like i_3, must be considered as a point of contact between I and U. Indeed, it may be doubtful in some cases whether u_3 has not been written for i_3. The passage of this u_3 into an approximate I is of the following nature:—First, a short O is changed into u_2. The genitive of the Greek imparisyllabic declension ends in -ος: for this the oldest Latin substitutes *-us*, as in *Castorus, nominus*, &c. compared with *Senatuos*, &c. Some of these old genitives remained to the end of the language, as *alius, ejus, hujus, illius*, &c. Again, the 1st pers. plur. of the Greek verb ended in -ομεν = -ομες: for this the old Romans wrote *-umus*, a form still preserved in *sumus* and *volumus*. Again, in old Latin the vowel of the crude form is preserved in the inflexions, as in *arcu-bus, optu-mus, pontu-fex*, &c. But in all three cases the later Latin exhibits an I: thus we have *Castoris, nominis*, &c.; *dicimus, scribimus,* &c.; *arcibus, optimus, pontifex,* &c. In these cases we observe that $U = 0$ passes into a simple I. But there are other instances in which the transition seems to go still further. As the reduplication-syllable is generally shorter than the root-syllable in the preterite of verbs, we should expect that the U, O in the first syllable of *cu-curri, mo-mordi, pu-pugi, tu-tudi*, would be an approximation rather to U_3. Then, again, in *cultus, culmen*, &c. from *colo, columen*, &c. the U is clearly less significant than O. But there are some cases in which we infer that the U, which is written, has less weight even than I. This might be inferred from *con-culco*, the secondary form of *calco*, which, according to the above table, should be either *con-cilco* or *con-celco;* and also from *difficultas, sepultus*, derived from *difficilis* and *sepelio*. The fact seems to be, that what would be I before R, becomes U_3 before L; so that U_3, I_3, are both ultimate forms of their respective vowels, and as such are in a state of convergence.

Accordingly, if we should seek to arrange the Latin vowels in regard to their comparative weight, we should, as the result of this inquiry, have the following order:

$\bar{A}$ (as in *musá*, &c.), $\bar{U}_1$, $\bar{I}_1$; A, O, U_2, I_2, E, U_3, I_3.

GREEK LETTERS.

The Greek letters subsequently employed by the Romans were Z, K, and Y. The period at which the first of these was introduced is doubtful; for while, on the one hand, we are told that Z is found in the Salian songs (Velius Longus, p. 2217: " Mihi videtur nec aliena sermoni fuisse z littera, cum inveniatur in carmine Saliari "), on the other hand we find that, even in words borrowed

§ 6. The Greek letters used by the Romans.

from the Greek, this letter is represented by *di,* as in *Sabadius* for Σέβαζος (Apulei. *Met.* viii. 170), *judaidiare* for *judaizare* (Commodian, *Instruct. adv. Gent.* c. xxxvii. 634), *trapedia* for *trapeza* (*Auctor. Rei Agrar.* p. 248), *schidia* for *schiza, oridia* for *oriza,* &c. (vide Schneid. *Elementarl.* i. p. 386; and Lobeck, *Aglaoph.* p. 296, note *l*). The fact seems to be, that the Romans had two different characters to express the two different values of the Greek z, which was a dental, either assibilated (as σδ), or softened (as δy). Now, in its latter use it becomes equivalent to the softened guttural; for the dental and guttural, when combined with *y,* which is the ultimate vocalisation of the gutturals, converge in the sound of our *j* or *sh* (*N. Crat.* pp. 126, 288). When, therefore, the Greek z more nearly approximates to the sound σδ, either this is preserved in the Latin transcriptions, as in *Mesdentius, Sdepherus,* for *Mezentius, Zephyrus* (Max. Victor. p. 1945); or the δ is assimilated to the σ, as in *Messentius, massa, Atticisso, comissor, badisso, malacisso,* &c. by the side of *Mezentius,* μάζα, Ἀττικίζω, κωμάζω, βαδίζω, μαλακίζω, &c.; or else one or other of the two component parts is omitted, as in *Saguntus* for *Zakynthus,* or *Medentius* for *Mezentius.* In this case, too, we may consider that the letter *x* occasionally steps in, as in *rixa* by the side of ἔρι[δ]ς. When, however, the Greek z is a *softened* δ, and therefore equivalent to a *softened guttural,* we find that it is represented either by the full combination *di,* as in the cases quoted above, or else by the vocalised guttural (*j*) only. Of this latter substitution there are numberless instances: such as, *Ju-piter,* Ζεὺς πατήρ; *jugum,* ζεῦγος; &c. Of these the most important are the cases connected with the first-quoted example, *Ju-piter = Dies-pater;* and I must take this opportunity of returning to one etymology belonging to this class, which has always appeared to me to open the way to a chain of the most interesting associations.

§ 6.]   ANALYSIS OF THE LATIN ALPHABET.   219

It has been shewn elsewhere (*N. Crat.* p. 130) how the Greek H, originally the mark of aspiration, came to be used as a sign for the long *e*. Out of that investigation it appeared—(1) that a short vowel aspirated may be equivalent to an unaspirated long vowel; (2) that the vocalised consonants *i* and *u* may change their place; (3) that these vocalised consonants may be absorbed into or represented by the long vowel only. To the instances given there, I will now add the iota subscriptum of the Greek dative, and the Ionic Greek absorption of υ after ω, as in θῶυμα, ἑωυτοῦ, &c.[1] These principles explain the connexion between *ἦπαρ, jecur* (Sanscr. *yakrit*); ἥμισυ, διάμεσος, *dimidius;* and between ἡμέρα = διάμερος, and *dies*[2] (comp. *diuturnus, juturna; Diana, Janus,* &c.). Now, besides ἡμέρα, we have an adjective ἥμερος, " civilised," "cultivated," &c. the regular antithesis of ἄγριος; and it has been suggested (ibid. p. 181), that this word was originally applied to a country through which there was a road or passage, a country divided by a road (διάμερος); just as ἄγριος was properly applied to a rude, open country, with nothing but ἄγροι. This is sufficiently proved by Æsch. *Eumen.* 13, 14: κελευθόποιοι παῖδες Ἡφαίστου, χθόνα ἀνήμερον τιθέντες ἡμερωμένην. Pind. *Isthm.* iii. 76 (iv. 97): ναυτιλίαισί τε πορθμὸν ἀμερώσατο. Herod. i. 126: ἐνθαῦτα ὁ Κῦρος (ἦν γὰρ ὁ χῶρος — ἀκανθώδης —) τοῦτόν σφι τὸν χῶρον προεῖπε ἐξημερῶσαι ἐν ἡμέρᾳ. iv. 118:

[1] In many editions of Herodotus we have these words written θῶυμα, ἑωϋτοῦ, &c.; but the accentuation of θῶυμα sufficiently proves that it is a dissyllable; and even if we had not this evidence, it would be contrary to all analogy to infer a resolution of a diphthong in a crasis, the sole object of which is to shorten the word. Why should τωὐτό be written, if it were a word of as many syllables as τὸ αὐτό?

[2] In the name of the city Ἱμέρα (another form of ἡμέρα, see Böckh's note on Pindar, *O.* xii. 13-21, p. 210), the preposition διά is represented by the aspirated ι. In the word *meri-die* also the syllables *ia* are contracted into *ī*. There is a similar contraction in *anti-quus, posti-cus,* from *antea, postea*.

τοὺς αἰεὶ ἐμποδὼν γινομένους ἡμεροῦται πάντας. In all of these passages the verb ἡμερόω implies making a clear passage or road; and in Plato (*Legg.* p. 761 A.) the adjective ἥμερος is used as a predicate of ὁδός: ὁδῶν τε ἐπιμελουμένους, ὅπως ὡς ἡμερώταται ἔκασται γίγνωνται.[1] That the Greeks connected road-making with civilisation in general, and with the peaceful commerce of man with man, appears from many passages (Aristotle, περὶ θαυμασίων ἀκουσμάτων, c. 85, p. 837, Bekk.; Thucydides, i. 2, compared with i. 13, &c.); and this is generally implied in all the legends relating to Hercules and Theseus. But it has not been sufficiently remarked that this road-making was also intimately connected with the cultivation of land. It may, however, be shewn, that as the Greek ἄγρος becomes ἥμερος when divided by a road, by a similar process the Latin *ager* becomes *jugerum* = *di-ager-um*.

Whenever a piece of unemployed ground—of *ager*, so called—was to be taken into use, whether for cultivation, or for the site of a city or a camp, the rules of the ancient *limitatio* were immediately applied. Now this very word *limitatio* signifies, the dividing of a certain piece of ground into main-roads (*viæ*) and cross-roads (*limites*); and the same primary notion is conveyed by *tem-plum*, so obviously derived from *tem-no*, Gr. τάμ-νω, comp. τέμενος, &c. For in all *limitation* the first thing done was to observe the *templum*, i. e., as we should say, to take the bearing by the compass.[2] Suppose the augur stood with his back to the north, then the line from north to south would be

---

[1] The word ἤπειρος = ἡ διαπέραν χώρα, furnishes another instance of the substitution of η for διά: comp. the epithet διαπρύσιος, Pind. *N.* iv. 51, where see the note.

[2] Most ancient nations seem to have connected the *regiones cœli* with the *regiones viarum*. Thus in old English "the milky way" was called "Watling-street," which was the name of one of the four great roads in this country; see Grimm, *Deutsche Myth.* p. 330, 2d ed.

called the *cardo*, as corresponding to the axis of the globe; and that from east to west, which cut the *cardo* at right angles, would be called the *decumanus*, or " tenth line." For both these lines repeated themselves according to the number of separate allotments into which the land was divided, or the number of separate streets in the city or camp.[1] Now the Roman *actus* or *fundus* = [120 feet][2] was the unit of subdivision; two of these *fundi* made a *jugerum* = *di-ager-um*, and two *jugera* constituted the *heredium* of a Roman patrician; consequently, 200 *jugera* made up the *ager limitatus* of a century of the old Roman populus (Fest. s. v. *Centuriatus*, p. 53). If this *ager limitatus*, then, were arranged as a square, we have, of course, for each side 20 × 120 feet. Supposing, then, a road between each two of the *fundi*,— which there must have been, as every two *fundi* made a *di-ager-um*,— the *cardo* which passed between the tenth and eleventh *fundus* would be properly called the *decumanus*, and it would consequently be the main road, and would be terminated by the main gate (*porta decumana*). The point at which the *decumanus* crossed the *cardo* was called *groma* or *gruma;* and here, in a city or camp, the two cross-roads seem to have spread themselves out into a kind of *forum*. There is as much probability in the supposition that the immortal name of Rome was derived from this ancient word, as

---

[1] It would seem that the word *sicilicus* (from *seco*) was properly and originally applied to this apportionment of land. In the Bantine Table (l. 25) we have *nep him pruhipid mais zicolois* x *nesimois;* which I have translated (above, p. 97), *ne in hoc prœhibeat* (i.e. *prœbeat*) *magis sicilicis* x *contiguis*. According to Klenze (*Abhandl.* p. 50) x *nesimois* = *decimis;* but I cannot understand why we should have an ordinal here. The root of *ne-simus* appears in *nahe*, *near*, *next*, &c.; and I would understand it of so many adjoining allotments. The *sicilicus* was 600 square feet, *i.e.* $\frac{1}{48}$ of the jugerum, or $\frac{1}{24}$ of the actus. Consequently, the 30 contiguous *sicilici* mentioned in l. 17 would be $\frac{5}{8}$ of the jugerum, or $\frac{5}{4}$ of the actus; and the 10 contiguous *sicilici* would, therefore, be $\frac{5}{24}$ of the former and $\frac{5}{12}$ of the latter.

there is in any of the numerous etymologies suggested by Festus (p. 266). From this it appears, that among the Romans it was the same thing to speak of a territory as divided by roads, and to call it cultivated, occupied, or built upon; and the *jugerum*, or divided *ager*, implied both. To the same principle we may refer the importance attached by the ancients to straight ploughing;[1] for the furrow was the first element of the road; and the *urbs* itself was only that space round which the plough had been formally and solemnly drawn.

The Romans were very sparing in their use of the Greek letter κ. It was occasionally employed to form the syllable *ka*, as in *kaput, kalumnia, Karthago, evokatus, Parkarum;* but in these instances it was considered quite superfluous; and Quinctilian thinks (i. 4, 9, and 7, 10) that its use ought to be restricted to those cases in which it serves as the conventional mark of an abbreviation, as in K.=*Kæso*, and K. or Kal.=*Kalendæ*.

The letter γ was never used by the Romans except as the transcription of υ in words derived either from or through the Greek; and it seems to have been a representative of those sounds which have been designated above by the characters u_1 and u_3, both of which involve an approximation to the sound of ι. Hence, in the French alphabet it is not improperly called "the Greek *i*" (*i grec*). In many words, rather connected with the Greek than derived from it, the υ is represented by ι, as in *cliens, in-clitus* (κλύω), *clipeus* (κρύπτω), *silva* (ὕλϝη), &c.; while in others the υ has become ε, as in *socer* (ἑκυρός), *remulco* (ῥυμουλκέω), *polenta* (παλυντή), &c. The Roman u_2 some-

---

[1] See Hesiod. *Op. et D.* 443:

ὅς κ' ἔργου μελετῶν ἰθεῖαν αὔλακ' ἐλαύνοι,
μηκέτι παπταίνων μεθ' ὁμήλικας.

Luke ix. 62; and comp. the tropical use of *delirare*.

§ 7.]   ANALYSIS OF THE LATIN ALPHABET.   223

times represents the common υ of the Greeks, as in *lupus*
(λύκος), *nunc* (νῦν), *fui* (φύω), &c.; sometimes the Greek
o, as in all nouns of the *o*-declension.

NUMERALS.

This examination of the Latin alphabet will not be
complete without some remarks on the signs which were
used by the Romans to denote the numeral adjectives.
Priscian, in his usual school-boy way, has endeavoured to
establish the connexion between the numeral signs as we
have them, and the ordinary Roman capitals. Thus, *quinque*, he tells us, is represented by V, because this is the
fifth vowel; *quinquaginta* is L, because, etymologically,
L and N may be interchanged, and N is πεντήκοντα in
Greek; *quingenta* is D, because this is the next letter to
C!—and so forth (Priscian, ii. p. 388, ed. Krehl).

§ 7.
The numeral signs.

Now there can be no doubt that the Roman numeral
signs are derived from the Tuscans; though in certain
cases a Roman capital has been substituted for an Etruscan character which does not correspond to it in value,
and though in these instances the figures are either inclined or reversed. The Etruscan characters are as follows:—

I, II, III, IIII, Λ, ΛI, ΛII, ΛIII, IX, X, &c.
1, 2, 3, 4, 5, 6, 7, 8, 9, 10.

XX, XXX, XXXX or XΤ, Τ, ΤX, &c.
20, 30, 40, 50, 60,

⊕, 8, Ɒ, ⊕, &c.
100, 1000, 5000, 10000.

It is sufficiently obvious that the first ten of these
characters are identical with the Roman figures, the Λ, &c.
being reversed; and as Τ is often written T, and as ⊥
L, frequently occur on Roman family coins, we may

recognise in this character the original of the Roman L, and therefore identify the Etruscan and Roman ciphers from 1 to 99. The Roman C and the Etruscan ⊕ do not appear to be connected; but the Etruscan 8, or, as it is also written ⟪Φ⟫, is clearly the same as the Roman ⟪⟫, ⟪Φ⟫, and cIɔ, for which M was subsequently written; and the same remark applies to the still higher numbers.

If, then, the Roman ciphers were derived from the Tuscans, it is obvious that we must seek in the Tuscan language for an interpretation. Now it cannot be doubted that the Tuscan numeral signs are either letters of the alphabet slightly changed, or combinations of such characters made according to fixed rules. Thus, Λ is the inverted V $=u$; ⟪Ͳ⟫ or T is an inverted $\psi = ch$; and $8 = f$. Since, therefore, the position of these letters in the organic alphabet does not correspond to their value as numeral signs, we must conclude that they represent the initials of the numerals in the Etruscan, just as M afterwards denoted *mille* in the Latin language. We do not know any Etruscan numeral, and therefore cannot pretend to any certainty on this subject; but this is the most probable inference. The manner in which the elementary signs are combined to form the intermediate numerals is more easily and safely investigated. The character denoting unity is perhaps selected from its simplicity; it is the natural and obvious *score* in every country. This character is combined with itself to form the next three digits, though four is sometimes expressed as $5-1$, according to the principle of subtraction so common among the Romans (comp. *duodeviginti*, &c.). The same plan is adopted to form the numerals between 5 and 10. The number 10 is represented by a combination of two V's—thus, X; and this figure enclosed in a circle indicates the multiplication of 10 by itself, or 100. The letter 8, or ⟪Φ⟫, being assumed as the representative of 1000, its half, or D, would indicate 500; and as multiplication by ten was indicated by a circle in the case of 100, on the same principle ⊕ would be 10,000, and its half or ⅅ would represent 5000.

These rules for the formation of one numeral from another are more obvious than the origin of the elementary numeral signs. But where certainty is not within our reach, we must be contented with a solution of those difficulties which may be submitted with safety to the searching analysis of philology.

CHAPTER VIII.

THE LATIN CASE-SYSTEM.

§ 1. Completeness of the Latin case-system. § 2. General scheme of the case-endings. § 3. Latin declensions. § 4. Hypothetical forms of the nominative and accusative plural. § 5. Existing forms—the genitive and dative. § 6. The accusative and ablative. § 7. The vocative and the neuter forms. § 8. Adverbs considered as cases of nouns.

§ 1.
Completeness
of the Latin
case-system.

THE system of cases, with which the Latin noun is furnished, is far more complete than that of the Greek declension. The Greek noun has no ablative case; its accusative has frequently lost its characteristic termination; the genitive is confused by the mixture of an ablative meaning; and the locative is almost lost. The greater number and distinctness of the Latin cases is due to the greater antiquity of the language, which had not yet begun to substitute prepositions for inflexions. As the language degenerates into the so-called Romance idioms, we find that its cases are gradually lost, and their place taken by a number of prefixes, which add indeed to the syntactical distinctness of the language, but purchase this advantage by sacrificing the etymological development.

In treating of the Latin cases, our attention is directed to three different aspects under which they may be considered. We may regard them either according to a general scheme derived from all the declensions, or as modified by those varieties in the termination of the crude form which constitute differences of declension; or we may take both of these together, and add to them those additional phenomena which are furnished by the adverb. A supplementary source of information respecting the cases may be derived from those nouns, whether substantive or adjective, which are obviously formed from the oblique cases of other nouns. Thus, we know that the original Greek genitive ended in -σιο (Sanscr. *sya*) from the form of the possessive adjective δημόσιος (Bopp, *Vergl. Gramm.* p. 294, note), and the genitive μέο is presumed in the old possessive μεός (see *N. Crat.* p. 164). Similarly, a case in *-ine*, analogous to the Sanscrit instrumental, may be inferred both from the particle *sine* and from the derivative forms *urbánus* (= *urbáinus*), &c., and *officina* (= *officiina*), &c.

If we confine ourselves to the forms of the noun, we get the following general scheme of the case-endings.

§ 2. General scheme of the case-endings.

SING.   PLUR.

Nom.   *s* (sometimes absorbed, assimilated,   [*s*]*es* (variously modified)
       or dropt by *visargah*)
Gen.   *is, jus, sis*   [*r*]*um*
Dat.   *i* or *bi* (the *b* is preserved only in   [*b*]*us* = *is*
       the pronouns)
Accus. *m*   [*m*]*s* (the singular *m* constantly absorbed)
Abl.   *a*[*d*] (the *d* is found only in old Latin) [*b*]*us* = *is*.

By taking the different crude forms according to the usual classification, we shall at once see how this scheme is modified and applied.

§ 3. Latin declensions.

CONSONANT-DECLENSION.

SING.   PLUR.

Nom.   *lapi*[*d*]*s*   *lapid*-[*s*]-*es* (= *és*)
Gen.   *lapid-is*   *lapide-rum* [1]
Dat.   *lapid-i*-[*bĭ*] (= *í*)   *lapid-i-bus*
Accus. *lapid-e-m*   *lapid-e*[*m*]*s* (= *és*)
Abl.   *lapid-e*[*d*]   *lapid-i-bus*

[1] Charisius, i. 40.

VOWEL-DECLENSIONS.

A

	Sing.	Plur.
Nom.	*familiă-[s]*	*familia-[sĕs]* (= *ai, æ*)
Gen.	*familia-is* (= *ás, āi, æ*)	*familia-rum*
Dat.	*familia-[b]i* (= *æ*)	*familia-bus* (= *ís*)[1]
Accus.	*familia-m*	*familia-[m]s* (= *ás*)
Abl.	*familia-[d]* (= *á*)	*familia-bus*

E

	Sing.	Plur.
Nom.	*die-s*	*die-[se]s*
Gen.	*die-i[s]*	*die-rum*
Dat.	*die-[b]i*	*die-bus*
Accus.	*die-[m]*	*die-[m]s*
Abl.	*die-[d]*	*die-bus*

I

	Sing.	Plur.
Nom.	*avi-s*	*avi-[sĕ]s* (= *és*)
Gen.	*avi-is* (= *avyis, avis*)	*avi-[r]um*
Dat.	*avi-[b]i* (= *aví*)	*avi-bus*
Accus.	*avi-m* (= *em*)	*avi-[m]s* (= *és*)
Abl.	*avi-[d]*	*avi-bus*

O

	Sing.	Plur.
Nom.	*avo-s*	*avo-ses* (= *aví*, as in gen. sing.)
Gen.	*avo-is* (or *sus* or *syo*, = *io*, = *í*)[2]	*avo-rum*
Dat.	*avo-[b]i* (= *ó*)	*avo-bus* (= *ís*)
Accus.	*avo-m*	*avo-[m]s* (= *ós*)
Abl.	*avo-[d]*	*avo-bus* (= *ís*)

[1] For the form in *-bus* comp. Orelli, *Inscr.* no. 1628, 1629, 4601, &c., and K. L. Schneider, *Formenlehre*, i. p. 25, sqq.

[2] As δημόσιο, δημόιο, δήμου, comp. the nom. plural.

U

	Sing.	Plur.
Nom.	fructu-s	fructu-ses (= ús)
Gen.	fructu-is (= ús)	fructu-[r]um
Dat.	fructu-[b]i (= ú)	fructu-bus
Accus.	fructu-m	fructu-[m]s (= ús)
Abl.	fructu-[d]	fructu-bus.

If now we compare these particular instances with the general scheme, we shall see that, taking all the varieties of the crude form, of which the above are specimens, there are only two assumptions in the general table,—namely, the original forms of the nominative and accusative plural. All the others are actually found, either in nouns or pronouns, at some epoch of the language.

§ 4. Hypothetical forms of the nominative and accusative plural.

With regard to the nominative and accusative plural, the assumed original forms are derived from a sound induction according to the principles of comparative philology.

And first with regard to the nominative plural. The sign of this case must have been originally -s throughout the declensions. Now it appears from general considerations, as well as from an induction of facts, that -s was also the sign of the nominative singular (*New Cratylus*, p. 317). Therefore the -s of the nominative plural, if it was to distinguish the form from the same case in the singular, cannot have been appended to the mere crude form of the noun; for then the nominatives singular and plural would have been one and the same inflexion. It must have been formed by adding the -s (with, of course, an intervening short vowel, for the Latin language does not tolerate a double-s at the end of a word) to the full form of the nominative, and thus constituting, as the total addition to the crude form, or the real termination, the syllable -ses. This view is supported, not only by the fact that the plurals *vo-bis*, *era-mus*, &c., actually stand in this relation to the singulars *ti-bi*, *era-m*, &c., but even more so by the analogy of the genitive singular. For in many cases the genitive singular is identical, in its secondary form, with the nominative plural: thus *familiæ*, *avi*, are the common forms of both cases. But *familiæ* is actually written *familiás = familiaěs*. Hence we may presume the same original form of the nominative plural *familiæ* (compare *dies*, &c). Now the original form of the nom. singular must have been *familiă-s;* consequently, if, when the nom. sing. was *familia*, the nom. plur. was *familia-ěs = familiæ*, it follows that when the nom. sing. was *familiă-s*, the nom. plur. must have been *familia-sěs*. The same follows from the form *avi*. I have preferred to treat the original form of the nominative plural as an assumption, and to support it by the arguments which I have just adduced; but if we remember that the original s of many Roman words was not changed into R till about the 4th century A.U.C. (above, Ch. VII. § 3), we might take the existence of such forms as *vi-res*, *spe-res* (which occurs in fragments of Ennius), and *gnaru-res* (which is found in Plautus, *Mostellaria*, i. 2, 17; *Pœnulus*, prol. 47), as a distinct confirmation of the theory. And here again the analogy of the genitive becomes applicable, as will be seen below (§ 5). The pronouns also supply a partial confirmation of the above induction; for though in common Latin we find a genitive singular in -*s* by the side of a nominative plural in -*i*, we learn from old inscriptions that there was also a nominative plural in -*s*: see *Senatus-Cons. de Bacch.* ll. 3, 7; *Lex Rom. Bant. Tab.* l. 21; Klenze *ad Leg. Servil.* p. 12.

Again, in regard to the accusative plural, which in all the above instances ends in -*s* preceded by a long vowel, we must infer that -*s* is the termination of the plural as such, from considerations of the same nature with those which have been just brought forward. We should also have no difficulty in supposing that the long vowel indicates the absorption of some consonant. This consonant can only be the -*m* of the accusative singular; for not only is this most probable *à priori*, but it is the only supposition which explains all the phenomena. Let us take the Greek, Latin, Sanscrit, and Gothic forms in a particular word; and we shall see that, while the Gothic alone preserves the outward marks of such a derivation of the accusative plural from the accusative singular, the only possible explanation of the other forms is the supposition that they were originally identical with the Gothic. Thus, λύκο-ν, *lupu-m, vrĭka-m, vulfa-n,* are the accusatives singular of synonymous words in these four languages. The plural of the Gothic *vulfa-n* is simply *vulfa-n-s*, whereas all the other forms strengthen the final vowel of the crude form, and drop one of the concluding consonants: λύκον becomes λύκους, *lupum* is converted into *lupós*, and *vrĭkam* into *vrĭkán*. The comparison of ὀδούς, &c. with *dens*, &c. shews us that λύκους may stand for λύκονς; and the analogy of τύπτων = τύπτον[τ]ς is sufficient to explain the change of *vrĭkans* into *vrĭkán*. If we add to this, that when the accusative singular has lost its final consonant, the plural accusative merely adds -*s* to the existing form of the singular (as in ἄνδρα[ν], τύπτοντα[ν], sing., ἄνδρα-ς, τύπτοντα-ς, plural), we have, it should seem, the most satisfactory evidence which the subject admits, in support of the assumed original form of the accusative plural.

Having thus justified the only hypothetical forms in the above scheme of cases, it will be desirable to make some remarks on the most striking peculiarities in the existing inflexions.

In the general scheme, the genitive singular is characterised by the terminations -*is*, -*sis*, or -*jus*; the gen. plural by the ending -*rum*, where the *r* is generally dropt, ex-

§ 5. Existing forms —the genitive and dative.

cept in the *a*, *e*, and *o* declensions, which constantly retain it. The difficulty here felt is, to connect the plural form with the singular. Struve's assertion (*über die Lat. Decl.* 3, 15), that the *r* is merely euphonic, would tend, if we assented to it, to complicate and increase this difficulty in no small degree. The comparative philologer cannot doubt that the original form of the genitive plural in the Indo-Germanic languages was that which is preserved in the Sanscrit -*sâm* = ΣΩΜ (see Müller *ad Varron. L. L.* viii. § 74, p. 192). This form, after the fourth century A. U. C., would appear in Latin as ROM, which was afterwards softened into RŬM. The Indians wrote -*nâm* for -*sâm* in many of their words, where the *n* represents the *s*, as in *vrĭkân* for *vrĭkás* = *vrĭkăm-s;* but in the pronouns, which generally preserve the authentic forms longer than the nouns, we have *tâ-sâm* = *istâ-rum*. The Greeks very often omitted an σ- between two vowels in a case like this; and as they wrote ἐλέγου for ἐλέγεσο, ἰχθυ-ες for ἰχθυσ-ες, so they gave us δημόιο, or ultimately δήμου, for the original δημόσιο, and μουσά-ων, or ultimately μουσῶν, for μουσάσων. That -*rum* is the proper and genuine form of the Latin genitive is proved not merely by the fact that the Romans actually wrote -*um* for -*orum* when it suited their convenience,[1] thereby shewing the reason for the omission of the *r* in the other declensions, but also by the fact that the *r* is found in the pronouns, the oldest and most immutable parts of speech, and that in the older state of the language even nouns of the other declensions retained the *r:* thus we hear of such words as *boverum*, *Joverum* (Varro, *L. L.* viii. § 74), *lapiderum*, *nucerum*, *regerum* (Cn. Gellius *apud Charisium*, i. 40). This evidence receives very striking confirmation from the analogy of the genitive singular. The most common characteristic of the genitive singular

---

[1] On this abbreviation, see Cicero's remarks in *Orator*, c. 46, § 155.

§ 5.]   THE LATIN CASE-SYSTEM.   233

is the termination *-is*. There are two reasons, however, which may induce us to doubt if this is the full and original form of the genitive-ending. First: the genitive-ending of the pronouns and oldest adjectives is not *-is*, but *-ius*: thus we have *cu-ius* or *quo-ius, ist-ius, un-ius, alter-ius*, &c.[1] Secondly: the possessive adjectives, which so often give us the true form of the genitive, end in *-ius*; as *prætor-ius*, or, what is the same thing, in *-ĕus*, as *virgin-eus*. It seems, however, that even this does not carry us back to the full and genuine type of the termination. The Sanscrit *vrĭkă-sya* compared with λυκόιο, and the possessive δημό-

[1] The personal pronouns *ego, nos*, and *tu, vos*, and the reflexive pronoun *se*, have properly speaking no genitive case. They express this relation by the derived or possessive pronouns *meus, noster; tuus, vester;* and *suus*. Sometimes these forms are regularly inflected through the cases, genders, and numbers, like other adjectives, and sometimes they are used as neuter nouns in the genitive singular. When the personality implied is emphatic, the latter is the proper usage; as in Ovid, *Heroid.* xiii. 166: *Si tibi cura mei, sit tibi cura tui.* Cic. *ad Fam.* xii. 17: *Grata mihi vehementer est memoria nostri tua.* Catil. iv. 9: *Habetis ducem memorem vestri, oblitum sui.* More generally, however, the genitive relation is expressed by the inflected possessive: as *petitio mea; amicus ille tuus; Cicero noster;* &c. And even in apposition with a genitive, as in Horat. i. *Serm.* iv. 23: *Mea scripta recitare timentis;* or in opposition to one, as Ovid, *Heroid.* vii. 134: *Parsque tui lateat corpore clausa meo.* By a singular attraction, the genitive plural of the possessive is in certain cases used where we should expect the genitive plural of the personal pronoun. Zumpt supposes that *nostrûm, vestrûm*, are used when the subject is signified; *nostri, vestri*, when the genitive denotes the object. When *omnium* precedes, *nostrûm, vestrûm*, are always preferred to *nostri, vestri;* as Cic. *Cat.* i. 7: *Patria est communis omnium nostrûm parens.* But we may have the inflected possessive before *omnium;* as in Cic. *Cat.* iv. 2: *Hi ad vestram omnium cædem Romæ restiterunt.* The impersonal verbs *interest* and *rêfert* not only employ these possessives as regular genitives, but also as inflected in the dative singular feminine to agree with *rei*, which is understood in *interest* and included in *rêfert = rei fert*. We have, however, in this use the forms *meâ, suâ*, &c., for *meæ, suæ*, &c., on the analogy of *post-hac* for *post-hæc*, &c. That the case is dative is proved not only by the competent testimony of Verrius (*apud Fest.* p. 282; see Müller, *Suppl. Annot.* p. 405), but also by many similar constructions. In Cato, *R. R.* c. 3, we have: *et rei et virtuti et gloriæ exit.*

σιος by the side of δημό-ιο, might lead us to suspect that the termination commenced with an *s,* which was subsequently absorbed; and this suspicion is confirmed by the fact, that there are in old Latin genitives ending in *-ris* = *-sis* where the *r* = *s* is not part of the crude form. Thus we have *sue-ris* for *suis* in the fragment of Plautus quoted by Festus, s. v. *Spetile,* p. 330: " Esto pernam, sumen *sueris,* spetile, callum, glandia." .Compare Varro, *L. L.* v. § 110, p. 44. And from the extant forms of the nominative plural in *-res* we may fairly infer that the genitive in *-ris* was not uncommon. Thus we have a perfect analogy between the genitives singular and plural; and the long vowel in the termination of the latter will be explained in the same way as the long vowel of the accusative plural: comp. the Sanscrit dual *-bhyâm* with the plural *-bhyas* or *-bhis.*

With regard to the dative singular, I need only refer to the Eugubine Tables, which give us, in the Latin writing, *ovi, vitlu,* instead of *ufeph, fitluph,* which appear in the corresponding passages of the Umbrian inscriptions.

§ 6.
The accusative and ablative.

The accusative and ablative require a more attentive consideration than has generally been bestowed upon them. The specimens of old Latin in Chap. VI. have sufficiently shewn that the characteristic of the Latin ablative was *-d,* or perhaps, at one period of the language, *-t.* The common sign of the accusative is *-m.* This corresponds strictly to the Sanscrit. The Greek language, however, being intolerant of *m* and *d* at the end of a word, has changed the *-m* into *-v,* and softened the *-d* of the ablative into *-ς.* The Greek language therefore affords no assistance to the philologer, when he is puzzled and perplexed, as he cannot but be, by the interchange and confusion of the locative, ablative, genitive, and objective notions, which have attached themselves to these two endings, which — being the one a labial, the other a dental—cannot have a common origin. First of all comes the fact, that in pronouns this dental termination, *-d* or *-t*, marks the neuter nominative-accusative of pronouns as well as the ablative: thus, *i-d, illu-d, quo-d*, &c. are never used as ablatives in common Latin; *me, te, se* (anciently *met, tet, set*, or *med, ted, sed; ego-met, me-met, ted-ipsum*, &c.), were both ablatives and accusatives; *sed*, which seems to be an ablative in its use as a conjunction, is an accusative in the *Senat.-Cons. de Bacch.* (ll. 13, 14.) Then, again, the termination *-m* is a regular locative in pronominal particles, such as *enim, jam*, &c. And the plural form used for the ablative is the same as the dative, *-bus* from *-bi*, which is a pure locative. Then, again, *-ĭ-nă* is the instrumental ending in Sanscrit; and *se* (=*sed*) is synonymous with *si-nĕ* in old Latin (above, Ch. VI. § 16). The form in *-na* or *-ina* in Sanscrit generally marks the instrumental case; but in the Italian languages *ne* seems to have indicated the locative case. Thus we have *pone* for *postne*, whence *pus-naies* in Umbrian; and the ethnical names *Romanus*, &c. seem to be derived from locatives. The Sanscrit neuter plural in *-nĭ* is probably a locative of the same kind. These and other difficulties of a similar nature are purely metaphysical. The solution of them which appears most satisfactory is that which would refer this interchange to the ultimate convergence of the ideas of location, causality, possession, derivation, &c., in the one great consciousness of objectivity. Our instinctive belief in an outer world—in something which is not self—assumes a number of different forms, according to the relations under which the objects present themselves to us: but still it is only one idea—the things are *there*, and as such are either located, presented, possessed; they are causes, instruments, occasions, as the case may be. Why should διά with the genitive signify "an instrument," with the accusative "an occasion" or "a cause?" Why should ὑπό with the genitive denote " causation," but with the dative mere " locality ?" Why should κατά with the genitive imply motion in a vertical line, but κατά with the accusative motion in an horizontal line ? These are questions which carry us back to the very foundations of all psychology ; and it is not the design of the present work to deal with such matters.[1]

§ 7.
The vocative and the neuter forms.

In the above scheme of the case-endings, and in the examples of the different declensions, I have omitted the vocative, because it is either the nominative, or, when it exists as such, is merely the crude form of the noun; and I have said nothing of nouns of the neuter gender, because the only distinction between these and other nouns consists in the circumstance that they have no nominative as distinct from the accusative[2] (see *N. Crat.* p. 314). The only remark which this part of the subject requires, is one connected with the last paragraph. All neuter nouns, to whatever declension they belong, form their plural nominative-accusative in *ă*. By the side of this we may place another general observation. All Greek nouns, whatever their crude form may be, have *ă* as the termination of their

---

[1] I have attempted to remove some of these difficulties in the *N. Crat.* (pp. 57 sqq., 157 sqq., 212 sqq., &c.). A young Cambridge philologer has published a second edition of my remarks, " with corrections," under the title of " A First Lesson in Psychology—Remarks upon certain Passages of the *New Cratylus.*" The subject will not, I fear, be simplified by the additional distinctions which he proposes to introduce.

[2] It is, perhaps, hardly necessary to say that in neuter nouns like *genus, tempus, robor,* &c., the *s* = *r* is not a nominative-ending, but the termination of the crude form, and consequently that the genitive-ending of these nouns is not *-ris* = *sis*, but *-is*. That the *s* in such words belongs to the crude form is clear from the derivatives *gener-osus, tempes-tas, robus-tus,* &c. The same may be said of the corresponding Greek forms in *-os* ; as ὅρος, which in its derivatives preserves the *-s* (as in ὀρές-βιος, &c.), though it has lost it in the cases ὅρεος for ὅρεσος, the σ being omitted, as it is in verbs (ἐλέγεσο = ἐλέγου) and nouns (δημόϊο for δημόσιο).

§ 7.]   THE LATIN CASE-SYSTEM.   237

accusative singular, when the regular -ν is omitted: thus we have ἄνδρᾰ for ἄνδρα-ν, and τύπτοντᾰ for τύπτοντα-ν. These two phenomena put together would lead us to the conclusion, that the plural nominative-accusative of Latin nouns originally terminated in a dental. That this was actually the case appears from the *Senatus-Consultum de Bacch.* (l. 24): *quei advorsum ea-d fecisent.* Consequently there was no real distinction of number in the objective cases of neuter nouns; and this is in harmony with the fact, that in Greek such nouns govern a singular verb.

Three of the pronouns exhibit a deviation from this form of the noun. The demonstrative *hi-c* makes its neuter *hæ-c;* and the relative *qui,* and the interrogative and indefinite *quis* (with their derivatives), have *quæ* in the neuter plural. If we compare the sing. fem. of these pronouns (*hæc, quæ*) with the corresponding forms in the other pronouns (*eă, istă,* &c.), we are induced to believe that the former must have been originally *hă, quă,* which having been strengthened by the addition of the other pronominal element *ce,* represented the loss of this, or of its final vowel, by a lengthening of the case-vowel. This supposition is not affected by the circumstance, that the vowel is equally lengthened whether the *-c* is appended or not; for there are other indubitable instances of the fact that a vowel, which has crept in as a modified pronunciation of a consonant, has taken its place at first by the side of the consonant which it ultimately supplants. This we know to have been the case with the French *u* considered as a substitute for *l;* for *alter* was written *aultre* before it became *autre; canales* appeared as *canaulx* before the word subsided into *canaux,* &c. Moreover there appear to have been cases of *hi-c* in which the *-c* was written after it had ceased to be pronounced: thus Varro has *hi-c* for *hi* (*L. L.* vi. § 73, p. 102), and *hæ-c* for *hæ* (*L. L.* v. §§ 75, 98, 137); and the latter spelling occurs also in Plautus

(*Aulul.* iii. 5, 59) and Terence (*Eun.* iii. 5, 34; *Phorm.* v. 8, 23). It seems, too, that the termination -*ce* was sometimes represented by a mere lengthening of the vowel *a* without any addition, as in *quā-propter*; sometimes the termination -*c* is appended without any additional vowel, as in *post-hac, advorsus hac*. The appearance of the former phenomenon in such forms as *inter-eā, post-eā*, &c., leads to the inference that the plural of *is* was also sometimes furnished with this appendix; and this inference is in some measure confirmed by the analogy of *post-eśa-k* in the Oscan language (see above, Ch. IV. § 4).

§ 8.
Adverbs considered as cases of nouns.

If now we add to the observations derived from the actual cases of the nouns and pronouns, the additional phenomena furnished by the adverbs, the subject of this chapter will have received all the examination of which it is capable.

Adverbs are, properly speaking, certain cases of pronouns and nouns, and under particular circumstances they are deduced from the participles or supines of verbs. Their syntactical use is as secondary predicates, inasmuch as they convey predication only through the verb of the sentence. The Greeks use their adjectives and participles for this purpose without any additional inflexion; but the Roman adverbs are always cases, and sometimes, if one may use the expression, double or superimposed cases of nominal or pronominal forms.

Pronominal adverbs are secondary predicates either of place or of time. The former indicate—(*a*) " locality," in which case they generally exhibit the locative endings -*bi* and -*m*: thus, from the demonstrative *is* and the relative *qui*, we have *i-bi* and *ubi*, originally *cubi*, comp. *ali-cubi*, &c.; the ending -*m* appears in *us-quam* or *uspiam*, &c.;— (*b*) " motion towards," in which case they end in -*o*: as *ul-tro*, " to a place beyond" (see Döderlein, *Syn. u. Etym.* iii. p. 105, sqq.); *quo*, " whither;" *eo*, " thither," &c.;

sometimes -*c* is appended: thus we have *illuc*, *istuc*, by the side of *illo*, *isto*;—(*c*) "motion from," in which case the ending is -*nde*, or -*nce*, -*nque*: thus we have *i-nde* from *is*, [*c*]*u-nde* from *qui*, *aliu-nde* from *alius*, *hi-nc* from *hi-c*, *illi-nc* from *ille*, *utri-nque* from *uter*;—(*d*) "the way," in which case we have a feminine ablative in -*á* agreeing with *viá* understood, as *quá*, *eá*, &c.

Pronominal adverbs of time generally end in -*m*, as -*tum*, *quum*; in -*nc*, -*nque*, as *tu-nc*, *cu-nque*; or in -*ndo*, -*nquam*, as *qua-ndo*, *nu-nquam*.

Adverbs derived from nouns adjective and substantive either end in *e*, *o*, or *ter*; or else are merely adjectives in the neuter objective case.

(*a*) Adverbs in *e* or *o*, anciently ending in -*ed* or -*od* (*N. Crat.* p. 324), are, in fact, ablative cases of adjectives: thus *valde*, originally *validod*; *bene*, originally *bonod*; *cito*, originally *citod*; *certe* or *certo*, originally *certod*, &c., are the ablative cases of *validus*, *bonus*, *citus*, *certus*, &c. respectively. The Greeks had a large class of adverbs of the same kind; but in these the final -*d* of the ablative has been softened down, according to the laws of Hellenism, into an -ς: thus, οὕτως, καλῶς, &c. represent the old forms of the ablative, οὗτοδ, καλόδ, &c. (see *N. Crat.* l. c.). There are two cases where this δ- seems still to exist, ἴδ-ιος and Ἀφροδ-ίτη (Sanscr. *Abhrád-itá*); and there is one instance in which the metre of Homer will not allow its modern representative to stand, namely, in those passages where ἕως is a trochee. The Sanscrit *tá-vat* compared with τέϝως might justify the supposition that the original form was ἄϝοδ; while the analogy of λαϝός, λέϝως, νάος, νέως, should authorise us to insert, even in our Hellenic text of Homer, the emendation ἄϝος for ἕως (comp. also Ἧως, Αὔως, Ἔως), whenever this particle is a trochee.[1]

[1] There can be little doubt that ἕως and τέως correspond to *yâvat* and

(b) The termination -*ter* is appended to adjectives of the third declension in the same way as $\genfrac{}{}{0pt}{}{-\bar{o}}{-\bar{e}}\}[d]$ is affixed to adjectives of the first and second declension. Thus, from *lenis* we have *leni-ter;* from *gravis*, *gravi-ter;* from *felix*, *felici-ter;* from *audax*, *audac-ter;* from *difficilis*, *difficul-ter;* and so on. The termination is, in fact, the same as that in -*tus*, which is appended to substantives and adjectives of the second declension: thus we have *cæli-tus, fundi-tus, radici-tus, antiqui-tus, divini-tus, humani-tus*, &c. This last, which is obviously the older form, answers to the Sanscrit -*tas*, -*thas*, -*das*, -*dhas*, on the one hand, and to the Greek -θεν on the other (compare the Greek first person plural in -μεν with the Latin in -*mus*). There is yet a third form in which it appears, namely, -*tim*, which is the termination of a most interesting class of participial adverbs; for I cannot consent to consider any of them as strictly formed from nouns; and though the verbs in all cases are not forthcoming, the adverbs themselves prove that they must have existed in part at least. Instances of this class of adverbs are *caterva-tim, carp-tim, grada-tim, priva-tim, punc-tim, separa-tim, vica-tim*. Compare with these the German participial forms in -*ingen*, and the Greek participial adverbs in -νδα, -νδην, -δην (*N. Crat.* p. 342, sqq.). The most striking result from a proper appreciation of the origin of adverbs in -*tim*, is the explanation which it supplies for those adverbs in -*ter* which are derived from active participles. The termination of the passive participle is already -*tus;* the adverb, therefore, is a locative case of the participle; for *caterva-tim* stands to *caterva-tus* in precisely the same relation as *par-tim* to *pars* (*par*[*t*]*s*) (*N. Crat.* pp. 215, 443). Simi-

távat respectively. Now as, by the side of λέως we have λαϝός and λᾶς, so by the side of ἕως we have ἇς (Pind. *O.* xi. 51; Aristoph. *Lysistr.* 173), which was also written ϝᾶς (*Tab. Heracl.* 2, 52, p. 207); and we may therefore infer the intermediate form ἇϝος = ἇϝοδ = *yá-vat*.

larly, *aman-ter*, *sapien-ter*, &c. are cases of the participles *amans*, *sapiens*, &c.; for the crude forms of these participles already contain the *t*. Now, if I am right in concluding that these terminations, -θεν, -*dhas*, -*ter*, -*tus*, -*tim*, &c. are lengthened forms of that dental which marks the ablative of the noun and the objective neuter of the pronoun (*N. Crat.* p. 326), most interesting conclusions may be drawn from this respecting the origin of the participle and of the passive person-endings of the Latin verb: for if the dental, which must be added to the noun to form the ablative case or adverb, is already included in the participle, it follows that the crude form of the participle is already an ablative or objective formation. That there is no essential distinction between the terminations -*tim* and -*ter*, and that the former is not restricted to participles of the passive formation, is clear from such forms as *pede-tentim*, &c. In fact, while the -*d* or -*t* alone are sufficient to express the ablative and participial relation (as in *cupi-dus*=*cupiens*; the terminations -δον, -δην, by the side of -νδον, -νδην; the participle τετυφότ[-ως] by the side of τύπτοντ-; and the adverbs in -*tus* by the side of those in -*nde*, both signifying " motion from "=" ablation "), yet we must admit that the strengthened form of the active participle, which contains the liquid as well as the mute dental, is no less ablative than those forms in which the mute appears alone; for there is no less opposition between *i-bi* and *i-nde* from *i-s*, than between αὐτό-θι and αὐτό-θεν from αὐτό-ς.[1] The participle, therefore, is an

---

[1] In the text I have merely put together some of the analogies suggested in my former work. Mr. Garnett, one of the soundest, and, at the same time, most original philologers in this country, has arrived at some results which are calculated to confirm and extend these views. In a letter to me (dated 3d May, 1842) he says: " I flatter myself that I can make it appear from a pretty copious induction that the Indo-Germanic present participle is formed upon the ablative case of the verbal noun [Sanscrit *tupat*], in much the same way as the pronoun possessive in Latin, German, &c., is formed

ablative or adverbial formation from a verbal root, expressing that which comes out of the action of a verb, *i.e.* the manner of it (*N. Crat.* p. 345); and differs only from these adverbs, and from the persons of the verb, in the circumstance, that it is not an immovable form, but one which is capable of regular flexion through the whole system of cases (*N. Crat.* p. 380).

Adverbs, used as conjunctions, are such as *jam* (from *is*), *enim* (Sanscr. *éna*), *ideo, tamen, igitur,* &c. These are, in fact, cases of different pronouns. Most of them are of obvious origin: *ideo* (comp. *adeo*) is equivalent to the Greek ἐπίτηδες (= ἐπὶ τάδεσιν, Buttmann), and from it is derived *idoneus* = *ideoneus* = Gr. ἐπιτήδειος. *Igitur* is the case in *-tur* (= *tus*, -θεν) from a pronoun which is found in Oscan, under the form of *esa*, the soft Latin *g* representing the sound of *ś* or *z*. In old Latin its signification was *i-nde*, " out of that" (Festus, p. 105; above, Chap. VI. § 7), which is the usual force of the termination -*tus* = θεν.

Some adverbs are merely cases of common nouns, which usage has made indeclinable. These appear sometimes as conjunctions, and sometimes as prepositions. *Instar, gratiá,* and *ergo,* may be compared with δίκην, χάριν, and ἕνεκα (see *N. Crat.* p. 350, sqq.). *Prope*[*d*] (cf. *propin-quus*) is the ablative of an old adjective, and *prop-ter* is its case in *-ter* = *tus* = θεν. *Penes* and *tenus* are forms of the same kind as *instar*, and contain the roots of *pen-d-ere, ten-d-ere*. *Clam* and *palam* are locatives of the same nature as *partim*, &c. The former, which was also written *calim*

---

upon the genitive of the personal. If I am not mistaken, this is calculated to throw an important light upon the organisation of the Indo-Germanic and many other languages." I gladly embrace this opportunity of correcting the oversight (in the *N. Crat.* p. 431) by which I have attributed to Dr. Prichard an important philological discovery, which is really due to his reviewer, Mr. Garnett (*Quarterly Review*, lvii. p. 100).

(Fest. p. 47), contains the root of *celo*, κλέπτω, καλύπτω, &c. *Palam* is the same case of an adjective connected with *palatum*, πύλη, &c. That it is a noun appears further from the fact, that it is used also with the preposition *in* (*in palam* = *aperte*, *Gloss. Isid.*), like *in-cassum;* comp. *pro-palam*. The same is the case with *coram* = *co'oram* (κατ' ὄμμα); comp. *co'minus*, *e'minus* (ἐκ χειρός). Sometimes the adverb is merely the crude form of the noun. We have examples of this in *simul*, *procul* (from *similis*, *procilis*); and the ancients wrote *facul* (Fest. p. 87) and *perfacul* (id. p. 214) for *faculter* or *facile*, and *perfacile*. Again, the full form of the noun is occasionally used as an adverb: in the XII. Tables we have *nox* for *noctu* (above, p. 164); and Virgil (*Æn.* i. 215; vii. 624) and other writers use *pars* for *partim*. There is an approximation to this usage in the indeclinable Greek θέμις (Buttmann, *Ausf. Sprachl.* i. p. 227).

To these instances of the adverbial use of nouns may, perhaps, be added the phrase by which the Romans designated the day of the month. Here the locative in *-m* of the day is inserted between the preposition and the word which denotes the standard of reckoning. Thus, " on the fourth day before the Nones of April," is expressed by, *ante* (*diem quartum*) *Nonas Apriles* = *quarto die ante Nonas Apriles*. And this whole expression is regarded as one word, which may be dependent on a preposition: thus we may say, *ex ante diem* iii. *Non. Jun. usque ad pridie Kal. Septembres*, or *differre aliquid in ante* xv. *Kal. Novembres.*

CHAPTER IX.

THE THEORY OF THE LATIN VERB.

§ 1. The Latin verb generally defective. § 2. The personal inflexions—their consistent anomalies. § 3. Doctrine of the Latin tenses. § 4. The substantive verbs. § 5. Verbs which may be regarded as parathetic compounds. § 6. Tenses of the vowel-verbs which are combinations of the same kind. § 7. Organic derivation of the tenses in the consonant-verb. § 8. Auxiliary tenses of the passive voice. § 9. The modal distinctions— their syntax. § 10. Forms of the infinitive and participle—how connected in derivation and meaning. § 11. The *gerundium* and *gerundivum* shewn to be active and present. § 12. The participle in -*úrus*. § 13. The past tense of the infinitive active. § 14. Differences of conjugation.

§ 1.
The Latin verb generally defective.

THE forms of the Latin verb are meagre and scanty in the same proportion as the cases of the nouns are multifarious and comprehensive. The deficiencies of the one are due to the same cause as the copiousness of the other. They both spring from the antiquity of the language. An idiom which has been long employed in literature will generally substitute prepositions for the inflexions of cases, and, by the employment of various syntactical devices, increase the expressiveness and significance of the verb. It is just in these particulars that the dialects formed from the Latin differ from their mother-speech, and in the same particulars they approximate to the syntactical distinctness of the Greek.

THE PERSON-ENDINGS.

§ 2.
The personal inflexions— their consistent anomalies.

The Latin person-endings are, however, on the whole, less mutilated than the corresponding inflexions in the Greek verb. This is because the person-endings are, in fact, case-endings of pronouns, by virtue of which every form of the finite verb becomes complete in itself (see

N. Crat. p. 429), and the case-endings, as has been already observed, are more perfect in Latin than in Greek.

The person-endings of the active verb, as they appear in classical Latin, are *-m*, *-s*, *-t*; *-mus*, *-tis*, *-nt*. But these forms are not maintained throughout all the tenses. The present indicative has dropt the characteristic *-m*, except in the two cases of *sum* and *inquam*. The sign of the first person singular is also wanting in the perfect indicative, and in the futures in *-bo* and *-ro*. The second person singular is represented by *-s* in every case but one — that of the perfect indicative, which substitutes *-s-ti*. The third singular is always *-t*; the first plural always *-mus*; the second plural always *-tis*, except in the perfect indicative, when it is *-s-tis*, to correspond with the singular of the same person; and the third plural is always *-nt*, though this is occasionally dropt in the third person plural of the perfect indicative, which, like the second persons, inserts an additional $r = s$ (below, p. 264). If we may judge from the *-to*, *-tote* of the imperative, these person-endings must have been originally ablative or causative inflexions of the pronouns. The original form of the imperative suffix in the singular number was *-tod* or *-tud*, which is unequivocally an ablative inflexion (above, Chap. VIII. § 6).

The person-endings of the passive verb present some difficulties to the inquiring philologist. In fact, only the third person, singular and plural, seems to have been preserved free from mutilation or suppression. The terminations of the passive should, according to the rules of sound philology, present themselves as inflexions or cases of the active person-endings. If, then, we compare the active *amat*, *amant*, *amare*, with the corresponding passive forms, *amatur*, *amantur*, *amarier*, we must conclude that *r*, connected with the active form by a short vowel, *e* or *u*, is the sign of the passive voice, and that this amounts to an inflexion of the active form analogous to the adverbs in -*ter* (*leni-ter, gnavi-ter*, &c.), -*tus* (*cæli-tus*, &c.), or -*tim* (*grada-tim*, &c.). According to this, the first persons *amor* and *amamur* are contractions of *amŏmĕr, amāmŭsĕr*, according to the Sanscrit analogy (comp. *bharê* with φέ-ρομαι, &c. *N. Crat.* pp. 436, 445). The second persons, *amaris* (*amare*) and *amamini*, are altogether different forms; they seem to be two verbals, or participial nouns, of the same kind respectively as the Latin and Greek active infinitives, *amare* = *amase* (compare *dic-sisse, es-se*, Gr. γέλαϊς, ὕψοϊς, &c.), and τυπτε-μέναι, which are, in fact, locative cases of passive participles. The verbal, which stands for the second person singular of the passive verb, was probably, in the first instance, a participle in -*sus;* compare *ver-sus, cur-sus*, &c. That which represents the second person plural is the plural of a form which is of very frequent occurrence in the Latin language (*N. Crat.* p. 495). The older form ended in -*minor*, and is preserved in the imperative, which in old Latin had a corresponding second person singular in -*mino:* thus we have *antestamino* (*Legg.* XII. *Tab.* i. Fr. 1, above, Ch. VI. § 7), *famino* (Fest. p. 87), *præfamino* (Cat. *R. R.* 135, 140), *fruimino* (*Inscr. Grut.*), for *antestare, fare, præfare, fruere;* as well as *arbitraminor* (Plaut. *Epid.* v. 2, 30) and *progrediminor* (id. *Pseud.* iii. 2, 70) for *arbitramini* and *progredimini*. The use of these verbals, with a fixed gender, and without any copula, to express passive predications referring to the second person, is one of the most singular features in the Latin language, and can only be compared to the Greek use of the infinitive to express the second person imperative.

THE TENSES.

§ 3. Doctrine of the Latin tenses. There is, perhaps, no one department of classical philology in which so little has been done as in the analysis and simplification of the Latin tenses. They are still arranged and designated as they were in the beginning;

and no one seems to have discerned the glaring errors inseparable from such a system. Even among the more enlightened, it is not yet agreed whether certain tenses are to be referred to the indicative or to the subjunctive mood, and forms of entirely different origin are placed together in the same category.

An accurate examination of all the forms in the Latin language will convince us that there are only two ways in which a tense can be formed from the root of a Latin verb. One is, by the addition of *s-;* the other, by the addition of *i-*. We find the same process in the Greek verb; but there it is regular and systematic, supplying us throughout with a complete series of primary and secondary, or definite and indefinite tenses.[1] In Greek, we say that the addition of σ- to the root forms the aorist and future, and the insertion of ι- indicates the conjunctive or optative mood. Moreover, we have in the Greek verb an augment, or syllable prefixed for the purpose of marking past time as such, and traces at least of the systematic employment of reduplication to designate the continuance of an action. As the ancient epic poetry of the Greeks neglects the augment, we may understand how it fell into desuetude among the Romans. The reduplication too,

---

[1] For the convenience of the reader, I will repeat here the distinctions which I have elsewhere quoted from J. L. Burnouf's *Méthode pour étudier la Langue Grecque*, p. 215, sqq.

PRIMARY TENSES.

The Present expresses	*simultaneity*	with reference to the present time	*je lis*
The Future	*posteriority*		*je lirai*
The Perfect	*anteriority*		*j'ai lu.*

SECONDARY TENSES.

The Imperfect expresses	*simultaneity*	with reference to some other time	*je lisais*[1]
The Aorist	*posteriority*		*je lus*[2]
The Pluperfect . . .	*anteriority*		*j'avais lu*[3]

[1] pendant que vous écriviez.   [2] après que vous eutes fini d'écrire.
[3] avant que vous eussiez écrit.

though common to all the old Italian languages, is of only partial application in the existing forms of the Latin verb. With regard to the value of the tenses in σ- and ι-, the same holds to a certain extent in Latin also; but while the principle is here susceptible of a double application, it is, on the other hand, interrupted by the operation of a system of composite tenses which is peculiar to the Latin language.

§ 4. The substantive verbs.

Before I proceed to examine the tense-system of the Romans, as it appears in all the complications of an ordinary verb, it will be as well to analyse, in the first instance, the substantive verb, which enters so largely into all temporal relations.

The Latin language has two verbs signifying "to be:" one contains the root *es-*, the other the root *fu-*.

The inflexions of *es-* are as follows:—

INDICATIVE PRESENT.

Actual form.	Ancient form.	Sanscrit.
'sum	*esum*[1]	*asmi*
es'	*essi*	*asi*
es't	*esti*	*asti*
'sumus	*esumus*	*smas*
es'tis	*esitis*	*st'a*
'sunt	*esunt*	*santi*

IMPERFECT.

eram	*ésam*	*ásam*
eras	*ésas*	*ásîs*
erat	*ésat*	*ásît*
eramus	*ésamus*	*ásma*
eratis	*ésatis*	*ástá*
erant	*ésant*	*ásan.*

[1] Varro, *L.L.* ix. 100, p. 231.

FUTURE or CONJUNCTIVE,

Formed by the insertion of the guttural element -*i*.

Actual forms.			Ancient form.	Sanscrit.
ero,	*'sim,*	*'siém* . .	*esyám* . .	*syám*
eris,	*'sis,*	*'siés* . . .	*esyás* . .	*syás*
erit,	*'sit,*	*'siét* . . .	*esyát* . .	*syát*
erimus,	*'símus,*	*'siémus* . .	*esyámus* .	*syáma*
eritis,	*'sítis,*	*'siétis* . .	*esyátis* . .	*syáta*
erunt,	*'sint,*	*'siént* . .	*esyánt* . .	*syus.*

INDEFINITE or PAST TENSE,

Formed from this last by the addition of -*să*.

Actual form.	Ancient form.
es-sem	*es-sa-yam*
es-ses	*es-sa-yas*
&c.	&c.

INFINITIVE,

Or locative of a verbal in -*sis*, expressing the action of the verb.[1]

es-se.

PARTICIPLE.

Nom. *'sen*[*t*]*s* (in *ab-sens, præ-sens,* &c.) originally *esen*[*t*]*s*
Gen. *'sentis* . . . . . *esentis*
&c. &c.

IMPERATIVE.

es,	*esto*	originally	*es,*	*estod*
	esto	. . .		*estod*
este,	*estote*	. . .	*esite,*	*esitote*
	sunto	. . .		*esunto.*

Throughout the Latin verb we may observe, as in the case of *ero* here, that the element *i* has vanished from the

---

[1] *N. Crat.* pp. 345, 492.

first person of the future; for *ero* does not really differ from *esum*, the present indicative. The explanation of this may be derived from the fact, that in English the first and other persons of the future belong to different forms: where an Englishman says, "I shall" of himself, he addresses another with "you will;" and conversely, where he asserts of another that "he shall," he tells him, "I will." The third person plural *erunt*, if it is not a mutilation of *era-font, era-hunt* (above, p. 68), is only another way of writing *erint; u₃* being substituted, as it so frequently is, for *i₃*, to which the qualifying *i* had been ultimately reduced. But besides the form of the future in *i*, we have in old Latin another expression of it in the inchoative form *esco* for *es-sco* (*Legg.* XII. *Tab. apud Gell.* XX. i. Tab. I. fr. 3. Lucret. i. 613. Festus, s. v. *escit*, p. 77; *superescit*, p. 302; *nec*, p. 162; *obescet*, p. 188; and Müller, *Suppl. Annot.* p. 386).

The inflexions of the verb *fu-* are the following:—

1st tense.	2d tense (*-si* inserted).	3d tense (*-i* inserted).
fu[*v*]*i* . .	*fu*[*v*]*e-syam* (*fueram*) . .	*fuyam* (*fuam*)
fu[*v*]*i-s-ti*	*fu*[*v*]*e-syas* (*fueras*) . .	*fuyas* (*fuas*)
fu[*v*]*it*	&c. &c.	&c.
fu[*v*]*imus*		
fu[*v*]*i-s-tis*		
fu[*v*]*e-r-unt*		

4th tense (both *-sa* and *-i*).	5th tense (*-sa-sa-i*).
fu[*v*]*e-syam* (*forem* and *fuerim*) .	*fu*[*v*]*i-sa-sa-im* (*fuissem*)
&c. &c.	&c. &c.

Participles, *fœtus* and *futurus*. Inchoative, *fœ-cundus* = *foi-cundus* = *fui-scundus*; comp. *ira-cundus* from *ira-scor*, *ju-cundus* for *juvi-scundus* from *juvo*, *vere-cundus* for *veri-scundus* from *veri-scor*, &c.

The conjugations of these two verbs furnish us with

specimens of verbs inflected through all their tenses without the aid of any foreign adjunct. But this is not the case with the great mass of verbs which constitute the staple of the Latin language. Although the flexion-forms in *s-* and *i-* appear in all these verbs, there is no one of them which is not indebted more or less to *fu-* for its active tenses; and all verbs form some tenses of their passive voice by calling in the aid of *es-*.

According to the ordinary classification of Latin verbs, there are three conjugations of vowel-verbs, in *a, e,* and *i,* and one conjugation of consonant-verbs, to which the verbs in *uo* belong. Now, as a general rule, we find that all vowel-verbs are secondary to nouns — in other words, they are derived from the crude forms of nouns. But many nouns are demonstrably secondary to consonant-verbs (below, § 14). Therefore we might infer, as a general rule, that the consonant-verb belonged to a class of forms older or more original than the vowel-verbs. This view is supported by a comparison of the tenses of the two sets of verbs: for while we find that *s-* often effects a primary variation in the consonant-verb, we observe that this insertion never takes place in the vowel-verb except in composite forms. The only tense in the consonant-verb which can be considered as a composite form is the imperfect; but the future does not correspond to this, as is the case in the vowel-verbs. Verbs in *io* partially approximate to the consonant-verbs in this respect.

§ 5. Verbs which may be regarded as parathetic compounds.

The next chapter will shew that the most remarkable feature in the pathology of the Latin language is the prevalent tendency to abbreviation by which it is characterised. Among many instances of this, we may especially advert to the practice of prefixing the crude form of one verb to some complete inflexion of another. Every one knows the meaning of such compounds as *vide-licet* (= *vi-*

dere licet), sci-licet (= scire licet), pate-facio (= patere facio), ven-eo (= venum eo, comp. venum-do on the analogy of per-eo, per-do), &c. There is a distinct class of verbs in -so, which are undoubtedly compounds of the same kind, as will appear from an examination of a few instances. The verb *si-n-o* has for its perfect *sivi*; and it is obvious that the *n* in the present is only a fulcrum of the same nature as that in *po-n-o*, root *pos-*; πί-νω, root πι-, &c. Now the verbs in -so, to which I refer, such as *arcesso, capesso, lacesso, quæro*, &c., all form their perfect in *-sivi*. We might therefore suppose, *a priori*, that the termination was nothing but the verb *sino*. But this is rendered almost certain by the meaning of *arcesso* or *accerso*, which is simply *accedere sino*.[1] Similarly, *capesso* = *capere sino*, *facesso* = *facere sino*, *lacesso* = *lacere sino*, &c. The infinitive of *in-quam* (above, p. 83) does not exist; but there can be little doubt that it is involved in *quæ-ro* or *quæ-so*, which means " I cause to speak," *i. e.* " I inquire."

§ 6. Tenses of the vowel-verbs which are combinations of the same kind.

Most of the tenses of the Latin vowel-verb seem to be composite forms of the same kind with those to which I have just referred; and the complete verbal inflexion, to which the crude form of the particular verb is prefixed, is no other than a tense of the verb of existence *fu-*, Lithuan. *bu-*, Sanscrit *bhú-* (see Bopp, *Vergl. Gram. vierte Abtheil.* pp. iv. and 804). This verb, as distinguished from *es-*, expresses " beginning of being," or " coming into being," like the Greek γίγνομαι. It is therefore well calculated to perform the functions of an auxiliary in the relation of time.

[1] I am not aware that any other scholar has suggested this explanation. Müller (*ad Fest.* p. 320) thinks that *arcesso* is the inchoative of *arceo* = *accieo*: but, in the first place, the reading in Festus is by no means certain (Huschke's *arce dantur* being, I think, an almost necessary correction); and, secondly, this would leave *accerso* unexplained.

§ 6.] THE THEORY OF THE LATIN VERB. 253

The vowel-verb has a present tense which preserves throughout the vowel of the crude form. From this is derived, with the addition of the element *i*, the present subjunctive, as it is called; and from that, by the insertion of *s*-, the imperfect of the same mood. Thus we have *amêm* = *ama-im*, *amarem* = *amasem* = *ama-sa-im*; *moneâm* = *mone-yam*, *monerem* = *monesem* = *monesyam*, &c. That *i* was the characteristic of the secondary or dependent mood is clear from the old forms *du-im* (*dêm*), *temper-im*, *ed-im*, *verber-im*, *car-im*, &c., which, however, are abbreviations from *du-yam*, *ed-yam*, &c. Comp. *sim* with the older form *siem*, and δίδοιμι, &c. with διδοίην, &c. The *i* is absorbed or included in *moneam*, *legam*, &c.; just as we have *nav-âlis* for *navi-alis*, *fin-âlis* for *fini-alis*, &c. (Benary, Römische Lautlehre, p. 95.) These are the only tenses which are formed by pronominal or organic additions to the root of the verb. Every other tense of the vowel-verb is a compound of the crude form of the verb and some tense of *fu*- or *bhu*-.

The futures of the vowel-verbs end in -*bo*, -*bis*, -*bit*, &c., with which we may compare *fio*, *fis*, *fit*, &c. The imperfect, which must be considered as an indefinite tense corresponding to the future, ends in -*êbam*, -*êbas*, -*êbat*, &c., where the initial must be regarded as an augment; for as *reg'-êbat* is the imperfect of the consonant-verb *reg'o*, not *regĕbat*, and as *audi-êbat* is the imperfect of *aud-io*, though *audi-bit* was the old future, it is clear that the suffix of the imperfect had something which did not belong to the crude form, but to the termination itself; it must therefore have been an augment, or the prefix which marks past time (see Benary, *l. c.* p. 29).

The perfect of the vowel-verbs is terminated by -*vi* or -*ui*. If we had any doubt as to the origin of this suffix, it would be removed by the analogy of *pot-ui* for *pot-fui* = *potis-fui*. Accordingly, *ama-vi* (= *ama-ui*), *mon-ui*, *audi-vi*

(=*audi-ui*), are simply *ama-fui* = *amare-fui*, *mon-fui* = *monere-fui*, and *audi-fui* = *audire-fui*.

Similarly, with regard to the tenses derived from the perfect, we find that the terminations repeat all the derivatives of *fui*: thus, *ama-uero* = *ama-fuero*; *ama-uisses* = *ama-fuisses*, &c.

§ 7.
Organic derivation of the tenses in the consonant-verb.

The consonant-verb, on the other hand, forms all its tenses, except the imperfect,[1] by a regular deduction from its own root. Thus we have *reg'o* [old fut. *reg-so*], 1 aor. *reg-si*; conjunct. pres. or precative, *regam* = *regyam*, *regas* = *regyas*, or, in a softer form, *regês* = *rege-is*, &c.; conj. imperf. or optat. *regerem* = *regesyam*; 2 aor. *reg-se-ro* = *reg-se-sim*; conjunc. 3 tens. *regsissem* = *reg-si-se-syam*. If we might draw an inference from the forms *facsit*, &c., which we find in old Latin, and from *fefakust*, &c., which appear in Oscan, we should conclude that the Italian consonant-verb originally possessed a complete establishment of definite and indefinite tenses, formed from the root by pronominal or organic addition, or by prefixing augments and reduplications after the manner of the genuine Greek and Sanscrit verbs. For example's sake, we may suppose the following scheme of tenses: root *pag*, pres. *pa-n-go-m*, impf. *e-pangam*, fut. *pan-g-sim*, 1 aor. *e-pangsim*, perf. *pe-pigi-m*, pl.-perf. *pe-pige-sam*, conj. *pangyam*, opt. *pangesyam*, 2 fut. *pepige-sim* or *pangse-sim*, past tense (derived from this) *pe-pigise-syam* or *pang-si-se-syam*.

§ 8.
Auxiliary tenses of the passive voice.

In the passive voice, those tenses which in the active depend upon *fui* and its derivatives are expressed by the passive participle and the tenses of *e-sum*. The other tenses construct the passive by the addition of the letter

[1] The loss of the imperfect, and the substitution of a compound tense, is accounted for by the practice of omitting the augment. Without this prefix the regular imperfect does not differ from the present.

$r = s$ to the person-endings of the active forms, with the exceptions mentioned before. The second person plural of the passive is of such rare occurrence, that we cannot draw any decided conclusions respecting it; but if such a form as *audi-êbamini* occurred, it would certainly occasion some difficulty; for one could scarcely understand how the *ê*, which seems to be the augment of the auxiliary suffix, could appear in this apparently participial form. I am not, however, aware that we have any instances of the kind; and *ama-bamini* is just as good a participle as *ama-bundus*: compare *ama-bi-lis*, &c.

Nor need we find any stumbling-block in the appendage of passive endings to this neuter auxiliary verb. For the construction of neuter verbs with a passive affix is common enough in Latin (e. g. *peccatur, ventum est*, &c.); and the passive infinitive itself furnishes us with an indubitable instance of a similar inflexion. We might suppose that the Latin future was occasionally formed periphrastically with *eo* as an auxiliary, like the Greek ἦα λέγων, Fr. *j'allois dire*, " I was going to say." If so, *amatum eo, amatum ire*, would be the active futures of the indicative and infinitive, to which the passive forms *amatum eor, amatum iri*, would correspond. The latter of these actually occurs, and, indeed, is the only known form of the passive infinitive future.

THE MOODS.

Properly speaking, there are only three main distinctions of mood in the forms of the Latin and Greek verb, namely, the indicative, the imperative, and the infinitive. The Greek grammars practically assign five distinct moods to the regular verb, namely, the indicative, imperative, conjunctive, optative, and infinitive. But it has been already proved (*N. Crat.* p. 475, sqq.), that, considered in their relation to one another and to the other moods, the Greek

§ 9. The modal distinctions—their syntax.

conjunctive and optative must be regarded as differing in tense only. The Latin grammarians are contented with four moods, namely, the indicative, subjunctive, imperative, and infinitive; and according to this arrangement, the present subjunctive Latin answers to the Greek conjunctive, while the imperfect subjunctive Latin finds its equivalent in the optative of the Greek verb: for instance, *scribo, ut discas* corresponds to γράφω, ἵνα μανθάνῃς, and *scripsi, ut disceres* to ἔγραψα, ἵνα μανθάνοις. If, however, we extend the syntactical comparison a little further, we shall perhaps be induced to conclude that there is not always the same modal distinction between the Latin indicative and subjunctive which we find in the opposition of the Greek indicative to the conjunctive + optative. Thus, to take one or two instances, among many which might be adduced, one of the first lessons which the Greek student has to learn is, to distinguish accurately between the four cases of protasis and apodosis, and, among these, more especially between the third, in which two optatives are used, and the fourth, in which two *past* tenses of the indicative are employed.[1] Now the Latin syntax makes

---

[1] This is, indeed, a very simple and obvious matter; but it may be convenient to some readers, if I subjoin a tabular comparison of the Greek and Latin usages in this respect. The classification is borrowed from Buttmann's *Mittlere Grammatik*, § 139 (p. 394, Lachmann's edition, 1833).

1. Possibility without the expression of uncertainty:

  εἴ τι ἔχει, δίδωσι (δός) = *si quid habet, dat (da)*.

2. Uncertainty with the prospect of decision:

  ἐάν τι ἔχωμεν, δώσομεν = *si quid habeamus, dabimus*.

3. Uncertainty without any such subordinate idea:

  εἴ τι ἔχοις, διδοίης ἄν = *si quid habeas, des*.

4. Impossibility, or when we wish to indicate that the thing is not so:

  (*a*) εἴ τι εἶχεν, ἐδίδου ἄν = *si quid haberet, daret*.

  (*b*) εἴ τι ἔσχεν, ἔδωκεν ἄν = *si quid habuisset, dedisset*.

The distinction between cases (3) and (4) is also observed in the expression

§ 9.] THE THEORY OF THE LATIN VERB. 257

no such distinction between the third and fourth cases, only taking care in the fourth case to use past tenses, and in the third case, where the hypothesis is possible, to employ present tenses of the subjunctive mood. Thus, *e. g.* in the third case: *si hoc nunc vociferari velim, me dies, vox, latera deficiant;* where we should have in Greek, εἰ τοῦτο ἐν τῷ παραυτίκα γεγωνεῖν ἐθέλοιμι, ἡμέρας ἄν μοι καὶ φωνῆς καὶ σθένους ἐνδεήσειεν. In the fourth case : (*a*) *si scirem, dicerem* = εἰ ἠπιστάμην, ἔλεγον ἄν. (*b*) *si voluissem plura, non negasses*=εἰ πλεόνων ἐπεθύμησα, οὐκ ἂν ἠρνήσω. And this confusion becomes greater still, when, by a rhetorical figure, the *impossible* is supposed *possible;* as in Ter. *Andr.* ii. 1, 10: *tu si hic sis, aliter sentias.* For in this instance the only difference between the two cases, which is one of tense, is overlooked. In the apodosis of case 4, b, the Romans sometimes used the plusquam-perfectum of the indicative, as in Seneca, *de Ira*, i. 11 : *perierat imperium, si Fabius tantum ausus esset, quantum ira suadebat;* and Horace, ii. *Carm.* 17, 27: *me truncus illapsus cerebro sustulerat, nisi Faunus ictum dextra levasset.* Sometimes the perfect was used in this apodosis, as in Juvenal, x. 123: *Antoni gladios potuit contemnere, si sic omnia dixisset.* Again, particles of time, like *donec*, require the subjunctive when future time is spoken of; as in Hor. i. *Epist.* 20, 10: *carus eris Romæ, donec te deserat ætas.* But this becomes a past tense of the indicative when past time is referred to; as in Hor. i. *Epist.* 10, 36: *cervus equum —pellebat—donec* [*equus*] *imploravit opes hominis frænumque recepit.* The confusion between the Latin indicative and subjunctive is also shewn by the use of the subjunctive present as a future indicative (a phenomenon equally remarkable in Greek, *N. Crat.* p. 480), and con-

of a wish: thus, *utinam salvus sis!* pronounces no opinion respecting the health of the party addressed; but *utinam salvus esses!* implies that he is no longer in good health.

S

versely by the employment of the periphrastic future (which is, after all, the same kind of form as the ordinary composite form of the future indicative) as an equivalent for a tense of the subjunctive mood. Thus Cicero uses *dicam* and *dicere instituo* in the same construction; *Phil.* i. 1: "*antequam* de republica *dicam* ea, quæ dicenda hoc tempore arbitror, exponam breviter consilium profectionis meæ." *Pro Murena*, 1: "*antequam* pro L. Murena *dicere instituo*, pro me ipso pauca dicam." And we have always the indicative in apodosis to the subjunctive when the future in *-rus* is used: *e. g.* Liv. xxxviii. 47: " si tribuni prohiberent, testes *citaturus fui*" (for "*citarem*"); and Cic. *Verr.* iii. 52: "illi ipsi aratores, qui remanserant, *relicturi* omnes agros *erant*" (for "*reliquissent*"), "nisi ad eos Metellus Roma literas misisset." The Romans also used the *futurum exactum*, which is generally accounted a tense of the subjunctive, exactly as the Greeks used their perfect indicative with καὶ δή in suppositions.

On the whole, it must be confessed that the Latin subjunctive, meaning by that term the set of tenses which are formed by the insertion of *-i-*, differs modally from the indicative only in this, that it is uniformly employed in dependent clauses where the idiom of the language repudiates the indicative; and it is not a little remarkable, that in almost all these cases—in all, except when final particles are used, or when an indirect question follows a past tense—the indicative is expressly required in Greek syntax. The title *subjunctive*, therefore, does but partially characterise the Latin tenses in *-i-*; and their right to a separate modal classification is scarcely less doubtful than that of the Greek optative as distinguished from the conjunctive.

The differences between the indicative, imperative, and infinitive equally exist between the two latter and the subjunctive. The indicative and subjunctive alone possess a complete apparatus of person-endings; the imperative being sometimes merely the crude form of the verb, and the infinitive being strictly impersonal.

§ 10. Forms of the infinitive and participle—how connected in derivation and meaning.

He who would investigate accurately the forms of the Latin language must always regard the infinitive as standing in intimate connexion with the participles. There are, in fact, three distinct forms of the Latin infinitive : (*a*) the residuum of an *abstractum verbale* in -*sis*, which remains uninflected ; (*b*) a similar verbal in -*tus*, of which two cases are employed ; (*c*) the participial word in -*ndus*, which is used both as three cases of the infinitive governing the object of the verb, and also as an adjective in concord with the object. There are also three forms of the participle : (*a*) one in -*ns* = *nts*, sometimes lengthened into -*ndus ;* (*β*) another in -*tus ;* and a third (*γ*) in -*rus*. The participle in -*ns* is always active ; its by-form in -*ndus* is properly active, though it often seems to be passive. The participle in -*tus* is always passive, except when derived from a deponent verb, in which case it corresponds in meaning to the Greek aorist middle. The participle in -*rus*, or rather in -*ū-rus*, is always active and future.

Now it is impossible to take an instructive view of these forms without considering them together. The participle in -*rus* (*γ*) is a derivative from the verbal in -*tus* (*b*) ; and it would be difficult to avoid identifying the participle in -*ndus* and the corresponding gerundial infinitive. In the following remarks, therefore, I shall presume, what has been proved elsewhere, the original identity of the infinitive and the participle.

That the verbal (*a*), which acts as the ordinary infinitive in *re* = *se*, is derived from the crude form of the verb by the addition of a pronominal ending *si*- or *sy*-, is clear, no less from the analogy of the Æolic Greek forms in -*ις*, where the *ι* is transposed (comp. *N. Crat.* pp. 492 and 496), than from the original form of the passive, which is -*rier* =

-*syer*, and not merely -*rer*. This infinitive, therefore, is the indeclinable state of a derivative precisely similar to the Greek nouns in -σις (πρᾶξις, ῥῆ-σις, &c.), which express the action of the verb. This Greek ending in -σις appears to have been the same in effect as another ending in -τύς, which, however, is of less frequent occurrence (ἐπη-τύς, ἐδη-τύς, ὀρχησ-τύς, &c.), but which may be compared with the Latin infinitive (*b*) in -*tum*, -*tu* (the *supine*, as it is called), and with the Sanscrit gerund in -*tvâ*. The verbal in -*tus*, which is assumed as the origin of these supines, must be carefully distinguished from the passive participle (β) in -*tus*. For, while the infinitive (*b*) is formed like the infinitive (*a*) by a suffix belonging to the *second* pronominal element (*N. Crat.* p. 345), so that the labial (u = v) is an essential part of the ending, the participle (β) has merely a dental suffix derived from the *third* pronominal element, and corresponding to the Greek endings in -τος, -νος, and the Latin -*tus* = *nis* (formerly -*nus*). In fact, the suffix of infinitive (*b*) is *tv*, that of participle (β) is *t-* only.

§ 11.
The *gerundium* and *gerundivum* shewn to be active and present.

The infinitive (*c*) and the participle (*a*) are, in fact, different, or apparently different, applications of one and the same form. In its infinitive use this verbal in -*ndus* is called by two names—the *gerundium* when it governs the object of the verb, and the *gerundivum* when it agrees with the object. Thus, in " consilium *capiendi* urbem," we have a *gerundium*; in " consilium urbis *capiendæ*," a *gerundivum*. As participles, the ordinary grammatical nomenclature most incorrectly distinguishes the form in -*ndus* as " a future passive," from the form -*n*[*t*]*s* considered as " a present active." The form in -*ndus* is never a future, and it bears no resemblance to the passive in *form*. The real difficulty is to explain to the student the seeming alternation of an active and passive *meaning* in these forms. Perhaps there is no better way of doing this than by di-

§ 11.]   THE THEORY OF THE LATIN VERB.   261

recting attention to the fact, that the difference between active and passive really becomes evanescent in the infinitive use of a verb. " He is a man to love"="he is a man to be loved;" " I give you this to eat"="I give you this to be eaten," &c.[1] The Greek active infinitives in -μεναι, -ναι, are really passive forms in their inflected use;[2] and that the Latin forms in -*ndus*, which seem to be passive in their use as *gerundiva*, are really only secondary forms of the participle in -*n*[*t*]*s*, appears not only from etymological considerations (*N. Crat.* p. 498), but also from their use both as active infinitives and active participles. When the *gerundivum* is passive, it generally seems to attach to itself the sense of *duty* or *obligation*. Thus, we should translate *delenda est Carthago*, " Carthage is *to be destroyed*"=" we ought to destroy Carthage;" and no one has taken the trouble to inquire whether this *oportet* is really contained in the *gerundivum*. If it is, all attempts at explanation must be unavailing. But since it is not necessary to seek in the participial form this notion, which may be conveyed by the substantive verb (e. g. *sapientis est seipsum nosse*), it is surely better to connect the *gerundivum* with the *gerundium*, and to reconcile the use of the one with the ordinary force of the

---

[1] We observe the same fact in the use of the participles in English and German. Thus, in Herefordshire, " a good-leapt horse" means " a good-leaping horse;" and in German there is no perceptible difference between *kam geritten* and *kam reitend*. See Mr. Lewis's *Glossary of Provincial Words used in Herefordshire*, p. 58; and Grimm, *D. Gr.* iv. p. 129.

[2] Conversely, the forms in -ντ-, which are always active when used in concord with a noun, are occasionally employed in that infinitive sense in which the differences of voice seem to be neglected. Thus we have, Soph. *Aj*. 579: θρηνεῖν ἐπῳδὰς πρὸς τομῶντι πήματι (" *ad vulnus quod secturam desideret*" s. " *secandum sit*"). *Œd. Col.* 1219: ὅταν τις ἐς πλέον πέσῃ τοῦ θέλοντος (" *quando quis cupiendi satietatem expleverit*" s. " *id quod cupiebat plene consecutus fuerit*"). Thucyd. i. 36: γνώτω τὸ μὲν δεδιὸς αὑτοῦ— τοὺς ἐναντίους μᾶλλον φοβῆσον (" *sciat timere illud suum—majorem adversariis metum incussurum esse*").

other. Supposing, therefore, that *da-ndus* is a secondary form of *da-n*[*t*]*s*, and synonymous with it, on the analogy of *Acraga*[*nt*]*s*, *Agrige-ntum;* *orie-n*[*t*]*s*, *oriu-ndus*, &c.; how do we get the phrase *da-nda est occasio*, " an opportunity is to be given," from *d-a-ndus* = *dan*[*t*]*s*, " giving?" Simply from the gerundial or infinitive use of the participle. Thus, (A) *da-ndus* = *da-n*[*t*]*s* signifies " giving;" (B) this, used as an infinitive, still retains its active signification, for *ad dandum opes* means " for giving riches" = " to give riches;" (c) when this is attracted into the case of the object, the sense is not altered, for *ad opes dandas* is precisely equivalent to *ad dandum opes;* (D) when, however, this attraction appears in the nominative case, the error at once takes root, and no one is willing to see that it is still merely an attraction from the infinitive or indeclinable use of the participle. Even here, however, the intransitive verb enables us to bring back the student to a consideration of the real principle. For one can hardly fail to see that *vivendum est* = *vivere est* i. q. *oportet vivere;* and that there may be no doubt as to the identity of the uninflected with the inflected gerund in this case, Horace has put them together in the same sentence: " nunc est *bibendum*, nunc pede libero *pulsanda* tellus," where it is obvious that *tellus pulsanda est* is no less equivalent to " oportet pulsare tellurem," than " bibendum est" is to " oportet bibere." At all events, his Greek original expressed both notions by the infinitive with χρή:

νῦν χρὴ μεθύσθην καί τινα πρὸς βίαν
πίνην, ἐπειδὴ κάτθανε Μύρσιλος.

(Alcæus, *Fr.* 20, p. 575, Bergk.)

This view of the case appears to me to remove most of the difficulties and confusions by which the subject of the gerund has hitherto been encumbered. There are two supplementary considerations which deserve to be adduced. The first is, that in the particular case where the *gerun-*

§ 11.]   THE THEORY OF THE LATIN VERB.   263

divum appears to be most emphatically passive—namely, when it implies that a thing is given out or commissioned *to be done*—it is found by the side of the active infinitive: thus, while we have such phrases as, " Antigonus Eumenem mortuum propinquis *sepeliendum* tradidit" (Corn. Nep. *Eum.* 13), we have by their side such as, " tristitiam et metus tradam protervis in mare Creticum *portare* ventis" (Hor. i. *Carm.* 26, 1). The other case is this; that the supines, which are only different cases of one and the same verbal, appear as active infinitives when the accusative is used (*-tum*), and as passive when the ablative is employed (*-tu*). Now, this seemingly passive use of the supine in *-tu* arises from the fact, that it appears only by the side of adjectives, in which case the active and passive forms of the infinitive are often used indifferently, and some adjectives take the supine in *-tu* when they expressly require an active infinitive, as in, " difficile est *dictu* (=*dicere*), quanto opere conciliet homines comitas affabilitasque sermonis" (Cic. *Off.* ii. 14). Now this supine, which is thus identical with the infinitive active, frequently alternates with the gerund; compare, for instance, *quid est tam jucundum auditu* (Cic. *de Or.* i. 8), with *verba ad audiendum jucunda* (id. ibid. i. 49).

But the form in *-ndus* is not only *active* in voice, but also *present* in tense. Thus, if we take a deponent verb, we often find a form in *-ndus* acting as a collateral to the common form in *-n*[*t*]*s*, and opposed with it to the form in *-tus*. For instance, *secundus* and *sequen*[*t*]*s* both signify " following," but *secutus* =" having followed." The same is the distinction between *morien*[*t*]*s, moriundus; orien*[*t*]*s, oriundus; irascen*[*t*]*s, ira*[*s*]*cundus,* &c. on the one hand, and *mortuus, ortus, iratus,* &c. on the other. This cannot be remarked in active verbs, because the Latin language has no active past participle. If, however, we turn to the gerundial use of the form in *-ndus,* we may observe a distinction of tense between it and the participle in *-tus* even in the case of active verbs. Thus *volvendus* is really a present tense in Virgil, *Æneid*. ix. 7: *volvenda dies, en, attulit ultro;* comp. Ennius (apud Varro, *L. L.* vii. § 104, p. 160, Müller), and Lucretius, v. 1275; because, in its inflected form, it is equivalent in meaning to *volvendo*. And the words of Livy (*præf. ad Hist.*): "quæ ante conditam condendamve urbem traduntur," can only mean " traditions derived from a period when the city was neither *built* nor *building*."

§ 12.
The participle in *-ŭrus*.

The participle (γ) in *-rus* or *-ūrus*, which always bears a future signification, is supported by an analogy in the Latin language which has no parallel either in Greek or Sanscrit. The Greek desiderative is formed from the ordinary future by the insertion of the element *i-*: thus δρά-ω, fut. δρά-σω, desiderative δρα-σείω. This desiderative is the common future in Sanscrit; though the Vêdas have a future, like the Greek, formed by the element *s-* only, without the addition of *i-*.[1] Now the regular future of *scribo* would be *scrip-so*, indicated by the aorist *scrip-si;* but the desiderative is *scripturio*. We may infer, then, that in the loss of the regular future of the Latin verb, the desiderative and future participle have been formed by the addition of the future $r=s$ and the desiderative $ri=si$, not to the crude form of the verb, but to the verbal in *-tus*.

§ 13.
The past tense of the infinitive active.

The past tense of the infinitive active ends in *-isse*, both when it corresponds to the Greek first aorist, as *scripsisse;* when it is the regular perfect, as *tetigisse;* and when it is a composite form, as *ama-visse = ama-fuisse*. It is to be recollected that in all these cases the same tense inserts an *-s = r* in the second person singular and second

[1] See Rosen, on the *Rig-Vêda Sanhita*, p. iv.

and third persons plural of the indicative mood. It is not improbable, then, that this doubling of the *-s* of the infinitive (*-s-se* instead of *-se*) is to be explained from the indicative mood (namely, as *fui-s-tis* instead of *fui-tis*, so *fui-s-se* instead of *fui-se* = *fuĕ-re* = *fore*), and that we have in both cases insertions similar to that by which *fuissem* is formed from *forem*. The supposition, that this additional *s* is designed to represent the lengthening of the penultimate syllable of the infinitive, is át least not very plausible.[1]

THE CONJUGATIONS.

§ 14. Differences of conjugation.

There is not much difficulty in the classification of the Latin verbs according to their conjugation, as it is called. We have three conjugations of vowel-verbs, in *a, e, i*, which are regularly contracted; and one conjugation of consonant-verbs, which retain their inflexions uncontracted. In the conjugations *u* is generally reckoned as a consonant, and this is sometimes the case with *i*. Now it is to be observed, that, in Latin as well as Greek, the vowel-verbs are all secondary or derivative forms, whereas the consonant-verbs are anterior to the corresponding nouns. The reasons for this have been given in the *New Cratylus*, p. 529; it will be sufficient in this place to shew that such is the case in the Latin language.

I. NOUNS DERIVED FROM VERBS.

Nouns of the E-declension are derived from consonant-verbs.

facere	*faci-es*
fidere	*fid-es*
con-spicere	*species*

Nouns of the U-declension are derived from consonant-verbs.

---

[1] Later forms, like *expugnassere*, result from a mistaken attempt to follow the Greek analogy (see Madvig, *Bemerkungen*, p. 41).

currere	currus
discedere . . .	discessus
gradi (aggredĕre, &c.) .	gradus
ludere	lusus
vertere	versus

Consonant-nouns are derived from consonant-verbs.

ducere	dux
legere	lex
pa-n-gere . . .	pax
regere	rex

II. VERBS DERIVED FROM NOUNS.

Verbs in A are derived (*a*) from nouns in A.

curare	cura
fugare	fuga
morari	mora
prædari	præda

(*b*) from nouns in I, in a causative sense.

celebrare . . .	celebris
ditare	ditis
gravare	gravis
levare	levis

Here the I of the crude form coalesces with the A, as in *funalis* for *funi-alis*, *navalis* for *navi-alis*, &c.

(*c*) from nouns in O.

bellare	bellum
donare	donum
numerare . . .	numerus
populare	populus
probare	probus
regnare	regnum
sanare	sanus

(*d*) from consonant-nouns.

fraudare	*fraus*
generare	*genus*
laborare	*labor*
laudare	*laus*
nominare	*nomen*
onerare	*onus*
orare	*os*
vocare	*vox*

This is particularly the case in compounds, as in *belligerare* from *belliger*, which is formed from *bellum* and *gerere*. And we must not overlook the fact, that nouns in A are formed in the same manner from consonant-verbs, not only in compounds, like *agri-cola*, *homi-cida*, &c., from *colere*, *cædo*, &c., but also in simple forms, as *ala*, " that which raises," from *alere*; *lingua*, " that which licks," from *lingu-ere*; *toga*, " that which covers," from *tegere*, &c.

Verbs in E are generally secondary extensions of simple roots. Some, like *lucere*, are derived from consonant-nouns. Not a few, like *ardere*, *favere*, *fulgere*, *pavere*, coexist with nouns in -*or*. The same, however, may be remarked of verbs in A: compare *amare*, *amor*.

Verbs in I are mostly derived from nouns of the I-declension. Thus we have

audire	*auris* = au<small>D</small>is
finire	*finis*
lenire	*lenis*
mollire	*mollis*
vestire	*vestis*

But this is by no means universal; for contracted verbs in I are derived from nouns with every variety of crude form. Thus we have *sepire* from *sepe*; *punire* from *pœna*; *blandiri* from *blandus*; *moliri* from *moles*; *sortiri* from *sors*; &c.

Verbs in E and I sometimes appear as secondary or intransitive forms of verbs in A. These seem to be either inchoatives in *-sco* or compounds in *-eo* (root *i*). Thus we have *durare, duresco; servare, servire;* &c.

Verbs in U, when this is really vocalised, are sometimes derived from nouns in U. Thus we have

acuere	*acu*
metuere	*metus*
tribuere	*tribus*

This may be regarded as a singular case; for no contraction is possible in a derivative verb of this kind. A noun of the I-declension occasionally forms a verb in A without any absorption of the I; thus we have *ab-brevi-are* from *brevis*, and *al-levi-are*, as well as *levare*, from *levis*.

CHAPTER X.

CONSTITUTION AND PATHOLOGY OF THE LATIN LANGUAGE.

§ 1. Genius of the Latin language. § 2. Abbreviations observable in the written forms. § 3. Ancient testimonies to the difference between the spoken and the written language. § 4. The poetry of the Augustan age does not represent the genuine Latin pronunciation; § 5. which is rather to be derived from an examination of the comic metres. § 6. The French language is the best modern representative of the spoken Latin. § 7. The modern Italian not equally so; and why. § 8. Different dialects of the French language. § 9. But all these dialects were closely related to the Latin. § 10. Leading distinctions between the Roman and Romance idioms. § 11. Importance and value of the Latin language.

§ 1. Genius of the Latin language.

EVERY language may be considered as an organic body, possessing within itself a principle of vitality, but also capable of disintegration and decay. We may therefore, without straining the metaphor, speak of its constitution, or power of continuing in a healthy state; and also of its pathology, or of the symptoms of that disease to which it is by its very nature more peculiarly liable.

Accordingly, if it were necessary to describe in one sentence the genius and constitution of the Latin language, one could not do this better than by defining it as a language which is always yearning after contraction. Whether this tendency is indicated in the written remains by the usual processes of synizesis, assimilation, and apocope; whether it appears in the slurring-over of syllables by which the scansion of the comic metres is effected; or whether we perceive it in the systematic abbreviations which mark the transition from the Roman to the Romance languages, it is still one and the same,—it is the type of the language in its infancy, its maturity, and its decay.

The most distinct and vivid picture of the Latin language is, therefore, to be derived from a consideration of this peculiarity, as developed—

I. In the written language of ancient Rome.

II. In the spoken language of ancient Rome, so far as we can discern it in the remains of the comedians.

III. In the modern languages (and particularly in the French) which are derived from the Latin.

§ 2. Abbreviations observable in the written forms.

I. With regard to the written forms in which the Latin language has been handed down to us, it would not, perhaps, be too large an assertion, if we said that every etymological difficulty arises more or less from this systematic abbreviation.

There are two ways in which this tendency manifests itself—in the loss of the termination, and in the coalition of syllables in the middle of the word.

When clipt or mutilated words are common in any language, the cause is to be sought in the strength and prominence of the single accent, which is generally thrown forward as far as possible, and in the impatience with which practical and busy men hurry through that part of their work which consists in talking. The rules of the Latin metrical system might have prepared us for something of the kind. It has been shewn in a former chapter (above, p. 174), that the triple recurrence of the ictus was the essential feature of the Saturnian verse, the thesis being observed or neglected at the pleasure of the composer. Similarly, the accentuated syllable of a word, or that on which the emphasis of pronunciation was allowed to fall, was supposed to represent the significance of the term, just as the weight of a body is considered to be collected at its centre of gravity; and the other syllables were slurred over or cast aside as superfluous and unnecessary incumbrances. As instances of this, one might adduce a number of syncopised forms of common words. We have *ac* for *atque, amavere* for *amaverunt, amare* for *amaris, cœl* for *cœlo, do* for *domo, dein* for *deinde, gau* for *gaudio, nec* for *neque, neu* for *neve, ni* for *nisi, pa* for *parte, po* for *populo, seu* for *sive*, &c.; and, not to speak of the *visárgah*, by which a final *s*, though written, was not pronounced (*N. Crat.* p. 317), we have a number of words in which the termination *-is* or *-us* was regularly abridged to *-ĕ*: such as, *ille, ipse, mage*, &c. for *ollus, ipsus, magis*, &c. The contemptuous familiarity with which the master addressed his slaves gave rise to a number of abbreviations of the Greek names of the latter. Thus, *Artemidorus* was called *Artemas* (Varro, *L. L.* viii. § 21), and *Demodorus* shrunk into *Demas* or *Dama* (Hor. ii. *Serm.* 5, 101; ibid. 6, 54).

But the hasty pronunciation of the Romans, so far as it was exhibited in the written forms of the language, appears chiefly in the omission of letters or syllables in the middle of words. If the hurried talker has time to pronounce more than one syllable, he would rather preserve the termination than any of the middle sounds. Indeed, the accent sometimes stands over the ruins of a number of syllables, which it has fused into one compound articulation. The following instances, selected from a very large number, may serve to illustrate this: *Ala* for *Axilla* (Cic. *Orat.* c. 45, § 153); *aula* (*olla*) for *auxilla; brúma* (s. c. *dies*), "the shortest day," from *brevimus; carcer* from *co-arceo; contaminare*, the derivative verb from *contagimen; contio* for *conventio; cunœ* for *cubinœ, dixti* for *dixisti, exilis* for *exigilis* (from *egeo*, cf. *exiguus*), *ímus* for *infimus, jusso* for *jussero, mala* for *maxilla, mollis* for *mobilis, omentum* for *opimentum, otium* for *opitium, Pollius* for *Publilius* (Nieb. *H. R.* i. n. 977), *paullus* for *pauxillus, prudens* for *providens, puella* for *puerula, qualus* for *quasillus, sacellum* for *sacraculum* (comp. *sakaraklúm Herekleís*=*sacellum Herculis*, in the *Cippus Abellanus*, l. 11), *solari* for *sublevari*, *sublimis* for *sublevimis* (cf. μετέωρος); *subtilis*, "fine-spun," for *subtexilis* (comp. *subtemen, tela*); *summus* for *supremus*, *tandem* for *tamendem*, *trucido* for *tauricido*, *vánus* for *vacanus*, *velum* for *vexillum*, &c. This is particularly remarkable in the flexion-forms of nouns and verbs; and as we have seen above, the complete forms cannot be restored until we have made good the losses occasioned by this systematic abbreviation. In some cases this abbreviation will appear in a compound, though the full form is retained in the simple word. Thus, although the gen. *cujus* retains the original termination, this has been shortened into ĭ in the compound: *cuĭ-cuĭ-modi* for *cujus-cujus-modi* (Cic. *ad Att.* iii. 22).

The Romans, however, were not satisfied with getting rapidly through their simple words. The same principle was applied to the compounds: thus *magis volo* was written *malo*, *non volo* became *nolo*, *postmurium* was shortened into *pomœrium*, and so forth; and not only so, but we also find that in the case of quasi-compounds, made up of two or more words, which are not amalgamated by the loss of inflexions into one whole, some part of the termination of the first word is regularly omitted, and thus the group is subjected to the domination of a single accent. It may be sufficient to mention such words as *audĭn* = *audisne*; *Ecere*, *Ecastor*, *Epol* = [per] *œdem Cereris, Castoris,* s. *Pollucis*;[1] *ho'die* = *hoc die*, *meridie* = *media die*, *multimodis* = *multis modis*, *nudiustertius* = *nunc dies tertius*, *omnimodis*

---

[1] It has been shewn above (p. 208) that the dentals, when preceded and followed by vowels, are frequently omitted in the French forms of Latin words; and it will be shewn below that D and T must have been dropt in the old pronunciation of some Latin words, such as *pater, modo, quidem*. The words *Epol* and *Ecastor* exhibit the same fact in the written forms of the old Latin language, and therefore complete the induction.

= *omnibus modis*, *refert* = *rei-fert*, *sis* = *si vis*, *sodes* = *si audes*, *tectifractis* = *tectis fractis*, *vasargenteis* = *vasibus argenteis*, &c. Then, again, we find a number of verbal juxtapositions, for we cannot term them compounds, belonging to the same class: such are *pate-facio* = *patere-facio*, *sci-licet* = *scire licet*, *vide-licet* = *videre-licet*, &c. It has been shewn above, that many verbs in -*do*, -*eo*, -*so*, may be explained in the same manner; and that a similar analysis may be applied to the secondary tenses of every verb.

It is not necessary to pursue this part of the subject any further; for we can scarcely read a page of Latin without finding some proofs of the general rule.[1]

II. But although there is much abbreviation in the written forms of the Latin language, the orthography of the Romans expressed much more than their articulation. This is more conspicuous in proportion as we take a more polished and advanced period of the language. Before proceeding to demonstrate this from the metres of the comedians, it will be convenient to adduce some passages, in which the difference between the written and the spoken language of ancient Rome is expressly recognised.

§ 3. Ancient testimonies to the difference between the spoken and the written language.

When Cicero's Crassus (*de Oratore*, iii. 11, § 41) is speaking of the true mode of pronouncing Latin, he says: "I do not like the separate letters to be either pronounced with pedantic accuracy, or slurred over too carelessly." This shews that, though an uneducated countryman might

---

[1] The reader might be referred for further instances to a paper on the "Ausfall oder Verwandlung der Consonanten durch Zusammenziehung oder Assimilation in der Lateinischen Sprache," in the *Rheinisch. Museum* for 1839 (pp. 42—81); but, although most of the words there enumerated are cases of contraction, the author, Professor Schwenck, has not been happy in his restorations. In the same volume of the *Rhein. Mus.*, p. 297, there is a criticism on Prof. Schwenck by Dr. Düntzer.

T

represent by his articulation too little of the written word, it would be a fault, on the other hand, if the scholar recollected too much of his spelling. Again, Suetonius, who had seen the chirograph of Augustus (*Vit. Octav.* c. 87), writes thus about his method of spelling (c. 88): " He did not strictly attend to orthography,—that is, the method and laws of writing as taught by the grammarians;—on the contrary, he seems rather to adopt the opinion of those who think that we should write just as we talk. For as to his often changing or omitting not letters only, but whole syllables, this is a common inaccuracy; nor would I remark the fact, did it not appear strange to me that he should have superseded a consular legate as being illiterate, because he saw in his handwriting *ixi* for *ipsi*." From this it is clear, that in the time of Augustus people did not pronounce as they wrote. Quintilian, too, expressly tells us (*Inst. Orat.* xi. 3, § 33), that, " although it is necessary, on the one hand, to articulate every *word*, yet it is wearisome and disgusting to take account of every letter, and as it were to reckon them up: for not only is the crasis of vowels very common, but even some of the consonants are disguised when a vowel follows;" and then he quotes the examples of both *ecthlipsis* and *synalœpha* in Virgil's *multum ille et terris*. From these and other passages which might be quoted, we conclude that the written language of Rome could not be taken as a standard of even the most exact and careful pronunciation of educated men living in the city itself, whose mode of pronouncing was strikingly different from that of the provincials (Cicero, *de Oratore*, iii. 11, § 43). Accordingly, the colloquialisms of the country people must have been still further removed from the written language of the day, and are less to be inferred from it.

The true way of considering the Latin language, if we

wish to realise to ourselves its spoken form, is to regard it as struggling with the fetters of the Greek metrical system.

The poetry of the Augustan age shews us, that the Greek rules of metre are observed with greater strictness by the Romans who adopted them than by the Greeks themselves. With the Roman poets the trochaic dipodia, that important rhythm in lyric poetry, always appears under the form of trochee + spondee; whereas in the Greek system there was nothing to prevent the dipodia from being pure. Take, for instance, the Sapphic verse: Horace's second foot is always a spondee, Sappho's as often a trochee. The same minute accuracy, or rather sameness, is observable in their *anacrusis*. In Horace's Alcaics the anacrusis at the beginning of the first three lines is rarely a short syllable; but in his Greek models he would as often find a short syllable as a long one.[1]

§ 4.
The poetry of the Augustan age does not represent the genuine Latin pronunciation;

---

[1] The remarks in the text refer to a mode of scanning the Sapphic and Alcaic stanzas, which is not in accordance with the common doctrine, but which is, I think, demonstrably correct. The Sapphic and Alcaic stanzas differ only in a varied arrangement of the same elements; and the three first lines of the Alcaic stanza begin with an anacrusis, which the Sapphic rhythm excludes. If we call the dactyl A, the trochee B, and the anacrusis x, the law of the verse appears in the following simple formulæ:

(1) Sapphic stanza: $2B + A + 2B$ (*ter*)
$2A$.

(2) Alcaic stanza: $x + 2B + 2A$ (*bis*)
$x + 4B$
$2A + 2B$.

Thus, for example, the Sapphic contains three lines like—*Jám sa|tís ter||rís nivis* || *átque* | *díræ* ||, and one like—*térruit* | *úrbem* ||; where it will be observed, the second member of the trochaic as well as the dactylic dipodia is always a spondee. The Alcaic has two lines like—*Vi|des ut* | *alta* || *stet nive* | *candidum* ||, one like—*Sil|vaé la|bóran*||*tés ge|luque* ||, and one like—*Flúmina* | *cónstite*||*rínt a|cúto*. With regard to the Sapphic verse, in particular, it will not perhaps be easy to correct errors which are sanctioned no less by

All this leads to the inference, that the poetry of the Augustan age was recited with a pedantic accuracy at variance with the genius of the language; and as the German opera-singers at the present day soften down their gutturals in order to accommodate their language to the flowing rhythm of Italian music, so the Romans, in the days of Horace and Virgil, were proud of their foreign fetters, and were glad to display the ascendancy which vanquished Greece had gained over the minds of her rude conquerors.

§ 5. *which is rather to be derived from an examination of the comic metres.*

This refined and mincing pronunciation was, of course, less compatible with the colloquialisms of comedy than with the elegant stiffness of copied heroic or lyric poetry. Consequently, though the comedians borrowed their metres from the Greeks, they were content to pronounce the words as they were uttered by the common people; and as the busy talkers of the forum were wont to clip and contract their words, so the syllables usually omitted in speaking were not taken into account on the comic stage. When, therefore, we can recognise the law of the verse in a Latin comedy, but find that the syllables, as they stand written in many of the lines, are more numerous than is necessary for the feet of the verse, we may safely conclude that the superfluous syllables were omitted in the pronunciation of the actor; and if by him, *a fortiori*, that they were habitually slurred over by the majority of his audience. This opinion will be confirmed, if we discover, on further inquiry, that the syllables so dispensed

the practice of schools than by the well-known jingle of the Anti-Jacobin; but it is not to be borne that this ignorance should exalt itself to dogmatism. In the last number of the *Classical Museum* (p. 338, sqq.) there is an article in which we are told that the Sapphic verse, "recited with the true metrical quantity and the natural spoken accent," will read thus: *Jáwm sattees | taérees || nivís autque | deéræ*, &c.; and that the following is a Sapphic of the same kind: *che il gran sepolcro libero di Christo!* And this is delivered, not as a modest suggestion, but as a decree of oracular wisdom.

with are not found in the corresponding forms exhibited by the modern idioms which derive their origin from the language of ancient Rome.

The following instances, few out of many, may be sufficient to establish this.[1] Let us first take some of the short imperatives, which are, by the nature of the case, especially liable to hurried pronunciation. As our *look!* has degenerated into *lo!*, and the Latin *vide* has become the Italian *ve'*, and the French *voi* or *v'* (in *voi-ci*, *v'la*); so in Terent. *Adelph.* ii. 2, 31, it is clear that we must pronounce the line:

Labáscit : ún' hoc hábyo : vé' si sát placet.

Here, also, we have Italian *abbio*. Similarly, as Cicero tells us,[2] that *cave ne eas* was pronounced *cauneas*, we see that the following line (*Phormio*, v. 1, 37) must be pronounced:

Sed pér deós atqu' hómmes, m'am éss' hanc, cáu resciscat quísquam.

This line also furnishes the French abbreviation *hommes;* and the form *mus* for *meus*, which, with its analogies, is reproduced in the French, Italian, and Spanish. The Troubadours wrote *mos, ma, mon*, for *meus, mea, meum;* and Ennius has *sas* for *suas*. The same sort of contraction has taken place in the Greek possessives: see *New Crat.* p. 164.

Then, again, as the French say *tai*, it is clear that *tace* is a single long syllable in the following line (*Adelph.* ii. 4, 16):

At ut ómne réddat—ómne réddet—taí-mod', ác suire hác—sequor.

Which line also furnishes us with the imperative *suire* for

---

[1] The reader, who desires a more copious induction, cannot do better than consult an excellent article on the subject in the *Journal of Education* (vol. ii. p. 344, sqq.), written, I believe, by Professor T. H. Key.

[2] *De Divin.* ii. 40, § 84 : " Quum M. Crassus exercitum Brundisii imponeret, quidam in portu, caricas Cauno advectas vendens, *Cauneas*, clamitabat. Dicamus, si placet, monitum ab eo Crassum, *caveret ne iret.*"

sequere, if we may in this case also follow the French analogy. In general there seems to have been a tendency towards softening down the guttural into its ultimate form, the vowel *i*. This has obviously taken place in *faire* and *œil*, derived from *facere* and *oculus;* and not only is the imperative *tace* a monosyllable, but also its indicative *tacet*, as in the following line (*Adelph.* iv. 5, 5):

Tait: cúr non lúd' hunc ál'quantísper mélyus est.

Where for *al'quantisper* compare Italian *alcuno*, and the French *aucun*, from *aliquis unus*. It can scarcely be doubted that *Adelphi*, iii. 2, 20, was pronounced as follows:

'Ad'lescént' ips' érip'r' œílos: pósthac praécip'tém darém;

and that in iii. 2, 37, *lacrymas* is a dissyllable after the analogy of *larme*, and of *serment* from *sacramentum*. Similarly, in *Heaut.* v. 5, 16, quoted below, as the ictus falls on *facile*, we may conclude that it was pronounced as a single long syllable. Festus tells us that there was a form *facul*, and *facile* appears as a mere *anacrusis* in the Scipio epitaph (c. 5); above, Ch. VI. § 20. Perhaps the most singular instance of this omission of the guttural is furnished by the French *faible* from *flexibilis;* for in this there is a double collapse.

The imperatives *abi, redi*, are monosyllables with the omission of the unnecessary *b* and *d* (*Adelph.* ii. 1, 13, and 36), and *jube* throws off its *b* (*Adelph.* v. 6, 1), as it does in the perfect, &c.

The phrase *bono animo es* is shortened for the same reason as the other imperatives. In Plautus (*Rudens*, iii. 3, 17) it forms a cretic:

'O salútis meaé spés tac' ác bón-ame és.

We observe the same sort of abbreviation in a number of nouns of common occurrence; such, for instance, as express the nearest degrees of family relationship. The compound *parricida* indicates a contraction of *pater* analogous to the French *père*, and the word was probably so pronounced in such lines as (*Adelph.* i. 1, 51):

> *Hoc pater ac dominus interest: hoc qui nequit;* i. e.
> *Hoc pére ac dónnus interést: hoc qui nequit.*

and (*Adelph.* i. 2, 46):

> *Natura tu illi pater es, consiliis ego;* i. e.
> *Natúra tú gli pére es, cónsiglís ego.*

where the ictus falls upon it. In the latter line, as *tu* is emphatic, an elision would be inadmissible; we must therefore pronounce *illi* either as the Italian *gli* or as the French *lui*, and this gives us another modern analogy. In the former line *dominus* is probably a dissyllable following the analogy of *domina*, which becomes *donna* in Italian, and *dame* in French. Similarly, *homines* is a monosyllable in the passage quoted above from the *Phormio; animus* becomes *ame; femina, femme*, &c.

That *puer* was often a monosyllable appears from the forms *por, pora*, which occur in inscriptions, from the compounds *Lucipor, Marcipor*, &c., and from the Spartan ποῖρ for παῖς. In *Heaut.* v. 5, 16, the old reading will stand if we may pronounce it thus:

> *Gnáte m'yó pol tí do púllam lépidam quám tu faíl amés.*

The Romans frequently omitted *b* in the middle of a word: this is most common in the dat. and abl. pl. of the first declension, and is also observable in the French derivatives; such as *où* and *y* from *ubi* and *ibi*. For the change of *puer* into *por*, we may also compare the transformation of *fuere* and *fuerent* into *fore, forent*.

Perhaps two of the most striking instances of this clipt pronunciation are afforded by the scansion of the particles *quidem* and *modo*, in both of which the *d* is omitted. With regard to the former even Bentley remarked that it must be frequently a monosyllable in Terence (*ad Andr.* i. 3,

20). The following reasons have been adduced to prove that it was so in general. (1) The analogy of *item*, shortened from *itidem*, will support the pronunciation of *qu'em* for *quidem*. (2) As it is an enclitic, and is regularly attached to certain words, in the same way as περ, γε, &c. in Greek, it seems reasonable to suppose that it would be peculiarly liable to curtailment. Now, if we retain the full form of *quidem* with some of these words, we alter their quantity, and so sacrifice the principal word in order to preserve a mere appendage. Thus, *ego-quidem*, or *eg-quidem*, is marked *ĕquĭdem* in books on Latin prosody, and *siquidem, quandoquidem*, are marked *sĭquĭdem, quandŏquĭdem*, although the true quantity of the separate words is *sī, quandō;* and though in other compounds—*quandōque, quandōcunque*—this quantity is invariably retained. It follows, therefore, that *quandoquidem* must have been pronounced *quandōqu'em; siquidem, sīqu'em;* and *equidem, ēqu'em;* just as *me quidem* must be scanned *mē qu'em* in Pers. i. 10:

> *Littera: per me quidem sint omnia protinus alba.*

In the same way it is manifest that *modo* must often have been a monosyllable: see *e. g.* Ter. Andr. ii. 1, 2, and ii. 4, 6. In the languages derived from the Latin the compound *quomodo* is represented by *como* Sp., *come* It., and *comme* Fr.; in which the *d* is omitted, and, in the last, as in the old French *cum* (below, § 9), the syllable is dropt altogether.

§ 6.
The French language is the best modern representative of the spoken Latin.

III. We may now pass, by a natural transition, to our third source of information respecting the constitution of the Latin language—that which exhibits it pathologically, or in its state of disorganisation or decay.

It will not be expected that I should here shew at length how the Romance languages were formed from the Latin. It will be sufficient to point out some of the reasons for believing that the French language is a better living representative of the pronunciation of the ancient Italians than the language which is now spoken in the peninsula itself; and, in conclusion, to state briefly what was the process of the disintegration, and in what degree the modern differed from the ancient form.

As the Romans successively conquered the different nations which formed the population of Italy, they gradually included within the limits of a single empire a number of different tribes, who spoke idioms, or dialects, differing but little from the language of the Romans themselves. It is not, therefore, surprising that a gradual amalgamation should have taken place, and that every Italian should have spoken, with only slight variations of accent, one and the same Latin language. The language of Rome itself—the language of government, of literature, and of law—would, of course, be independent of these minor differences. Every educated man and every public functionary would refer to this unvarying standard, and would speak or write, in some cases with pedantic accuracy, the language of the senate-house and the forum. Accordingly, the inhabitants of the provinces, *i.e.* the foreign subjects of the Empire, would hear nothing but pure Roman Latin; and, if they learned the language of their rulers at all, they would at least learn it in the best form. Their position in this respect differed materially from that of colonists, even in ancient times. The colonists of our day, and especially the English emigrants, present a natural contrast to the case of the Roman provincials. For, while the colonists who sailed from Corinth or Athens were of all classes—οἱ τυχόντες—our modern colonists are generally those who are either not able to live at home, or, at all events, who practise trades inconsistent with a high amount of educational polish. We find, therefore, that colonial English represents only the vulgar colloquial language of the mother-country; whereas the Roman provincials spoke a language derived — imperfectly, it might be, but still derived — from the polished and elegant diction of proconsuls, jurisconsults, and publicani.

The Gauls, in particular, were remarkable for their tendency to assimilate themselves, in their language and usages, to the Romans. In an inconceivably short space of time the province of Gallia was completely Romanised.[1] Their own language was out of the pale of civilisation: in fact, they had no mother-tongue to struggle for. A language is only dear to us when we know its capabilities, and when it is hallowed by a thousand connexions with our civilisation, our literature, and our comforts. So long as it merely lisps the inarticulate utterances of half-educated men, it has no hold upon the hearts of those who speak it, and it is readily neglected or thrown aside in favour of the more cultivated idiom, which, while it finds names for luxuries of civilisation before unknown, also opens a communication with those who appear as the heralds of moral and intellectual regeneration. The Greeks and the Jews had good reasons for loving the language of their ancestors, and could never be induced to forget or relinquish the flowing rhythms of their poets or the noble energy of their prose writers. The case was not so with the provincials of Gaul. Without any anterior predilections, and with a mobility of character which still distinguishes their modern representatives, they speedily adopted the manners and the words of the Romans; and it is probable that in the time of the Empire there was no more difference between the gramma-

---

[1] How completely this was the case even in Cicero's time may be inferred from what he says in his *Orat. pro Fonteio*, 1, § 1: " Referta Gallia negotiatorum est, plena civium Romanorum. Nemo Gallorum sine cive Romano quidquam negotii gerit; nummus in Gallia nullus sine civium Romanorum tabulis commovetur," &c. For the literary culture of Gaul some hundred years later, the reader may consult the commentators on Juvenal, i. 44, vii. 147, 8, xv. 111.

tical Latin of Lyons and Rome, than there is now between the grammatical French of St. Petersburg and Paris.

From what I have just said, it should appear that the Latin spoken in Gaul was upon the whole better and purer than the Latin spoken in the municipal districts of Italy during the time of the Empire. Let us, however, suppose that they were only equally good. Then, if it can be shewn that the disturbing causes were greater and more efficacious in Italy than in Gaul, we shall still have a greater surplus of good Latinity in the latter.

§ 7. The modern Italian not equally so; and why.

Before the Italian language revived as a vehicle of literary communication, the peninsula had been subjected to a series of invasions which had modified and corrupted in no slight degree the speech of the country people. This was effected not only by the influence of the conquerors, but also by the infusion of a considerable amount of foreign population. In Lombardy and other parts, where the invaders formed a permanent settlement, the change was most sensibly and durably felt; whereas Tuscany, which had been screened by its position from any permanent or extensive occupation by the northern tribes, was not exposed to this corruption of its familiar language, and its greater wealth, its commerce, and its independence, preserved among its inhabitants a residuum of the old Latin literature and civilisation.

When, therefore, vernacular composition revived in Italy, it was emphatically Tuscan. It is true that the new literary language spread itself over the whole of Italy, and that there were varieties of accent in the different districts.[1]

[1] On these differences of Italian articulation Matthæus Ægyptius writes as follows (*ad S. C. de Bacch.* p. 145): "Quosdam audias ore adstricto, et inter dentes, dimidiata verba tanquam invitos, et cum quadam parsimonia efferre, ut Ligures: quosdam ore patulo et laxo, claraque et sonora voce animi sensus effundere, ut Neapolitani faciunt: medios inter hos Senenses,

Still, however, a purity of Tuscan phraseology is essential to literary correctness; and whatever a man's native accent may be, he must accommodate it to this court-language. It follows, therefore, that the pronunciation of modern Italian must be syllabic. In other words, it must be more akin to the studied accuracy with which the Romans of the Augustan age pronounced their Græcised poetry, than to the natural articulation of the ancient Italians. It has been truly said, that the Italian language cannot be pronounced both well and quickly. This is only another expression of the fact, that a literary language, which is not natural, can only be articulated syllabically. The qualification of *lingua Toscana in bocca Romana* is another illustration of the same fact; for here we have a recognition of the truth, that the modern Italian is a written language to be pronounced according to its syllables, and that of the accents, in which it can be pronounced, the best and sweetest is that of a well-educated inhabitant of the pontifical metropolis.

§ 8.
Dialects of the French language.

Very different was the case of the Gauls. After living for several hundred years under the dominion and influence of the Romans, and having lost their Celtic language and in a great measure their Celtic character, they were invaded and partially conquered by a confederation of German warriors, who called themselves *Franks*, a name indicating their bold and martial character.[1] The domination

queis Musa dedit ore rotundo loqui. Adderem Florentinos nisi ex imo gutture pronuntiantes originem adhuc ostenderent Phœniciam."

[1] It has usually been supposed that the word *Frank* denotes "free-man," so that "French" and "Latin" would, when referred to their etymology, appear as synonymous terms. This is not, however, the original meaning of the word *Frank;* though, in a secondary sense, the word has borne this signification. In the Teutonic languages, to which it belongs, the word *fra-n-k,* or *frak*, is equivalent to *ferox*, and signifies "bold," "warlike," "intrepid" (see Thierry, *Lettres sur l'Histoire de France,* Lettr. vi. p. 436, Bruxelles

of these rude conquerors did not destroy the Roman texture of the language which was spoken by the inhabitants of Gaul. At first both the conquerors and the conquered retained their own idioms; and the *lingua Francisca*, or *Francica*, of the German invaders flourished by the side of the *lingua Gallica*, or *Gallicana*, of the conquered provincials. In time, however, as there was much more literary culture among the latter, and as the priests and scholars of the age were all furnished by the district in which the Franks had settled, the standard of diction would be sought in the language of the more educated class, and the Roman language, more or less corrupted, would gradually become the medium of communication between the conquerors and the conquered.

As might have been expected, this gradual adoption of the Roman language by the Teutonic invaders gave rise to a number of dialects. Of these the most refined and polished was that which was spoken by the inhabitants of the south-eastern district of France. Many causes conspired to give this idiom an earlier development. The south-eastern provincials were more completely Romanised in the first instance;[1] they were less subjected to foreign invasion than the other inhabitants of France; the Burgundians and Visigoths, who settled among them, were more adapted to social life than their German brethren, and more readily assimilated their language and customs

---

ed.). Ethnical names, in addition to their primitive meaning, are often used as expressive of certain qualities, whether the use is complimentary or not. *Assassin, Gascon, Vandal,* and *Goth,* are attributive words in our own language; the word *Slave* has been derived from the low estate of the *Sclavonians;* and even in ancient times, Κάρ, Κρής, Παφλάγων, Μυσός, Συβαρίτης, Σκύθης, &c., were terms significant of qualities. The German confederacy of the *Franks* seems to have corresponded to that of the *Iscævones;* those of the Saxons and Thuringians to the *Ingævones* and *Herminones* respectively.

[1] It is right, perhaps, to say, that Marseilles in particular was rather Græcised than Romanised: see Cic. *pro Flacco,* 26, § 36.

to those of their subjects; and when at length Provence became a part of the Frankish dominions, their conquerors were no longer unruly German barbarians, but the civilised and Romanised subjects of a regular monarchy. The happy climate of Provence, and the wealth and commerce of the people, contributed to foster and encourage those arts which can only flourish in a genial soil; and we are not to wonder if the provincials outstript the northern Gauls in intellectual tastes as well as in physical comforts.

The connexion between Provence and Catalonia tended to increase the civilisation of the latter. But, in reference to the present object, to discover a Romance language which shall most accurately represent the spoken language of the Romans, we may safely dismiss the Spaniards; whose language, already corrupted by the invasions of the Suevians and Visigoths, has been still further disorganised by the pervading and durable influence of the highly civilised Arabians.

The people of Provence were keenly sensible of the difference between their own language and that of their Franco-Gallic rulers. The names by which they distinguished their own country and that of the French referred to the differences of the idioms spoken in them. It is singular that this difference should have been expressed in terms of the affirmative particle, which they had respectively adopted. Drawing a line through Dauphiné, Lyonnais, Auvergne, Limousin, Perigord, and Saintonge, the country to the south of this was called *Langue d'oc*, the district to the north of the line was termed *Langue d'oyl*. Now, although the differences between the *Langue d'oc* and the *Langue d'oyl* consisted mainly in the greater or less development of the Latin element in each, it is to be remembered that these affirmative particles are both due to their Teutonic affinities.[1] And here is the inconsist-

---

[1] According to Grimm (*D. Gramm.* iii. p. 768), *oyl* is *ja il*, and *oc* is *ja*

ency; the words *oc* and *oyl* are equally Frankish or German, and yet the people of the *Langue d'oc* distinguished their language from that of the *Langue d'oyl* by calling it *Roman, lemozi, provensalesc;* and they termed themselves *Provinciales,* i. e. *Romanæ Provinciæ inquilini,* as distinguished from the *Francigenæ* of the north.

§ 9.
But all these dialects were closely related to the Latin.

But whatever were the distinctions between the languages of the northern and southern inhabitants of the province of Gaul, it is clear that the language of the whole country was to the middle of the ninth century A. D. a very near approximation to the Latin. We have the original of an oath which was sworn at Strasburg in 842 A. D., by Lodewig, king of Germany. This interesting document, which is expressly stated to have been in the *Romana lingua,* is in the following words:[1]—" *Pro*

ich; the only difference between them being, that the affirmative is combined with the first person in the one case, and with the third person in the other. To me it appears that *oyl* is simply the affirmative *wel* or *wohl* (for this power of the initial *o* see above, p. 37), and that *oc* is the German *auch=etiam* (*Phil. Mus.* ii. p. 345).

[1] Nithardi *Hist. ap. Scr. Rer. Francic.* vii. p. 26, quoted by Thierry, *Lettres sur l'Histoire de France* (lettr. xi). Substituting the Latin words which come nearest in etymology to the words of this fragment, we have : *Pro Dei amore et pro Christiano populo et nostro communi salvamento, de isto die in ab-ante, in quantum Deus sapere et posse mihi donabit, sic salvare habeo ego ecc' istum meum fratrem Carolum, et in adjutu et in quaque una causa, sic quomodo homo per directum suum fratrem salvare debitus est, in eo quod ille mihi alterum sic faciet; et ab Lothario nullum placitum numquam prendere habeo, quod, mea voluntate, ecc' isti meo fratri Carolo in damno sit.* It is not necessary to enter upon any lengthened discussion of the corrupt Latinity of these words. That *salvar-ai,* &c., are *salvare-habeo,* &c., is well known (*N. Crat.* p. 454). It appears from the oldest forms of the words that the French *cel, cest* (*cist*), Italian *quello, questo,* are the compounds *ecc' ille* and *ecc' iste* respectively. For, as in Provençal we have *aisso,* in old French *aezo,* into which *ço* enters, so we have *icel* and *icest,* anterior to *cel* and *cest.* Similarly *ici* is *ecc' ibi.* Of *altresì,* which is common in Italian, Varchi says : " *Altresì* è Provenzale, non Ispagniuolo, e gli antichi nostri scrivano *altresie,* e non *altresì.*" Comp. *altrettale, altrettanto.*

Deu amor et pro Christian poblo et nostro commun salvament, dist di en avant, in quant Deus savir et podir me dunat, si salvarai io cist meon fradre Karle, et in adjuda et in cadhuna cosa, si cum om per dreit son fradre salvar dist, in o quid il mi altresi fazet: et ab Ludher nul plaid numquam prindrai, qui, meon vol, cist meon fradre Karle, in damno sit." It appears from the context of the history, that the oath was couched in this language in order that it might be understood by the French subjects of Karl, le Chauve. It was, therefore, the common language of the country; and as it is free from Germanisms, and exhibits only those corruptions of the Latin for which it is easy to account, it furnishes us with a distinct confirmation of the opinion, that we ought to seek in the language of France for the best modern representative of the language of ancient Italy.

The difference between the modern Italian, considered as the offspring of the new Tuscan literature, and the old French, regarded as a scion of the Roman language which was spoken in the province of Gaul, consists in the fact to which I have already adverted—namely, that the former would reproduce the mincing and pedantic pronunciation of the literary Romans, while the latter would retain the genuine colloquial utterance of the free colonists of the empire. It is worthy of observation that the French language itself enables us to illustrate this difference. If we examine the French language as it is, we shall often find double forms of derivatives from the Latin. Now, in every one of these cases it is remarkable that the older word—that which belongs to the oldest and most genuine vocabulary—differs most from the written form or syllabic pronunciation of the Latin original. Thus, *chez, chose, hôtel, naif, Noel, pitié, pousser,* from *casa, causa, hospes, nativus, natalis, pietas, expulsare,* are older forms than *case, cause, hôpital, native, natal, piété, expulser.* (See

A. W. Schlegel, *Observations sur la Langue et la Littérature Prov.* p. 44.) The fact is, that the latter were derived from the written, the former from the spoken language.

§ 10. Leading distinctions between the Roman and Romance idioms.

The manner in which the transition from the Latin language to the French may be supposed to have taken place is well known, and very easily described. In this place we must be contented with a few brief remarks; for it would be an idle attempt to discuss as a secondary matter the details of a subject which admits of such ample illustration, and which has already been treated at great length, though with various degrees of success, by Diez, Raynouard, Schlegel, Ampère, Fuchs, and Lewis.

The tendency of the spoken Latin language to clip and mutilate itself began at an early period to militate against the regularity of the grammatical forms. With regard to the verbs, it has been shewn above that the organic inflexions had been in a great measure superseded by secondary or compound tenses before the commencement of the classical age; and that the person-endings are obliterated, or deformed by inconsistencies, in the oldest specimens of the written language. In regard to the verbs, then, the change from the Roman to the Romance is merely a further development of that which was already in operation. The Roman case-system was in itself more complete than the conjugation of the verb; and therefore we may expect to find greater changes in the French noun as compared with the Latin. In general it may be remarked, that when the tendency to abbreviation has commenced its action on the flexional forms of a language, certain devices are at once adopted for the purpose of preventing any syntactical obscurity. Indeed, the logical or syntactical development of a language is generally benefited by the change; and where the etymological organisation becomes imperfect, the literary capabilities of the particular idiom are extended and confirmed.

There is good reason for believing, that in the spoken language of the ancient Italians the difference between the subjective and objective cases of the noun was at an early period neglected or overlooked (see Lepsius, *ad Inscript.* p. 120). At any rate, it is clear that this was the first step towards the breaking up of the Roman case-system. The accusative case was substituted for the nominative, and all the subordinate relations were expressed by prefixing prepositions to this new crude form of the noun. We observe a tendency of the same kind in vulgar English; and perhaps this passage from the subject to the object may be explained on general principles, without any reference to the want of grammatical education on the part of those in whom it is most observable. Connected with this employment of prepositions to give definiteness to the crude forms of nouns, is the use of the old Roman demonstratives *ille* and *ipse* to mark a definite object, as contrasted with *unus* and *aliquis-unus*, which denote indifference. This is, of course, identical with the use of the definitive article in the Greek and other languages; and the Romance languages owe much of their acknowledged perspicuity to this adaptation. It is true that the artifice is not applied with the logical subtilty by which the employment of the Greek article is distinguished; but any deficiency in this respect is amply compensated by the strictly logical order of the sentences in which the words are arranged.

It is not necessary in this place to say much on the subject of the Romance verb. Where the tenses have preserved the forms of the Latin verb, we observe a systematic abbreviation. Labials are absorbed, according to the practice so remarkable in Latin; final syllables are dropt, and the accent is thrown forward. Generally, however, the number of compound or auxiliary tenses is very much increased. In addition to the verbs *sum* and *fui*, we find that *habeo* and *sto* are regularly pressed into the service. Verbs in their first formation construct their perfect and future tenses with the aid of *habeo;* for the past participle with *habeo* makes up the former (as *j'ai aimé = ego habeo amatum*), and the regular future consists of a combination of the same verb with the infinitive (as *j'aimer-ai = ego habeo amare*). On these and similar forms see *New Cratylus*, p. 538, and compare Latham's *English Grammar*, § 352, sqq.

§ 11. Importance and value of the Latin language.

In the preceding pages I have endeavoured to write the history of the Latin language, and to characterise its peculiarities, from the earliest period of its existence down to the present time, when it is represented by a number of daughters, all resembling their mother more or less, and all possessing in some degree her beauties and defects. Of these, it can hardly be doubted that the French is the most authentic as well as the most important representative of the family. The Latin and French languages stand related to one another, not only in the connexion of affinity, but still more so in the important position which they have occupied as political and literary organs of communication. They have both striven to become the common language of civilised and educated men; and they have had singular recommendations for the office which they partially assumed. For power of condensation, for lucid perspicuity, and for the practical exposition of common matters, there are few idioms which can compete with the Latin or the French. In many particulars they fall far behind the Greek and the German; in many more they are surpassed by the English; and it seems now to be determined that neither Cæsar nor Napoleon was destined to reverse the decree of Providence, that man, though the one reasoning and speaking creature, should, in different parts of the world, express his thoughts in different languages. If there is one idiom which seems both worthy and likely to include within it the articulate utterances of all the world, it is our own,—for we, too, " are sprung of earth's first blood," and the sun never sets upon our Saxondom. Still we ought not to neglect or discourage the study of the old Roman language: though it will never again become the spoken language of Europe, there is no reason why it should not resume its place as the organ of literary communication,—why, with its powers of conciseness and abbreviation, and with its appropriation of all the conventional terms of science and art, it should not still flow from the pens of those who have truths and facts to communicate, and who are not careful to invest or disguise them in the embellishments of some modern and fashionable style. This at least is certain, that the Latin language has struck its roots so deeply and so permanently in our own language, that we cannot extirpate it, even if we would; for we must know Latin, if we would thoroughly understand our own mother-tongue; and those who are least learned, and most disposed to undervalue classical attainments, are most of all liable to further what others would call the corruption of our language, by the introduction of new terms formed after a Latin model.

INDICES.

I.

ETHNICAL NAMES, AND NAMES OF PLACES.

Æqui, 4.
Agathyrsi, 27.
Αἰθίοψ, 25.
Alba, 4.
Apulus, 4.
Ἄριοι, 28.
Asia, 29.
Auruncus, Αὔσων, 4.
Cascus, 4.
Etruscus, 11.
Frank, 284.
Herminones, 285.
Iguvium, 48.
Ingævones, 285.
Ἴων, Javan, 24, 29.

Larissa, 12.
Latinus, 5, 44.
Lithuanian, 44.
Μαιδοί, 27.
Massagetæ, 29.
Opicus, Oscus, 3.
Πάρθος, 27.
Πελασγός, 24.
Πέλοψ, 25.
Quirites, 43.
Rasena, 16.
Rhoxolani, 30.
Roma, 43.
Romanus, 235.
Sabinus, 6.

Sacæ, 29.
Sauromatæ, 29, 46.
Saxon, 29.
Sclavonian, 45, 285.
Scolotæ, 41.
Σκύθαι, 27, 29.
Ταρασένα, 16.[1]
Terracina, 13, 16.
Thracians, 27.
Thyrea, Thyræon, 12.
Τυῤῥηνός, 11.
Tuscus, 11.[2]
Umbri, 7.
Volscus, 4.

II.

SCYTHIAN WORDS.

aba, 39.
Apia, 36.
araxa, 39.
Araxes, 35.
arima, 38.
Arimaspi, 38.
Artimpasa, 37.
Borysthenes, 34.
brix-aba, 39.

Dan-ubius, 33.
Dnieper, 34.
Dniester, 33.
dun, 33.
Eri-danus, 35.
Exam-pæus, 40.
Ger-rus, 34.
Grou-casus, 39.
halinda, 39.

Hypa-caris, 34.
Hypan-is, 34.
Is-ter, 32.
masadas, 37.
Octa-masadas, 37.
Oito-surus, 37.
Oior-pata, 38.
Panticapes, 34.
Papæus, 36.

[1] Comp. *Tursni*, Vermiglioli, *Iscr. Per.* i. p. 279.
[2] Comp. Abeken, *Mittelitalien*, p. 127.

294   INDICES.

pata, 37, 38.
phru, 39.
phry-xa, 39.
Porata, 33.
Rha, 35.

Rho-danus, 35.
Sparga-pises, Sparga-pithes, 38.
spu, 38.
Tabiti, 36.

Tami-masadas, 37.
Tana-is, 34.
Temerinda, 37.
Tyres, 33.
xa, 39.

III.

UMBRIAN WORDS.

The Alphabetical List in pp. 68, 69, and the following.

abrons, 60.
ahaltru, 70.
anzeriates, 57.
ape, 54.
arsie, 55.
arsmo, 66.
arepes, 62.
arveitu, 52.
arves, 62.
arvia, 60.
buf, 59.
dersecus, 66.
dupursus, 68.
enetu, 57.
enumek, 63.
erar, erer, 65.
erus, 54.
este, 57.
etre, 68.
feitu, 60.
ferine, 60.
festira, 51.
fos, 65.
fri, 66.
frite, 65.
frosetom, 55.
furenr, 52.
futu, fututo, 54.
habe, &c., 55.
heris, 60.
heritu, 61, 67.

kapire, 52.
karetu, 54.
Krapuvius, 59.
kupifiatu, 54.
kurnase, 63.
kutef, 54, 62.
mers, 65.
nep, 67.
nome, 54.
okris, 54, 61.
orer, 66.
paker, 65.
parfa, 63.
peica, peiqu, 63.
pepe, 70.
pernaies, 57.
persei, 66.
persklum, 57.
pesetom, 55.
peturpursus, 68.
pihatu, 51.
pir, 67.
poplu, 54.
portatu, 65.
pre, 58.
prumum, 68.
prusesetu, 50.
pufe, 54, 58.
pune, pus, pusnaies, 54, 57.

punus, 70.
purtinsus, 54.
pusei, puze, 54, 56.
pustru, 54.
sevum, 62.
skrehto, skreihtor, 55.
stahito, 51.
steplatu, 63.
subator, 66.
subokau, suboko, 65.
sue-pis, 65.
tases, 62.
tertie, 68.
tera, 51, 65.
tesenakes, 59.
tesva, 51, 64.
titis, 71.
tota, 54, 62.
tover, 55.
treplanes, 58.
tuplak, tupler, tuves, 68.
vatuva, 60.
vehiies, 58.
veres, 58.
vitlup, 53.
ulo, 65.
uru, 65.

INDICES.

IV.

OSCAN WORDS.

The Alphabetical List in pp. 74-86, and the following.

æteis, 93.
aisken, 96.
aktud, 94.
akum, 97.
allo, 96.
amirikatud, 96.
amnud, 91.
ampert, 93.
angit, anget, 89.
anter, 89.
atrud, 96.
araget, aragetud, 89.
Ausil, 84.
Bansæ, 95.
Bantins, 95.
brateis, 91.
Degetasius, 89.
deivaid, deivast, 90.
dikust, 93.
egmazum, 97.
eituam, eituas, 93.
eizazunk, 97.
embratur, 8.
estud, 92, 96.
esuf, 95.
esak, 91.
etanto, 92.
famelo, 96.
fefakust, 92.
flusare, 59.
fortis, 92.
fuid, fust, 97.
Herekleis, 272.
herest, 93.
hipid, 91.

him, 97.
iok, ionk, 90.
izik, 96.
kadeis, 91.
karneis, 90.
kastro, 93.
kebnust, 96.
kensam, kensaum, 95.
kensazet, 96.
kenstom, 96.
kenstur, 95.
keus, 95.
kom, 94.
komenei, 90.
komono, 90.
kontrud, 92.
kvaísstur, 52.
ligis, ligud, 96.
likitud, 89.
maimas, 90.
mais, 90.
mallum, malud, 90.
manimasepum, 97.
meddisud (pru-), 96.
medikatud, 96.
mesene, 59.
minstreis, 93.
molta, 89.
moltaum, 92.
neip, nep, 97.
nesimois, 97.
op, 94, 96.
pa, 96.
pam, 94.

pertemust, 90.
perum, 90.
petiropert, 94.
piei, 91.
pis, 83, 90.
pod, 91, 92.
poizad, 95.
pomtis, 94.
pon, 95.
post-esak, 91.
præfukus, 96.
præsentid, 96.
preivatud, 94.
pru, 94.
pruhipid, 91.
prumedikatud, 96.
pruter, 94.
puf, 95.
Q[uæstor], 89.
sakaraklum, 272.
senateis, 90.
set, 97.
siom, 90.
sipus, 94.
skriftas, 97.
suæ, 90.
tadait, 92.
tanginud, 90.
toutiko, 92, 96.
valæmom, 92.
vinkter, 96.
urust, 94.
ust, 95.
uzet, 95.
zikolom, 94.

V.

ETRUSCAN WORDS.

The Alphabetical Lists in pp. 113-125, 132, 133, and the following.

Ancaria, 111.
Apulu, Aplu, 109.
Aril, 124.
Aritimis, 39, 129.
Aruns, 71.
Ausil, 108.
ceca, 129.
Ceres, 111.
chfinchfe, 122.
clen, 130.
Elchsntre, 102.
epana, 127.
Epure, 109, 128.
erai, 127.
etera, 129.
ethe, 127.
Feronia, 108.
fuius, 128.
helefu, 127, 135.
Janus, 106.
Juno, 107.

Jupetrul, 128.
Kalairu, 128.
kethuma, 127.
Kupra, 77, 107.
Lar, 112.
lauchme, 71.
lisiai, 127.
Mantus, 110.
maram, 127.
Mars, 108.
mathu, 127, 206.
Matuta, 109.
Menerfa, 108.
Merqurius, 112.
mi, 127.
nastav, 127.
Nethuns, 109, 127.
ni, 127.
Nortia, 111.
phleres, 129.
Phupluns, 136.

Porsena, 16.
Rasne, 16.
Saturnus, 108.
Secstinal, 103.
Sethlans, 108.
sie, 127.
Soranus, 109.
Sothina, 109.
Summanus, 106.
Tanaquil, 103, 134.
Thalna, 107.
Thana, 134.
Thipurenai, 127.
Tina, 105.
turce, 129.
Turms, 112.
Vedius, 107.
Vertumnus, 108.
Usil, 84.
Utuze, 103.

VI.

GREEK WORDS.

ἄγριος, 219.
ἄδην, 207.
αἰθή, αἰθός, 37.
αἱρέω, 61.
αἶσα, 37, 113.
αἰών, 114.
ἅλις, 207.
ἀμείνων, 120.
ἄμπειρα, 144.
ἄναξ, 204.
Ἀπία, 36.
ἄργος, 12.
Ἄρης, 195.
Ἄρτεμις, 39. 129.
ἀσύφηλος, 124.

Ἀφροδίτη, 239.
βλίττω, 191.
Βερενίκη, 35.
Βόσπορος, 35.
βοῦς, 116.
βύργος, 35.
γελέοντες, 119.
γλυκυρρίζα, 202.
δαήρ, 207.
δάκρυον, 207.
δαλίς, 77.
δαλός, 207.
δαπάνη, 127.
δαψιλής, 207.
δειλός, 207.

δεινός, 78.
δημόσιος, 227, 232.
διχομηνία, 118.
δνοφεραί, 191.
δῶρον, 207.
ἔζεσθαι, 204.
εἰ, 204.
εἴκων, 118.
ἐλεύθερος, 5, 45.
ἐλλός, 204.
ἕπομαι, 204.
ἔρις, 204.
ἔως, 239.
Ζεύς, 105.
ἥλιος, σελήνη, 84, 108.

ἥμερος, 219.
θάλασσα, 203.
θαρρεῖν, 206.
θέμις, indecl., 243.
θήρ, 193, 206.
θῆτες, 95.
θύρα, 206.
θώρηξ, 207.
θῶυμα, 219.
ἴδιος, 239.
Ἱμέρα, 219.
καλός, 207.
κλύω, 45.
κυννῶ, 202.
κόσμος, 202.
κραναός, 79.
κρύσταλλος, 39.
λάμος, &c., 113.
λίτρα, 5.
μάντις, 110, 195.
μαστός, 44.
μάτην, 121.

μέθυ, 207.
μέλας, 24.
μεός, 227.
μεσημβρία, 191.
μύριοι, 215.
ναθμός, 127.
νέω, 109.
ξένος, 153.
Ὀαρίων, 195.
ὄασις, 37.
ὀδούς, 208.
Ὀδυσσεύς, 103.
οἶστρος, 37, 202.
παρθένος, 193.
πασάσθαι, 70.
πατήρ, 36.
πέλιος, πελιδνός, 25.
πίνω, 70, 252.
πλήρης, 207.
ποῖρ, 279.
πόλις, 62.
πρύλεες, 215.

ῥεῖθρον, 123.
ῥοῖβδος, 202.
σίφων, 124.
Σοωδίνα, 109.
στυφελός, 194.
σχέτλιος, 204.
τάλις, 107.
τερμίς, 112.
τίς, 105.
τῖφος, 36.
τραχύς, 13.
τύραννος, 12.
τύρσις, 11.
ὕπνος, 204.
φολκός, 193.
χαμαί, 127, 198.
χαοί, 4.
χάρμη, 204.
χήν, 116.
χίλιοι, 215.
χλωρός, 118.

VII.
LATIN WORDS.

accerso, 207, 252.
accuso, &c., 215.
acerra, 167.
acervus, 139.
actus, 94, 221.
adoro, 164, 209.
adulo, 209.
æger, 214.
aeneus, ahenus, 51.
æreus, æneus, 207.
æstimo, 214.
æternus, 108, 114.
ala, 267.
ambitus, 159.
amicus, 207.
amo, 39.
amœnus, 120.
ampirvo, 145.
ancilla, 111.
anguis, 117.
annus, 123.

antiquus, 219.
ara, 113.
arcera, 150.
arcesso, 207, 252.
assiduus, 150.
augur, 214.
aula, 271.
auris, 207.
axo, 57.
bellum, 191.
berber, 140.
berbex, 39.
bitumen, 191.
bonus, 191, 195.
bruma, 271.
calvitur, 149.
canus, candidus, 39, 74.
capesso, 252.
caput, 39, 194.
carcer, 271.

caterva, 139.
cauneas, 277.
cerus manus, 120, 143.
ceva, 116.
choroiaulodos, 143.
cimeterium, 216.
cippus, 194.
clam, calim, 243.
cliens, 222.
clipeus, 222.
cœna, 74.
cohors, 51.
colonia, 200.
cominus, eminus, 243.
comissari, 50.
compascuus, 160.
concapes, 158.
contio, 208, 271.
contaminare, 271.
coquus, 200.
coram, 243.

INDICES.

corvus, 116.
cosol, 173.
crus, 122.
cuicuimodi, 272.
cujus, &c., 200, 233.
culmen, 130.
cunæ, 271.
cupidus, 241.
curia, curiatius, 76.
decumanus, 221.
deliro, 222.
denuntio, 185.
dequim, 180.
dextra, 65.
dice, 141.
diffensus, 153.
difficultas, 217.
dissicentes, 66.
divido, 118.
donum, 207.
dumtaxat, 181.
dunque, 143.
Ecastor, &c., 272.
elementum, 102.
enim, 96.
enos, 139.
equidem, 280.
equus, 38, 201.
escit, 250.
esum, 248.
exiguus, 271.
exilis, 271.
existimo, 213, 214.
explodo, 216.
facie, 141.
facul, 178, 243, 279.
fagus, 190.
Fatua, 117.
fatuus, 60.
febris, 117.
fera, 193.
fero, 190.
finalis, 253.
findo, 118, 208.
folium, 190.
forent, 279.
foveo, 117.
frangere, 190.

fraudem frausus, 165.
frustra, ¶121.
fui, 250, 252.
fundus, 221.
Gaius, 197.
Gnæus, 197.
gena, 196.
generosus, 236.
genus, 196.
glisco, 130.
globus, 44, 195.
gnarures, 230.
granum, 196.
gruma, 43, 221.
heluo, 127.
Herminius, 76.
herus, 76.
hibernus, 195, 198.
hir, 61.
hodie, 272.
homo, 76.
honestus, 204.
Horatius, 76.
hortus, 160, 198.
hospes, 152.
hostis, 152.
humus, 127, 198.
ideo, idoneus, 242.
idus, 118.
igitur, 149, 242.
illud, &c., 235.
im, 181.
imperator, 81.
imus, 271.
inclitus, 222.
inde, 238.
inquam, 83, 252.
inquilinus, 200.
instar, 242.
invitus, 62.
iracundus, 250, 263.
item, 280.
iterum, 129, 206.
judaidiare, 218.
jugerum, 94, 220.
jurgium, 161.
lacesso, 252.
lacryma, 207.

lanius, 118.
lapiderum, 232.
lappa, 194.
largus, 112.
levir, 206.
librarius, 180.
ligare, 207.
limes, 220.
lingua, 207, 267.
lira, 119.
lorica, 207.
luærvem, 139.
ludus, 120.
lupus, 202.
luridus, 118.
luuci, 185.
lympha, 207.
mala, 110, 271.
Marcipor, &c. 279.
massa, 50.
meditor, 207.
mei, &c., 233.
melior, 195.
mentum, 110.
mergus, 66.
meridie, 272.
mile, miles, 215.
minister, 93.
modo, 280.
mollis, 271.
multimodis, 272.
musso, 50.
nanxitor, 156.
narro, 44, 69.
navalis, 253.
nec, 67, 214.
negotium, 67.
negritu[do], 67, 214.
negumo, 144.
nequinont, 202.
Nero, 82.
nostri, nostrum, 233.
nudiustertius, 272.
nuncupo, 157.
nuntius, 208.
obedio, 216.
obliquus, 119, 209.
obrussa, 50.

INDICES. 299

obstinere, 60, 144.
occultus, 201.
officina, 227.
olfacit, 207.
olim, 146.
ollus, 271.
omentum, 271.
omnimodis, 272.
onustus, 204.
oppidum, oppido, 62.
ops, 3.
oscines, 64.
oses, 143.
otium, 271.
pagunt, 151.
palam, 243.
pars, parti, partus, 181, 242.
patefacio, 252, 273.
paullus, 271.
pectuscum, 20.
penes, 242.
pergo, 214.
pipulo, 83, 162.
pleores, 140.
plorare, 145.
plumbum, 195.
polenta, 222.
pono, 208.
populus, 136.
portus, 153.
posthac, &c., 91, 233.
pravus, 39.
prœlium, 215.
proficiscor, 212.
proletarius, 150.
promulgare, 195.
propinquus, 207, 242.
procul, 243.
propter, 242.
prosper, 194.
prudens, 271.
puella, 271.
puer, 279.
puniceus, 194.
purgo, 57.
quæro, 252.
qualus, 271.

quandoquidem, 280.
ques, 154, 182, 230.
quidem, 280.
quomodo, 280.
quoquus, 200.
quorsus, 111.
radere genas, 167.
redantruo, 144.
refert, 233.
remulco, 222.
repudio, 174.
ricinium, 167.
rixa, 104, 204, 218.
robustus, 236.
rota, 206.
ruber, 5.
ruma, 43.
rupitia, 163.
rursus, 111.
sacellum, 272.
sanates, 150.
sarpta, 159.
scilicet, 252, 273.
scribere, 190.
secundus, secutus, 263.
securis, 75.
sed, sine, 155, 168, 235.
sedulum, 180.
Semones, 140.
sempiternus, 108.
sestertius, 159.
severus, 7, 62.
sibus, 94.
sicilicus, 94, 221.
silva, 222.
simul, 204, 243.
sino, 252.
siremps, 186.
sis = si vis, 273.
socer, 222.
sodes, 273.
solari, 272.
sollemnis, 124.
sonticus, 152.
speres, 230.
squama, 201.
Spurius, 77, 214.
sterno, 208.

stipulus, 63.
strenuus, 85.
suad, 90.
sublimis, 272.
subtilis, 272.
sueres, 234.
summus, 272.
tædet, tardus, 92.
tandem, 272.
tectifractis, 273.
tellus, 62.
tempestas, 236.
templum, 220.
tenebræ, 191.
tenus, 242.
terra, 62.
Tiberis, 130.
Titus, 71, 76.
toga, 124, 267.
topper, 194.
torquular, 200.
tot, 62.
totus, 62.
trebla, 58.
tripudium, 143, 174.
trucido, 272.
tuber, 195.
ultro, 238.
urvo, 94.
vanus, 272.
vasargenteis, 273.
vaticinari, 195.
vehemens, 70.
veneo, venumdo, 252.
venilia, 24.
Venus, 195.
verecundus, 250, 263.
veru, 193.
vestri, vestrum, 233.
videlicet, 252, 273.
vicus, vicinus, 160.
villa, 160.
vires, 230.
virgo, 93.
vitricus, 193.
vitta, 37.
vivus, 66, 201.

VIII.
FRENCH WORDS.

abeille, 203.
aigre, 203.
aimé, 208.
aimerai, 290.
ame, 278.
apôtre, 209.
assez, 208.
aucun, 210, 278.
avant, 287.
aveugle, 203.
aumône, 210.
aune, 210.
avoir, 194.
avril, 194.
autel, 210.
biais, 209.
bougre, 45, 210.
cage, 192.
case, 288.
cause, 288.
cel, cet, 287.
chacun, 287.
Châlons, 208.
chambre, 191.
changer, 192.
chaste, 203.
cheoir, 202.
cheval, 202.
cheveu, 194.
chez, 202, 288.
chien, 202.
chose, 288.
combler, 191.
comme, 280, 287.
corbeille, 203.
dame, 279.
diacre, 209.

Dijon, 192.
dit, 203.
droit, 287.
epître, 209.
esclave, 45.
évêque, 194.
expulser, 288.
faible, 278.
faire, 278.
faisons, 203.
femme, 279.
feu (*focus*), 203.
feu (*felix*), 210.
foi, 208.
fois, 203.
gué, 208.
guerre, 200.
hommes, 277.
hôpital, 288.
hors, 193.
hôtel, 288.
Huguenot, 208.
ici, 287.
jeu, 203.
larme, 203, 278.
lieu, 203.
lièvre, 194.
liquorice, 202.
lire, 203.
Loire, 203.
loisir, 203.
lui, 279.
maigre, 203.
mais, maitre, 90, 203.
minuit, 208.
naif, 288.
natal, 288.

natif, 288.
noel, 288.
nombre, 191.
nu, 208.
nuire, 203.
oc, 237.
œil, 278.
œuvre, 194.
ou, 279.
ouvrir, 194.
oyl, 287.
pauvre, 194.
père, 208, 279.
persifler, 124.
peu, 203.
piété, 288.
pirouetter, 145.
pitié, 288.
plaisir, 203.
poids, 95.
poitrine, 203.
pousser, 288.
queue, 208.
rage, 192.
recevoir, 194.
roche, 194.
rougir, 192.
sache, 194.
serment, 203, 278.
siffler, 124.
suivre, 277.
tai, tait, 277.
titre, 210.
vie, 208.
voici, voila, 277.
voir, 208.
y, 279.

THE END.

Made in the USA
Monee, IL
03 May 2026